Hidden in Plain Sight: The Legacy of Slavery

"Hidden in Plain Sight" tells the story of black oppression in America, shedding light on a history often overlooked or conveniently forgotten. This book presents a collection of narratives that reveal the struggles of black people who endure the weight of systemic racism, discrimination, and injustice.

Within these pages, you will encounter a people whose lives have been deeply impacted by the pervasive grip of oppression. Their stories paint a vivid and unflinching picture of the harsh realities endured by generations of African Americans throughout history. From the days of slavery and the dehumanizing era of Jim Crow to the challenges faced today, these narratives expose the profound injustices that have shaped the black experience.

Exploring the intricate complexities of racial identity, the book examines the intergenerational impact of oppression and delves into the social, cultural, and psychological repercussions of systemic racism. Each chapter presents a profound exploration of the multifaceted dimensions of black oppression, urging readers to empathize, reflect, and engage in vital conversations about racial inequality.

Through these narratives, we confront the uncomfortable truths of America's past and present, urging readers to challenge their own biases and actively contribute to the ongoing fight for justice and equality. "Hidden in Plain Sight" serves as a catalyst for awareness and change, encouraging readers to recognize the pervasive nature of black oppression and actively dismantle the systemic barriers that hinder progress and perpetuate injustice.

"Hidden in Plain Sight" offers a powerful exploration of black oppression in America. It serves as a reminder that the struggle for liberation is ongoing and that acknowledging these stories of oppression is essential to shaping a more equitable future for all.

African Diaspora, the Middle Passage, and the Trans-Atlantic Slave Trade

- This tragedy was responsible for forcibly displacing an estimated 12 million Africans from their homeland over 400 years ago.

Involvement of Black People in Transatlantic Slave Trade

- African kingdoms actively participated in the dark commerce of buying and selling human cargo.

Slavery in America

- Slavery became an entrenched part of American society during this period since it provided an opportunity for wealthy landowners to gain access to free labor from Africans who had been taken from their homelands against their will.

The Reconstruction Era

- In addition to restoring order within states that were part of the Confederacy, there was also an effort to secure civil rights for newly freed African Americans.

The Jim Crow Era

- Jim Crow laws were enacted in the late 19th century in the Southern United States to enforce racial segregation between white and Black citizens. These laws mandated the segregation of public facilities such as schools, transportation, bathrooms, restaurants, and restrooms.

Reparations for Slavery

- Reparations acknowledge the wrongs of slavery and provide a way to rectify them, including restitution payments to descendants of slaves, investing in the African American community with resources such as education, healthcare, and housing.

Black Wall Street aka Greenwood, Oklahoma

- On May 31st and June 1st, 1921, a mob of white supremacists descended on Greenwood, Oklahoma with an intent to terrorize and destroy the area's affluent African American neighborhood known as 'Black Wall Street'. The attack was swift and violent, resulting in countless deaths, extensive property damage, and leaving nearly 10,000 African Americans homeless.

The Brutality of Colonizers

- They would massacre entire villages, raze crops and homes, and brutally punish anyone who dared to resist.

The Genocide of Native Americans

- For hundreds of years, Indigenous people have suffered under oppressive policies that sought to erase their culture and assimilate them into white society.

The Banning of Black History

- Black history has been systematically dismissed for centuries, with the banning of books, speeches, and other works that told these stories.

The Great Migration

- The Great Migration was one of the largest population movements in American history, with over 6 million African Americans leaving the South between 1916 and 1970.

Social Promotion and the Black Community

- Social promotion is a term used to describe the practice of moving students from one academic grade to another without mastering all the required skills for their current grade level.

Black on Black Racism

- This type of racism occurs when members of the same racial group discriminate against each other due to differences in class, education level, or identity.

Crime in the Black Community

- People of color living in poverty are often ensnared in a cycle of criminalization and incarceration that affects generations of families.

Classism within the Black Community

- Despite being part of a larger minority group, members of the black community are still divided among themselves by socio-economic status and other factors.

Black on white Crimes

- Despite progress over the last few decades in terms of civil rights and racial equality, Black on White crime remains an issue today.

White Exodus aka White Flight

- An ongoing trend of white people leaving urban areas for suburban or rural locations.

White Privilege

- White privilege, or the unearned advantages granted to people based solely on their skin color, has been a part of society for centuries.

Healthcare Disparities Faced by Black Americans

- African Americans are more likely than whites to suffer from preventable diseases and illnesses due to inadequate healthcare.

Undiagnosed Mental Illness in the Black Community

- Mental health issues in the Black community are often brushed under the rug, leaving many people undiagnosed and struggling with their mental wellbeing.

Racial Disparities in Maternal and Infant Health

- Black women are more likely to die due to childbirth related complications than White women.

Infant Mortality among Black Babies

- Black infants are two-and-a-half times more likely than white infants to die during their first year of life.

The Sexualization of Black Women and Girls in America

- Studies have shown that this hyper sexualization leads to an increased risk of developing depression, anxiety, low self-esteem, body dissatisfaction, and eating disorders.

Sex Trafficking in the African American Community

- African Americans make up 40% of all human trafficking cases reported in the United States despite comprising only 13% of the population.

Difference between Racism and Racial Bias

- Racism is defined as an ideology based on the belief that certain social groups are inherently superior or inferior to others, while racial bias is defined as an unconscious or conscious preference for one race over another without any rational basis.

Microaggressions and Exclusionary Behaviors

- Microaggressions are subtle, often unintentional comments or actions that communicate hostility or disrespect to a member of a marginalized group. Exclusionary behaviors are deliberate acts designed to exclude people from an environment, activity, or opportunity based on their membership in a particular group.

Pseudoscientific Racism

- Pseudoscientific racism is the belief that certain races or ethnicities are inherently superior or inferior to others based on unscientific claims, unsupported theories, and reductionist views.

Stereotypes

- Studies have shown that black students in the United States are four times more likely to be suspended than their white peers, indicating that schools can have a bias against them due to racial stereotypes.

Critical Race Theory (CRT)

- Race and Intersectionality are core concepts within CRT because racism exists both as an individual prejudice or bias as well as a system which institutionalizes these practices across society.

Racial Profiling

- Occurs when individuals are selected for investigation based on their race or ethnicity rather than evidence of criminal activity.

The War on Drugs Effect on the Black Community

- It has resulted in mass incarceration, disproportionate sentencing, diminished economic opportunity, reduced social mobility, increased poverty rates, racial profiling, police brutality and misguided policy priorities.

Discriminatory Restrictive Covenants

- Historically, these types of agreements were used to block African Americans from living in certain neighborhoods and working at specific jobs as part of discriminatory practices.

Gentrification

- Gentrification often brings with it improvements like new infrastructure and businesses, as well as increased property values, but these positives come at a cost.

Gerrymandering

- Gerrymandering is a process used to manipulate the boundaries of electoral districts, to give an advantage to a particular political party or group.

The Electoral College

- We will cover what exactly the Electoral College is, how it works, its role in deciding presidential elections and some of the arguments for and against it.

Voter Suppression

- Voter suppression has been used throughout history to disproportionately deny certain groups of people their right to vote.

Redlining

- Redlining is the systematic denial of resources, services, and opportunities based on race or geography.

Hate Groups

- A hate group is defined as an organized group or movement that advocates and practices hatred, hostility, or violence towards members of a race, ethnicity, nation, religion, gender identity, sexual orientation, or any other designated sector of society.

The Great Replacement Theory

- This theory suggests that non-white immigrants are replacing the white population in Europe and North America, but there is no concrete proof to back up this claim.

White Supremacy

- White supremacy is not just a set of beliefs; it is also an oppressive system which has been used by those in power as a tool for subjugating minority groups.

Ku Klux Klan

- KKK members used fear tactics such as physical violence, assassination threats and economic intimidation to deter African Americans from voting or engaging in other political activities.

Neo-Nazism

- Neo-Nazism is an ideology that combines elements of white supremacy, nationalism, and anti-Semitism - all of which are rooted in Nazi Germany's totalitarian regime.

Non-State Armed Groups

- Generally speaking, NSAGs are organizations that challenge the authority of a legitimate state and use violence to achieve their goals.

The Aryan Brotherhood

- The Aryan Brotherhood is an organized prison gang formed in 1964 by white inmates in California prisons with racist ideologies at its core. It seeks to maintain white supremacy by engaging in criminal activities.

American Hypocrisy

- From racism and gender inequality to foreign policy contradictions, there are many examples of American hypocrisy that have been exposed over the years.

White Christian Nationalism

- It was established to preserve what were seen as traditional values and beliefs by attempting to maintain an idealized version of American Christianity that focused on white racial supremacy and exclusionary policies.

Police Street Gangs

- They are organized groups of law enforcement officers who operate outside the scope of their professional duties and use their power to engage in criminal activity.

Black Historical Moments

- From the abolition of slavery to the elections of Barack Obama and Kamala Harris, these events have made a lasting impact on our society that will never be forgotten.

The Contributions of Black People in America

- Despite centuries of oppression and discrimination, black people around the country have worked tirelessly to make a positive difference in society – and continue doing so today.

Contributions of Black Soldiers in American History

- The contributions of Black soldiers to our nation's history are far reaching and innumerable, from their service during wartime to their impact on civil rights movements and culture.

NAACP

- Originally founded in 1909, the National Association for the Advancement of Colored People (NAACP) is a leading civil rights advocacy organization that has been on the frontlines in defending people of color against racism and discrimination.

HBCUs

- The establishment of HBCUs provided an invaluable space where students could learn without fear of discrimination or persecution based on race while being surrounded by like-minded peers from similar backgrounds and experiences.

Black Fraternities and Sororities

- From academic excellence to community service, leadership development to an unbreakable network of support - the impact of black fraternities and sororities can be felt everywhere.

The Black Elite

- In the United States, African Americans make up just 13% of the population, but hold 48% of all top-level executive positions in Fortune 500 companies.

The Black Panther Movement

- Founded in 1966, the BPP was a revolutionary organization focused on protecting and empowering African American communities.

Black Lives Matter

- The Black Lives Matter movement began in 2013 after the acquittal of George Zimmerman in the shooting death of Trayvon Martin.

What Is Antifa?

- Antifa is a political movement that has gained significant attention in recent years, due to its stance against fascism and white supremacy. It is a controversial subject with strong opinions on both sides of the debate.

Call to Action to Save Black History Studies in Our Schools

- The lack of Black history studies in our schools is a symptom of a larger problem: systemic racism. It is not enough to simply add more Black history studies into the curriculum; we also need to ensure that these courses are being taught in an inclusive environment, free from bias and discrimination.

Call to Action for Young Black Children to Become Activist for Social Change

- Now is the time for young Black children to step up and make a change. It is an exciting time to be alive: with so many tools at our fingertips, there are plenty of ways to create awareness and act.

Resources for Young Black Children

- Empowering black children to become social activists is an important endeavor. Here are some resources that can guide and inspire them on their journey.

Hidden in Plain Sight: The Legacy of Slavery

"Hidden in Plain Sight" tells the story of black oppression in America, shedding light on a history often overlooked or conveniently forgotten. This book presents a collection of narratives that reveal the struggles of black people who endure the weight of systemic racism, discrimination, and injustice.

Within these pages, you will encounter a people whose lives have been deeply impacted by the pervasive grip of oppression. Their stories paint a vivid and unflinching picture of the harsh realities endured by generations of African Americans throughout history. From the days of slavery and the dehumanizing era of Jim Crow to the challenges faced today, these narratives expose the profound injustices that have shaped the black experience.

Exploring the intricate complexities of racial identity, the book examines the intergenerational impact of oppression and delves into the social, cultural, and psychological repercussions of systemic racism. Each chapter presents a profound exploration of the multifaceted dimensions of black oppression, urging readers to empathize, reflect, and engage in vital conversations about racial inequality.

Through these narratives, we confront the uncomfortable truths of America's past and present, urging readers to challenge their own biases and actively contribute to the ongoing fight for justice and equality. "Hidden in Plain Sight" serves as a catalyst for awareness and change, encouraging readers to recognize the pervasive nature of black oppression and actively dismantle the systemic barriers that hinder progress and perpetuate injustice.

"Hidden in Plain Sight" offers a powerful exploration of black oppression in America. It serves as a reminder that the struggle for liberation is ongoing and that acknowledging these stories of oppression is essential to shaping a more equitable future for all.

John Angus Scantling Jr.

African Diaspora, the Middle Passage, and the Trans-Atlantic Slave Trade

African Diaspora , the term most commonly refers to the descendants of the black West and Central Africans who were enslaved and shipped to the Americas via the Atlantic slave trade between the 16th and 19th centuries, with their largest populations in Brazil, Colombia, Dominican Republic, the United States, and Haiti (in that order).

This tragedy was responsible for forcibly displacing an estimated 12 million Africans from their homeland over 400 years ago.

The Middle Passage, which was the journey of these captives across the Atlantic to be sold into enslavement, is remembered as one of history's most brutal episodes.

In this article, we will examine how this devastating event came to be and its effects on humanity today.

We'll also explore what can be done in order to ensure such atrocities are never repeated again.

Causes of the African Diaspora

You may wonder how the African Diaspora, middle passage, and trans-Atlantic slave trade came to be - let's explore the causes!

The major cause of the African Diaspora was a combination of political changes, economic needs, and religious beliefs. During this period in history, African nations were vulnerable to outside influences due to internal conflict and instability. As a result, European countries took advantage of these weaknesses by offering lucrative trading opportunities in exchange for enslaved Africans.

Additionally, Europeans used their religious beliefs as justification for enslaving Africans because they believed it was their divine right to do so. Furthermore, many European countries saw slavery as an efficient way to increase their wealth and power. Thus, these three factors combined created the perfect environment for the African Diaspora to take place.

The Middle Passage was then a journey of suffering that Africans had no choice but to endure during this dark period of history. Here, hundreds of thousands of enslaved people were taken from Africa with little food or water on ships where sickness spread quickly amongst them. Many did not survive this horrific journey across the Atlantic Ocean due to overcrowding and harsh conditions on board.

Those who made it through arrived in America only to face more oppression under slavery until eventual emancipation in 1865 when slavery was abolished throughout United States territories.

This is especially tragic considering that many enslaved people were ripped away from families and loved ones without ever being able to see them again; all while being forced into labor against their will and having their basic rights stripped away from them for centuries until emancipation could finally be achieved after years of struggle and sacrifice by those brave enough to stand up against it.

To sum it up: The African Diaspora began due to a variety of political, economic, and religious forces that triggered one of the most significant tragedies in human history – The Trans-Atlantic Slave Trade – which created immense suffering across generations until abolition could be reached at last. Consequently, paving the way for today's descendants whose ancestors survived such unfathomable hardships brought about by this cruel practice so long ago.

The Middle Passage: A Journey of Suffering

Your journey across the tumultuous sea was one of sheer misery and pain, a seemingly endless voyage of despair. The Middle Passage was the route taken by slave ships to transport African captives from their homeland to the New World.

This treacherous journey across the Atlantic Ocean in cramped and unsanitary vessels lasted anywhere from a few weeks to several months, often resulting in death or illness for many enslaved Africans due to overcrowding, poor nutrition, disease, violence, and lack of fresh air. You were considered little more than cargo as you were treated like animals with no regard for your health or safety.

The conditions on these voyages were abysmal; you had limited provisions of food that provided insufficient nourishment as well as water that was contaminated with urine and feces. Furthermore, there were no medical supplies available if you fell ill or injured yourself.

There was also rampant physical abuse by crew members against African captives who dared to resist captivity; this included whipping, shackling and other forms of torture aimed at breaking down your spirit until submission became inevitable.

The horrors of the Middle Passage left an indelible mark on those who survived it; they carried psychological trauma from witnessing unspeakable brutality inflicted upon fellow human beings while experiencing such extreme suffering themselves. The fear still lingers today among many descendants of African slaves whose ancestors endured these traumatic ordeal generations ago; but despite its enduring legacy, we must never forget what happened during this dark period in our history so that we can move forward into a better future free from oppression and exploitation.

With this knowledge comes the power to challenge injustice wherever it may be found—and bring about true freedom for all people everywhere without exception.

Trans-Atlantic Slave Trade: Exploitation and Abuse

The Trans-Atlantic Slave Trade saw the exploitation and abuse of countless individuals, forcing them into a life of servitude that was marred by immense suffering and cruelty. It was an inhumane practice that robbed millions of their freedom and humanity through physical, emotional, sexual, and psychological violence.

The conditions they were subjected to on board ships during the Middle Passage were particularly horrific; overcrowded cargo holds where malnutrition, dehydration, disease, exhaustion, and death were commonplace. In addition to these subjugation onboard ships, enslaved Africans suffered immensely upon arrival in the New World, with many being separated from family members or sold at auctions as commodities.

This dehumanizing system of oppression caused African people to endure immeasurable pain and suffering throughout its duration, although it is impossible to estimate how much anguish was endured over such a long period of time.

The Trans-Atlantic Slave Trade was an atrocity that haunts us still today as we grapple with its legacy in our society – one filled with inequity and prejudice against people with African heritage. The shocking human cost of this trade can be seen when looking at some of the statistics, which estimate that between 1525–1866, 12 million Africans were taken from Africa for enslavement in the Americas – only 10 million survived the journey due to various deaths along the way.

This vast number serves as a stark reminder of how devastating this practice was for those who experienced it firsthand. To move forward, we must strive towards understanding these injustices so we can build a better future free from discrimination based on race or ethnicity.

The Atlantic Slave Trade in Numbers

The harrowing reality of the Atlantic slave trade is evident in the staggering numbers associated with it, with an estimated 12 million people uprooted from their homes and only 10 million surviving the journey.

To put this into perspective, it can be broken down as follows: Approximately 20% of those who were captured by slave traders did not survive the Middle Passage. Of those enslaved Africans that arrived in the New World, about 15% died within the first year due to disease or overwork. About 10 million slaves eventually reached their destinations alive but still had a long road of servitude and mistreatment ahead of them regardless if they stayed in Africa or elsewhere in the world.

This mass migration and displacement created social, economic, political, and cultural changes in both Africa and its Diaspora that would last for centuries after slavery was abolished. The effects were catastrophic for countless generations of African people; from separation of families to erasure of cultural heritage to physical suffering—all at the hands of greed-driven individuals who sought nothing more than wealth through human exploitation.

It's no surprise then why many have described it as one of history's greatest tragedies. These atrocities are still being felt today by descendants around the world—a reminder that what happened during this period should never be forgotten or repeated again.

The Disastrous Effects of the Slave Trade

You can't ignore the disastrous consequences of human exploitation that have been echoed through generations, even centuries later. The Atlantic Slave Trade was a tragedy on an unimaginable scale, resulting in millions of lives lost and numerous families torn apart. Enslaved people were ripped from their homes and forced into horrific living conditions where they were treated as less than human and subjected to physical, emotional, and spiritual abuse. People's humanity was taken away from them in incredibly cruel ways with no regard for their life or dignity.

The effects of this atrocity have been felt across continents for centuries, with the African Diaspora reaching all corners of the world throughout history. Many Africans had to cope with a feeling of loss and displacement as they struggled to make sense of their new reality in unfamiliar places. The trauma experienced by enslaved Africans has been passed through generations, leaving many still dealing with its repercussions today.

This is only part of the story, though. We cannot talk about the Atlantic Slave Trade without recognizing its immense global impact, connecting Europe, Africa, and America together in an unprecedented way that changed these regions forever. To fully understand the legacy of this dark period in history, we need to look at how it has come to shape our present-day world. This task will be explored further in the next section: "The Trans-Atlantic Slave Trade: A Global Phenomenon."

The Trans-Atlantic Slave Trade: A Global Phenomenon

Exploring the Trans-Atlantic Slave Trade is like uncovering a global phenomenon that has forever transformed the lives of countless people around the world. The slave trade was an immense and complex network of commerce, involving merchants, traders, and shippers from Europe, Africa, and North America.

Moreover, it's estimated that between 12 million and 15 million Africans were enslaved and forced to embark on this treacherous journey across the Atlantic Ocean. This human trafficking created deep ripples in African societies through its devastating impact on culture, economy, politics, and social life.

It altered African cultures by weakening family bonds as many individuals were forcibly separated from their families. Economically speaking, it caused Africa to lose much of its labor force resulting in loss of productivity which impeded agricultural development during this period.

Politically speaking, it weakened powerful empires that had once controlled large swaths of land due to decreased population numbers brought about by enslavement practices. Socially speaking it caused widespread psychological trauma due to horrific conditions endured along the Middle Passage voyage as well as physical torture once reaching their place of enslavement abroad.

The Trans-Atlantic Slave Trade is a reminder that human suffering can have lasting implications for generations to come; ramifications which are still being felt today in countries all across the globe--from Angola to Brazil to Haiti and beyond.

As we move forward examining how these effects resonated within African societies specifically, we must keep in mind both its long term consequences upon those who survived as well as what was lost with those who didn't make it home alive or at all...

The Impact of the Slave Trade on African Societies

Uncovering the effects of this global phenomenon on societies across the world has been a harrowing journey, with its lasting repercussions still felt today. The Trans-Atlantic Slave Trade had a profound impact on African societies and cultures, resulting in significant losses in population, freedom and social organization.

The most obvious consequence was the immense loss of life due to capture, confinement and transport of enslaved Africans to the Americas. An estimated 12 million Africans were moved across the Middle Passage between 1525 and 1866, leading to an alarming decrease in population numbers back in Africa. In addition, millions more died during capture or from inadequate living conditions while being transported overseas. This resulted in a large-scale disruption of traditional family structures as families were broken apart by slave traders' raids.

Moreover, traditionally communal societies operating under decentralized systems of governance which had relied heavily on kinship networks were now subject to centralized control by foreign entities – such as European trading companies – who could manipulate prices for their own benefit. Consequently, African economies suffered greatly as they were forced into new markets that benefited Europe instead of themselves. This further weakened already fragile political states and disrupted what few social services they had been able to provide their citizens prior to this point in time. It is clear that this trade drastically changed African societies forever; it would take centuries before many could begin to heal from its devastating effects.

The Trans-Atlantic Slave Trade left behind not only a legacy of physical destruction but also psychological trauma for generations born after it ended: feelings of shame and inferiority have been passed down through families who experienced displacement and enslavement firsthand, creating an emotional burden that continues even today.

Impact	Description	Consequence
Losses	Population numbers decreased drastically	Disruption
	Traditional family structures broken up	Weakening
	Economies suffered from manipulation by foreign entities	Control

The African Slave Trade and its Legacy in the Americas

Discovering the far-reaching consequences of the African Diaspora in the Americas reveals a complex legacy of resilience, adaptation, and identity. Africans brought with them their heritage and melded it with European influences to shape distinct identities in the New World.

Every aspect of life was affected by this massive movement: from foodways to spiritual beliefs, Africans left an indelible mark on the American landscape. Here are three ways in which we can see this impact today:

- The proliferation of African-American music genres such as jazz, blues, hip hop, and R&B;
- The presence of West and Central African words and phrases that have been incorporated into modern English;
- The adoption of certain religious customs like Voodoo or Santeria which were born out of syncretism between Christianity and traditional African faiths.

Overall, it is clear that the transatlantic slave trade had a profound impact on both Africa's history as well as its diasporic communities across the globe. This legacy has not only shaped our culture but also gives us insight into how people can adapt under even the most oppressive circumstances – something that resonates powerfully today as we continue to grapple with racism and inequality around the world.

As we move forward in understanding this shared history, it's essential to bear witness to its enduring legacy while at the same time striving for a more just future for all peoples regardless of race or creed. With this recognition comes an obligation to work towards dismantling systems rooted in oppression so that everyone may live free from fear and prejudice.

The Abolition of the Trans-Atlantic Slave Trade

Witnessing the atrocities of the Trans-Atlantic Slave Trade sparked a powerful movement to abolish it and free countless individuals from its clutches, forever changing our world for the better.

Abolitionists around the world, including Britain's Thomas Clarkson and William Wilberforce, led a campaign that successfully pressured British Parliament to pass legislation outlawing the slave trade in 1807. This was followed by similar acts by other European countries over time. The United States also took action in 1820 and 1822 when Congress passed legislation prohibiting slavery on vessels registered in US ports, as well as limiting American participation in slave trading.

The impact of this monumental achievement was felt all across the Atlantic Ocean where millions of Africans were freed from bondage and able to start new lives with dignity.

The abolition of the trans-Atlantic slave trade marked an important victory for human rights, but unfortunately did not end slavery itself or its legacy of racism which continues to plague societies today. As such, it's essential we build upon these successes and strive towards creating a more just society where everyone has equal opportunities regardless of race or background.

This meaningful step forward set into motion a domino effect that ultimately changed history forever; however, its impact on African lives was still yet to be seen. With abolition now firmly established, attention turned towards addressing how best to help those affected by centuries of oppression...

The Impact of Abolition on African Lives

Unraveling the cruel effects of slavery, abolition brought hope to those whose lives had been forever altered by its devastating legacy. But for many, freedom was not a tangible reality.

Although they weren't subject to enslavement anymore, African people still faced discrimination and prejudice in their everyday lives. They were denied access to education and economic resources, struggling to survive in societies that refused them basic rights and privileges. This made it difficult for formerly enslaved Africans to build better lives for themselves and their families despite the hopes inspired by emancipation.

The abolition of the Trans-Atlantic Slave Trade did not end all forms of oppression against African people; yet it did allow them to form new identities after centuries of suffering under enslavers' rule. Through this process, African cultures around the world began revitalizing their traditions as they reconnected with their ancestral roots and reclaimed a sense of community identity. This led to the development of vibrant cultural movements like Afro futurism, which blended together elements from traditional African culture with modern technology.

As African descendants built upon these connections between liberation and identity formation, they created powerful legacies that continue to shape our shared histories today. This shift towards redefining what it means to be an African descendant also transformed how we understand the impact of enslavement on global history - both in terms of its humanitarian costs as well as its lasting political ramifications.

By recognizing how deeply slavery had impacted generations across continents, we can begin addressing how best we can work towards repairing these systemic damages while also embracing new opportunities for building a brighter future together - one rooted in equity instead of injustice. With this collective vision in mind, let's explore further how the African Diaspora has left an indelible mark on world history today.

The Impact of the African Diaspora on World History

You can explore how the African Diaspora has shaped world history in remarkable ways, impacting generations across continents to this day.

From the trade of goods and resources to the spread of culture and language, the African Diaspora has left an indelible mark on all corners of the globe. Not only did millions of people face displacement through forced labor during the trans-Atlantic slave trade, but those who survived were able to create a unique identity for themselves in new countries by incorporating their own cultural practices into new societies.

This influence is still evident today as people from around the world celebrate holidays that were once celebrated exclusively by Africans in their home country. The consequences of slavery and exploitation due to racism and imperialism are still felt today as descendants try to reclaim their lost heritage.

By studying genealogy, it's possible to trace one's ancestry back centuries and even uncover family connections between different nations. Additionally, many African religions have been blended with other traditions around the world, creating a unique blend of spirituality that is found nowhere else on earth.

The struggle for civil rights also owes much to activists whose ancestors were forcibly removed from their homeland during slavery times as they fought for equality in a foreign land. The African Diaspora has made its presence known through art, music, literature, cuisine and more; these contributions continue to enrich our lives every day with color, flavor and beauty beyond what we could ever imagine.

We must not forget this legacy when looking at issues such as poverty or inequality; rather than simply blaming those affected for their circumstances we should recognize that racism and oppression created a system where some are given opportunities while others are denied them outright. With this understanding in mind, we can strive towards justice now more than ever before--moving forward into a brighter future for generations yet unborn.

The Legacy of the African Diaspora in the Present Day

Today, the profound legacy of the African Diaspora can still be felt in countless ways, from cultural practices to spiritual beliefs and beyond.

- **Cultural Practices:** The traditions, music, cuisine, artistry, and language of many different cultures all over the world have been shaped by the influence of African diasporic communities. This is particularly evident in the United States, where both African-American and Afro-Caribbean culture has had a major impact on American society and continues to do so today.

- **Spiritual Beliefs:** Many people around the world who are descended from those forcibly displaced during the Middle Passage have held onto their traditional spiritual beliefs despite centuries of oppression and marginalization. These religions include Vodou (Haiti), Santeria (Cuba), Candomblé (Brazil), Orisha worship (Yoruba) amongst many others that are practiced in various forms across Latin America as well as other parts of the world.

- **Political & Social Movements:** In recent years, there has been an increased awareness about issues related to racism and social justice which can be traced back to many political movements that were led by members of the African Diaspora. These movements, such as Marcus Garvey's Universal Negro Improvement Association or Martin Luther King Jr's civil rights movement, have helped shape public discourse around these topics globally while also sparking conversations about how we should address systemic inequality throughout our societies.

The legacy of this critical period in history continues to reverberate in our present-day lives for better or worse - from its effects on global politics to personal identity formation - making it essential for us all to understand its impact on a deeper level. As such, further exploration into how this issue has impacted individuals as well as entire nations is necessary if we are to begin unraveling its complex implications for all involved parties throughout history and into our modern times.

This leads us into tackling a new subtopic - the global impact of the transatlantic slave trade - which will be discussed in further detail below.

The Global Impact of the Trans-Atlantic Slave Trade

Discovering the global impact of the Trans-Atlantic Slave Trade can be a powerful experience, allowing us to gain insight into how this event has affected individuals and nations across time.

The enslavement of millions of Africans had devastating effects on African country economies, resulting in long-term underdevelopment and poverty. It's argued that profits from the slave trade provided capital for industrialization in Europe and North America, contributing to a widening gap between rich countries and poor countries today.

It also created an enduring legacy of racism and inequality throughout the world, with many societies still struggling to overcome its damaging consequences. The Trans-Atlantic Slave Trade caused deep psychological trauma among generations of black people, which manifested itself through social disconnection and family disruption.

This has had long-lasting implications for identity formation, self-esteem, economic opportunities, and access to education and healthcare; all factors that are essential for meaningful inclusion in our society today. Moreover, there is evidence that suggests links between colonialism imposed by Europeans during slavery times through exploitative labor practices, which have led to socio-economic disparities between African countries compared with their European former colonizers.

The fight for reparations and justice are still ongoing processes as we strive to confront this dark page in human history head-on. Racism and discrimination continue to blight our lives even today as they are deeply embedded within our collective consciousness - a reminder that without acknowledgement or apology from those responsible, healing will remain incomplete as we attempt to rebuild bridges broken by years of oppression inflicted upon so many innocent victims whose stories remain largely untold throughout history books globally.

The Fight for Reparations and Justice

Since the end of the Trans-Atlantic Slave Trade, efforts have been made to seek restitution for those who suffered in its wake. This has taken many forms, from advocacy and awareness campaigns to legal action and reparations.

We've seen a long history of struggle as groups strive to secure justice for generations of people subjected to this great tragedy. Although some progress has been made in recent years, activists continue to push for greater recognition and compensation.

This includes demands for an official apology from countries that profited from slavery – such as Britain and the United States – alongside calls for financial reparations. Supporters have pointed out that these payments could help repair some of the economic damage caused by centuries of inequality and exploitation, while also providing a measure of redress after so many years without justice or acknowledgement.

From peaceful protests to legal challenges, we can see how countless individuals around the world are working together towards a better future; one where all victims of this terrible crime are given their due respect and recompense.

Now's not only a time to look back on our collective history but also a time when we can learn meaningful lessons from it and work towards preventing another similar tragedy from occurring again.

Lessons from History: How to Prevent another Tragedy

You can learn from the past to help prevent another tragedy like this, and together we must strive for a better future.

One of the most important lessons we can take away from the African Diaspora, Middle Passage, and Trans-Atlantic Slave Trade is that unchecked power is dangerous. It's essential to ensure that all individuals have their rights protected by law, regardless of race or economic standing. We also need to be aware of how certain systems of oppression are perpetuated through generations and can negatively impact people for years or even centuries afterwards. This means that laws shouldn't only protect those currently affected but also make sure that their descendants aren't faced with similar injustices in the future.

Another lesson is that ignorance doesn't equate to innocence; it just makes us complicit in injustice. As citizens of a country, we have an obligation to educate ourselves on current events and ongoing issues around the world so that we can speak out against unjust actions when they occur. We must use our voices to demand accountability from our leaders so that no one group will suffer disproportionately due to exploitative policies or practices.

We must also recognize how interconnected society is today and how every decision made affects people around the world—for better or for worse. The repercussions of any action taken should be weighed carefully before being implemented as part of policy-making processes in order to ensure justice for all those involved now and in the future.

By taking these measures seriously, we can work towards creating a more equal world where everyone has access to basic human rights without fear of exploitation or oppression based on their identity or circumstances.

Frequently Asked Questions

How is the African Diaspora still affecting people today?

We're still feeling the effects of the African Diaspora today. Millions of people were taken from their homes and sent to live in foreign lands through the trans-Atlantic slave trade. This created an undeniable ripple effect that is still felt centuries later. Despite all odds, these individuals have persevered and continue to strive for equality and social justice. Their legacy has forever changed our world in ways both large and small, making it a better place for us all.

What efforts are being made to fight for reparations and justice?

We, the people of today's world, have been working hard to fight for reparations and justice for those affected by the Trans-Atlantic Slave Trade.

According to statistics, more than 12.5 million Africans were enslaved during the Middle Passage and over 1.8 million died at sea.

Our goal is to ensure that all those affected are properly compensated and honored for their suffering.

We're working to raise awareness about this issue through educational programs in schools and other institutions, advocating for legislation that would provide financial compensation or reparations, and pushing governments around the globe to recognize and accept responsibility for their role in this horrific event.

What are the long-term effects of the African slave trade?

We, as a collective African Diaspora, have had to face the long-term effects of the African slave trade for centuries. This cruel system was responsible for ripping families apart and leaving lasting physical, emotional, and psychological scars on generations to come.

Not only did it disrupt our culture and heritage, but it also caused immense economic hardship due to the loss of human capital. Many African nations are still struggling with these consequences today - from economic disparities between different regions to unequal access to resources and education.

We must continue fighting for reparations and justice in order to break this cycle of oppression.

How did the abolition of the trans-Atlantic slave trade impact African lives?

We never truly imagined the drastic effects that abolishing the trans-atlantic slave trade would have on African lives. It was like a floodgate of freedom had been opened, transforming an entire continent within moments!

Freeing millions of people after centuries of suffering and oppression, it gave Africans the chance to reclaim their lives and futures. This new, unapologetic freedom allowed them to shape their own destinies in ways previously impossible, enabling them with newfound opportunities for education, work, and social justice that ultimately changed generations to come.

What can be done to prevent another tragedy like the trans-Atlantic slave trade?

We must learn from the mistakes of the past and take concrete steps to ensure a tragedy like the trans-Atlantic slave trade never happens again.

We should start by educating ourselves about the horrors of slavery and its lasting effects, as well as identifying any present-day systems that uphold oppression.

To prevent future exploitation, we need to create laws and regulations that protect vulnerable populations around the world. Additionally, programs must be in place to support victims of human trafficking and provide greater access to economic opportunities for those at risk of being enslaved.

Finally, it's essential for us to hold governments accountable and demand transparency when it comes to labor practices. By doing so, we can help ensure no one ever experiences such suffering again.

Conclusion

We've seen the devastating effects of the African Diaspora, the Middle Passage, and the Trans-Atlantic slave trade.

It's estimated that over 12.5 million Africans were taken from their homes and forced into slavery – with only 10.7 million surviving to reach their destinations.

This tragedy left an indelible mark on history, its consequences still reverberating today.

We must continue to fight for reparations and justice for our brothers and sisters who suffered so greatly at the hands of these atrocities.

We must remember this dark chapter in history so that we never repeat such a heinous crime against humanity again.

Involvement of Black People in Transatlantic Slave Trade

We have long known that the Transatlantic Slave Trade was a horrific practice responsible for the displacement and suffering of millions of people. But what is often forgotten is the involvement of black people in this enterprise. By looking at its various aspects, we can gain a better understanding of how they were involved in it, as well as the far-reaching impact it had on African societies and African-American identity.

In this article, we will explore the role African kingdoms, captives, traders, brokers, European merchants and even the United States played in this dark chapter of history. Additionally, we will look at how it continues to affect us today.

The Role of African Kingdoms in the Slave Trade

African kingdoms actively participated in the dark commerce of buying and selling human cargo. They were eager to enter into trade agreements with Europeans, as it enabled them to access goods they wouldn't have otherwise. African kings benefited financially from trading captives, whether through receiving money or goods in exchange for slaves.

By providing a reliable source of labor, they also increased their political power in the region. The influence of Europeans made slavery increasingly commonplace and accepted by many African rulers as a legitimate form of social control. This allowed for the slave trade to become entrenched in local economies throughout Africa, particularly along the west coast and on islands off its shores.

Throughout this period, there was no single unified policy on slavery among African kingdoms; instead, each ruler had their own policies regarding how slaves were acquired and treated within their realm. Captives taken during wars or raids were often sold into slavery as a form of punishment or repayment for debts owed by individual or family members; these people often didn't receive any compensation for being enslaved.

Alternatively, some individuals willingly entered into slavery out of poverty or desperation—a reality that some European traders exploited by making false promises about opportunities available abroad with potential buyers. For instance, there are records of European traders convincing Africans that if they left their homeland they could make enough money to buy land back home upon returning; however, this rarely happened due to enslavement becoming a permanent status once captured and transported across the Atlantic Ocean.

Awareness campaigns against slaving activities became prominent at various points throughout history among both Europeans and Africans; however, these efforts largely failed in eliminating the practice due to its deeply entrenched nature throughout multiple societies across different continents over centuries-long periods of time.

Nevertheless, such initiatives remain significant insofar as they demonstrate how wrongs can be recognized even when global systems sustain them—a lesson that continues to be relevant today given similar issues related to human exploitation still occurring around the world today.

The Role of African Captives in the Slave Trade

Captives were an integral part of the horrific journey across the Atlantic, enduring unimaginable hardships. Men and women from African countries were often tricked into slavery by foreign traders who promised them freedom or goods in exchange for labor. Those captured often faced a grueling march to the coast, with harsh conditions that led to many fatalities during transit.

When they arrived at the slave markets, captives would be inspected and sold as commodities for prices ranging from several hundred dollars to a few thousand dollars each. The majority of captives sent across the Atlantic came from West Africa, due to its proximity to Europe and its abundance of natural resources. In areas such as Benin, Ghana, Angola, Nigeria and Senegal, locals were routinely abducted by captors who then sold them to foreign traders for profit.

The transatlantic journey was long and arduous with many perishing aboard overcrowded ships due to malnutrition or disease outbreaks; those that survived endured miserable living conditions on plantations when they arrived in America or Europe. In addition to physical suffering inflicted upon those enslaved, cultural traditions were also forced out of existence because captives had no access to their traditional practices while working on plantations or ships abroad.

As a result of this cultural displacement, African people lost much of their history along with their identities as members of distinct cultures; these losses are still felt today by descendants whose ancestors suffered through this dark period in history. Moving forward into our understanding of the role of African traders in the slave trade, we must acknowledge how both sides perpetrated this great injustice against humanity.

The Role of African Traders in the Slave Trade

You may not have heard much about it, but African traders played an essential role in the heinous transatlantic slave trade. Throughout history, these traders were responsible for capturing and selling millions of Africans into slavery. Here are a few key points to consider regarding their involvement:

- African traders usually operated in small networks or family-based groups that spanned various kingdoms and regions located along the West African coast.

- They would capture people from villages and sell them to Europeans who had come to Africa for slaves.

- Some African traders even used deceitful tactics, such as capturing individuals under false pretenses with promises of employment or marriage only to later sell them into slavery instead.

The profits that could be made through this practice were so attractive that often times the African rulers allowed it or even actively encouraged it, resulting in an increase of captives being sold by African traders over time.

This contributed significantly to the large numbers of men, women, and children being shipped off across the Atlantic Ocean as part of the transatlantic slave trade system, which caused irreparable damage on many generations of Africans both physically and psychologically. With this, we can see how pivotal role African traders had in igniting one of the darkest chapters in our world's history, making it clear that they shouldn't be overlooked when seeking answers about this period in time.

As we move forward in understanding these events, it's important to keep in mind the great influence that African brokers had on shaping its outcome as well.

The Role of African Brokers in the Slave Trade

Captured and sold into a life of servitude, countless Africans were betrayed by the opportunistic African brokers who profited off of the lucrative slave trade. As intermediaries between African traders and European merchants, these brokers facilitated the exchange of slaves for manufactured goods. The transaction was highly profitable for all parties involved, but it came at an immense cost to those whose lives were taken away from them.

Participants	Brokers	Traders	Merchants
Roles	Played a key role in facilitating transactions between African traders and European merchants.	Engaged in small-scale trading with local communities on the coast.	Had the resources and connections to purchase large numbers of slaves from brokers or directly from traders.
Motivations	Highly motivated by profits gained through the slave trade.	Mainly acquired captives as payment for debts owed by villages or individuals to other villages or individuals.	Profited greatly from exporting commodities produced with labor provided by enslaved people across the Atlantic Ocean.
Impact	Enabled economies of scale, increasing profitability and efficiency for all parties involved.	Facilitated the initial acquisition of captives, acting as intermediaries.	Held significant power in transatlantic slave trading operations, having access to larger amounts of capital than African traders or brokers. Their influence allowed for a quicker acquisition of slaves without extensive travel throughout Africa.
Overall Result	Despite their role, European merchants ultimately held more power over transatlantic slave trading operations due to greater access to capital.	Brokers connected different parties involved, making it easier for Europeans to acquire slaves quickly.	European merchants, with tremendous power, had a significant impact on this shameful chapter in human history, influencing and dominating transatlantic slave trading operations. Transitioning into a discussion about their role highlights their greater influence.

The role played by African brokers in this process is undeniable - they allowed for economies of scale that increased both profitability and efficiency. By connecting different parties involved in this abhorrent practice, they made it easier for Europeans to acquire slaves quickly without having to travel extensively throughout Africa. In spite of their involvement, however, it was ultimately European merchants who held most of the power over transatlantic slave trading operations; they had access to larger amounts of capital than either African traders or brokers did. Transitioning into a discussion about 'the role of European merchants in the slave trade' then reveals how such tremendous power enabled them to have an even greater impact on this shameful chapter in human history.

The Role of European Merchants in the Slave Trade

You may be aware of the pivotal role African brokers played in the transatlantic slave trade, however, it is important to recognize that European merchants held significant power and influence over the process. These merchants were largely responsible for obtaining slaves from African traders, transporting them across the Atlantic Ocean, and then selling them in the Americas. This was a lucrative business venture for European merchants as they were able to make a considerable profit out of each transaction.

European merchants not only profited from this human trafficking but also used their influence to gain access to other resources such as gold, ivory, and spices which could also be sold in Europe for a large sum of money. Furthermore, many of these merchants had investments in sugar plantations across South America so they could increase their overall profits by supplying labor with enslaved Africans.

The involvement of European merchants was essential in ensuring that demand for slaves remained high throughout much of Europe's history. Without their participation in the trading networks between Africa and the Americas, it is unlikely that slavery would have become as widespread or profitable as it did during this period.

Transitioning into subsequent topics about the role of European governments in the slave trade, one can see how different governments sought to regulate or promote this industry through various means such as taxation laws or even protectionist policies.

The Role of European Governments in the Slave Trade

European governments played a crucial role in perpetuating the horrors of slavery, profiting immensely from the suffering of millions. Throughout Europe, governments actively promoted and protected the slave trade, providing subsidies to merchants or companies involved in its activities.

In particular, Britain and France invested heavily in the industry by offering tax exemptions and other incentives to those who traded slaves. This allowed them to control much of the transatlantic slave trade until 1807 when both countries abolished it.

Governments also mandated that enslaved people be brought into their colonies as labor for agricultural production and domestic work. Many European countries used legal systems to ensure that enslaved people could not own property or sue in court, thus denying any possibility of freedom or justice for them.

Furthermore, European powers were responsible for negotiating treaties with African states that allowed merchants to acquire slaves directly from African traders without intervention from government officials. This enabled Europeans to bring even more enslaved Africans across the Atlantic Ocean against their will.

European governments provided a powerful economic incentive for enslaving African people by making sure there was a steady supply of cheap labor available through this system of exploitation. By allowing this large-scale human trafficking, these governments were complicit in promoting an institution which caused immense suffering and injustice on an unimaginable scale throughout centuries of history.

As such, they must bear responsibility for their involvement in this atrocity before moving forward with its legacy today.

The Role of the United States in the Slave Trade

You played a part in the slave trade tragedy, too; with its subsidies and treaties, America acted as an enabler of this harrowing injustice.

The United States was heavily involved in the transatlantic slave trade from 1790 to 1808. This period saw the importation of more than 600,000 African captives into American territory. Nearly 200 ships sailed from U.S. ports to Africa for slaves every year. Slave trading became a lucrative business for many Americans — especially those living in New England. Slave traders could expect profits of up to 50 percent on their investments. This enabled many parts of the nation to have access to cheap labor resources.

The role that US citizens played in Atlantic slavery was not limited to simply providing markets and labor sources. In some cases, they were directly involved in buying and transporting slaves across the ocean via ships or financing expeditions and brokers operating out of US-controlled ports. American merchants also established networks with African merchants who supplied them with enslaved people for sale on US soil.

These activities helped fuel an international market based on human bondage that had devastating consequences for millions of Africans over centuries. Furthermore, it is estimated that around 2 million people died during the Middle Passage due to horrific conditions aboard slave vessels crossing the Atlantic Ocean from Africa to America or other destinations such as Brazil or Cuba.

The impact of these losses can still be felt today by descendants of those who suffered under this system. As a result, one could say that United States citizens were deeply complicit in perpetuating the transatlantic slave trade through their actions and economic interests which continue to affect generations today.

The Impact of the Slave Trade on African Societies

The transatlantic slave trade had a devastating impact on African societies, leaving lasting effects that can still be felt today. Millions of African people were taken from their homes and sold into slavery during the course of the transatlantic slave trade, leading to a massive disruption in the social structure of many African societies. This disruption was further compounded by the loss of natural resources and agricultural knowledge as enslaved Africans were forced onto ships and shipped out to work in other countries.

The economic impact of this mass displacement was significant, as it resulted in a substantial decrease in Africa's population size and labor force, leading to underdevelopment throughout much of the continent. In addition, the cultural and spiritual traditions that many enslaved Africans were forced to abandon or modify also had long-term implications for African societies.

Impact	Description
Economic	Decrease in population size and labor force; Underdevelopment throughout much of the continent.
Cultural & Spiritual Traditions	Forced abandonment or modification with long-term implications for African societies.
Social Structure	Massive disruption due to mass displacement resulting from enslavement.

This tragic episode in human history has left an indelible mark on both African society and its descendants around the world. Today, many communities are still struggling with its legacy – both economically and culturally – while others have managed to build upon it as a means of survival and expression. As we move forward into a new era, we must remember what happened during this period so that we can ensure that such atrocities never happen again. By honoring those who suffered through this period we can better understand our own role in continuing to create an equitable society for all people across the globe.

The Impact of the Slave Trade on African-American Identity

The transatlantic slave trade drastically shaped the identity of African-Americans, leaving an undeniable imprint on their culture and heritage.

From a cultural standpoint, the slave trade had a profound effect on African-American identity by introducing elements of African cultures into the Western world through music, language, religious beliefs and practices. It also forged deep bonds between members of enslaved communities that were based on shared experiences of oppression. The trade established new cultural norms that blended various aspects of both African and European cultures, and created a unique social structure with distinct codes of behavior and communication among those who were enslaved.

From an economic perspective, the effects of slavery have been far-reaching as well. The labor exploitation associated with slavery allowed for great wealth disparities between white Americans and African-Americans which persist to this day in many parts of America. Additionally, the lack of investment in resources such as education for those who were enslaved meant that they lacked opportunities to acquire meaningful employment after emancipation, leading to further poverty among black Americans even after the abolition of slavery itself.

This has resulted in persistent patterns of inequality based on race which are still very much alive today in some contexts. The legacy of enslavement continues to be felt today both psychologically and socially as its effects linger long after formal emancipation was declared nearly two centuries ago. Through these lasting impacts, it is clear that the transatlantic slave trade has had an immense impact on African-American identity throughout history - one which will continue to be felt for generations to come.

The Continuing Legacy of the Slave Trade

You feel the lasting effects of the slave trade deeply, as it continues to shape African-American identity even today.

Historical trauma and systemic racism are both results of the transatlantic slave trade and still have a significant influence on how black people experience life in America. This is evidenced by lower educational attainment rates, greater unemployment levels, and higher poverty levels among African-Americans compared to their white counterparts. Furthermore, laws like redlining that barred black people from buying homes or taking out loans in certain neighborhoods continue to limit access to economic opportunities for black people even today.

Moreover, the symbolism of slavery still carries power. Monuments honoring Confederate soldiers who fought against the liberation of slaves remain standing in many southern states while monuments dedicated to enslaved Africans remain largely absent from public spaces. The presence of these symbols perpetuate a culture which diminishes the experiences and contributions of African-Americans throughout history.

The legacy of slavery will never be fully erased; its impact has been so profound that it can be felt deeply generations later. Despite progress made since then, America remains an unequal society where race still determines one's destiny more often than not.

It's therefore essential that we acknowledge this legacy if we hope to ever truly move past it and create an equitable society for all Americans regardless of race or ethnicity.

Frequently Asked Questions

What was the role of the Middle Passage in the Transatlantic Slave Trade?

We, as historians, have long studied the role of the Middle Passage in the Transatlantic Slave Trade. This section of the voyage was especially significant due to its location between Africa and America.

During this time, enslaved Africans were transported across the Atlantic Ocean from their homeland to a new life in North and South America. The estimated death toll for individuals on Middle Passage ships ranged from 13-20%.

Additionally, millions of people experienced immense suffering during these voyages due to overcrowding and lack of sanitation aboard ships. As such, it's clear that the Middle Passage played an integral role in facilitating one of history's largest diasporas.

How did the Transatlantic Slave Trade affect other countries around the world?

Weaving a tangled web of destruction, the transatlantic slave trade had devastating effects on various countries around the world. From Europe to Africa to the Americas, no corner of the globe was spared from its insidious reach.

Countries like Portugal and Britain profited greatly off of this system, while others such as Angola and West Africa suffered immense loss in terms of population and economic stability.

On top of that, it caused an unprecedented disruption to African cultures with entire generations separated by seas and continents due to forced relocation.

The transatlantic slave trade not only left a lasting imprint on humanity but also serves as a reminder that history must not be repeated for any country or people.

How did the Transatlantic Slave Trade influence the global economy?

We've seen how the transatlantic slave trade had a profound effect on countries around the world, but what of its influence on the global economy?

It's hard to estimate just how much of an impact it had, but we can make some educated guesses. The Atlantic slave trade was responsible for introducing vast amounts of wealth into Europe and America. This influx of money helped shape their economies in a number of ways, from providing capital for investment projects to creating new markets and labor forces.

Additionally, the slave trade created new opportunities in industries such as agriculture, manufacturing, and transportation. Not only did this help to stimulate economic growth in Europe and America, but it had ripple effects that reached other parts of the world as well.

What are some of the long-term effects of the Transatlantic Slave Trade?

We've seen the far-reaching effects of the Transatlantic Slave Trade on the global economy, but its long-term implications are just as significant.

The enslavement of millions of Africans and their descendants had a deep and lasting impact on societies throughout Europe, the Americas, and Africa. Economically, many countries in Africa were stripped of human capital which stunted economic growth and resulted in lost potential wealth.

Additionally, legacies of racism still linger today due to historical injustices perpetuated by slave traders. Socially, communities were disrupted through displacement and forced labor that caused damage to family structures and traditions.

Finally, psychologically there have been wide-ranging effects resulting from the trauma experienced by those affected by this dark period in history.

What is the connection between the Transatlantic Slave Trade and modern-day racism?

We acknowledge the connection between the transatlantic slave trade and modern-day racism. The slave trade had a lasting impact on people of African descent, both in terms of their political, economic, social, and cultural status.

This has resulted in an ongoing legacy of racism that has affected generations since then. The transatlantic slave trade was a form of institutionalized racial oppression which continues to shape how societies view people from different backgrounds today.

This is why it's important for us to recognize its consequences and take action to address them.

Conclusion

We've seen how the involvement of African people in the Transatlantic Slave Trade was multifaceted. Africans suffered greatly as victims of the slave trade, but they also played a role in its perpetuation.

African kings and traders acted as brokers, captives were kidnapped, and European merchants profited from it all. The slave trade had devastating effects on African societies, while also leaving an indelible mark on African-American identity.

One example of this is the life story of Olaudah Equiano (1745 - 1797), a former slave who published his autobiography in London to great acclaim. His narrative drew attention to the horrors experienced by slaves during their passage across the Atlantic and helped foster greater public awareness about slavery's reality.

This legacy continues to impact how we understand both African history and contemporary society today.

Slavery in America

We've all heard the stories: a group of people taken from their homes and families, forced to work against their will, and treated as property.

It's not a pleasant image, but it's one that has been part of American history since the very beginning.

In this article, we'll take a look at the origins of slavery in America, how it grew over time, and its legacy today.

We'll also examine current issues related to slavery in America and discuss ways that we can work together to address these problems.

It's an uncomfortable topic for sure, but an important conversation to have – so let's get started!

Origins of Slavery in America

The enslavement of thousands of people brought to the US against their will began a legacy of oppression and injustice that continues to this day.

The earliest records of enslaved individuals in what's now the United States date back to 1619, when 20 African captives were sold as indentured servants in Jamestown, Virginia. This marked the beginning of slavery in America, and throughout the 17th century, more African slaves were imported into British colonies as demand for labor increased.

By 1680, there were approximately 6,000 black slaves in America, and by 1750 that number had risen to over 200,000. Slavery became an entrenched part of American society during this period since it provided an opportunity for wealthy landowners to gain access to free labor from Africans who had been taken from their homelands against their will.

Laws were created which severely limited the rights of African Americans and enabled them to be treated like property and commodities. This included laws preventing interracial marriage and laws limiting freedom of movement for those living under bondage. The horrific conditions endured by slave laborers would ultimately spark a civil war which saw the abolition of slavery across the US in 1865 with President Lincoln's Emancipation Proclamation.

However, even after emancipation was declared, many former slaves still faced discrimination, segregation, and poverty due to systemic racism within American society. Thus while slavery may have ended on paper at least, its effects continue to linger today throughout all aspects of our society - from economic disparities between blacks and whites, lack of access to education or healthcare resources as well as ongoing issues with police brutality against minorities nationwide.

To address these inequalities, we must first recognize how they are rooted in America's history with slavery before we can move forward towards greater equality moving forward.

The Growth of the Slave Trade

With the demand for labor on the rise, more and more people were being taken from their homes to work against their will. As a result, the slave trade in America dramatically increased throughout the 17th and 18th centuries.

The Trans-Atlantic Slave Trade was driven by economic forces in Europe, the demand for labor in America, and horrific conditions on ships and during transport. Slaves were usually brought from Africa to South America or Caribbean islands before arriving at North American ports. Some slaves were also transported within America itself, when colonial powers needed additional labor forces.

The cruel practice of slavery saw millions of people forcibly removed from their families and homeland so they could be sold into a life of servitude. Enslavement did not just take away these individuals' freedom – it caused untold suffering as human lives were treated like commodities with no rights or respect for basic humanity.

This devastating legacy still affects many African Americans today, as they continue to battle injustices related to this shameful history of slavery in America. To better understand this struggle, we must now turn our attention to examining what life was like for slaves who lived and worked on plantations.

Life of Slaves on the Plantation

You can only imagine the daily struggles and injustices endured by those living and working on plantations, like that of the hypothetical slave Mary who was separated from her family at a young age and forced to work for no pay.

On these plantations, slaves were treated as less than human, with some owners not providing them with adequate food or clothing. They often lacked basic medical care and were subject to physical abuse if they did not meet their masters' demands. Slaves worked long days in grueling conditions doing back-breaking labor without any respite or sense of control over their lives.

Life on the plantation for slaves was one marred by trauma, pain, and suffering due to the oppressive nature of their circumstances. Slaves had no legal rights or protections under the law and faced harsh punishments for any perceived disobedience or insubordination.

Moreover, because they could be sold away from their families at any time, many slaves experienced an unrelenting grief as they endured constant separations from loved ones.

The horrors of slavery are difficult to describe in words but must be acknowledged in order to understand its lasting legacy today. To move forward towards true equality between all people requires us to first confront our nation's history honestly—an effort which begins by understanding fully how enslaved people lived during this era of American history before transitioning into a discussion about the abolition movement that followed it.

The Abolition Movement

Gain a deeper understanding of how humanity triumphed over injustice by exploring the inspiring story of the abolition movement. The fight to end slavery began with a few brave people who saw that all human beings should have the same rights and freedoms. Through their courage, the anti-slavery movement became one of the most powerful reform movements in American history.

Reformers used petitions, speeches, and writings to argue for an end to slavery and organize boycotts against slaveholders. Many also risked their own safety to help slaves escape from bondage by creating networks known as "The Underground Railroad."

The turning point in the fight against slavery came in 1863 when President Abraham Lincoln issued his Emancipation Proclamation which declared all persons held as slaves within any state or designated part of a state were then 'forever free.' After this landmark ruling, many African Americans joined Union forces in fighting against Confederate states and helped turn the tide in favor of freedom during America's Civil War.

Even though emancipation marked a major victory for those fighting for justice, it was not until 1865 when Congress passed the Thirteenth Amendment that slavery was finally abolished throughout America.

This momentous achievement inspired other countries around the world to follow suit and take similar steps towards ending racial discrimination everywhere. By bringing together people from across society on both sides of an issue, this powerful movement showed what can be achieved when citizens come together with a shared goal—a lesson that reverberates even today as we look forward towards continuing progress on issues like civil rights and immigration reform.

With its legacy still alive today, it's clear that our nation will never forget the impact made by those who fought so hard for freedom during this monumental time period in our history – paving way for us now to explore what kind of economic impact slavery had on our nation.

The Impact of Slavery on the Economy

Explore how the unjust institution of slavery had an undeniable economic influence on our nation, and see how it still affects us today. Slavery provided a source of labor for plantations which enabled the US to become a major exporter of agricultural goods. It also contributed to the growing divide between North and South with regard to industrialization.

Here are three ways that slavery had a significant economic impact:

- The slave trade was an important source of revenue for both business owners and traders who transported enslaved Africans across the Atlantic Ocean.

- Slave labor allowed for more efficient production processes, as enslaved people were considered property without rights or wages, making them far cheaper than free laborers.

- Slavery also encouraged racial discrimination by creating an entrenched system in which white landowners held power over African slaves and their descendants—a legacy that continues to shape our society today.

Slavery left its mark on many aspects of our economy, from labor practices to social structures to consumer trends across the country. Its effects are still felt in America today—not only through institutional racism but also through persistent wealth inequality that disproportionately impacts Black Americans compared with their white counterparts.

As we look towards understanding the role religion played in facilitating this era of American history, it's critical that we consider these ongoing injustices caused by centuries-old slave labor. Only then can we create meaningful change going forward.

The Role of Religion in Slavery

We've long sought to make sense of the morally reprehensible institution of slavery. Religion was used to justify the unjust, inhumane institution of slavery and continues to shape our society today. Religious beliefs were often fused with the concept of racial supremacy, allowing for slaves to be dehumanized and treated as subhuman. This entrenched the idea that white people had a god-given right to dominate black people.

Some religious institutions actively supported slavery; slaveholders argued that their actions were divinely ordained by God and justified through religious scripture. At the same time, there was a strong contingent of abolitionists who believed that slavery could not be reconciled with Christian morality and argued against it on moral grounds. They drew upon passages from the Bible which spoke out against oppression and highlighted God's love for all people regardless of race or status in society.

Despite these efforts, it would take an entire civil war before slavery could finally be abolished in America. The legacy of religion's role in justifying enslavement is still felt today. Despite its abolishment over 150 years ago, racism persists in our society due to deeply ingrained prejudices perpetuated by centuries-old ideologies which deemed one group superior over another based on skin color alone.

As we move into exploring 'slavery in the Civil War,' we must continue examining this complex history if we're ever going to come together as a nation united against racism and prejudice.

Slavery in the Civil War

You can gain insight into the devastating impact of slavery by exploring how it was used to support the Civil War. Slavery played a large role in causing and perpetuating the Civil War, as it had divided many Americans on both sides of the conflict.

The Confederacy's reliance on enslaved labor resulted in their successful production of foodstuffs and other materials for war efforts, while Union forces sought to abolish slavery and free those held captive. In addition, some African Americans were enlisted to fight for the Union cause; despite facing discrimination from white soldiers, in particular Confederate troops who viewed them as traitors against their former enslavers.

The war itself led to an even greater number of casualties among those fighting than any other American conflict before or since; much of this death toll was due to disease brought on by inadequate nutrition and sanitation amongst soldiers during battle. However, mortality rates for slaves also increased significantly due to forced labor conditions imposed upon them by their captors during this time period.

In short, whether in terms of its direct role in causing or sustaining the war effort or its deleterious effect upon those serving at either side's behest, slavery had a devastating impact on all involved with the Civil War.

This legacy continues today, making it important to understand how slavery shaped America's history so that we may better grapple with its effects still present within our society. As such, exploring its influence during the Civil War is essential for gaining clarity as we move towards understanding and overcoming the legacy of slavery in America.

The Legacy of Slavery in America

The lingering effects of a dark past still haunt the nation, symbolized by the shadows of oppression that haven't been fully cast away.

The legacy of slavery in America is an ever-present reminder of the country's difficult history, and it has had profound implications on modern American society.

Today, its reverberations can still be felt across political, economic, and social spheres:

- Political – Many African Americans are underrepresented or excluded from government bodies at all levels. Racial bias in voting laws continues to suppress Black voices in politics.

- Economic – Systemic racism has resulted in lower wages and higher unemployment rates for African Americans compared to their white counterparts. Additionally, Black communities tend to receive fewer resources for economic development projects.

- Social – Structural racism persists through inequitable education systems and public health disparities between whites and Blacks due to a lack of comprehensive healthcare access.

- Legal – The criminal justice system disproportionately incarcerates people of color while maintaining harsher sentences than those for white defendants convicted of similar crimes.

These lasting consequences have caused tremendous amounts of injustice throughout our nation's history and continue to deny many African Americans basic human rights today.

Transcending this entrenched legacy requires a long-term commitment from individuals and institutions alike to address current issues related to slavery in America.

Current Issues Related to Slavery in America

You feel the reverberations of a dark past in today's society, an echo of injustice that still lingers and demands attention. The legacy of slavery is still very much present in America, from issues such as racism to modern-day labor exploitation and human trafficking. These problems have been exacerbated by centuries of systemic oppression and discrimination against African Americans.

The current economic inequalities between Black and white communities are profoundly rooted in more than 400 years of slavery. The issue of reparations for descendants of slaves is also a controversial topic that remains unresolved. Some believe that it would be a form of justice while others argue that it would be too costly or impossible to measure the extent to which people have been affected by slavery.

Still other issues include the lack of access to education for those who descend from slaves, as well as disparities in criminal sentencing between whites and Blacks despite similar offenses being committed. The effects can be seen all around us: from drug addiction to poverty levels, they are all linked back to the injustices suffered by our ancestors during chattel enslavement.

As a nation, we must continue facing this injustice head on and work together towards creating lasting solutions so that future generations won't have to grapple with these same issues any longer - transitioning into taking action against slavery in America is the only way forward.

Taking Action Against Slavery in America

We know that current issues related to slavery in America are still very prevalent. But what can we do to take action against it?

We must start by being informed about the issue and understanding the scope of the problem. There are several organizations and initiatives dedicated to combating slavery in America.

This includes organizations that provide legal services, shelter, education, and other resources to victims of modern-day slavery. These organizations also work towards raising awareness about human trafficking and educating others on ways to prevent it from occurring.

We can also take steps on an individual level to fight against slavery in America. By supporting anti-slavery initiatives with donations or volunteering our time, we can make a difference by helping to provide resources for those affected by this form of exploitation.

Additionally, we can help spread awareness through social media campaigns or speaking out on behalf of victims in our communities. Taking these small actions together can have a big impact when it comes to bringing an end to this injustice once and for all.

Conclusion

We've come a long way since the days of slavery in America, but it still exists. We must take action and speak out against this injustice if we want to see real change. Its legacy continues to haunt us with economic inequality and racism.

As we look back at our history, let's use pathos to evoke an emotional response in order to fuel our passion for anti-slavery efforts. Together, we can make sure that no one ever has to experience the horrors of slavery again.

The Reconstruction Era

We've all heard the theory that Reconstruction was a period of great progress for African Americans in the United States, but how much of this is true?

The Reconstruction Era was an important period of reform between 1865 and 1877, following the end of the Civil War.

During this time, federal legislation was passed to secure civil rights for those who had been formerly enslaved.

In this article, we'll explore how these changes were made and examine their lasting impact on our nation today.

It's sure to be an interesting journey as we uncover what really happened during this turbulent period in American history.

Causes of the Reconstruction Era

Following the end of the U.S. Civil War, a period of rebuilding and reform ensued, resulting in a major shift in the nation's history. This time was known as the Reconstruction Era and it was spurred by multiple causes stemming from both sides of the war.

In addition to restoring order within states that were part of the Confederacy, there was also an effort to secure civil rights for newly freed African-Americans. The passage of landmark legislation such as the 13th Amendment ended slavery permanently and marked a new chapter in American history.

The 13th Amendment

You ratified the 13th Amendment in 1865, ending slavery in the United States once and for all. With this step forward, our nation marked a turning point in history that still resonates today.

We succeeded at tearing down centuries of injustice and oppression by stepping into a new era of freedom and equality. The 13th Amendment granted emancipation to millions of African Americans, while providing legal protection against involuntary servitude.

It also abolished any form of slavery or indentured servitude - except as punishment for crime - across the entire country. This monumental change was key to laying a foundation for further reforms during Reconstruction such as the 14th Amendment.

The 14th Amendment

The 14th Amendment continued the legacy of freedom and equality, ensuring all citizens equal protection under the law. This Amendment had far-reaching implications that allowed African Americans to be seen as more than just property but as citizens with inalienable rights.

The Amendment declared:

- All persons born or naturalized in the United States are American citizens.
- No state can deny a citizen due process of law and equal protection under the law.
- Any person who's been deprived of their civil rights must have legal recourse for justice.

These three points granted African Americans unprecedented access to civil liberties, such as voting rights and equal representation before the government, allowing them to finally experience true freedom within society.

Through this amendment, we've seen a massive shift toward greater racial equity and social justice that's helped forge a stronger union for generations to come. With this empowering sense of safety now ingrained in our collective identity, it's time to look at how the 15th Amendment furthers these goals even more!

The 15th Amendment

You now have the right to vote, regardless of race, thanks to the 15th Amendment. The Amendment was passed in 1870 as part of the Reconstruction Era and prohibited any state from denying a citizen the right to vote due to their race.

This marked a major milestone in civil rights history that had been hard-fought for by African Americans since the abolishment of slavery. It served as one more step towards ensuring they could fully participate in civic life and exercise their constitutional rights.

The 15th Amendment has since become an integral part of our democracy and is still reflected today in federal voting laws protecting citizens from discrimination based on race or color. Its passing was also instrumental in creating new opportunities for black Americans during Reconstruction, paving the way for them to build better lives for themselves and their families.

With this amendment's success, we can look forward with optimism to continued progress towards equal rights for all citizens. To further these efforts, attention now turns towards 'the freedman's bureau' – an organization established after the Civil War with a mission of aiding newly freed slaves.

The Freedman's Bureau

Discover how the Freedman's Bureau helped newly freed slaves gain access to resources, education, and employment opportunities after the Civil War.

Established in 1865, the Freedman's Bureau provided vital aid to over four million formerly enslaved African Americans. It distributed food, clothing, and fuel to destitute families; organized schools for former slaves in 17 states; worked with employers to create wage labor contracts; advised freedmen on leasing land; and established hospitals and refugee camps.

The bureau also sought justice for those who were unjustly imprisoned or persecuted by state laws. Those attempting to reduce slavery-related abuses were given legal assistance from Freedman's Bureau attorneys.

By helping newly freed slaves transition into their new lives as citizens of a free nation, the Freedman's Bureau played an essential role in making sure that they got off on the right foot. Its impact was felt far beyond its end in 1872, leaving a lasting legacy of hope and equality for all African Americans.

With these successes under their belt, it's now time to explore how another post-Civil War movement - the Ku Klux Klan - affected Reconstruction efforts across America.

The Ku Klux Klan

Experience how the Ku Klux Klan, a post-Civil War white supremacist group, affected Reconstruction efforts across America.

From 1866 to 1871, the Klan terrorized African Americans in the South by committing acts of violence and intimidation to restore white supremacy. Severe beatings were common tactics used by Klansmen to suppress black voting rights.

Lynching was used as a form of vigilante justice against African Americans who challenged Jim Crow laws. Many citizens were forced off their land due to economic intimidation and threats of violence from members of the KKK.

Racial discrimination in employment opportunities became more widespread during this time period due to fear of reprisal from Klan members if businesses hired African American workers. The effects that the Ku Klux Klan had on Reconstruction efforts were far-reaching and devastating for many African Americans living in the South at this time period.

We can only imagine what life must have been like for those individuals who faced such hatred and oppression every day without any legal recourse or protection from these violent hate groups. As we move forward into our discussion about 'the reconstruction acts', it's important to remember how these terrible injustices affected so many people throughout our nation's history.

The Reconstruction Acts

Explore how the Reconstruction Acts of 1867-1868 sought to restore civil rights and rebuild America after the devastating effects of the Ku Klux Klan, bringing a glimmer of hope in a time of despair.

The series of laws, known as the Reconstruction Acts, allowed for military control over former Confederate states. Each state was required to ratify amendments to the United States Constitution that abolished slavery and granted voting rights to African Americans. This was an unprecedented move in American history, although some argued it went too far.

Regardless, the Reconstruction Acts provided stability and safety for those who had been denied civil rights for so long. As such, it allowed them to begin rebuilding their lives and have faith that brighter days were ahead. With this newfound sense of security came optimism that they could build a better future for themselves and their families – something they hadn't had since before the Civil War began.

Despite its flaws, these acts brought a renewed sense of hope at a time when many felt powerless against hate groups like the Ku Klux Klan.

Moving forward from here, we'll now look at how Andrew Johnson's impeachment impacted this period in American history.

The Impeachment of President Andrew Johnson

You could say that the impeachment of President Andrew Johnson in 1868 was like a thunderbolt striking in an otherwise peaceful Reconstruction-era sky.

It was a period of seemingly insurmountable disagreements between Democrats and Republicans, with both sides wanting to prove their dominance over the other.

President Johnson had become increasingly hostile towards Congress, leading to him being impeached by the House of Representatives on 11 articles of impeachment.

Although he was acquitted by the Senate by one vote, this event marked a major turning point in the era and left many people feeling uncertain about what would come next.

The outcome of this incident set up a precarious situation for future negotiations—one which would eventually be resolved through what became known as the Compromise of 1877.

The Compromise of 1877

The Compromise of 1877 was a pivotal agreement between two opposing sides, an event that would shape the future of American politics. It was negotiated by a group of politicians in Washington, D.C., and it effectively ended the Reconstruction Era by allowing Southern states to regain control over their own affairs while guaranteeing limited civil rights protections for African Americans.

The Compromise also included provisions for military withdrawal from former Confederate states, and it allowed Rutherford B. Hayes to become president after a contested election result. This compromise marked the end of Reconstruction as well as its legacy: racial injustice continued to be rampant in the South despite the new laws put in place by Congress.

As such, this momentous event serves as a reminder of how far we still have to go when it comes to ensuring justice and equality for all people. With this in mind, let's now turn our attention to looking at the legacy of reconstruction left behind by this historic agreement.

The Legacy of Reconstruction

The Compromise of 1877 may have marked the end of Reconstruction, but it left behind a legacy that continues to impact us today. In many ways, this period of history is responsible for shaping our modern society and attitudes toward race.

For example, laws enacted during Reconstruction aimed to promote racial equality had lasting effects on voting rights, education opportunities, and economic development in the South. Furthermore, efforts to increase public safety during Reconstruction led to the creation of new government agencies and organizations like the Freedmen's Bureau that are still active today.

Despite these positive changes, many Americans continue to struggle with racism and inequality as a result of Reconstruction-era policies. Segregation practices such as Jim Crow laws were born out of the post-war era and remain embedded in certain aspects of our culture even now. Similarly, some economists believe that the unequal distribution of resources among African-Americans has roots in Reconstruction-era legislation which created disparities between black and white communities.

Clearly, though nearly 150 years old, the legacy of Reconstruction lives on—for better or worse—in American life today.

Frequently Asked Questions

What was the impact of the Reconstruction Era on African-American rights?

We're living in a time when African-American rights have come a long way. We can attribute much of this progress to the Reconstruction Era, which had a significant and lasting impact on African-American rights.

During this period, laws were passed to protect African Americans' right to vote and own property, while also granting them access to education and civil rights. Additionally, many organizations were formed with the intention of advocating for equal rights for all citizens regardless of race or background.

The Reconstruction Era set an important precedent that has been influential in modern civil rights movements across the United States.

How did the Reconstruction Acts affect the economy in the South?

We believe the Reconstruction Acts had a significant impact on the economy of the South.

The laws were designed to help rebuild and modernize the Southern economy, which was devastated by the Civil War.

They provided for investment in infrastructure such as railroads, bridges, and harbors, as well as providing new banking systems to support local businesses.

Additionally, these acts enabled African-Americans to participate fully in economic life through land grants, access to credit and capital markets, and protection from discriminatory practices.

Ultimately, this helped promote an economic recovery that would benefit all citizens of the South.

What were the effects of the Ku Klux Klan on African-Americans?

We shudder to think about the impact that the Ku Klux Klan had on African-Americans during Reconstruction.

In fact, in 1871 alone, there were nearly 2,000 reported acts of violence and terror inflicted against African Americans – an average of five per day – perpetrated by the Klan or their sympathizers.

This was a shocking act of cruelty and injustice that had long-lasting effects on individuals and communities throughout the South.

It's a reminder that we must remain vigilant in our fight for equality so that such atrocities aren't repeated.

How did the Impeachment of President Andrew Johnson affect the Reconstruction Era?

The impeachment of President Andrew Johnson in 1868 had far-reaching effects on the Reconstruction era. It set a precedent that presidents can be impeached and removed from office. It weakened the power of Congress to establish federal policy. This shift in power away from the presidency allowed for more progress to be made with Reconstruction efforts. Congress was now able to pass legislation regarding civil rights without presidential approval. The end result was African-Americans gaining greater access to voting rights, education, and employment opportunities during this period.

How did the Compromise of 1877 change the course of the Reconstruction Era?

We all understand the importance of compromise. The Compromise of 1877 was no different, and it had a significant impact on the course of history.

This deal between Democrats and Republicans ended the Reconstruction Era in the United States, as it resulted in federal troops being removed from remaining Southern states. It also legitimized Republican Rutherford B. Hayes's presidential election victory and marked an end to years of intense political struggles between North and South over civil rights and voting rights for African Americans.

Ultimately, this compromise set up a new era that diminished African American civil liberties by allowing state governments to implement segregationist laws.

Conclusion

We've seen the immense impact of the Reconstruction Era.

From the passage of Amendments to protect the civil rights of African Americans to the landmark Compromise of 1877, the changes wrought by this period have been truly remarkable.

It's hard to overstate how far we've come since then; it's like night and day!

We owe much to those brave individuals who fought for justice and equality during this time, and we must never forget their legacy.

Let us continue to strive towards a better future, one that is built on respect and understanding for all people.

The Jim Crow Era

We've all heard about the Jim Crow era, but what was it really like? During this time period in American history, laws and customs enforced racial segregation between Black and white Americans.

In this article, we'll explore the origins of Jim Crow laws, as well as their impact on African-Americans. We'll also take a look at how these laws manifested in education, transportation, healthcare and social life.

You'll learn about the fight for desegregation and the legacy of Jim Crow Laws that still persists today. So join us as we take a deep dive into this difficult but important part of our nation's history.

Origins of Jim Crow Laws

As segregation spread, so too did the laws that codified it, creating a system of restrictions and oppression that would be known as the Jim Crow era.

Jim Crow laws were enacted in the late 19th century in the Southern United States to enforce racial segregation between white and black citizens. These laws mandated the segregation of public facilities such as schools, transportation, bathrooms, restaurants, and restrooms. They also had numerous other effects on African-Americans' lives.

For example, they ensured legal discrimination by making it illegal for black Americans to vote or serve on juries. The Jim Crow era saw widespread violence against African-Americans and resulted in countless deaths due to lynching or mob justice.

It wasn't until 1964 when Congress passed the Civil Rights Act that these laws began to be overturned. As this dark period of American history was coming to an end, its devastating impact on African-Americans was just beginning to be felt.

Impact on African-Americans

You can feel the weight of oppression and discrimination that African-Americans experienced during the Jim Crow era. From disenfranchisement to racial segregation, African-Americans faced a multitude of injustices. They were systematically excluded from full participation in society with little recourse for recourse or recompense.

The impact was far-reaching. African-Americans were denied their basic human dignity and hindered from achieving their full potential on multiple levels. This led directly into the next phase of Jim Crow which was segregation in education.

During this time period, African-Americans experienced the following injustices:

1) Denial of voting rights through literacy tests, poll taxes, grandfather clauses, and other methods

2) Separation in public facilities such as restaurants, bathrooms, transportation systems, and schools
3) Segregation in housing markets through restrictive covenants and other tactics
4) Unequal access to healthcare services.

Overall, the weight of these injustices had a profound impact on African-American communities.

Segregation in Education

The Jim Crow era saw African-Americans segregated in education, a weighty injustice that barred them from achieving their full potential and robbed them of their innate dignity.

Schools, universities, and other educational institutions were strictly divided by race. This meant that black students had to attend separate schools with fewer resources than those attended by white students. They often had inferior facilities and outdated textbooks, which kept them from receiving the same quality of education as whites.

This prevented many talented African-Americans from pursuing higher education or professional careers. It was also emotionally damaging for many African-American students who were deprived of the opportunity to study alongside peers of different backgrounds and cultures.

The effects of this segregation were far reaching and long lasting, making it difficult for African-Americans to access equal opportunities even after the Jim Crow era ended.

These injustices in education further highlight the systemic racism experienced by African Americans during the Jim Crow era.

As we move on to explore segregation in transportation, it's clear that these oppressive policies weren't just limited to one area but rather encompassed all aspects of life for African Americans at the time.

Segregation in Transportation

We, African Americans, were subject to discrimination and unequal access during the Jim Crow era on all modes of transportation. We were limited to segregated cars with separate facilities and often separated into different sections on railroads. These cars had lower quality services than those for whites.

On city buses, we faced segregated seating. However, some bus companies allowed us to sit where we pleased. Still, white passengers sometimes harassed us if they saw us in the wrong seat.

This restricted our freedom of movement and created a climate of fear and intimidation as we traveled from place to place. The same level of discrimination continued even when it came time for medical care, as segregation in healthcare was just another form of oppression African Americans faced during the Jim Crow era.

Segregation in Healthcare

During the dark times of segregation, it felt like African Americans were blocked from receiving proper medical care, as if a wall of discrimination was standing in their way. Hospitals and other healthcare facilities did not treat them with the same respect or level of care as white patients. In many cases, they would be turned away and denied access to services altogether.

Even when they were able to receive treatment, it would often be done in separate areas that lacked adequate resources and staff. This inequality created an even larger divide between African Americans and whites during this time period. It was clear that the Jim Crow Era had wrought deep barriers between races when it came to accessing healthcare.

This only highlighted how deeply entrenched racism was in society at the time, making it almost impossible for African Americans to secure quality medical care. As a result, many African Americans had to rely on makeshift solutions such as home remedies provided by family members and friends instead of professional help — a situation which could have been avoided with greater equality in access to quality healthcare services.

Moving forward from this difficult period, we must strive for progress towards racial justice within our healthcare system so that all can benefit from its necessary services equally.

Segregation in Religion

You can still feel the sting of segregation in religion today, as many places of worship remain divided along racial lines.

During the Jim Crow era, African Americans were prohibited from attending white churches, and vice versa.

Even though these laws have been abolished, some churches continue to practice segregation in their congregations or by providing separate entrances for blacks and whites.

This further perpetuates the idea that one race is superior to another.

It's important to acknowledge the legacy of discrimination that exists in religious institutions so we can begin to move past it.

We must recognize how this type of segregation has hurt all communities and take steps towards creating an inclusive environment where everyone feels welcome regardless of race or ethnicity.

Only then will we be able to create a society where all people are truly equal—one free from oppression and prejudice.

Segregation in Social Life

We feel the effects of segregation in social life today, with unequal access to resources and opportunities depending on race or ethnicity. During the Jim Crow era, this inequality was heavily enforced through legal means that perpetuated white supremacy and racism.

The consequences of the Jim Crow era reached far beyond just the south:

- In Northern states, segregation was often not written into law but still occurred through informal practices such as 'redlining' neighborhoods and denying loans to certain people based on their race.

- In Western states, Native American reservations were denied basic services from state governments, which had a devastating effect on economic development for many years to come.

Despite tremendous progress since then, these legacies remain embedded in our society today.

The story of our nation's past can never be fully told without understanding how entrenched segregation has been in our history. But by recognizing this reality and taking meaningful steps towards equality, we can ensure a brighter future for all Americans.

As we look at Jim Crow laws in the North next, let's keep this goal firmly in mind.

Jim Crow Laws in the North

The past struggles of certain communities have left an indelible mark on the nation, and efforts must be taken to right these wrongs in order to achieve real progress.

The Jim Crow laws were not limited to the Southern United States, but were enacted in Northern states as well. These laws enforced racial segregation through a variety of methods, including legalized discrimination in education, housing, employment, and public accommodations. African Americans living in Northern states often faced similar injustices that their Southern counterparts did under Jim Crow Laws.

These laws denied African Americans their civil rights and freedoms, making it even more difficult for them to gain economic security and social acceptance in society. As a result of such oppressive legislation, many African Americans were forced into poverty or had little choice but to migrate from the North seeking better opportunities elsewhere.

Thus, it is evident that Jim Crow laws had far-reaching effects on numerous communities throughout the country—not just those residing below the Mason-Dixon Line.

As we continue our discussion of this era of American history, it is important to note how black individuals fought against these unjust laws in hopes of achieving true freedom and equality for all citizens. The fight for desegregation was a long and arduous one—with black leaders at its forefront leading the charge towards justice and equal rights for all people regardless of race or creed.

The Fight for Desegregation

Striving for a better tomorrow, the fight for desegregation was a long and difficult road - but where there's a will, there's a way.

African Americans took to the streets in defiance of Jim Crow laws, knowing that they were risking their safety to do so. Their courage and unwavering commitment to justice inspired many people of all races to join them in their struggle.

Marches, protests, boycotts, and sit-ins helped raise awareness about civil rights issues throughout the nation. However, it wasn't until the Supreme Court ruled in favor of Brown v Board of Education that school segregation was declared unconstitutional.

This landmark decision sparked an even more determined effort among civil rights activists who saw this as an opportunity to push for other forms of equal access. Despite fierce opposition from those who wanted things to stay as they were, progress was made through both legal action and grassroots efforts.

As individuals continue fighting for justice and equality today, it is important to remember that without this brave fight for desegregation during the Jim Crow era, none of these successes would have been possible.

With that in mind, we turn our attention toward understanding the legacy left by these oppressive laws.

The Legacy of Jim Crow Laws

You can still feel the weight of Jim Crow laws today, a legacy that continues to limit opportunities for many and deny justice to those who should have it. While the civil rights movement of the 1950s and 60s brought an end to legal segregation by race, its effects linger in our society.

The legacy of Jim Crow is wide-reaching and far-reaching:

- In terms of economic opportunity, many people are denied access to high-paying jobs due to their race or ethnicity.

- Educational disparities between black and white children still exist, preventing them from reaching their full potential.

- In terms of criminal justice, the disproportionate incarceration rate of African Americans persists despite reforms in sentencing guidelines. Black people are more likely to be stopped by police than any other group in America.

- In terms of healthcare disparities, African Americans face higher rates of chronic illnesses such as diabetes, hypertension, asthma, and HIV/AIDS due to limited access to quality healthcare services. Infant mortality rates for non-Hispanic blacks continue to be higher than those for white infants in most states.

It is clear that the legacy of Jim Crow lives on today – even though it may not always look like it did before – continuing to impede progress towards racial equality.

Frequently Asked Questions

How did Jim Crow laws affect other minority groups?

We all know how damaging the Jim Crow era was for African Americans, but what about other minority groups?

It's true that Jim Crow laws unfairly impacted African Americans most heavily, but other minorities were also affected.

From Native American tribes to Mexican-Americans and even Chinese immigrants, the segregation of the Jim Crow era had a lasting impact on many different cultures.

The effects of this era are still felt today - from unequal access to education and housing to employment discrimination.

Although there's still much progress to be made in protecting the rights of all minority groups, it's important to remember that we must look back at the events of history in order to move forward together.

What led to the passage of Jim Crow laws?

We've all heard of Jim Crow laws, but how did they come to be? The passage of these laws was largely driven by the end of Reconstruction in the late 19th century.

After the Civil War, African Americans were granted full citizenship rights, including voting and civil liberties. But with Reconstruction ending and new state legislatures passing laws that would limit these rights, many began turning to segregationist policies as a way to maintain social control.

This led to a wave of Jim Crow laws that sought to keep African Americans from certain public spaces and denied them access to basic services like healthcare and education.

How did the civil rights movement challenge Jim Crow laws?

We've been fighting for our civil rights since the dawn of time - but the civil rights movement in the 1950s and 60s was a watershed moment that forever changed the course of history. Through peaceful protests, boycotts, sit-ins, and rallies, Black Americans challenged Jim Crow laws head on.

In a world where they were systematically denied access to education, employment opportunities and public services because of their skin color, they bravely stood up to demand recognition as equals in society. We watched in awe as activists like Rosa Parks and Martin Luther King Jr. made tremendous strides towards dismantling segregation.

Their courage is nothing short of heroic - inspiring millions across the nation to march against injustice with an unwavering resolve that would ultimately pave the way for a more equitable future.

What were the economic consequences of Jim Crow laws?

We've seen the devastating economic consequences of Jim Crow laws for decades. These discriminatory laws denied African Americans access to resources, jobs, and educational opportunities that were available to white citizens in the United States.

This system of racial segregation had a profound impact on African Americans' ability to build wealth, gain economic security, and improve their standard of living. In addition, the effects were felt beyond the individuals directly affected by these laws; communities across the country suffered from reduced tax revenues due to decreased spending power among African American citizens.

The Jim Crow era was a time when inequality had an immense effect on our society's economic landscape.

What were the legal precedents for Jim Crow laws?

We all know that laws are put in place to protect us, but how did the legal precedents for Jim Crow Laws come about?

This dark period of history has a long and complicated origin story. It began with the Supreme Court ruling on Dred Scott v. Sandford in 1857, which declared that African Americans were not citizens and had no rights under the Constitution.

Following this decision, states started to pass segregation laws that limited where African Americans could live, go to school, or even eat. These statutes formed the legal foundation for Jim Crow Laws, which would go on to be enforced across much of the country until 1965.

Conclusion

We've seen how the Jim Crow era greatly impacted African-Americans throughout the US. Segregation became commonplace in education, transportation, healthcare, and social life.

Despite being outlawed in 1964, its legacy still remains today - a 2018 study found that black children are 2.5 times more likely to live in poverty than white children.

The fight for desegregation is ongoing; it's up to us to make sure the Jim Crow era doesn't repeat itself.

Let's continue to strive towards a society where everyone has equal opportunities and rights no matter their race or background.

Reparations for Slavery

We, the authors of this article, are here to discuss reparations for slavery. This is a topic of great importance with moral and economic implications that must be fully considered.

In this article we will provide an overview of the historical context surrounding the issue, as well as examine its moral implications. We'll look at both sides of the debate around reparations, exploring the arguments for and against them.

Additionally, we'll consider the economics behind potential solutions and obstacles to reparations in order to assess their feasibility. Finally, we'll explore international perspectives on reparations and their implications in the United States today.

Historical Context

You may not be aware of the long history of oppression and injustice that led to the discussion of reparations for slavery.

The Atlantic Slave Trade took millions of Africans from their homes and stripped them of their culture, language, family, and freedom in order to make them commodities for labor in North America.

For centuries after, African Americans were systematically oppressed through segregation laws and denied basic human rights such as education, housing, voting rights, employment opportunities, legal protection from violence and discrimination.

This deep-seated legacy of racism has caused generational trauma that still affects African Americans today.

The Civil Rights Movement helped to end some forms of legalized racial discrimination but structural racism remains pervasive in many aspects of society.

African Americans continue to face unequal access to economic resources, educational opportunities, healthcare services and legal protection due to systemic racism embedded in our policies and institutions.

Furthermore, the economic legacy of slavery continues with disparities between white households' wealth compared to black households' wealth widening since 1995 despite large gains made by Black Americans over this period.

These historical injustices must be addressed if we are ever going to have a truly equitable society where all people are treated with respect regardless of race or ethnicity.

To do so requires an honest reckoning with our past which can only come when we recognize the unique suffering experienced by those affected by the legacy of slavery in America - a recognition that is essential if we are ever going move beyond it.

Moving forward then requires us to consider not just the moral implications but also practical solutions for how best to provide redress for these historic wrongs.

Moral Implications

It's an absolute travesty that such atrocities have been allowed to go on for so long without proper redress! The moral implications of slavery are far-reaching and devastating.

The legacy of racial injustice, inequality, and oppression is still felt by many generations of African-Americans today. By denying reparations for slavery, we are effectively ignoring the wrongs done to past generations and perpetuating a cycle of racism in our society.

The horrific treatment of enslaved Africans during the slave trade was a clear violation of human rights. Laws were passed to protect their rights, but they weren't enforced due to the power dynamics between whites and blacks at that time. This lack of justice practically solidified racial distinctions between African-Americans and other Americans, which has caused lasting harm throughout history.

There is no question that reparations for slavery are necessary if we are going to make progress towards true racial equality in this country. Reparations would be a tangible way to address the wrongs done in the past and provide much-needed economic support to those who have been historically disadvantaged by racism and discrimination.

Without meaningful efforts towards rectifying these injustices, it seems unlikely that real progress will be made anytime soon. As such, it's vital that we take steps towards providing reparations for slavery as soon as possible in order to begin repairing the damage done by centuries of oppressive racism in America.

The Case for Reparations

You recognize that the case for reparations is an essential step towards true racial equality in this country, and one that can't be ignored or put off any longer.

Slavery has had a lasting impact on the African American community, and its effects are still felt today. Reparations acknowledge the wrongs of slavery and provide a way to rectify them, including restitution payments to descendants of slaves, investing in the African American community with resources such as education, healthcare, and housing.

Making these investments wouldn't only seek to reverse centuries of harm caused by slavery but also provide tangible benefits to those who've been historically disadvantaged.

Financial compensation alone wouldn't fully address the legacy of slavery, however. In addition to economic aid, efforts must be made to repair relationships between races that have been strained due to prejudice and discrimination over hundreds of years.

This could include public apologies from government officials as well as other symbolic gestures such as commemoration days dedicated to recognizing those affected by slavery.

In examining reparations for slavery, we must acknowledge both its potential for good and its limitations. While financial compensation or other forms of restitution may help alleviate economic inequality faced by African Americans today, it won't erase racism or heal deep cultural divides overnight.

Although there are many obstacles standing in our way, we must continue striving towards a future where everyone can live free from oppression and prejudice regardless of race or ethnicity.

The Case against Reparations

It's understandable to be concerned about the potential drawbacks of a reparation plan, especially when considering its long-term implications. Some have argued that it would be difficult and costly to accurately identify all individuals who could receive reparations and to properly distribute them. Others worry that the process of offering reparations could become politicized, leading to delays or even a lack of action from lawmakers.

Additionally, there is the question of whether or not reparations are really an effective way to address historical wrongs:

- Offering monetary compensation might not serve as an adequate means for addressing centuries-old injustice and oppression on an individual level.

- Reparations may also place an unfair financial burden on present-day taxpayers who had no part in perpetuating past injustices against African Americans.

- Furthermore, some argue that granting reparations could lead to divisions among racial groups since it may imply that one group should pay another for their suffering and loss instead of striving together towards a shared goal of equality for all people regardless of race or ethnicity.

These are important questions with complex answers which need careful consideration before any decisions can be made about implementing a reparation program in the United States.

To move forward productively and address these issues effectively, we must first explore the economics behind such a program and its possible outcomes for both current generations and those yet unborn.

The Economics of Reparations

Understanding the economic implications of reparations is essential for determining whether such a program would be beneficial or detrimental in the long term. It's imperative to consider both the costs and potential benefits of various reparation proposals.

On one hand, programs like debt relief or direct payments can come with substantial financial burdens that would need to be funded either by taxpayers or philanthropic institutions. On the other hand, reparations have been proposed as a way to close existing income gaps between white and black households, which could potentially increase economic growth over time if successful.

It's important to note that these costs and benefits are not necessarily limited to those directly affected by slavery. Reparations may also lead to positive externalities for other members of society as well, such as increased access to educational opportunities or improved public health outcomes. Additionally, there could also be unintended consequences that must be weighed when considering the implementation of any reparation scheme.

As such, it's clear that any attempt at evaluating the economics of reparations requires a comprehensive analysis of all possible impacts associated with implementing such a program. Moving forward, we must prioritize this work in order to better understand if and how reparations should play an important role in addressing America's legacy of racial injustice and inequality.

Priorities for Reparations

To truly address America's legacy of racial injustice and inequality, it's essential to prioritize the implementation of reparations that can benefit both those affected directly by slavery and other members of society.

The allocation of resources for reparations should reflect a careful assessment of the current economic conditions, as well as an understanding of how best to use limited resources to effect equitable change.

In order for reparations to have a lasting impact on those who are still suffering from the effects of slavery and systemic racism, policy makers must focus on initiatives that will create sustainable economic opportunities, invest in education programs, provide access to healthcare services, and promote legal reforms aimed at eliminating discrimination.

This requires a comprehensive approach that takes into account not only financial costs but also social costs associated with providing meaningful assistance for those who were enslaved or disenfranchised.

It is also important to consider how existing social policies such as welfare reform may affect efforts toward achieving reparations.

An effective strategy would seek to identify how government policies can be amended or modified in order to better serve this goal.

Moving forward, governments need to take responsibility for their role in perpetuating the injustice caused by slavery and develop strategies that prioritize long-term solutions over short-term fixes.

This will require a thorough evaluation of structural inequalities embedded within our current systems so that any potential reparations initiatives can be implemented in ways that are equitable and justifiable.

With these considerations in mind, we must confront any obstacles standing between us and meaningful progress towards true justice for all Americans.

Obstacles to Reparations

We've identified the key priorities for reparations, such as providing financial compensation and restitution for victims of slavery and their descendants, including an apology from the government. Now we turn to examine some of the obstacles associated with delivering these reparations.

First, there's a lack of consensus on who should be eligible for reparations. Some argue that only those directly affected by the slave trade should receive them, while others say that all people of African descent or anyone living in poverty should be included. Furthermore, it's unclear how much money would need to be allocated in order to provide adequate reparations - estimates range from hundreds of billions to trillions of dollars.

Second, it may prove difficult to identify and locate individuals or families eligible for reparations due to incomplete documentation and records left behind by slave owners and traders. Additionally, many countries are resistant to paying out large sums of money in compensation for past wrongs due to strained public finances or because they feel no sense of responsibility towards this issue.

Finally, there has been little progress made at an international level towards recognizing collective responsibility for slavery or introducing a global framework for compensating its victims. International courts have largely avoided this issue. Few governments have publicly committed themselves to providing any form of monetary compensation. Intergovernmental organizations have failed to make any headway on this. Multilateral agreements are also lacking in this regard. As such, addressing these obstacles will require considerable political will across numerous jurisdictions if meaningful progress is ever going to be made on providing reparations at an international level.

International Perspectives on Reparations

Gaining an appreciation of different perspectives on reparations from around the world is critical to finding a solution that can satisfy all parties.

European countries such as Germany, France, and the United Kingdom have acknowledged the injustice of slavery and supported initiatives like The Foundation for the Memory of Slavery in Paris, which was established to promote research and education about slavery. However, these countries haven't taken steps towards providing financial reparations to descendants of former slaves.

In other parts of the world, there has been more open discussion about reparations for victims of slavery and colonialism. African countries like Nigeria have pursued legal action against Britain in international courts seeking compensation for their economic losses due to colonial rule. While this case is yet to be resolved, it serves as an example that many African nations are taking proactive strides towards achieving justice through reparations.

In Latin America too, there has been a push for recognition and redressment by indigenous people who suffered under colonial rule. In recent years, Bolivia declared its independence day from Spanish colonization a national holiday in order to commemorate those who died during Spanish colonization 500 years ago. Such movements demonstrate a renewed commitment by former colonies toward respecting their history and seeking justice through reparations for past wrongs.

As we consider how best to move forward with reparations in the United States next, understanding these global efforts is essential in identifying potential solutions that can bring justice across borders.

Reparations in the United States

Having discussed the international perspectives on reparations for slavery, we'll now focus on the United States.

While some countries such as Germany and Canada have offered formal apologies and reparations to their citizens of African descent, most countries in the Western Hemisphere have yet to do so.

In the United States, there's been a long history of discussions and debates around providing reparations, but no actual action has been taken.

There are various reasons why reparations for slavery haven't occurred in the U.S., including a lack of political will among elected officials and policymakers; resistance from white Americans who feel they shouldn't be held responsible for something that occurred before their time; and difficulty pinpointing exactly who would receive compensation or how much it would cost.

Additionally, some argue that offering monetary compensation is inadequate to address systemic racism because it fails to address underlying structural issues that continue to disproportionately impact African-Americans today.

Despite these challenges, there remains strong support among many groups in favor of providing reparations for slavery as an important step towards racial justice.

Supporters point out that direct payments could help close economic disparities between Blacks and whites by providing additional resources to Black communities which have experienced centuries of discrimination and disenfranchisement due to American chattel slavery.

Furthermore, they argue that paying reparations could also serve as a symbolic gesture of atonement for past wrongs—recognition of America's shared history with respect to race relations.

With this discussion in mind, let's consider what potential solutions could exist within the U.S context to rectify this systemically unjust situation.

Potential Solutions

Taking action on the issue of racial injustice can be intimidating, but there are a few potential solutions that could make a meaningful difference.

One is for governments to offer financial reparations to African Americans whose ancestors were slaves in the United States. Such reparations would provide direct financial restitution, which many argue is necessary to truly address the harm done by centuries of slavery and systemic racism.

Another potential solution is for governments to enact legislation that gives preferential treatment to certain minority groups when it comes to job opportunities, education programs, and housing initiatives. This approach has been used in some countries with success, though it remains controversial as it may give advantages to certain groups over others.

Finally, there is an ongoing movement towards greater public accountability and transparency when it comes to issues of race and discrimination in society. This includes efforts such as creating better data collection on race-based disparities in areas such as health care or criminal justice reform initiatives like bail reform or police body cameras.

Taking these steps towards greater transparency can help ensure that laws are followed fairly across all communities and go a long way towards addressing structural racism and inequality within our society.

Frequently Asked Questions

What is the legal definition of reparations?

We, as a society, have been asking ourselves: what's the legal definition of reparations? Well, it turns out that reparations are defined as any form of compensation or restitution for harm caused by an individual or group.

This could include financial payments and/or non-financial measures such as apologies, recognition, memorialization, education programs, and other forms of support. Reparations can be awarded to individuals or groups who have suffered physical or psychological harm due to wrongful actions by another person or institution.

In this way, reparations provide critical assistance for those affected by past wrongs in order to restore their dignity and sense of justice.

Who is eligible to receive reparations?

We've been discussing who's eligible to receive reparations.

Generally speaking, a person or group of people must meet certain criteria to be considered eligible for reparations. This can include experiencing direct or indirect harm due to the actions of another party or being part of a group that's suffered discrimination and injustice in the past.

In some cases, eligibility may also depend on being able to prove a connection between present-day challenges and an historic injustice.

Eligibility requirements will vary depending on the specific reparation program being discussed.

What form would reparations take?

We're exploring the question of what form reparations would take. One possible solution could be providing financial compensation to those affected by slavery, such as descendants of slaves or communities that were disproportionately affected by the legacy of slavery.

Another option could be creating educational programs designed to close gaps in resources and opportunity for those who have been historically deprived because of their race.

Finally, investments in infrastructure and economic development initiatives could help to create a greater sense of equity in communities that have suffered from systemic racism and poverty.

What countries have already implemented reparations?

We've seen a recent surge in countries taking action to implement reparations for those affected by slavery. As of now, the United Kingdom, Germany, and Norway are among some of the first countries to take steps towards implementing reparations payments.

The UK has made an official apology as well as offering financial compensation and health care access to British Caribbean nationals who were living in the UK when laws around immigration changed in 1962.

Germany has set up a fund specifically for people whose ancestors were victims of colonial violence and forced labor during German colonialism.

Norway has also offered funds for social projects that will benefit communities descended from those harmed by Norwegian slave trading between 1650-1851.

How would reparations be funded?

We're facing a tough question: how should reparations be funded? Some ideas include direct transfer of funds or government-sponsored programs and policies. Regardless of the solution, it's clear that this issue requires significant resources. To fund this effort, we need to be creative and consider options like leveraging private investments or tapping into existing economic structures. Achieving real progress towards meaningful reparations demands us to step beyond our comfort zone and embrace innovative ideas.

Conclusion

We've considered the history, moral implications, economics, and international perspectives of reparations for slavery.

It's clear that while there are many obstacles to overcome, reparations are an essential step in the pursuit of justice.

We can view this process as a bridge leading to a better future - one where we finally face our shameful past and begin to repair the wounds inflicted by centuries of oppression.

To truly make progress on this issue, it's time to move beyond rhetoric and take practical steps towards implementing meaningful change.

Only then will we be able to leave behind a legacy of true equity and fairness for generations to come.

Black Wall Street aka Greenwood, Oklahoma

We've all heard of Wall Street, but what about Black Wall Street? It sounds like a far-fetched mythical place. But it was very real and had an important role in the history of America.

It's a story that is both inspiring and heartbreaking, filled with incredible success and devastating tragedy. Black Wall Street was the nickname given to Greenwood, Oklahoma in the early 1900s.

This small African American community blossomed into one of the most successful suburbs in America during its time – boasting over 600 businesses, two newspapers, several hotels, movie theaters and more! The thriving business district soon earned Greenwood the title of "the Negro Wall Street" among other nicknames by its citizens.

However, this success would be cut short when violence erupted on May 31st 1921 in what has come to be known as Tulsa Race Massacre.

The Rise of Greenwood, Oklahoma

In the early 1900s, Greenwood, Oklahoma rose from near-obscurity to become a thriving business hub. It was led by African American entrepreneurs and became known as "Black Wall Street" for its economic prosperity.

This remarkable community was built on the hard work of freed slaves who made their way to Oklahoma after the Civil War ended. Despite facing racism and discrimination, these individuals worked together to create something special—a place that offered safety, opportunity, and a chance for success.

The energy in Greenwood was palpable; it was an oasis of hope in a world that didn't always make it easy for African Americans to succeed. As Black Wall Street grew in prominence, more businesses opened up and more people began calling it home. It was truly a remarkable example of what can be achieved when everyone works together towards a common goal.

With this newfound strength and stability came even greater potential—and with potential comes growth.

The Growth of Black Wall Street

You've heard of it, but what kind of success did this place reach? Experience a remarkable journey through its rise and prosperity.

Black Wall Street soon became the heart of Greenwood, Oklahoma - the hub for African-American owned businesses in the early 1900s. The area was bustling with activity: barbershops, grocery stores, movie theaters, restaurants, and many other establishments that provided an economic base for black citizens.

The atmosphere of Greenwood was one of unity and safety - people were friendly to each other regardless of race or background. Businesses flourished as more black entrepreneurs moved into town to take advantage of the opportunity to own their own space and make their mark on history. As Greenwood grew in size and population, so too did its influence on African-American culture; it had become a symbol of black pride throughout America.

The success story of Black Wall Street didn't just happen overnight; it was built upon hard work, dedication, and determination by its residents who refused to let racism or segregation stop them from achieving greatness. With support from organizations like the NAACP (National Association for the Advancement of Colored People), Black Wall Street managed to create an environment where racial equality could be enjoyed without fear or prejudice from outsiders.

This made way for some extraordinary examples of wealth among African-Americans that would not have been possible elsewhere in America at the time - paving a path towards financial freedom for generations to come. Soaring into new heights with pride and confidence, these achievements showed just how far a collective effort can go when given the right conditions – setting up Greenwood's elite class as they took things even further into prosperity.

The Greenwood Elite

Experience the remarkable success of Greenwood's elite class and explore how they achieved financial freedom, taking their city to soaring heights. Through hard work and determination, this prosperous African American community flourished in the early 1900s.

Businesses ranging from pharmacies to banks to beauty salons were owned by members of Greenwood's elite class with a wide variety of backgrounds. The following are a few key takeaways that show just how successful these individuals were:

- They owned more than 600 businesses, making up over one-third of Tulsa's business district.
- They had an average wealth of around $50,000 each, which was more than double the national average at the time.
- Many of them had achieved upper middle-class status after only a few years in Tulsa.

The success story of Greenwood's elite class was a shining example for generations to come and made clear that economic mobility is achievable for all people - regardless of race or background. And yet this remarkable prosperity would eventually be destroyed...

The Tulsa Race Massacre

The Tulsa Race Massacre tragically destroyed this remarkable success story, shattering hopes of economic mobility for the African-American community. They were left devastated and digitally excluded from the American dream.

On May 31st and June 1st, 1921, a mob of white supremacists descended on Greenwood, Oklahoma with an intent to terrorize and destroy the area's affluent African-American neighborhood known as 'Black Wall Street'. The attack was swift and violent, resulting in countless deaths, extensive property damage, and leaving nearly 10,000 African Americans homeless.

Devastatingly, the event was largely ignored by history until recently when its significance has finally been acknowledged. As we reflect upon this tragic event, it is clear that while progress is being made towards achieving true equality in America, there is still much work to be done in order to ensure that such horrific acts never occur again.

In light of this tragedy, we must now turn our attention to examining the aftermath of the massacre.

The Aftermath of the Massacre

After the devastating attack, Greenwood was left with a broken spirit - a void that could never be filled. The survivors of the massacre were traumatized by what they had experienced and faced years of injustice, poverty, and neglect in its aftermath.

The destruction caused by the mob was immense; more than 1,200 homes were destroyed and over 35 square blocks of businesses and residences were reduced to rubble. While some survivors banded together to rebuild their community, others moved away from Tulsa or left Oklahoma altogether, unable to forget or forgive what had happened.

Despite their efforts, the legacy of 'Black Wall Street' would never be fully recovered. Despite these tragic losses, it's important to recognize that Greenwood represented an inspiring example of African American achievement and resilience that paved the way for future generations.

Thus, even though the massacre marked an end for 'Black Wall Street', it also serves as an enduring reminder of how far African Americans have come since then - and how much further they still have left to go.

With this in mind, it's essential to consider the impact this tragedy has had on black communities across America today.

The Impact of Black Wall Street

The impact of Black Wall Street is still felt today, with African Americans owning less than 2% of all businesses in the United States. The legacy of the massacre has had a long-lasting and devastating effect on generations of African Americans to come.

From the destruction of Greenwood, to systematic discrimination in loan applications and business opportunities, it's clear that this tragedy had a major effect on black business owners:

- Limited Access to Financial Resources:

- Denied access to capital from banks and other financial institutions

- Unfavorable terms for loans when they were able to acquire them

- Systemic Discrimination:

- Difficulties competing with white businesses for contracts and other opportunities

- Unequal access to markets or customers due to segregation laws

These issues continue today, with many African American entrepreneurs facing similar obstacles as their predecessors did almost 100 years ago. This demonstrates how powerful and lasting the effects of Black Wall Street were, even after its destruction.

As we move forward into the future, it'll be important for us to remember this history and ensure that minority business owners have equal access to resources so that they can pursue their dreams without being hindered by systemic racism.

The Legacy of Black Wall Street

We've learned about the impact of Black Wall Street and its tragic downfall. But what remains of its legacy?

Although much was lost in the Tulsa Race Massacre, many African-Americans were able to rebuild their lives and businesses in Greenwood. It is a testament to their strength and resilience that they were able to make something out of the ruins of their former homes, businesses, and churches.

After so much loss, it is inspiring to think that Black Wall Street was able to leave behind something positive for generations to come.

The legacy of Black Wall Street speaks for itself: it demonstrates that African-Americans could create an economic powerhouse when given the chance. This gives us hope for a better future where everyone has an equal opportunity to succeed financially, regardless of race or background.

We must remember this lesson as we look towards the resurgence of Greenwood and other efforts to bring economic justice back into our communities.

The Resurgence of Greenwood

You can see the strength and determination of the African-American community in Greenwood's resurgence. It shows that they aren't deterred by past injustices and are ready to thrive again. The legacy of Black Wall Street is living on in Greenwood today in a different way. Businesses are being revitalized, new entrepreneurs are coming into the area, and people from around the world come to experience its unique culture.

This resilience speaks volumes about just how much Greenwood has been through while still maintaining its spirit and character. As we look forward, there's no doubt that with continued investment and support from all corners of society, Greenwood will continue to be a shining example of what can happen when communities unite and work together for progress.

Thus, it's only fitting that we recognize this tremendous resurgence by honoring the survivors of the Tulsa Race Massacre with a Centennial Commission.

The Tulsa Race Massacre Centennial Commission

Experience Greenwood's past and present as you join in honoring the survivors of the Tulsa Race Massacre with the Centennial Commission.

The Centennial Commission is a dedicated group of individuals who are committed to recognizing and commemorating one of America's most horrific acts of racial violence.

They recognize that this event has had a lasting impact on generations and strive to ensure it will never be forgotten.

Through their efforts, they are helping people learn about what happened during the massacre so we can all understand its true significance.

As part of their mission, they also work to support businesses in Greenwood and promote economic development in an effort to help rebuild what was lost 100 years ago.

The Centennial Commission is creating a powerful platform for healing and understanding by providing accessible education programs, public events, memorials, monuments and other initiatives that connect us all to this history while building bridges between today's generations.

By joining forces with them, we can start to rediscover the history of Black Wall Street, honor those who experienced it firsthand, and commit ourselves to ensuring such tragedies never again occur.

Rediscovering the History of Black Wall Street

Discover the rich cultural heritage and vibrant legacy of "Black Wall Street," a once-thriving community in Tulsa, Oklahoma's Greenwood neighborhood. This economic hub allowed African Americans to thrive independently during a time of racial injustice. It boasted over 600 businesses, including grocery stores, banks, movie theaters, churches, and more.

The area provided its residents with much-needed resources and opportunities for financial success. Homeownership rates were higher than surrounding white neighborhoods. Educational institutions like Langston University produced some of the most sought-after graduates in the nation. There were numerous entertainment venues that showcased black culture and musical acts from around the world.

The legacy of Black Wall Street is one worth celebrating and studying for its immense impact on American history. It serves as an example of true resilience in the face of adversity and an important reminder that economic development can be achieved even under oppressive conditions. By rediscovering this remarkable story, we can empower people today who may have otherwise been forgotten or ignored by society.

Frequently Asked Questions

How can people today help to preserve the legacy of Black Wall Street?

We have an opportunity to use our collective power to preserve the legacy of Black Wall Street.

We can create a movement that will speak louder than any words ever could - a movement that will honor the courage, strength, and resilience displayed by generations before us.

By educating ourselves about this rich history, we can build on its foundation and ensure it lives on for generations to come.

Through our actions, we can take steps towards equality and justice like never before - abolishing systems that oppress minorities and promoting economic growth in previously underserved communities.

Let's join together in solidarity to make sure the impact of Black Wall Street is felt not only today but every day into the future.

With every step forward, let's remember: This is bigger than us; this is a legacy worth preserving with all our might!

What can be done to ensure that the events of the Tulsa Race Massacre are not repeated?

We must take action to ensure the events of the Tulsa Race Massacre aren't repeated.

We must recognize our past mistakes, learn from them, and strive for a better future. We can do this by educating ourselves and others about what happened to make sure it's not forgotten.

Additionally, we should work together with local governments and communities to promote understanding and acceptance between different groups of people. By doing this, we can create an environment where incidents like the Tulsa Race Massacre can't occur again.

How can the Greenwood Elite be celebrated today?

We celebrate the Greenwood Elite today in various ways. As a reminder of their resilience, courage, and determination to succeed against all odds, we honor them with events such as symposiums and seminars that bring their stories to life.

We also recognize their economic achievements by continuing to promote small businesses within communities and encouraging individuals from diverse backgrounds to participate in entrepreneurship.

Finally, we use education to ensure that the memory of these brave individuals lives on for generations to come.

What are the benefits of the Tulsa Race Massacre Centennial Commission?

We're proud to bring you a plethora of benefits through the Tulsa Race Massacre Centennial Commission! Our mission is all about honoring those affected by this tragedy and ensuring that everyone in Tulsa can feel safe and secure in their community.

We offer a wide range of initiatives, such as educational programs, public events, commemorative projects, and more. Through these efforts, we aim to help people better understand the history of this event and its impact on the city.

We also provide a platform to honor the victims and survivors, and we hope to bring a bit of lightheartedness to this dark chapter in history.

Overall, the Tulsa Race Massacre Centennial Commission is dedicated to bringing relief and healing to those affected by this tragic event.

How can the history of Black Wall Street be taught in classrooms?

We understand the importance of teaching young people about the history of our society. That's why we're discussing how classroom instruction can cover the phenomenon of Black Wall Street.

This topic allows us to explore how certain communities have been able to build and thrive despite systemic racism, and is essential for understanding modern-day disparities. It also provides an opportunity to discuss economic success within marginalized communities, and how that has helped shape our nation today.

By learning about this powerful moment in history, students gain a better appreciation for America's past and present.

Conclusion

We can never forget the tragedy that befell Greenwood and its vibrant Black Wall Street. We owe it to those who lost their lives, homes, and businesses to ensure their legacy is not forgotten.

It's up to us to remember what was taken from them and use it as a reminder of how far we've come, but also how much further we need to go in terms of equality for all. Through the Tulsa Race Massacre Centennial Commission and other initiatives, we hope that one day this anachronism of racism will be a distant memory in our collective history.

Let's rise together in honor of Black Wall Street.

The Brutality of Colonizers

We have all heard the stories about the brutalities perpetrated by colonizers. But they are often only partially told, leaving us with a skewed understanding of how colonization has shaped our history and identity.

To fully understand the horror inflicted on colonized people, we must delve into the specifics of what exactly constituted their oppression: military violence, mass incarceration, economic exploitation, and cultural erasure, and forced relocation, loss of self-determination and destruction of cultural heritage.

The physical abuse, exploitation of natural resources and subjugation that accompanied colonial rule left an indelible mark on generations to come.

In this article we will explore in detail these atrocities to gain an appreciation for just how awful colonization was for its victims.

Military Violence

You've probably heard stories of colonizers' military violence, and it's not a pleasant picture. Colonizers used their superior military might to oppress native populations, often with devastating results. They would massacre entire villages, raze crops and homes, and brutally punish anyone who dared to resist.

Wars of attrition were waged with the intent of wiping out existing cultures in order to make way for colonial rule. This type of violence left lasting effects on native populations that are still felt today.

Military violence was also used as a tool of subjugation once colonies had been established. Laws were imposed by force in order to maintain control over local populations, often involving harsh punishments for those who didn't comply or challenged the ruling powers. The enforcement of these laws was brutal, and could include torture, public humiliation or execution depending on the severity of the offense committed.

This generated fear among local populations which aided colonists in maintaining their power over them indefinitely. But this form of control wasn't limited to those living within colonial borders; many colonizers sought to extend their influence beyond their own countries through naval blockades and invasions into foreign territories which further increased their domination over other nations.

This expansionist agenda eventually led to some of the bloodiest wars in history as colonizing forces clashed against each other vying for global supremacy. To transition from this topic without writing 'step', it's important to remember that while military violence has been used throughout history by many different actors; its use by colonizers stands out due to its brutality and destructive consequences that continue even after colonialism has ended.

Mass Incarceration

Mass incarceration is an extreme example of how colonizers have deprived people of their freedom and rights! Despite the fact that many countries that were once colonized have become independent, the practice of mass incarceration has been used to continue to oppress certain ethnicities or groups.

The idea behind mass incarceration is to detain a large number of people from a particular group in order to control them for political or economic purposes. This has been done in countries such as the United States, where African Americans have disproportionately been targeted by law enforcement agencies for arrest and detention. In addition, there are also other forms of oppression such as racial profiling which can lead to increased rates of incarceration for some minority populations.

As a result, mass incarceration has had a lasting effect on these communities by creating feelings of mistrust towards authority figures and weakening social networks within neighborhoods. Furthermore, it has resulted in overcrowding in prisons and jails leading to poorer conditions for inmates with no access to proper medical care or rehabilitative programs.

This form of oppressive policymaking is yet another way colonizers have sought to maintain power over those they seek to subjugate. The effects of mass incarceration can be seen not just through physical confinement but also through economic exploitation. Many former prisoners are unable to find employment after their release due to discrimination based upon their criminal record, leading them into poverty and further marginalization from society.

Economic Exploitation

Economic exploitation is a form of oppression that disproportionately affects minority populations, leaving them unable to find gainful employment after their release from prison and forcing them into poverty.

Colonizers have long sought to take advantage of any resources available, including the labor of those they colonize. This often leads to extreme deprivation for the colonized population in terms of their right to self-determination and economic security.

The exploitative nature of colonial rule has forced many people into situations where they are unable to make decisions for themselves or access necessary resources. This economic exploitation is also compounded by the fact that colonizers often actively work against the economic interests of those they oppress.

Examples can be seen throughout history, such as when colonizers used indentured servitude or other forms of debt bondage as a means to extract resources from people who had no choice but to obey their commands. As a result, many indigenous communities have been left without adequate access to education, healthcare, and basic necessities due to the lack of capital generated by oppressive systems put in place by colonial powers.

The legacy of this type of exploitation continues today in various forms; for example, through exploitative practices like wage theft that prevent workers from receiving fair compensation for their labor or through discriminatory policies that limit opportunities for certain racial and ethnic groups.

It is an unfortunate reality that many marginalized communities face daily, with little chance at improving their situation until systemic change is achieved. To truly combat this injustice, it is essential that we recognize its existence and strive towards creating equitable societies where everyone enjoys equal protection under the law regardless of race or ethnicity.

Cultural erasure must also be addressed in order for true progress towards achieving justice and equality to occur.

Cultural Erasure

You're likely already familiar with how cultural erasure can be a devastating consequence of colonization, but what you may not be aware of is the extent to which it has dehumanized those affected by it. Cultural erasure involves a colonizer's attempts to make a group of people forget their traditions, language, and even identity in order to conform to the colonizers' standards. This process can be violent and traumatic as it strips individuals of their sense of self-worth and belonging.

Moreover, colonial powers have sought to suppress native beliefs and practices in an effort to erase any trace of their existence from the public sphere. This includes outlawing traditional ceremonies, replacing indigenous languages with that of the colonizers, destroying sacred artifacts or sites associated with native culture, and rewriting history books so as to paint natives as uncivilized savages.

The effects of cultural erasure have been far reaching; it has caused tremendous psychological harm as well as long-term physical damage due to displacement from traditional lands and resources. It is also worth noting that this process continues today in various forms around the world – making its legacy one that shouldn't go unrecognized or forgotten.

Transitioning now into forced relocation: this phenomenon saw millions uprooted from their homes against their will...

Forced Relocation

Forced relocation has resulted in millions of people being displaced from their homes, with an estimated 12 million people forcibly relocated during the Transatlantic Slave Trade alone. Colonizers throughout history have used forced relocation as a way to gain control and access to land and resources, often at the expense of indigenous populations. This often includes separation of families or communities, forced displacement into unfamiliar environments, loss of cultural identity or heritage, and disruption of traditional economic practices.

The effects of such relocations can be devastating for those who are displaced, leading to physical and psychological trauma that can last for generations. In addition, colonizers sometimes disregard indigenous rights when relocating populations, which strips away autonomy and self-determination and further exacerbates suffering. Consequently, it can take decades or even centuries for these communities to fully recover from forced relocation due to colonizer brutality.

Such repercussions are still being felt today around the world as a result of colonial policies of long ago. Transitioning into subsequent sections about 'disregard for indigenous rights', it is important to recognize how this pervasive practice has had lasting impacts on entire nations and their people.

Disregard for Indigenous Rights

The disregard for indigenous rights often associated with colonialism has had far-reaching and devastating consequences on the autonomy and self-determination of native populations. Colonizers would often deny native peoples their traditional forms of governance, instead imposing systems that had no understanding or respect for existing cultures. This denial of autonomy and self-determination led to an increasing sense of powerlessness among these communities, as they were unable to protect themselves or their land from exploitation by colonizers.

Furthermore, indigenous people's rights to land ownership were often ignored through the practice of terra nullius – a doctrine which states that land is legally owned by whoever first claims it – allowing colonizers to seize large amounts of land without paying any compensation.

This blatant disregard for indigenous rights created a legacy of inequality between colonizer and native populations which continues to this day. In many countries, even where colonization has ended long ago, indigenous people still suffer from poverty, social exclusion and racism due to the systemic discrimination that was built into colonial societies.

Moreover, even when governments attempt to recognize indigenous rights in law, this recognition is not always enforced in practice. Without meaningful legal protections that ensure fair access to resources and participation in decision making processes, there can be no true self-determination for native populations who are continuously denied justice under colonial laws.

These circumstances have resulted in profound losses for many native cultures around the world; examples include language loss due to oppressive assimilation policies imposed by colonizers as well as cultural practices being suppressed or outlawed by foreign governments who fail to recognize their significance or value.

Moving forward then requires an acknowledgement of the injustices perpetrated against indigenous peoples throughout history and a commitment from all nations involved in colonialism towards reparative action such as financial restitution and increased political representation within government structures.

Loss of Self-Determination

The disregard for Indigenous rights that characterizes the brutality of colonizers has led to a significant loss of self-determination. Colonizers have consistently denied Indigenous peoples agency over their own lives, cultures, and livelihoods. This lack of autonomy has resulted in an inability for many Indigenous communities to shape their respective futures according to their values and beliefs.

Colonizers have used a variety of tools to ensure that they remain in control. For example, they've sought to undermine traditional forms of governance by imposing external systems or laws on Indigenous nations. They've also usurped land from communities without permission or compensation, infringing upon the right to land ownership and independent economic development. Additionally, they've prohibited access to resources such as education which could help empower individuals within these groups and expand their capacity for self-determination.

These practices are not only detrimental to the present-day status of Indigenous people but also serve as a legacy of ignorance and oppression that will continue into future generations if left unaddressed. It's imperative that we recognize our collective responsibility in upholding the rights of all people - regardless of race or background - so that everyone can attain equal opportunities for life satisfaction and freedom from discrimination.

To deny any one group this chance at true autonomy is an injustice that cannot be tolerated any longer; it's time we move towards a more equitable tomorrow by allowing all people the same opportunity for self-determined success.

With this goal in mind, we now turn our attention towards examining how colonizers' brutality has impacted cultural heritage.

Destruction of Cultural Heritage

You can see the destruction of cultural heritage in the way colonizers have denied Indigenous peoples access to resources, land ownership, and traditional forms of governance. This has led to a dramatic shift in how these communities interact with their environment and how they practice their culture.

Colonizers have destroyed sacred sites, banned ceremonies, and restricted language use; all of which served as important aspects of Indigenous cultures before colonialism.

- Colonizers have taken away access to ancestral lands which kept many traditions alive and tied generations together.
- They've replaced traditional forms of education with Eurocentric curricula that ignored or erased Indigenous histories and knowledge systems.
- Language suppression has been used to strip away lifeways, customs, values, spiritual beliefs, and oral histories for centuries.

- Forced relocation is another tool colonizers have used to disrupt connections between people and place by disrupting or erasing physical ties between people's history and culture on the land they are forced from.

The systematic stripping of cultural heritage has had devastating effects on Indigenous Communities around the world including the loss of identity both individually and collectively as well as an inability to pass down wisdom through generations due to disruptions caused by colonization practices such as intergenerational trauma leading directly into physical abuse inflicted upon these populations by colonizers in brutal attempts at subjugation that continues today.

Physical Abuse

Physical abuse inflicted upon Indigenous communities by colonizers is a devastating consequence of colonization, wreaking havoc on generations and robbing them of their cultural heritage. Colonizers often used physical force to enforce their rule, with no regard for the people they were subjugating. The violence perpetrated against Indigenous populations included beatings, mutilation, and murder.

While many colonizers believed the physical punishment was necessary for proper governance, others saw it as a way to take advantage of and intimidate those they sought to control. The effects of this physical abuse were far-reaching—not only did it cause direct harm to its victims but also left lasting psychological scars that continue to affect generations today.

This violence destroyed trust between Native Americans and settlers, making cooperation difficult if not impossible in some cases. Moreover, this type of oppression has created an environment in which Indigenous people feel powerless in the face of authority figures or anyone who represents potential threats or danger.

This situation has been further exacerbated by the exploitation of natural resources from Indigenous lands without any form of compensation or recognition for the original inhabitants. Such disregard for the basic rights and dignity of Native peoples has had serious ramifications that are still felt even centuries later.

In addition to environmental degradation caused by resource extraction activities, Indigenous communities have suffered economic losses due to displacement from traditional lands as well as restrictions on their access to resources such as water and timber.

Exploitation of Natural Resources

Exploitation of natural resources from Indigenous lands without any regard for their inhabitants has had devastating consequences, leading to environmental degradation and economic losses. Colonizers have long sought to extract minerals, oil, gas, and timber from Indigenous territories as a way of advancing their own interests. This has been done in an unbalanced manner that ignores the rights of the locals and disregards any environmental impact.

In some cases, this exploitation has led to a complete depletion of natural resources such as fish stocks or forests which are essential to local communities for food security and other livelihoods activities. These exploitative practices have also caused significant damage to the environment through deforestation, pollution, soil erosion, water contamination and many more. These effects can be felt decades after extraction activities have stopped as it takes time for ecosystems to regenerate naturally.

Furthermore, this type of exploitation often leaves Indigenous peoples with no control over how their land is managed or what kind of development projects can take place on it, furthering the marginalization they already experience within colonizing countries. The effects of resource exploitation by colonizers are still being felt today in many parts of the world.

Indigenous communities continue to suffer due to lack of access to traditional sources of sustenance while at the same time dealing with environmental destruction caused by outside forces with little recognition or reparation from governments or corporations involved in these activities. It is clear that this form of colonization has been incredibly damaging not just on human populations but also on entire ecosystems around the world that may never recover fully from its effects.

Frequently Asked Questions

What are the long-term effects of colonization on indigenous peoples?

We've all heard the stories about how colonization has affected Indigenous peoples, but what are its long-term effects?

Well, let us not sugarcoat it: Colonization has had a devastating impact on Indigenous peoples. From loss of land and resources to cultural erasure and assimilation policies, the damage done by colonizers is undeniable.

This legacy continues to be felt today in various ways, such as through disparities in health outcomes, economic inequality, displacement, and more.

It's our responsibility to recognize these injustices and work together to create meaningful solutions that strengthen Indigenous communities.

How has colonization impacted the mental health of indigenous populations?

For many indigenous populations, colonization has had a severe impact on their mental health. Studies conducted in the US, Australia, and Canada found that those who live on reserves or reservations have higher levels of depression and suicide than those who don't.

This is likely due to the disruption of cultural practices, displacement from ancestral land, economic disenfranchisement, and racism experienced by Indigenous people as a result of colonization. Additionally, the intergenerational trauma stemming from past violence inflicted by colonizers continues to affect Indigenous communities today.

What is the most effective way to address the legacy of colonization?

We believe the most effective way to address the legacy of colonization is through an intersectional approach.

This means recognizing how different forms of oppression are intertwined and cannot be addressed in isolation.

It also involves acknowledging the historical context and taking responsibility for past injustices.

Such an approach can help create equitable systems that promote justice, respect, and healing for all people impacted by colonialism.

How has colonization impacted the traditional relationship between indigenous peoples and the environment?

We've seen the impacts of colonization on traditional relationships between indigenous peoples and the environment. Colonization has caused a disruption in traditional stewardship practices, resulting in an erosion of cultural knowledge and connection to land.

This has led to changes in how indigenous communities interact with their local ecosystems, including shifts in management approaches such as conservation and subsistence activities. Indigenous populations have also been forced to adopt new technologies that can be detrimental to natural resources, while facing displacement from ancestral lands as a result of colonialism.

Consequently, there's a need for renewed focus on rebuilding these traditional relationships through policies that empower indigenous people to restore their relationship with the environment.

What is the best way to restore the rights of indigenous peoples?

We believe that the best way to restore the rights of indigenous peoples is through a commitment to reconciliation and reparations. This includes working with local governments and engaging in meaningful dialogue with indigenous communities to address their needs, providing access to housing, education, and health care services, and recognizing traditional land claims.

Moreover, it's important for both parties to create an environment of mutual understanding and respect in order to build trust between them. Finally, there should be tangible efforts made by all involved towards undoing the damage done by colonization over centuries.

Conclusion

We've seen the brutality of colonizers, from military violence and mass incarceration to economic exploitation and cultural erasure. Forced relocation, loss of self-determination, destruction of cultural heritage, physical abuse, and exploitation of natural resources are all legacies that cannot be forgotten.

The juxtaposition between what was lost and what remains is stark. Our collective memories will continue to honor those who sacrificed for freedom while recognizing the harsh realities they faced in pursuit of their autonomy.

We must use this knowledge to create a better future where our right to self-determination is respected and defended.

The Genocide of Native Americans

Native Americans have been subjected to centuries of mistreatment and genocide by the US government.

For hundreds of years, Indigenous people have suffered under oppressive policies that sought to erase their culture and assimilate them into white society.

From the Doctrine of Discovery through the Trail of Tears and Wounded Knee Massacre, Native Americans have experienced numerous injustices at the hands of the US government.

The long-term consequences are still being felt today as many Native Americans struggle with poverty, health issues, and lack of access to resources.

This article will examine these events in detail to provide a comprehensive understanding of this dark chapter in our nation's history.

History of Indigenous-US Government Relations

The US government has had a long and complicated relationship with Indigenous peoples, one that has unfortunately had devastating effects. From the early days of colonization to broken treaties and forced assimilation policies, the United States' history with Native Americans is filled with injustices.

The Trail of Tears – an event where thousands of Cherokee were forcibly removed from their ancestral lands – serves as a vivid reminder of the oppression they have faced. Generational trauma continues to haunt many indigenous communities due to the physical, emotional, and spiritual violence inflicted on them by settlers and government officials alike.

This relationship between Native Americans and the US government has resulted in countless tragedies, including genocidal actions committed against tribal nations throughout American history. In spite of this dark past, many Indigenous people are striving for justice through recognition of their rights as sovereign nations today.

The Doctrine of Discovery

You may not know, but the Doctrine of Discovery was responsible for taking away over 90 million acres of land from Indigenous people in North America. This doctrine was a legal principle that set out how European nations could claim ownership over lands inhabited by Indigenous peoples. It served as a way to legitimize the colonization process, allowing Europeans to take control over land and resources without any recognition or consent from its original inhabitants.

The Doctrine of Discovery has had a devastating effect on Indigenous populations throughout history. It denied them their right to self-determination and autonomy. It violated their traditional beliefs and customs. It led to countless deaths due to displacement, disease, and violence. And it continues to cause harm through its legacy today in the form of poverty, health disparities, and other systemic issues.

As we remember this tragic history, we must also strive for a better future—one in which all people are respected equally and where justice is restored for Native American communities.

Forced Removal and Relocation

Tragically, millions of Indigenous peoples were forcibly removed from their ancestral homelands, uprooting them from their beloved communities and heritage in a heartbreaking act of dispossession.

This policy of forced removal and relocation was part of an effort to reduce the population size and control Native American land.

These measures had devastating consequences for Indigenous peoples, as they were exiled from their homes, separated from family members, and subjected to cruel conditions during transport. Additionally, many did not survive the journey due to lack of food or exposure to disease.

As such, this policy resulted in an alarming amount of death and displacement among Native Americans across North America.

The United States government implemented these policies with little regard for human rights or compassion towards the Indigenous people who lived on the land long before it was colonized by Europeans.

This forced removal led to extreme levels of trauma that have been passed down through generations—a legacy still felt today by Native American communities all over the world.

In spite of this difficult history, many tribes have bravely held onto their culture and identity despite immense odds against them—a testament to their remarkable resilience in the face of adversity.

The Indian Removal Act of 1830

You're invited to explore the Indian Removal Act of 1830, an act that forced millions of Indigenous people away from their homes and into an unfamiliar world, leaving behind a lasting legacy of dispossession. This Act was signed into law by President Andrew Jackson on May 28, 1830 and resulted in the relocation of Native American nations living east of the Mississippi River to Indian Territory west of the river. This illegal act was driven by a desire for western expansion and largely ignored Indigenous rights.

Here are five facts about this unjust policy:

- The Indian Removal Act of 1830 authorized the President to negotiate with Indigenous nations in order to exchange their ancestral homelands for land west of the Mississippi River.

- It allowed for states and private citizens to buy or occupy Native American land without consent from tribal nations.

- It led to military campaigns against those who refused to move and caused thousands of deaths due to starvation, exposure, or illness during removal processes from their homelands.

- Many tribes lost vast amounts of land as well as their traditional way-of-life as a result of this policy - including Cherokee Nation's loss more than 50 million acres across several states they had inhabited since antiquity.

- The Indian Removal Act was overturned in 1832 when Congress passed legislation that prohibited further removals except when absolutely necessary in order for settlers and commercial interests looking for resources such as timber or minerals on tribal lands which were often taken without adequate compensation being paid back to tribes affected by these acts.

Its important today that we remember this history not only out respect for Native Americans but also so we can be mindful going forward on how our actions may affect other communities around us - both now and in the future.

The Trail of Tears

The Trail of Tears was a tragic event in US history that saw thousands of Indigenous people forcibly relocated from their ancestral homelands to an unfamiliar world. This relocation was ordered by the Indian Removal Act of 1830. It entailed an arduous journey for many Native Americans and resulted in the deaths of thousands due to starvation and disease.

The Trail of Tears represented a major blow to tribal sovereignty, autonomy, and cultural identity. Native Americans were stripped away from their homes and forced into the unknown. While the death count is impossible to accurately determine, it is estimated that approximately 4,000 Cherokee people perished during this period due to harsh weather conditions, inadequate food supplies, and poor living conditions while on route to Oklahoma.

It is an event that has left a long-lasting impression on American history. It speaks volumes about our nation's treatment of indigenous peoples. Through understanding the tragedy of the Trail of Tears, we can learn more about our collective past with empathy and respect towards those who have suffered great losses throughout our shared history.

The Indian Appropriations Act of 1851

The Indian Appropriations Act of 1851 saw the US government make significant changes to their approach towards Native American land rights and sovereignty. This act, signed into law by President Millard Fillmore, granted the federal government power to purchase tribal lands from Native Americans for resettlement. It also gave the government authority to manage and oversee any funds allocated towards Native American tribes.

This meant that the US could now dictate how much funding they wanted to provide to each tribe in order to help them survive on their newly acquired reservations. As a result of this new legislation, many tribes were forcibly relocated away from their ancestral lands and had little choice but to adhere to its terms.

This shift in policy marked a major turning point in the way Native American tribes were treated by the US government after centuries of mistreatment. The Indian Appropriations Act not only stripped these nations of their autonomy, but it also reduced them to mere wards of the state who had no say in how they managed their own affairs or resources.

Despite this difficult reality, many tribal members found ways to survive on these new reservations while preserving some semblance of their culture and identity through traditional practices and spiritual observances.

Assimilation Policies

In the late 19th and early 20th centuries, the US government adopted assimilation policies that sought to erase Indigenous cultures and identities by forcing Native populations onto reservations and into American society. These policies were seen as a way of "civilizing" Indigenous people to fit within mainstream society.

Assimilation was a systematic attempt to eradicate Indigenous culture, language, customs, traditions, and beliefs. Native Americans were required to take on English names and abandon their spiritual practices in favor of Christianity. Their children were placed in boarding schools where they were taught western values and forbidden from speaking their native languages or engaging in traditional activities.

The Indian Citizenship Act of 1924 provided citizenship status for all Native Americans born within US borders but stripped them of tribal rights. Native Americans who assimilated were moved away from reservations and encouraged to adopt white lifestyles. These assimilation policies caused immense harm to communities across the United States and continue to reverberate today as many struggle with the effects of cultural erasure while trying to reclaim lost heritage.

Wounded Knee Massacre

You may not have heard of the Wounded Knee Massacre, yet it resulted in the death of 300 Lakota Sioux people in 1890 - nearly one third of their population at that time.

The massacre was a result of an attempt by the US military to disarm members of the tribe. Sadly, tensions between Native Americans and white settlers had been escalating for decades prior to this event and culminated with a conflict between two groups near Wounded Knee Creek on December 29th, 1890.

Tragically, it's believed that as many as 350 innocent Native American men, women and children were killed during this incident by US troops.

This event marked a grim chapter in history and serves as an example of how fear can lead to devastating consequences for all involved.

To this day, Native Americans continue to remember those who lost their lives in the Wounded Knee Massacre through memorials and remembrance ceremonies.

Long-Term Consequences

Experience the devastating consequences of fear and prejudice that linger even today, as a reminder of the Wounded Knee Massacre.

The genocide of Native Americans has had long-term effects on their culture and heritage. Survivors still carry deep emotional scars from the impact of this tragedy, which caused many to feel isolated from their own communities.

It also left them feeling disconnected from society at large due to further marginalization and stereotypes. This has resulted in a lack of recognition for their rich history, as well as an overall lack of understanding about what happened at Wounded Knee.

As time passes, these issues have become more important to address in order to get closer to true reconciliation between native peoples and non-native settlers. Education is essential when it comes to understanding the gravity behind the massacre and its ongoing repercussions—only then can we truly honor those who were affected by this tragedy.

Modern Day Struggles of Native Americans

Today, the struggles of indigenous people are still ongoing, with devastating effects that can't be overstated.

From poverty and disparities in access to health care to unequal opportunities for economic development and education, Native Americans face a range of issues that have been prevalent since colonization.

Here are three current challenges faced by many contemporary Native American tribes:

- A lack of access to financial resources and capital needed for economic development on reservations.

- An inability to adequately protect tribal land from environmental destruction due to limited legal authority.

- The continued prevalence of discrimination and racism against Native Americans in public institutions such as schools, hospitals, and police departments.

These struggles are daunting but not insurmountable.

Indigenous communities continue to strive for self-determination, cultural survival, and social justice through lobbying efforts at the local, state, and federal level as well as grassroots organizing initiatives led by young activists determined to do their part in creating a more equitable future for all Native communities.

Frequently Asked Questions

How is the genocide of Native Americans commemorated today?

Today, the genocide of Native Americans is commemorated in a variety of ways. Many tribes across the United States host events to honor the memory and legacy of those who were lost. These gatherings often include traditional singing and dancing, as well as storytelling, to keep their stories alive.

There are also monuments dedicated to Native Americans around the country that serve as important reminders of our troubled history. Finally, there've been recent efforts to recognize tribes through official government acknowledgments, helping to restore some justice for this long-neglected group of people.

What actions are being taken to address the devastating effects of the genocide?

In the United States, efforts are underway to address the devastating effects of genocide against Native Americans. According to a recent study by the National Congress of American Indians, over 2 million people in 574 federally recognized tribes are actively working to preserve their culture and fight for justice.

From advocating for tribal sovereignty and treaty rights to providing services such as healthcare and education, these communities have come together to ensure that their heritage is respected and honored. Through these brave efforts, they continue to make strides towards healing from generations of trauma inflicted by colonialism.

How did Native Americans resist assimilation policies?

Native Americans have long sought to preserve their cultural identities and traditions, often in the face of assimilation policies that threaten these practices.

In particular, many tribes resisted by engaging in acts of civil disobedience, like refusing to send children to boarding schools meant to forcibly assimilate them. Other forms of resistance included establishing independent schools on reservations or setting up alternative government structures.

Still other tribes worked hard to pass laws that would protect their rights and ensure they had access to resources like healthcare and education. By standing up for their rights, Native Americans continue the fight against assimilation policies today.

What are some of the cultural practices that have been lost due to the genocide?

Native American culture has been dramatically impacted by colonialism and the genocide of Native Americans. Many cultural practices, such as traditional ceremonies, languages, music, and art forms have been lost due to the oppression of Native Americans.

Additionally, many tribal nations have had their land taken away or forced into reservations that further limited their access to traditional resources and cultural practices. The loss of these elements has left a lasting impact on the culture and heritage of Native American communities across the continent.

What are the legal rights of Native Americans today?

In the United States, Native Americans are legally recognized as citizens who enjoy many of the same rights and privileges as all other citizens.

Today, Native Americans have their own tribal governments and reservations which are sovereign entities within the American legal system. These tribal governments provide access to a variety of services including health care, housing, education and more for members of their tribe.

They also have the right to vote in federal elections and participate in local politics. Despite this progress, there's still much work left to be done to ensure that all Native Americans can fully exercise their legal rights.

Symbolically speaking, it's important to remember that by protecting the rights of Native Americans we are honoring the memories of those who were lost during the genocide of native peoples in America's past.

Conclusion

Native Americans have faced centuries of genocide and oppression at the hands of the US government, resulting in long-term consequences that continue to this day.

From forced removal and relocation, assimilation policies, and massacres such as Wounded Knee, Native Americans have been denied their rights time and time again.

Yet despite facing immense odds, they still demonstrate resilience by standing up for their culture and identity—a juxtaposition that provides a glimpse into the strength of Indigenous peoples.

While much progress has been made in recent years, it's clear that there's still a long way to go until true justice can be achieved.

The Banning Of Black History

We, the authors, are here to speak for those unheard. We are here to shed light on the injustice of the banning of black history in our educational system and beyond.

Our hearts ache as we consider what a tragedy it is that such a fundamental part of American heritage has been denied its rightful place in our schools. Our minds boggle at the thought of how much knowledge and understanding has been lost due to this ban.

It's time to take a stand; it's time for change! Let us examine together the impact that this ban has had on education, society, economy, family dynamics and racial identity.

Historical Context for the Banning of Black History

It's heartbreaking to think of a time when our nation actively tried to suppress and erase the stories of people who had been so wrongfully oppressed. Black history has been systematically dismissed for centuries, with the banning of books, speeches, and other works that told these stories. Such censorship was part of an effort to further subjugate African Americans and prevent them from gaining equal footing in society.

In addition, the dominant culture ignored or actively denied contributions made by African Americans throughout our history. This led to a complete absence of black history in schools and textbooks, leaving generations without access to accurate information about their cultural heritage or role models that could inspire them.

Though some progress has been made since then, it's clear that we still have a long way to go when it comes to restoring justice and equity for African Americans today. It's not enough just to recognize past injustices; we must work together as a society towards meaningful reparations that provide tangible benefits for individuals who have suffered decades—even centuries—of oppression.

To do this, we first need to understand the full scope of what happened in order for us all to move forward together in solidarity. That means continuing our work towards uncovering hidden histories and amplifying voices that have gone unheard for too long. We must commit ourselves fully towards recognizing the immense value of every person's story - even if it doesn't conform to our own - so that everyone can be seen equally in our shared narrative.

Only then can we begin the journey towards true reconciliation between all members of our society and create a future rooted firmly in equity and justice for all people. To achieve this goal, we must start by exploring the impact of the banning of black history in education today.

The Impact of the Banning of Black History in Education

You're missing out on an important part of our collective knowledge when you don't learn about the accomplishments of a certain group in education. The banning of black history has had far-reaching impacts on both the educational system and society at large, which can't be overstated.

The impact of this ban can be seen in three main areas:

- In terms of access to information: By not teaching black history, students are denied access to valuable information that would otherwise help to broaden their understanding of the world and its history. This can lead to a lack of appreciation for diversity and different cultures, as well as a limited view of reality.

- In terms of learning outcomes: When black history isn't taught in school, it can lead to lower academic performance among those students who are deprived from learning about their own culture or the cultures and histories of others. This can have a direct effect on graduation rates and other measures associated with educational success.

- In terms of representation: A lack of representation in any field will limit opportunities for members from those communities who may otherwise excel if they had access to equal resources. With no representation in schools or universities, there's less chance for members from these communities to gain exposure and recognition for their work or ideas.

The banning of black history has also had an effect on society at large by perpetuating stereotypes and furthering existing divisions between different groups based on race, class, gender, etc. This makes it more difficult for people from these backgrounds to gain acceptance into mainstream society.

The Impact of the Banning of Black History on Society

By not teaching about the accomplishments of a certain group in education, you're missing out on an important part of our collective knowledge that could help bridge divides between different communities.

When black history is banned from schools, it sends a message to students and society at large that this part of our shared history is not important or relevant to our current lives. This can lead to feelings of alienation and erasure for those who are affected by the ban, as well as a lack of understanding and appreciation for their heritage among those outside the affected group.

This can also lead to increased distrust between groups in society due to a feeling that one's culture is seen as less than worthy. As a result, this can create further division within our communities rather than facilitate unity and understanding.

In turn, this leads to an even bigger impact on society as a whole. By not recognizing the importance of black history in our education system, we are perpetuating systemic racism and inequality at all levels.

The Impact of the Banning of Black History on the Economy

The exclusion of certain cultural contributions from the curriculum can have a devastating effect on our economy. This is evidenced by the fact that African American-owned businesses are disproportionately impacted when resources are scarce. For example, after the 2008 financial crisis, black-owned businesses were more than twice as likely to go out of business compared to white-owned businesses.

The lack of access to capital and resources for African Americans perpetuates economic inequality throughout society. This has been particularly true in terms of education attainment and quality job opportunities. Additionally, black households tend to have less savings and wealth than their white counterparts due to systemic racism and discrimination in the labor market.

Not only does this create disparities in wages, it also reduces business formation among African Americans which limits employment opportunities for others within their communities. The ramifications of these imbalances go far beyond economics; they extend into family dynamics with long lasting impacts that are felt generationally.

Therefore, it's essential that we recognize the importance of teaching about black history in order to ensure racial equity and promote economic justice for all people.

The Impact of the Banning of Black History on Family Dynamics

Learning about the contributions of African Americans in our past can have a positive impact on family dynamics, enabling generations to come to understand and value their cultural heritage. It allows families to better recognize the diversity that exists within their own households and encourages them to explore different cultures and customs. This can help create an environment of mutual respect where everyone's identity is valued. It also promotes open dialogue between family members, which facilitates honest communication and understanding between generations.

Acknowledging black history as part of American history helps us understand why certain institutions or laws exist today that may not necessarily be beneficial for people of color, making it easier for families to address these issues together. It also provides an opportunity for parents to teach their children the importance of striving for equality — something that has been a key component in the struggle for civil rights throughout our nation's history.

The banning of black history has deprived many families from experiencing this type of learning together, making it more difficult for them to form strong bonds based on shared knowledge and appreciation for different cultures. This lack of awareness can lead to feelings of isolation among those whose ancestry was affected by slavery or other forms of discrimination in America's past, hindering the progress they wish to make towards racial justice today.

With this in mind, it's important now more than ever that we acknowledge how vital it is to pass down stories from one generation to another so that we can continue breaking down barriers associated with race, class, gender, sexual orientation, religion, etc., allowing us all collectively move forward towards true equality.

Moving into the next section about the impact of the banning of black history on mental health, it's clear that there are far-reaching implications when discussing this subject matter – not only economically but also emotionally as well.

The Impact of the Banning of Black History on Mental Health

Experiencing a lack of recognition for one's cultural heritage can have detrimental effects on mental health, leading to feelings of isolation and disconnection from the world. This is especially true when it comes to the banning of black history in education systems.

Without access to accurate information about their cultural background, many African Americans are left with only stereotypes and negative perceptions of their identity. This can lead to low self-esteem and a sense of disconnection that can be difficult to overcome.

The banning of black history also reinforces the idea that African American culture is not as important or valid as other cultures, making it difficult for individuals to feel proud and empowered by their heritage. Not being able to learn about the accomplishments and contributions made by people who look like them can be disheartening and create an environment where individuals do not feel seen or appreciated.

These feelings can carry over into other areas of life, creating barriers between individuals and others around them due to a lack of understanding or appreciation for their unique backgrounds.

As such, recognizing the impact that banning black history has on mental health is essential for promoting positive change within our society. Moving forward, it's important that we recognize the importance of this issue in order to create an inclusive environment where everyone feels accepted regardless of race or culture.

The Impact of the Banning of Black History on Racial Identity

You may feel like a part of your identity is missing when you're not able to explore and celebrate the achievements and contributions of people from your background. This lack of recognition can make it difficult for you to develop a sense of pride in your culture, leaving you feeling disconnected and unseen.

The banning of black history can cause erosion in racial identity - making it difficult for individuals to find a place in society or even identify with their own race. It creates an environment where individuals are denied access to information about how their ancestors have shaped the world around them.

Individuals who don't know much about their past may struggle with figuring out what makes them unique and how they fit into the larger picture. They may also be less likely to understand the context behind current events that involve race, as well as be able to form meaningful connections with others who share similar backgrounds.

When children don't learn about Black history, they become disconnected from their own heritage which can lead to feelings of isolation, shame, anger, guilt, and frustration. Without learning about important figures within one's culture or having access to diverse perspectives on historical events such as slavery or civil rights movements, people are deprived of developing a strong sense of self-identity or being able to relate positively with other races and cultures.

Lastly, when cultural awareness is absent from education systems it perpetuates systemic racism by furthering ignorance towards Black people's histories and struggles.

The banning of black history has far-reaching consequences on racial identity that cannot be understated; without education on minority groups' contributions there exists an oppressive environment that undermines our collective ability to appreciate each other's backgrounds and experiences. This leads us smoothly into considering the debate around reinstating black history in education which will be discussed next...

The Debate around Reinstating Black History in Education

The debate around reinstating a fuller perspective of minority contributions in the classroom is one that has been ongoing for generations, with passionate advocates on both sides. On one side, there are those who believe that it is important to recognize the significant contributions of black history and its figures throughout history, not just in America but across the world. On the other side, there are those who feel that implementing such measures will lead to too much emphasis being placed on race instead of on merit or academic achievement.

Argument For Reinstatement	Argument Against Reinstatement
Celebrates diversity and inclusion	Reinforces racial divide
Creates a richer understanding of our shared past	Places too much emphasis on race over merit
Recognizes the achievements of black people	Unfairly privileges some cultures over others

At its core, this debate is really about what students should learn in school and how they should be taught about it. It's about having an appreciation for different cultures and perspectives while also recognizing how systemic racism has prevented certain groups from achieving their potential for centuries. Ultimately, it comes down to how we view History itself – as an objective account of facts or as a narrative crafted by those in power? The answer lies somewhere in between these two extremes; however, both sides can agree that Black History needs to be acknowledged and discussed openly if we are ever going to move forward together as a society. With this in mind, alternative solutions must be explored which can provide an equitable platform for all voices without reinforcing any existing divides.

Alternative Solutions to the Banning of Black History

Discovering alternative solutions to the inequality of minority contributions in education is a must, so that we can collectively move forward and progress as one with an appreciation for different cultures and perspectives.

One potential solution could be incorporating multiculturalism into all aspects of the curriculum, from history classes to science classes. This would ensure that students have exposure to a range of backgrounds and ideas, allowing them to gain a better understanding of different perspectives.

Additionally, implementing anti-bias curriculums within the classroom can help students recognize their own biases and develop the skills necessary for interacting with people from various backgrounds without judgment or fear.

Another way to address this issue is by providing more diverse representation in educational materials such as textbooks, films, and other media sources used in school. By ensuring these resources cover multiple viewpoints on any given topic, students will become more aware of how history is often shaped by societal power dynamics.

This will create an environment where everyone feels represented while also giving teachers the opportunity to explore difficult topics like prejudice and racism in order to discuss its effects on society today.

In order to combat unequal representations of minority contributions within education systems, we must take steps towards creating learning spaces that are inclusive and equitable for all students regardless of their race or background. Through increased diversity in educational materials and engaging anti-bias curriculums, we can strive towards creating a more just learning environment for generations to come.

With these measures put into place, we can begin working towards restoring Black History back into our schools while simultaneously encouraging mutual respect among all cultures within our society.

Recommendations for Reinstating Black History in Education

Now that we've come up with alternative solutions to the banning of black history in education, it's time to discuss how to reinstate this important topic into curriculums. We believe there are several recommended steps for achieving this goal:

- Increase awareness and education of black history among educators and administrators.

- Incorporate more diverse authors, books, and perspectives into school libraries.

- Require classes be taught by instructors who have knowledge on a variety of cultures and can teach from multiple perspectives.

- Develop curriculum standards that ensure representation of all cultures' stories are being told accurately, fairly, and without bias.

- Create student-led initiatives that bring attention to forgotten histories or events in order to properly remember them going forward.

By taking these steps together as educators, students, administrators, parents, and community members, we can work towards creating an inclusive educational system. This system should allow all students to feel respected and represented within their learning environment. Let's strive for an educational system where every person has the opportunity to learn about different aspects of the human experience with equal respect given to each culture's unique set of values. This would provide our children with a sense of understanding not just limited to one culture but rather all cultures they may encounter throughout their lives.

Frequently Asked Questions

What led to the banning of Black History in the first place?

We're interested in what led to the banning of black history in the first place. To understand this, it's important to look at the roots of racism in our society, which have been present since long before any laws were enacted.

Racism has been used as a way to oppress and marginalize people of color, often by denying them access to education or resources that would allow them to learn about their own heritage and cultural history. This means that many aspects of black history and culture were not taught in schools, nor was it given any recognition or validation in mainstream media or other public forums.

Over time, this created an environment where black history was systematically erased from the public consciousness – leading eventually to its complete banishment from educational institutions and other public spaces.

Are there any current efforts to reverse the banning of Black History?

We're witnessing a resurgence of interest in Black History. Though it's been banned for many years, current efforts are underway to reverse this trend.

In fact, over the past year alone, there's been a 66% increase in the number of people searching for information about African American history online. This indicates that people are becoming more aware and engaged with this topic.

This is an encouraging sign that'll hopefully lead to further progress towards rectifying the injustices of the past.

How does the banning of Black History influence public opinion?

We believe that the banning of black history has a significant effect on public opinion. It creates a perception of inferiority and powerlessness, which can lead to feelings of resentment or even anger among minority groups. This further perpetuates racism in society, leading to distrust between races and creating an atmosphere of distrust and hostility.

The banning of black history also serves to erase important parts of our collective history, leaving us with incomplete perspectives and understanding about our shared past. Through this erasure, we risk losing valuable information that could help us better understand our present and future relationships with one another.

How has the banning of Black History affected the way that Black people view their own history?

We, as black people, have been completely robbed of our history. When we try to look back and learn more about our culture and heritage, it feels like something is missing - like a great big hole in the middle of the story.

We can feel the immense weight of all that has been taken away from us. Despite this injustice, we still find strength in looking back on our rich history with pride and passion.

Our ancestors may not be able to tell their stories today because of the banning of black history, but their legacies live on through us. They inspire us to continue fighting for truth and justice so that one day we may proudly know every bit of our own unique heritage.

How has the banning of Black History changed the way that people of other races view Black History?

We believe that the banning of black history has had a significant effect on how people of other races view black history.

With limited access to accurate information about the accomplishments and struggles of African Americans, many people have adopted myths and stereotypes as facts.

This lack of education contributes to a racial divide, as it prevents people from understanding the history and culture of African American communities.

As a result, we're seeing an increase in racism and discrimination among different races.

It's essential that we make sure everyone has access to accurate information about black history so that we can move towards true equality for all races.

Conclusion

We've seen the devastating consequences of banning black history from education. It has had a negative impact on society, economy, family dynamics, and racial identity.

We find ourselves in an uncomfortable debate about how to reinstate black history into our classrooms. Juxtaposing ideas, such as alternative solutions and recommendations for reinstatement against the already existing problems, is a powerful tool when approaching this issue.

We must work together to develop effective strategies that will ensure black history is not only taught but celebrated in our schools. Only then can we create a more equitable learning experience for everyone.

The Great Migration

In the early 20th century, we experienced an unprecedented phenomenon that would forever change the course of history. Dubbed 'The Great Migration', this mass relocation of African-Americans from the rural South to cities in the North was a historic exodus.

It was sparked by a desire for economic opportunity and freedom from oppressive conditions such as segregation and discrimination, but it had far-reaching implications that continue to shape our society today.

From family dynamics to education, businesses to civil rights, this incredible movement created lasting ripple effects across generations.

Let's take an in-depth look into The Great Migration and all its complexities.

Reasons for the Migration

You may be wondering why so many people decided to leave their homes and embark on this journey - let's explore the reasons for the migration.

The Great Migration was one of the largest population movements in American history, with over 6 million African Americans leaving the South between 1916 and 1970. Though some were driven by economic opportunities, most were seeking refuge from oppressive laws and violence in an effort to secure better lives for themselves and their families.

In addition, they were promised job opportunities as part of a larger narrative of freedom, equality, and opportunity that was being promoted in the North at this time.

Discrimination against African Americans had been deeply entrenched into law since before Reconstruction. Segregation remained firmly in place after emancipation; Jim Crow laws made it illegal for black people to vote or attend integrated schools while reinforcing racial segregation throughout society.

Racial violence also played a huge role in driving this mass exodus: lynchings became all too common during this period, creating a culture of fear that forced many African Americans out of their homes and into unfamiliar places where they could live without fear of persecution or death.

The promise of economic stability was another major factor behind the Great Migration. With industrialization taking hold across much of America, northern cities offered jobs that paid decent wages which often couldn't be found back home; although discrimination persisted even in these areas, there were often less discriminatory practices than those experienced in Southern states making it easier for them to get hired or find housing if they moved northward.

As word spread about these economic opportunities, thousands more followed suit each year until millions had left behind everything they knew to build new lives elsewhere. This influx created vibrant communities whose influence can still be seen today – from music to literature to civil rights activism – making it one of the greatest moments in modern American history.

Economic Opportunities in the North

The North offered African Americans a chance to pursue economic opportunities that weren't available in the South. The promise of better wages, more job security, and fewer racial restrictions provided an incentive for people to leave their homes during the Great Migration in search of a better life. This desire was so strong that many African American families sold what they owned and made the journey north despite having no guarantee of success.

In cities like New York, Detroit, Chicago, and Philadelphia, there were countless jobs to be had in factories as well as other industries such as construction and transportation. At first glance, these positions appeared lucrative - wages compared favorably to those paid in Southern states - but often came with long hours, little job security, or benefits. Furthermore, black workers were sometimes hired for the most dangerous tasks and rarely promoted into managerial roles regardless of their capabilities.

Despite this inequality, African Americans still sought out jobs in the North. It offered a greater degree of freedom than what was available in the former Confederate states. Even though they would face discrimination and segregation wherever they went, at least they could choose where they wanted to live. Instead of being bound by Jim Crow laws, which limited their rights even further. As such, many African Americans saw hope for a better existence, although it would come at a great cost both financially and emotionally. Leaving home meant potentially never seeing family members again.

The next section will focus on how discrimination and segregation followed African-Americans from south to north during this period.

Discrimination and Segregation in the North

Discrimination and segregation followed African-Americans to the North like a dark cloud, stifling any hope of a brighter future. Even in states such as Ohio, Illinois, and Michigan where African-American migration was highest, racial segregation remained rampant.

- Housing opportunities were limited to certain areas; properties were often overvalued for black buyers or rental agreements had stringent conditions that made it difficult to obtain housing.
- Employment options were also limited. African-Americans were barred from certain professions or relegated to the lowest paying jobs.
- Education opportunities were severely restricted; separate schools with fewer resources allocated than those for white students perpetuated disparities in educational quality.
- Social exclusion was widespread; many restaurants, theaters and other businesses refused service based on race alone.
- Racial violence was an ever present threat; lynchings and mob violence occurred frequently throughout this period of history.

The oppressive atmosphere of discrimination and segregation cast a pall on the hopes of African-Americans looking for economic opportunity in Northern cities but still they persisted, laying down roots that would begin to form the foundation of thriving communities despite the adversity faced by African-American migrants during this time period.

Through hard work and resilience, these communities developed institutions that allowed them greater access to education, employment opportunities, housing availability, and much more - leading into a new era of hope for generations yet unborn.

Impact on African-American Businesses

Experience the impact of discrimination and segregation on African-American businesses as they struggled to survive in an oppressive atmosphere.

During the Great Migration, many Black entrepreneurs looked to expand their business into newly accessible Northern cities. However, these business owners were met with a major roadblock: institutional racism.

Through restrictive covenants and discriminatory zoning ordinances, African-Americans were excluded from certain commercial districts and denied access to capital needed to build new businesses. Even when successful businesses did open up in predominantly white neighborhoods, they often faced boycotts from white customers or false accusations of criminal activity meant to drive them out of town.

The lack of economic opportunity for Black businesses was further compounded by unfair labor practices that limited wages for Black workers. This created an environment where many African-Americans could not afford goods and services being offered by other black entrepreneurs due to lack of available funds.

Despite all these challenges, some African-American business owners persisted against the odds and found ways to succeed in spite of the systemic oppression they faced every day. These courageous individuals demonstrated the potential for economic growth within their communities if given equal opportunities under the law.

They laid the foundation for future generations of African-American business leaders who would continue striving for success despite adversity. As we turn our attention towards exploring how this period impacted African American education in the North, it's important to remember those who persevered through challenging times and kept their dreams alive.

African-American Education in the North

Amidst the obstacles of systemic racism, African-American education in the North still flourished as a beacon of hope for future generations. During this time period, many African-Americans had very limited access to quality educational opportunities due to segregation and discrimination.

However, with the assistance of organizations like the NAACP and later programs such as Brown v. Board of Education, African-American students in Northern states were able to attend schools that provided them with a better education than those available to their counterparts in Southern states. This was especially the case for college and university level institutions where talented African-American students could receive a higher level of instruction from faculty members who were dedicated to providing an equitable learning experience for all students regardless of race or ethnicity.

In addition, many organizations offered financial aid and other resources that allowed more African-Americans to pursue higher education in the North despite facing economic hardship caused by racial inequality. Although these advancements did not completely eliminate disparities between black and white educational attainment levels in northern states, they laid down an important foundation for future progress.

Without question, African-American education in the North made significant strides during The Great Migration which would ultimately help shape politics and culture across America today. As we now move into examining how this affected African-American politics, we must remember that the foundations set during this time have been crucial in helping create lasting change within our society.

Impact on African-American Politics

The African-American political experience was drastically altered by the Great Migration. During the period of mass migration, millions of African Americans left the South and sought opportunities in northern cities. This shift in population had a dramatic impact on politics throughout the country.

In particular, the African-American presence in northern cities allowed for increased political representation and influence. With their newfound collective power, black citizens were able to build coalitions and organize politically to pursue their own interests. This rise of Black Power resulted in more equitable laws being passed that could benefit all members of society regardless of race or ethnicity.

Though there were still major issues facing African Americans as they navigated new social environments, they were now better equipped to confront those challenges through organized action rather than be limited by oppressive state laws as before. With this newfound freedom came a wave of changes to shape how American democracy functions today—changes that would continue to evolve over time due to advances made during The Great Migration.

By creating an environment where African Americans could have a stronger voice in politics, this movement changed the way we think about civil rights and justice for all citizens. As such, it's clear that The Great Migration had a lasting impact on our current understanding of democracy and its importance for every person regardless of race or creed.

Changes in Family Dynamics

With the large-scale movement of African Americans to Northern cities, family dynamics within the Black community underwent significant changes. During the Great Migration, many families were split up as some members moved north for better job opportunities and wages while others stayed in the South. This separation caused a shift in traditional family roles and responsibilities. Women took on more prominent roles in their households and became primary breadwinners. The migration also led to an increase in single-parent households as many men left for work without their spouses or children.

The changes in family dynamics brought about by the Great Migration had both positive and negative effects on African American communities. On one hand, it enabled African Americans to escape oppressive conditions and gain economic independence. On the other hand, it caused a breakdown of traditional familial structures that had provided stability to generations of African Americans for centuries before them.

The legacy of this period remains with us today. From higher rates of single-parent households among African American families to a greater emphasis on individualism rather than collective support systems within these communities – all resulting from this great wave of migration over 100 years ago. This lasting impact continues to shape how African American families live and interact even today.

The Legacy of the Great Migration

The Great Migration left a lasting imprint on African American families, reshaping them like clay in the hands of a master potter. As generations of African Americans moved from rural areas to urban ones, they faced new challenges such as wage inequality and segregation. Yet the Great Migration also offered opportunities that changed family dynamics for generations.

The changes in family roles, economics, education, and more were felt by African American communities across the country. The Great Migration allowed African Americans to seek out better economic opportunities for themselves and their families. For many, moving away from farms and small towns meant increased access to higher wages and wealth-building opportunities which could provide greater financial security for their descendants.

With higher wages came new educational possibilities; black families were able to send children to college or trade school far more frequently than before the migration began. African American women experienced dramatic shifts in expectations during this time period as well. Prior to the migration, women were largely relegated to housekeeping roles but now had a chance at full-time employment or even careers outside of the home.

This shift was both empowering and disorienting as traditional gender roles shifted drastically with new economic realities imposed by the Great Migration. The legacy of the Great Migration is deeply woven into African American culture today; its effects are still felt through shifts in family dynamics that continue today – including those related to gender roles, economics, education, and more – all shaped by those first brave souls who made the trek northward over a century ago.

As we move forward into understanding how these changes have impacted us as individuals and our collective community over time, one thing is certain: The Great Migration has been an integral part of our history that continues to shape us today.

The Long-Term Impact of the Great Migration

You've likely been affected by the Great Migration in some way, whether through changes in family dynamics, roles, economics, or education - and this long-lasting legacy continues to shape us today.

The Great Migration has had far-reaching consequences for both African Americans who moved during this time as well as those who were left behind. It has resulted in a massive shift of population and resources from rural areas to urban centers. It has caused profound social and economic shifts within both the black communities left behind and those that moved northward. It has also created new opportunities for African American people to pursue their dreams of upward mobility but also brought with it many challenges.

The impact of the Great Migration can still be seen across generations today – studies suggest that children born into families with members who participated in the Great Migration are more likely to achieve higher levels of educational attainment than those whose families did not participate.

As we move forward, it's important to remember that while there may have been tremendous opportunity associated with the movement northward for African Americans during this period, there were also immense challenges faced by migrants which must be acknowledged if we're truly going to understand the full scope of its historical significance.

With an awareness of these complexities, we can begin to grapple with how best to learn from our collective history and use these insights to create a better future for all.

Challenges Faced by the Migrants

Although the promise of a better life was alluring, the Great Migration brought with it many hardships for African Americans as they relocated to urban centers. Discrimination in employment, housing, education and social opportunities were just some of the issues they encountered. Many cities' infrastructure was not able to keep up with the influx of migrants. This lack of resources led to overcrowding and inadequate housing conditions, such as dilapidated buildings with multiple families living in one apartment. Additionally, racial prejudice and segregation prevented Black people from accessing quality healthcare and educational opportunities.

Challenge	Description	Solution
Employment	Job discrimination and limited access to opportunities	Activism through labor unions & civil rights organizations
Housing	Overcrowded living spaces due to a lack of homes	Formation of tenant's unions & advocacy groups
Education	Lack of equal access to schools & post-secondary institutions due to segregation	Development of Historically Black Colleges & Universities (HBCUs)

The challenges faced by African Americans during the Great Migration had serious consequences that still reverberate today. The disparities created then have left an enduring mark on generations past and present; yet despite these obstacles, Black folks helped create vibrant communities across America, paving the way for future progress. As a result of their resilience, courage and determination we can now look back at this era with admiration while also recognizing what more needs to be done moving forward.

Frequently Asked Questions

What were the primary motivations behind the Great Migration?

We, as a people, have historically been driven by the desire to better ourselves. The Great Migration was no different.

African Americans in the early 20th century were motivated by a range of factors including economic opportunity, social justice, and freedom from oppression. The promise of higher wages, access to education, and greater civil rights for African Americans spurred a mass exodus from the rural South to cities in the North and Midwest.

This movement for improvement changed American society forever, providing more opportunities for generations to come.

How did the Great Migration affect the African-American population in the South?

We, the African-American population in the South, were profoundly affected by the Great Migration. It was a period of time where millions of us journeyed from our homes in search of better opportunities and improved lives.

During this time, we faced many challenges as we left behind family, friends, and familiar places to move to unfamiliar environments with different cultures and ways of life. Despite these difficulties, many of us found success through new jobs and greater economic stability which ultimately provided for our families.

The Great Migration had a monumental impact on us and continues to shape our culture today.

Was there a difference in the economic opportunities offered to African-Americans in the North vs. the South?

We've seen a stark contrast in economic opportunities offered to African-Americans between the north and south.

In the south, many African-Americans were unable to take advantage of advances in industry because they were denied access to jobs, or had low wages due to discrimination.

Conversely, in the North there was greater job availability as well as better wages for African-Americans that enabled them to build wealth and move up into the middle class.

The Great Migration saw millions of African-Americans leave the South for these more plentiful economic opportunities in Northern cities, which has had an immense impact on their lives and communities.

How did the Great Migration help to shape African-American culture?

We believe that the Great Migration of African-Americans from the South to the North had an enormous impact on African-American culture.

Despite some popular beliefs, this migration wasn't merely a means for economic opportunity - it also opened up new cultural expression and opportunities for social growth.

By leaving behind oppressive and segregated conditions of the South, African-Americans were able to create their own unique sense of identity in Northern cities.

This newfound freedom allowed them to pursue creative endeavors such as music, art, literature, and theater, which blossomed with new ideas and influences from diverse cultures.

The end result was an enriched landscape of vibrant culture that has shaped the American experience as we know it today.

What were the long-term consequences of the Great Migration?

We experienced a major shift in population over the course of the 20th century, with millions of African-Americans leaving the South to seek out opportunities and better lives in other parts of the country.

This massive movement, known as The Great Migration, had long-term consequences that are still felt today. These include an increase in racial tensions between whites and blacks in both urban areas which saw large influxes of black residents, as well as an economic divide due to differences in income levels between those who stayed behind and those who moved away.

Additionally, there's been a lasting impact on African-American culture due to the influx of different people and ideas into new communities.

Conclusion

We, the great migrants, have come so far and endured much in our search for a better future. Our journey has been long and difficult, but we won't forget those who came before us or the legacy of strength they left behind.

We're now ready to embark on a new chapter of progress and prosperity - one that's built on the courage and determination of all those who chose to take a chance and forge ahead.

This allegory speaks to our collective resilience in the face of adversity. We've faced immense challenges since leaving our homes; yet, through it all, we've persevered with hope in our hearts.

Our story is an inspiration for generations to come: no matter how hard life may seem at times, we can always find the strength within ourselves to overcome whatever obstacles may stand in our way.

Social Promotion and the Black Community

We all know the adage that "education is the key to success" — but for many African American students, this isn't always true.

Social promotion is a practice in which students are advanced to the next grade level despite their lack of mastery of content and skills.

This has far-reaching implications for the black community, as it can lead to lower educational outcomes and create an achievement gap between white and black students.

In this article, we explore the effects of social promotion in the African American community, its impact on educational outcomes, strategies to improve these outcomes, and alternatives to social promotion.

What is Social Promotion?

You have the power to reach success, no matter what obstacles stand in your way.

Social promotion is a term used to describe the practice of moving students from one academic grade to another without mastering all of the required skills for their current grade level. This method has been implemented as a means of addressing students' academic deficiencies and improving student motivation and engagement. It also serves as an alternative to retaining students at their current grade level or assigning them to summer school programs.

Social promotion has been met with mixed reactions from various stakeholders, such as parents, teachers, administrators, politicians, and other members of the educational system. Supporters argue that social promotion is beneficial for those students who are struggling academically due to factors outside their control, like poverty or lack of access to resources. Opponents argue that it does not adequately prepare students for higher levels of learning or equip them with necessary skills.

The effects of social promotion on African American students have been closely studied in recent years in an effort to determine if this policy helps or hinders these populations' academic success. Studies indicate that while social promotion may be beneficial for some African American students, it can also lead to disengagement and lower grades due to lack of sufficient preparation for more advanced coursework. In addition, many experts believe that by encouraging socially promoted students rather than challenging them academically, we are sending a message that mediocrity is acceptable, which can limit potential achievement later in life.

Moving forward, then, it is essential that we ensure all members of our society have access to quality education opportunities regardless of race or economic status, so everyone can reach their full potential.

The Effects of Social Promotion on African American Students

Receiving a pass-through grade, rather than being held back, can have a lasting impact on African American students' education. This is especially true in the case of social promotion, which is when an individual student progresses to the next grade level without meeting all of the criteria for that level; often this occurs because there aren't enough resources or opportunities available to help them meet those requirements.

Social promotion is a common practice in many school districts across the United States and can be beneficial for African American students who may face challenges due to poverty or limited access to quality educational materials. On one hand, it provides these students with an opportunity they wouldn't otherwise have had; however, it also comes with some risks.

The primary risk associated with social promotion is that it may lead to unpreparedness for higher levels of learning. Students who are passed through grades without mastering the skills necessary for success may experience gaps in their knowledge as they advance further in their studies. This can cause frustration and difficulty understanding new concepts at each stage of learning, leading to lower test scores and ultimately making it more difficult for these students to succeed academically.

Additionally, if a student's peers are more advanced than them due to better educational opportunities or more rigorous coursework outside of school, they may find themselves feeling increasingly isolated and left behind as their classmates continue advancing ahead of them.

These problems can create long-term academic challenges that have far-reaching implications not just for African American students but also for their entire communities. Low levels of academic achievement among any population will limit economic potential and stifle overall societal growth. This means that while social promotion offers short-term gains by allowing some disadvantaged students access to additional educational opportunities, its long-term effects could potentially be detrimental if steps aren't taken to ensure that these same students receive sufficient support along their educational journey so they can reach their full academic potentials.

Transitioning into discussing "the implications of social promotion in the African American community," then, requires us first to consider how best we might make sure every African American student has what he/she needs - in terms of both resources and guidance - to reach his/her fullest potential throughout life's journey beyond high school graduation.

The Implications of Social Promotion in the African American Community

It's no secret that the impacts of social promotion are far reaching and can have lasting effects on African American students' academic success. With this in mind, it's important to recognize the implications of such a practice in this population and take steps to ensure they have what they need to succeed.

Social promotion fails to address many of the underlying issues faced by African Americans, such as poverty, racism, and lack of access to high-quality education. As a result, those who are promoted may still be unprepared for the next grade level or even fall behind their peers academically. This can lead to increased frustration and feelings of inadequacy among students who may already feel like outsiders in an educational system that is not designed for them.

Additionally, there can be long-term consequences associated with social promotion for African American students. Studies have shown that these students often struggle more than their white counterparts when placed into classrooms where they are ill-prepared or given less attention from teachers due to their perceived lower academic potential. This can lead to significant disparities in educational outcomes between black and white students which only further existing racial achievement gaps.

We must acknowledge that social promotion has its unintended consequences if we want all children—especially those of color—to receive quality education and reach their full potentials.

It's critical that schools provide all students with resources and support geared towards helping them succeed both inside and outside the classroom so that everyone has equal opportunity for success regardless of race or background.

Moving forward, it is necessary for educators to examine ways in which social promotion can be used responsibly while also providing targeted interventions for struggling students so that every child has an equitable chance at achieving academic excellence.

The Impact of Social Promotion on Educational Outcomes

You can't underestimate the incredible impact social promotion has on educational outcomes-- it's truly massive! African American students, in particular, have been disproportionately impacted by this practice. For example, research has shown that Black children are much more likely to be held back a grade due to poor academic performance than their white peers. This causes them to fall behind academically and is often accompanied by feelings of shame or inadequacy.

Furthermore, when these students are socially promoted, they may not have had the opportunity to develop basic skills needed for their age-appropriate grade level. As a result, they face difficulty catching up with their classmates and struggle with self-esteem issues.

The long-term consequences of social promotion for African American students can be especially damaging. Studies show that those who repeat a grade in elementary school are likely to experience lower academic achievement later on in life and may even drop out of high school altogether. Additionally, it can lead to other negative outcomes such as increased behavior problems and mental health struggles like depression and anxiety.

It's clear then that social promotion is having an immense effect on educational outcomes among African Americans—one that should not be taken lightly or ignored.

These findings reveal how essential it is for educators to work together with families and the community at large in order to ensure all students receive the necessary resources and support they need in order to succeed academically regardless of race or background. With the right combination of interventions tailored specifically for each student's individual needs, we can create an equitable environment where everyone has equal access to quality education—and ultimately put an end to disparities caused by social promotion once and for all.

Moving forward, understanding the current state of social promotion in the African American community will be key if we hope to break down systemic barriers that prevent our youth from achieving success both inside and outside the classroom.

The Current State of Social Promotion in the African American Community

Gaining a better understanding of the current state of educational outcomes for African Americans is essential in order to create an equitable environment and ultimately break down systemic barriers.

Social promotion, the practice of advancing a student to the next grade level despite academic performance, has been used as a way to keep students from being held back due to gaps in their education. This has been especially beneficial for African American students who have historically faced more challenges academically due to systemic racism.

Despite this benefit, social promotion also carries with it some unintended consequences that are important to consider when making decisions about how best to support African American students in their educational journey.

The advantages of social promotion include providing students who may be struggling academically with an opportunity to continue their progress without having to repeat coursework or fall behind their peers. It can also help reduce the stigma associated with repeating a grade and provide additional motivation for students who may need extra time or resources in order to succeed.

However, there are also potential drawbacks which must be taken into account, such as increased class sizes and lower overall academic achievement levels due to not challenging students enough or holding them accountable for meeting expectations.

It is clear that social promotion has both positives and negatives when applied within the African American community; but what is even more important is ensuring that all students receive the necessary support they need regardless of race or socio-economic background in order to achieve success in school and life.

With this goal in mind, it is essential that educators understand the nuances behind social promotion so they can make informed decisions about what strategies best serve their student populations moving forward.

As we move ahead, we must continue striving towards creating equitable learning environments where all individuals can reach their full potentials no matter their starting point.

The Advantages and Disadvantages of Social Promotion

Navigating the pros and cons of social promotion can be a tricky tightrope to walk, but it's important to remember that every child deserves an equal chance at success - don't throw out the baby with the bathwater.

On one hand, social promotion is a great idea on paper: instead of being held back for failing a single subject or year level, students are moved up with their peers despite academic shortcomings. This can help prevent student disengagement and boost morale in the classroom.

However, this approach has its drawbacks too. It could lead to a low-quality education for those who have been promoted without having achieved necessary levels of mastery in core subjects. It could cause overcrowding as more students pass through each grade. It may also reduce motivation and focus among those who have advanced without adequate preparation.

Social promotion is an issue that requires thoughtful consideration from all stakeholders involved. It is essential that we create systems which help children reach their educational potential while ensuring high standards are met. We must strive to provide our African American youth with the equitable access they require to succeed academically while ensuring our expectations remain achievable and reasonable across all grade levels.

By taking these factors into account when considering social promotion policies, we can ensure our young people receive the best possible education while maintaining their enthusiasm and engagement in learning. As we move forward into strategies aimed at improving educational outcomes for African American students, let's continue doing so with diligence and care.

Strategies to Improve Educational Outcomes for African American Students

Gaining equitable access to education is essential for African American students to reach their potential - let's work together to make sure they get it.

To do that, both parents and schools need to be involved in the effort. Parents can provide a supportive home environment that fosters learning and encourages positive academic behaviors, while schools should strive for a curriculum that is tailored toward the needs of African American students and promotes critical thinking skills.

Additionally, school systems should focus on closing achievement gaps between African American students and their white peers by providing more resources as well as hiring teachers who are sensitive to racial issues.

Furthermore, we must promote an anti-racist culture in our schools so that all students feel safe and supported. This includes engaging with conversations surrounding racism, advocating for policies that support diversity initiatives, and implementing effective discipline strategies that recognize implicit bias.

Furthermore, community organizations can play an important role in helping African American children develop social-emotional skills such as resilience and self-advocacy which will help them succeed academically later on in life.

In order for African American students to have access to quality educational opportunities they need both parents and schools working together towards this goal. It's only through collaborative efforts from everyone involved that these disparities can be addressed effectively - let's move forward with determination so all children have the same chance at success no matter their background or skin color!

As we look ahead towards the role of parents and schools in addressing social promotion, it's clear this problem can't be solved without meaningful collaboration from all parties involved.

The Role of Parents and Schools in Addressing Social Promotion

You can help African American students succeed by joining forces with schools to address the challenge of social promotion. Allude to a team effort that will create a bridge between parents and educators, so that everyone is working together towards a common goal for success.

When it comes to social promotion, there should be active dialogue between parents and educators regarding the expectations of both parties in order to ensure that all children are given the same opportunity for academic success. Parents need to provide support for their children by reinforcing positive behaviors and attitudes at home while educators must work with families on how best to create meaningful learning experiences in the classroom.

By involving families in school-based activities such as parent-teacher conferences, open houses, and special events, schools can build relationships with families and foster an environment of collaboration among parents and teachers. Additionally, providing resources such as tutoring programs or after-school activities can give students access to educational opportunities beyond what they may receive during regular school hours.

Schools should also seek out funding sources from government agencies or non-profit organizations that could provide additional support services for struggling students who may benefit from extra attention outside of class time.

These strategies can help close the achievement gap between African American students and their peers by setting high standards for all students regardless of race or economic background. It's essential that we work together - parents, teachers, administrators - to make sure every student has an equal chance at achieving their goals in life through education.

With this concerted effort, we can give our African American youth the tools necessary for success now and into adulthood—and ultimately break down barriers associated with social promotion once and for all.

The Role of Government and Policy in Addressing Social Promotion

Government and policy makers have a critical role to play in ensuring that all students, regardless of race or economic background, are given the same opportunity for success - it's time to make sure everyone has an equal chance.

To reach this goal requires understanding the unique challenges faced by African American communities when it comes to social promotion. This includes:

- Ensuring adequate funding for schools in order to provide quality educational opportunities
- Addressing disparities in access to resources such as technology and curriculum materials
- Implementing more effective accountability measures that focus on improving student performance rather than punishing schools
- Developing support systems that address underlying issues such as poverty and discrimination
- Increasing teacher diversity so students can better identify with those teaching them

The solutions must go beyond simply passing laws or providing additional funds; they must be designed with an understanding of how racism affects communities and creates barriers to success.

This means creating policies that recognize the unique needs of African American students and their families, while also acknowledging systemic inequities that have been perpetuated for generations. By making these changes, government officials can ensure social promotion does not become a tool used against Black students but instead is part of a larger effort to improve equity outcomes.

Rather than widening the gap between those who succeed and those who do not, let's work together towards creating a society where everyone has an equal opportunity for success.

With this goal in mind, we can move forward towards exploring alternatives to social promotion in the African American community.

Alternatives to Social Promotion in the African American Community

When it comes to providing students with the best chance for success, creating alternatives to social promotion is essential in order to ensure all students have equitable access to educational opportunities.

In the African American community, this is especially true given its long-standing history of systemic racism. It's important for there to be a focus on creating and implementing alternative methods of assessment which are both culturally relevant and developmentally appropriate for African American students.

This could include more holistic assessments such as portfolios, projects, and student self-reflection that allow teachers and administrators to measure academic progress in a more comprehensive manner. It's also necessary for educators and school leaders in the African American community to create an environment where these alternatives can be successful.

This requires building positive relationships between teachers, administrators, parents, guardians, and other stakeholders so that they're all invested in helping African American children reach their full potential. Additionally, it's beneficial when schools provide additional resources such as tutoring programs or afterschool activities which can help support student learning outside of classroom instruction.

For social promotion alternatives to be successful within the African American community, it takes a collective effort from everyone involved in order for students' needs to be met in an effective way. By ensuring there are adequate resources available along with meaningful assessments which accurately reflect each student's individual abilities and potential growth areas, we can give every child an opportunity to succeed regardless of their race or background.

Frequently Asked Questions

What are the long-term implications of social promotion for African American students?

We're confronted with a troubling reality. The long-term implications of social promotion for African American students can be far-reaching and devastating.

Like a dark cloud looming on the horizon, this phenomenon can cast a shadow on their futures, impacting not only their academic development but also their life chances.

Social promotion may lead to an inability to keep up with course material, which in turn could create feelings of alienation or frustration in the classroom environment.

Furthermore, these students may end up graduating without having acquired the necessary skills and knowledge needed to pursue further education or even gainful employment.

To make matters worse, this lack of preparation can have lasting effects that reverberate throughout generations, perpetuating inequities within our society.

It's therefore essential that we recognize the importance of addressing this issue head on by providing appropriate support services and mentorship opportunities for African American youth who are at risk of being socially promoted.

Is there evidence that social promotion has a positive or negative effect on African American students' academic performance?

We've been looking into the effects of social promotion on African American students' academic performance.

While there has been no definitive answer to this question, research studies suggest that the potential effects could be both positive and negative.

On one hand, social promotion may increase students' confidence and sense of belonging in their school community. On the other hand, it could lead to a gap in necessary educational skills that would otherwise be acquired if the student was held back.

Ultimately, further research is needed in order to gain more insight into how social promotion affects African American students' academic performance.

Are there any studies that compare the effectiveness of social promotion vs. traditional grading methods?

We've been exploring the effectiveness of social promotion versus traditional grading methods. Studies have shown that both approaches can be beneficial for African American students, depending on the individual student's needs and learning style.

However, there is limited research comparing the two approaches in terms of their overall effectiveness. Some studies suggest that social promotion may be more effective in helping African American students reach their academic goals, while others indicate that traditional grading methods may be better suited to certain types of learners.

Ultimately, it's important to consider each student's unique needs when deciding which approach will best support their academic success.

What are the best strategies for parents and teachers to use when addressing social promotion?

We've all heard of social promotion, and many of us have concerns about its efficacy. But did you know that studies show that students who are socially promoted achieve higher levels of success than those who fail classes?

This means it's important for parents and teachers to consider the best strategies when addressing social promotion in the classroom. It's essential to look beyond grades and find ways to engage students with meaningful learning experiences.

A key strategy is to create an inclusive environment where every student feels valued, respected, and empowered to succeed.

What alternatives to social promotion are available for African American students?

When it comes to alternatives to social promotion for African American students, there are a variety of options. Schools can provide additional tutoring or summer school programs that focus on helping students catch up on material they may have missed during the regular school year.

Schools can also look into alternative assessment methods such as portfolios and projects that demonstrate mastery in subject areas instead of relying solely on traditional tests.

Finally, research has shown the importance of providing culturally relevant curriculum to all students, especially those from underrepresented backgrounds - this could be an effective way to help close any achievement gaps while demonstrating respect for each student's unique cultural background.

Conclusion

We've seen the effects of social promotion on African American students and communities, and it's clear that something needs to change.

We need to work together as parents, schools, policy makers, and community members to create better educational outcomes for our young people.

By investing in alternative approaches to education that recognize the unique needs of our African American students, we can help ensure they have the resources they need to reach their full potential.

Our efforts will pay off – not just for our young people but for all of us who share a common future.

Together, let's make sure every student has an opportunity to succeed!

Black on Black Racism

We, as a society, are facing an issue that has been present since our country's inception: racism. Racism is defined by oppression and discrimination based on the social construct of race.

One form of racism that has become increasingly prominent in recent years is black on black racism. This type of racism occurs when members of the same racial group discriminate against each other due to differences in class, education level, or identity. It is an insidious and divisive force that can have far-reaching effects within the Black community.

In this article, we will explore the history, prevalence, impact, and strategies for overcoming black on black racism. We will also discuss ways in which individuals can take action against systemic racism and institutional oppression to create positive change in our society.

History of Black on Black Racism

The history of prejudice and discrimination against members of the same race has been a long, painful one that continues to this day. Black on black racism is no exception; it can be seen throughout our country's history, from slavery up until today.

The first instance of black on black racism occurred during the slave trade when African Americans were divided into various castes based on their skin color or origin. This division created an atmosphere of competition and hatred between those with lighter skin tones and those with darker skin tones. In some cases, slave owners used this animosity to prevent slaves from forming unions or rebelling against their masters.

In the years following emancipation, African Americans still faced racial discrimination even within their own communities. In many parts of the United States, blacks were denied access to businesses owned by whites and discriminated against in hiring practices for jobs in both public and private sectors. Additionally, there were discriminatory policies such as Jim Crow laws which further marginalized African Americans within their own communities by preventing them from participating in certain activities or attending certain places.

These examples demonstrate how deeply ingrained prejudice can be in a society - regardless if it is among different races or within the same race. Unfortunately, these historical events have had lasting effects that are felt well into today's world where we see continued instances of black on black racism occurring across different contexts including education, housing, employment opportunities and more.

Rather than being solely a consequence of external factors such as white supremacy or institutionalized racism, a closer look reveals that internalized attitudes towards other members of one's own racial group also play a role in perpetuating this type of oppression. Moving forward, we must strive to recognize these internal biases so that we may work together to bring about lasting change for all people impacted by racism and injustice regardless of race or ethnicity.

Prevalence of Black on Black Racism

Despite the belief that all communities of color are united in their struggle against racism, many people of color have experienced and witnessed firsthand the prevalence of prejudice within their own communities.

For example, a recent survey found that nearly half of African American respondents had experienced discrimination from someone within their own race. This is in line with other studies which have shown that black Americans may be more likely to experience racism from other members of their community than any other racial group.

It's not just limited to the United States either; similar phenomena can also be seen across countries such as Brazil, where black people are discriminated against by members of their own race due to light skin privilege.

The impact of this kind of prejudice can extend well beyond a single incident or even a lifetime; it has been argued that it can contribute to larger social disparities between different shades within the same racial group.

Take for example educational attainment: Black students who attend predominately white schools often face higher levels of exclusion than those attending predominantly black schools, leading to lower graduation rates overall and creating long-term educational inequality. The same could be said for access to employment opportunities, housing, healthcare and other resources - all these issues can stem from a community-wide attitude towards darker skinned individuals among some parts of the population.

This kind of systemic racism has far-reaching consequences on both an individual level and on society as a whole - making it imperative for us to understand its scope and implications in order to effectively address it moving forward.

Without understanding how deeply rooted this issue is in our culture, we cannot hope to create meaningful change in terms of greater acceptance and inclusion for people regardless or race or skin tone. As such, exploring the impact black on black racism has on individuals and society should be our next step forward.

Impact of Black on Black Racism

You may not be aware, but prejudice within one's own racial group can have a huge impact on individuals and society as a whole. This kind of racism, often referred to as 'black on black racism', is an issue that often goes unaddressed due to its complexity and the difficulty in finding a solution.

The impacts of this type of racism are wide-ranging:

- It creates feelings of mistrust among members of the same race;

- It reinforces stereotypes about certain ethnic groups;

- It increases tension between different communities within the African-American community.

These issues lead to further division within the population and can ultimately result in decreased economic opportunities, lower educational attainment levels, and higher rates for poverty among African Americans.

By recognizing these issues, we can better understand how to work towards solutions that benefit everyone in our society, regardless of their skin color or cultural background. In doing so, we move closer to achieving true racial equity and social justice for all people - an outcome that would benefit us all.

Racial and Social Division within the Black Community

Even within its own community, racial and social divisions continue to plague African-Americans, perpetuating inequality and injustice. This is largely due to the fact that African-Americans aren't a homogenous group; rather, they come from different socioeconomic backgrounds and have diverse experiences with race.

In addition, African Americans have vastly different levels of access to opportunities such as education or employment. As a result of these disparities and unequal access to resources, some members of the black community hold positions of privilege while others struggle for basic necessities.

The effects are compounded by the use of discriminatory language and attitudes towards those who may be lower on the socio-economic ladder than those in more privileged positions. Such actions can create an environment where certain members of the African American community feel excluded or unwelcome in their own communities due to their perceived class status or lack of financial security.

Furthermore, this hinders efforts at creating an inclusive society that values all people equally regardless of race or class background. In light of this, it's vital for African Americans to recognize how differences between individuals within the same ethnic group can lead to systemic inequality if not addressed properly.

Moreover, it's important for members of all races to strive towards understanding one another's perspectives so that everyone may benefit from mutual respect and unity moving forward into a brighter future—one free from racism and division among its citizens regardless of their background or identity.

To do this successfully requires breaking down existing barriers through dialogue and understanding how these social divisions impact us all emotionally as well as economically. Discriminatory language and attitudes must be challenged if we want true justice for all citizens in our society today.

Discriminatory Language and Attitudes

Discriminatory language and attitudes can create a climate of hostility that is so oppressive it feels like a mountain of bricks crushing down on you. This type of discrimination is unfortunately still very prevalent in the Black community today.

Whether its derogatory terms used to describe skin color or negative stereotypes about certain parts of the African Diaspora, discriminatory language and attitudes have an undeniable impact on how members of the Black community interact with each other and view themselves. On top of that, these words often carry connotations rooted in centuries old systems of oppression that further exacerbate tensions between different groups within the African Diaspora.

The use of derogatory terms has become normalized by some members of the Black community, which makes it all the more difficult to address this issue head-on without being accused as someone who doesn't understand their culture or heritage. While there are many ways to combat this type of discrimination among Blacks, one important step is recognizing its existence and understanding why it exists in order to start a dialogue about its implications on our collective identity as well as individual identities within our communities.

Intersectionality plays an important role in dismantling discriminatory language and attitudes among blacks since we must first look at how power dynamics intersect within our communities before making any progress towards true unity. Understanding the underlying causes behind these issues opens up space for meaningful conversations that will ultimately lead us towards a more inclusive future free from oppressive speech and behavior patterns.

Transitioning into cultural appropriation, we must remember that respect for all cultures begins with understanding our own deeply entrenched histories and recognizing how they play out in modern day interactions between different people across social classes, genders, sexualities, religions, races, etc.

Cultural Appropriation

We've observed how discriminatory language and attitudes can be damaging to the black community, but there's another form of racism that we must consider: cultural appropriation.

Cultural appropriation is when members of a dominant culture take elements from a minority culture without understanding or respecting their significance.

For example, in the 1920s, white women wearing African-style headwraps became popularized as "flapper" fashion while black women were expected to keep their hair natural or wear conservative styles like buns or braids. This remains true today; certain hairstyles are associated with privileged people while those same styles are seen as inappropriate for less privileged communities.

Another example of cultural appropriation is when non-black people use slang terms developed by African Americans such as "on fleek" or "lit" without knowing their origins or giving credit to the creators. This undermines the experiences and expressions of black people who faced oppression due to racism, yet still created unique forms of communication and artistry to express themselves and find joy in spite of it all.

Furthermore, it commodifies elements from these cultures that often carry deep spiritual meaning without context or respect for its roots – ultimately leading to further erasure and exploitation of minority groups.

In short, cultural appropriation perpetuates stereotypes surrounding minorities while simultaneously denying them credit for their creativity and contributions to society – reinforcing oppressive systems which make it difficult for marginalized communities like African Americans to gain recognition for their work.

Moving forward we must strive towards recognizing how our words, actions, and consumption choices can perpetuate racist ideologies even if they don't necessarily appear overtly hostile on the surface level. We should instead aim towards educating ourselves on minority cultures so that we may appreciate them authentically rather than appropriating them out of ignorance or selfishness.

Let us now turn our attention towards exploring how this lack of representation manifests in media and entertainment outlets...

Lack of Representation in Media and Entertainment

You may not be aware of the lack of representation for minority groups in media and entertainment, yet it's a pervasive issue that contributes to racism.

In many cases, people of color are marginalized or not represented at all. This includes actors, directors, writers, etc., which results in fewer opportunities for minorities to tell their stories and share their perspectives.

Even when African Americans are represented in media and entertainment, they often lack depth and nuance. They can be reduced to stereotypes or token characters who only appear on-screen for brief moments. Their roles can be limited to certain genres such as comedies or action films. They may have little input into the story's narrative or creative direction. The content produced can reinforce negative images of black people instead of celebrating positive aspects of culture and identity.

This lack of representation has long-term implications that contribute to racism within our society by denying visibility to minorities who don't conform with mainstream ideals and standards set by white creators. It also perpetuates damaging beliefs about black people that remain unchecked since there is no counterbalance from people with lived experience or knowledge of the subject matter at hand.

From this arises systemic racism and institutional oppression—topics worthy of deeper exploration, which will be discussed further in the subsequent section.

Systemic Racism and Institutional Oppression

Uncovering the truth behind theories of systemic racism and institutional oppression can reveal how prevalent these issues are in modern society. Systemic racism is defined as a series of structures, policies, ideologies, practices, and actions that result in inequitable outcomes or opportunities for certain races and ethnicities. Institutional oppression refers to discrimination created by laws, regulations, or other forms of government-sanctioned policies that create an unequal society. These policies are often set up with the intention to protect certain groups but end up creating further disparities between them.

Systemic racism has been used as a tool to maintain those who have power over others for centuries. It takes many forms such as denying people access to education or job opportunities because of their race. This type of discrimination has caused people from minority backgrounds to be unable to access resources they need for upward mobility like quality housing or financial aid. Similarly, institutional oppression occurs when governments use oppressive tactics against minority groups such as immigration laws that target particular nationalities or restrictions on voting rights based on ethnicity.

These systems ultimately work together to keep the status quo in place which perpetuates inequality throughout all aspects of life including economic stability and educational opportunity. As we learn more about these mechanisms, we can begin addressing them through advocacy efforts and policy changes so they no longer hold individuals back from reaching their full potentials regardless of race or ethnicity.

To move forward with overcoming black on black racism, it requires understanding these complicated dynamics and finding ways to create more equitable systems that provide all people equal opportunity regardless of background.

Strategies for Overcoming Black on Black Racism

You can take steps to address black on black racism and create a more equitable society by understanding the complex dynamics at work and advocating for policy changes that promote equality.

Firstly, it's important to recognize that there are numerous factors which contribute to black on black racism, including:

- Historical legacies of oppression;
- A lack of representation in decision-making bodies; and
- Inequitable access to resources within communities of color.

In order to move forward with solutions, it's essential to acknowledge these underlying causes without placing blame on individuals or groups.

Additionally, education programs must be implemented in order to challenge existing stereotypes and promote respect for cultural differences among members of the same community.

Finally, meaningful dialogue between people from different racial backgrounds should be encouraged in order to bridge divides and create a shared sense of responsibility for addressing systemic issues such as racism.

To accomplish this task, we must commit ourselves to engaging in honest conversations about race and working together towards shared goals of justice and equity.

Transitioning into actionable strategies that can be taken against racism will require an even greater level of collaboration between individuals and organizations alike.

Ways to Take Action in the Fight Against Racism

Having outlined strategies for overcoming black on black racism, it is now important to consider ways to take action in the fight against racism. To achieve this, a structural approach should be taken that takes into account the systemic and institutional barriers that are prevalent in many societies. We must first recognize our individual role in dismantling these structures, and then work together with communities of color to create meaningful change.

Action	Impact
Challenge Injustices	Increased Awareness & Understanding of Racism
Educate Others	Empowerment & Solidarity Amongst Communities of Color
Advocate for Change	Creation of Structural Reforms at the Local Level
Promote Diversity	Improve Inclusivity Across Different Communities

Taking action can be done through various methods that rely on challenging injustices, educating others, advocating for change at the local level, and promoting diversity in all aspects of life. Challenging injustices means recognizing when prejudices manifest themselves in everyday situations and calling out those who perpetuate them. Educating others involves using resources such as books, films or podcasts to build a better understanding of systemic racism within society. Advocating for change is an effective way to drive substantial reform by engaging with local decision makers and ensuring their commitment to tackling racial injustice. Finally, promoting diversity across different communities can help break down stereotypes about race by celebrating differences through literature, art or music.

It is clear that the fight against racism requires collective effort from individuals and organizations alike who strive towards creating a more equitable world where everyone has access to equal opportunities regardless of their background or race. This can only be achieved if we actively challenge existing structures while also working together with marginalized communities so they have the necessary tools needed to combat prejudice head-on.

Frequently Asked Questions

Are there any common misconceptions about Black on Black racism?

We've all heard the phrase 'birds of a feather flock together', and when it comes to racism, this idiom is often used to perpetuate a common misconception.

This idea that people of color cannot be racist towards one another ignores the reality that racism exists in every group, regardless of race.

While there are certainly some unique dynamics between different races when it comes to prejudice and discrimination, black on black racism exists just as much as racism between other racial groups.

Studies have found that black people hold implicit biases against their own racial group just like any other race does.

We must recognize these biases in our own communities if we hope to create an equitable society for all.

How does Black on Black racism differ from racism experienced from other racial groups?

We often hear the term 'black on black racism' used to refer to incidents of discrimination or prejudice between members of the same racial group. However, it's important to recognize that this type of racism differs from that experienced from other racial groups in several ways.

Black on black racism can be more subtle and harder to detect than bias coming from outside sources, as its perpetrators may not necessarily have malicious intent but rather a lack of understanding about societal privilege and power dynamics. Additionally, its effects can be more long-lasting due to the unique sense of exclusion felt by being discriminated against by one's own group.

As such, greater attention needs to be paid to recognizing and addressing this form of racism in order to ensure equality for everyone.

What are the long-term effects of Black on Black racism?

We all know the damaging effects of racism, but what about black on black racism? It's a form of prejudice and discrimination that has long-term implications for everyone involved.

To put it simply, when members of a minority group turn against one another, they are creating a ripple effect that can be felt by all. From feelings of exclusion and betrayal to an overall sense of mistrust among their peers, these issues can undermine the progress made by the African American community as a whole.

The consequences are far-reaching and often more subtle than those experienced from other racial groups, making it even harder to combat. All in all, black on black racism is an insidious problem with serious repercussions that shouldn't be overlooked.

What are the most effective strategies for addressing Black on Black racism?

We believe the most effective strategies for addressing racism are those that focus on education, empathy, and collaboration.

These strategies involve teaching people of all backgrounds about the history of racism and discrimination to gain a better understanding of its effects.

Additionally, creating open dialogue between different racial groups can help build bridges and foster empathy.

Finally, working together to create policies and initiatives that promote inclusivity will be essential for creating lasting change.

We'll need to educate ourselves and each other, talk openly and honestly, and work together to create a more just and equitable society.

How can individuals take action to promote racial equality and end Black on Black racism?

We as individuals can take action to promote racial equality and end black on black racism.

First, we can educate ourselves and others through reading books, articles, and watching documentaries that explore the history of racial injustice in our society.

Additionally, we should support organizations dedicated to combating racism by donating money or volunteering our time.

Furthermore, we should use our platforms such as social media to spread awareness about issues like racial bias and inequality.

Finally, it's important to have meaningful conversations with family members and peers about race so that they may become more aware of their own biases as well as those of others around them.

Conclusion

We've come to the conclusion that the effects of black on black racism are significant.

It has created a deep racial and social division within the black community, as well as oppressive language and attitudes.

The irony is that despite this divide, we still face systemic racism from external sources.

We can no longer be complacent in accepting these disparities; it's time for us to take action.

Our voices matter, and together we must create a united front against all forms of racism.

We have the power to make real change if we stand together with courage, resilience, and an unwavering commitment to justice and equality for all people of color.

Crime in the Black Community

Crime in the black community is a complex issue that has been entrenched in American society for centuries. We must investigate the underlying social, economic, and political influences that have contributed to this phenomenon to understand how we can create meaningful change.

In this article, we'll explore the historical context of crime in the black community as well as its systematic inequalities, media representation, economic insecurity, poor education system, racial profiling by law enforcement, over-policing and mass incarceration.

Additionally, we'll consider potential solutions for creating a safer and more equitable future.

Historical Context

The long-standing tension between law enforcement and minority groups has been a harsh reality for generations. This is especially true in the Black community, where distrust of police officers and other authority figures runs deep.

Part of this distrust stems from the fact that African Americans have faced systemic racism since their arrival to America, including enslavement, segregation, and discrimination. These injustices have caused negative perceptions of law enforcement among many African Americans who had to endure racialized policing practices throughout history.

Unfortunately, these issues still persist today despite recent efforts to improve police-community relations. Overpolicing in Black neighborhoods continues to be a problem that disproportionately affects the African American community. Incidents like the death of George Floyd have highlighted how people of color are more likely than white people to experience excessive force from police officers and suffer dire consequences as a result.

These events demonstrate why many African Americans lack faith in the justice system due to systematic inequalities that remain entrenched in our society today. To address this issue – and the wider issue of crime in the Black community – it's necessary for us to take an honest look at how historical injustice has shaped current conditions, and take steps towards meaningful change moving forward.

Systematic Inequalities

You're facing a truly staggering level of unfairness when it comes to systematic inequalities. From disparities in educational opportunities, employment access, and police interactions, the black community is disproportionately affected by unequal systems within our society.

Research shows that African Americans are more likely than any other racial group to be arrested and incarcerated for criminal activity; however, this is due less to criminality and more to systemic racism combined with economic marginalization. People of color living in poverty are often ensnared in a cycle of criminalization and incarceration that affects generations of families. This has created an environment where people from the black community have fewer chances for upward mobility and long-term success due to systemic injustice.

The effects of these inequalities are not limited solely to the justice system either; they extend into every area of life from health care access to job opportunities. Black people suffer from higher unemployment levels than white counterparts with similar qualifications, as well as lower wages overall despite having equal training or schooling backgrounds. Additionally, studies show that minorities struggle with obtaining quality medical care since many physicians have unconscious racial biases which lead them to provide poorer treatment options for patients who do not fit their stereotypical expectations.

These systematic injustices create a pervasive inequality among minority populations that limits their ability to achieve successful lives regardless of their ambition or intelligence level. It's clear from the data presented here that racism continues to exist in multiple forms throughout our society and needs decisive action if we hope to make progress towards addressing it on both institutional and individual levels.

Media representation is just one element of creating meaningful change but an important one nonetheless...

Media Representation

Media representation can be a powerful tool for challenging systemic racism and creating meaningful change, helping to provide diverse, accurate portrayals of people of color that go beyond stereotypes. This can help to improve public understanding of the plight of black communities in America, while also inspiring action towards greater justice and equity.

The media has an important role in shaping how we perceive ourselves and others, so it's vital that depictions accurately reflect the breadth and complexity of the lived experiences of African Americans. Unfortunately, this is often not the case; many popular films, television shows, books, or other forms of entertainment display one-dimensional characters who are reduced to simplistic archetypes.

These negative images perpetuate damaging stereotypes which create further stigma about black people even within black communities themselves. By perpetuating these stereotypes through media outlets such as news programs or fictionalized accounts, audiences are presented with an oversimplified version of reality that does not accurately represent the actual life experiences of those affected by racism and prejudice. As a result, viewers may have difficulty recognizing their own bias when it comes to issues around race. This lack of awareness can prevent people from understanding how their actions may contribute to racial injustice on both systemic and individual levels.

Additionally, when stories focus on crime within black communities without providing any context or solutions, they may end up reinforcing existing prejudices rather than helping to dispel them. It's essential that more balanced narratives be created with nuanced portrayals showing how structural factors drive criminal behavior in marginalized populations while also exploring possible avenues towards positive change.

Without such nuanced representations, it can be difficult for outsiders to recognize their complicity in perpetuating inequality - something essential if progress towards greater justice is ever going to be achieved.

Economic Insecurity

Economic insecurity in marginalized populations can be a noose around their necks, strangling the chances of achieving success and stability. In the black community, this economic insecurity is evident in:

- The lack of equal access to job opportunities
- Lower wages than whites on average
- Higher rates of poverty
- Fewer assets leading to less generational wealth

The effects of these disparities are wide-reaching and long-lasting. They create an uneven playing field that further entrenches inequality along racial lines while ensuring the cycle continues for future generations as well. To break this cycle, meaningful progress must be made to improve education and job training. This will enable individuals to have better access to gainful employment, allowing them to build financial security for themselves and their families. This is especially true within the black community, where poor educational systems can often lead to even further economic hardship down the line.

Poor Education System

Poor educational systems can often have devastating effects on an individual's economic future, trapping them in a cycle of poverty and insecurity.

In the black community, this has been exacerbated by inadequate funding for schools in lower-income neighborhoods and a lack of qualified teachers. This has resulted in students not receiving the education they need to succeed in college or get well-paying jobs.

Furthermore, it is difficult for students to access resources and extracurricular activities that could help them develop skills that would be marketable after graduation. Without these educational opportunities, many young people are unable to gain meaningful employment, leaving them with few options other than low wage jobs or illegal activities.

The lack of quality job opportunities further entraps individuals in cycles of poverty and crime as they struggle to support themselves and their families. In addition, poor education systems create an environment where graduates lack the qualifications employers often look for when hiring new employees.

All of these factors combined contribute to higher unemployment rates among African Americans and poorer outcomes overall compared to white Americans. This disparity only serves to widen the economic gap between racially segregated communities, further creating an unequal playing field with far-reaching consequences for generations to come.

As such, change must be made at all levels - from improved school funding and teacher training programs to increased job opportunities - if real progress is going to be achieved towards eliminating crime within the black community caused by economic inequality due to the lack of quality job opportunities.

Lack of Quality Job Opportunities

The lack of quality job opportunities can be a major barrier for individuals to achieving economic stability, leaving them with few options other than low-paying jobs or desperate measures.

This is particularly true in the black community, where there are often fewer resources available to help people secure gainful employment. African Americans are more likely to be unemployed than any other racial group, and those who do have jobs often earn lower wages than white employees.

This wage gap further entrenches poverty within the black community as it becomes increasingly difficult for individuals to find better paying work that can provide stability and financial security. Without access to good job opportunities, many people turn to crime as a means of providing for themselves and their families.

As such, the unequal distribution of employment opportunities contributes significantly to high levels of crime in the black community. Without adequate support and resources from employers and society at large, this cycle will remain difficult to break – not only perpetuating existing poverty but creating new challenges for future generations.

Racial profiling by law enforcement then compounds these issues even further.

Racial Profiling by Law Enforcement

Racial profiling by law enforcement is a huge issue that continues to plague our society, often resulting in unfair treatment towards those of minority backgrounds. Unfortunately, this discrimination has been all too common for centuries, and it's high time we put an end to it.

The effects of racial profiling are far-reaching. It can lead to increased rates of imprisonment without due process, lack of trust between the police and the community they serve, and an overall negative perception of law enforcement. It also disproportionately affects Black people more than any other group.

In addition to these long-lasting psychological impacts, there's also a financial effect on members of the black community who have been targeted by racial profiling. This includes paying costly fines or legal fees for minor offenses they may not have committed if not for their race being taken into account by law enforcement officers.

Without proper oversight and accountability from government agencies, racial profiling will remain a major problem with serious implications for many individuals.

Over-Policing

You're constantly being watched and judged, simply because of the color of your skin. Over-policing has become an oppressive reality for too many people, and it's time to put a stop to it. Over-policing is defined as the disproportionate presence of police in certain communities or in relation to particular individuals compared to others. This means that people of color are more likely to be stopped by law enforcement than their white counterparts, even when they have not done anything wrong.

Examples	Impact on Community	Ways To Combat
Targeting low-income neighborhoods for drug sweeps and traffic stops	Fosters distrust between community members & law enforcement; leads to feelings of insecurity & fear at home; damaging relationships with local government	- Establish clear rules regarding acceptable levels of policing. - Invest in non-police methods such as youth outreach programs & social services. - Create better police training protocols around community engagement & de-escalation techniques.
Allowing false accusations against black citizens without investigation	Creates a culture where racism goes unchecked; creates an environment where racist profiling is seen as normal behavior by law enforcement officers, leading to civil rights violations and wrongful imprisonment	- Improve officer recruitment processes to ensure only qualified candidates represent the department. - Increase efforts towards diversifying police departments to reflect the populations they serve. - Establish civilian oversight boards to investigate complaints about police misconduct, including racial profiling.

Over-policing affects entire communities, not just individuals who may have been targeted directly. It erodes public trust in institutions meant to protect them, leaving everyone feeling unsafe and uncertain about their future. Furthermore, over-policing does nothing but fuel further injustice since it disproportionately targets marginalized groups who already face systemic oppression due their race or economic status. It's time we recognize this problem for what it is - institutional racism - and take action against it before its effects can do any more damage. Without meaningful reform, our criminal justice system will continue perpetuate systemic discrimination rather than provide safety and security for all citizens regardless of race or class status. As we look ahead towards solutions like investing in non-police resources such as social services and improving officer recruitment processes, let us remember one thing: change starts with us.

Mass Incarceration

You're facing an alarming reality: mass incarceration, which disproportionately affects people of color. This issue is often overlooked as it's not a glamorous subject matter. However, it's an important one to consider when discussing crime in the Black community.

Mass incarceration is defined as the large-scale imprisonment of individuals within a society over long periods of time. It has become increasingly prevalent in recent years due to tough-on-crime policies, such as mandatory minimum sentences and three strikes laws.

Here are two key points that drive this phenomenon:

- Racial Inequality: People of color are more likely than whites to be arrested for drug offenses even though both groups use drugs at similar rates. Furthermore, African Americans receive longer sentences for similar crimes than other races do; this contributes heavily to their increased chance of being incarcerated.

- Poverty: Individuals from low-income communities lack financial resources and support systems that can provide them with opportunities that may otherwise reduce their chances of committing a crime or going back to prison if they have been convicted.

The current criminal justice system does little to address these issues because they remain primarily rooted in systemic racism and poverty—both deeply entrenched problems in America today. As a result, many people get trapped in the cycle of recidivism without any hope for reform or progress towards rehabilitation or reintegration into society after release from prison.

Moving forward, potential solutions must be explored in order to combat mass incarceration and its effects on the Black community.

Potential Solutions

You can help reduce the effects of mass incarceration by exploring potential solutions that focus on addressing systemic racism and poverty.

One potential solution is to invest in education and job training, especially for those who have already been incarcerated. Not only does this give individuals a chance to gain employment or career skills, but it also reduces the likelihood of recidivism.

Another potential solution is to reform sentencing laws, such as reducing mandatory minimum sentences and eliminating racial disparities in sentencing guidelines. This has proven effective in many states already and could be implemented nationwide with the right support from legislators.

A third approach would be to remove economic barriers for formerly incarcerated individuals; this could include providing access to housing, healthcare services, and other resources that are often denied due to prior convictions.

Finally, it's important for communities to understand how mass incarceration affects their neighborhoods so they can work together towards developing alternative methods of justice that prioritize rehabilitation over punishment. By collaborating with local organizations and advocating for policy changes at all levels of government, we can make a meaningful difference in reducing crime rates within our communities.

Frequently Asked Questions

How can the black community be supported in overcoming systemic inequalities?

We believe that the black community can be supported in overcoming systemic inequalities by focusing on education, economic development, and criminal justice reform.

Education initiatives should focus on providing access to quality educational opportunities for all students regardless of race or background.

Economic development efforts should include expanding job and business creation in the black community, as well as providing training and mentorship programs.

Lastly, criminal justice reforms should ensure that those accused of crimes are treated fairly and equitably based on their circumstances.

These measures will help create a more equitable society for everyone.

What strategies can be used to challenge media representation of the black community?

We believe that challenging media representation of the black community starts with taking a critical look at how our stories are being told.

We need to question why certain narratives are presented, who's telling them, and what values they reflect.

We must also be mindful of the ways in which these stories can perpetuate harmful stereotypes or create false impressions about our community.

By actively engaging in conversations around media representation, we can begin to shape and redefine how the black community is depicted.

How can economic insecurity in the black community be addressed?

We, as a society, have to come together to address the economic insecurity in the black community. This is essential for creating a level playing field and ensuring that everyone has access to opportunity.

To put it simply, we need to break down the barriers that have been preventing people of color from achieving financial stability and security. This can be done through initiatives such as job training programs, increasing access to capital for small business owners, providing incentives for companies that hire minority workers, increasing educational resources in underserved communities, and investing in public transportation infrastructure.

All of these steps are necessary for empowering African Americans and other minorities with the tools they need to secure a better future.

How can law enforcement be held accountable for racial profiling?

We believe that law enforcement should be held accountable for racial profiling. To do this, we must work to establish a system of checks and balances that hold members of the police force responsible for their actions.

This includes developing better oversight measures by increasing transparency and accountability within police departments, as well as creating independent review boards to investigate complaints of racial profiling.

Furthermore, we must actively combat racism in policing by implementing anti-racism training for officers and encouraging diversity in hiring practices. Such measures will help ensure that law enforcement is held accountable for any instances of racial profiling.

What are the long-term effects of mass incarceration on the black community?

We've seen a drastic rise in the number of people incarcerated, particularly in the Black community. According to recent statistics, over 30% of people in prisons are made up of African Americans despite them making up only 13% of the population.

This has had profound implications for Black communities across America, from breaking apart families and reducing economic stability to creating a culture where crime is seen as inevitable.

Long-term effects have included an increase in poverty rates and a decrease in educational attainment due to inadequate resources and access to opportunities.

This mass incarceration crisis has further perpetuated systemic racism and continues to be an issue that needs immediate attention if we want to make real change for these communities.

Conclusion

We've seen the effects of racism and systemic inequalities on the Black community. From the historical context to media representation, economic insecurity, and poor education system. Racial profiling by law enforcement and mass incarceration. It's clear that more needs to be done to help our brothers and sisters.

Interesting to note, African Americans are incarcerated 5 times greater than whites yet only make up 13% of the population. This statistic speaks volumes about institutional racism in our society.

We need an overhaul of our justice system as well as more investment in education and resources for those affected. It's time for change.

Classism within the Black Community

We, as a society, have a tendency to stereotype and classify people according to their status in life. Sadly, this has led to the prevalence of classism within the black community.

In fact, studies show that the median wealth for black households is only 8% of white households – an alarming statistic which demonstrates how pervasive and damaging classism can be.

Classism refers to prejudice or discrimination based on one's social or economic status. This type of discrimination has been around for centuries and continues to persist today within many marginalized communities – including the black community.

Through this article, we aim to explore the causes and effects of classism within the black community and discuss ways on how it can be addressed moving forward.

Understanding Classism

You may not be aware of it, but social hierarchies exist even among people who share the same background. Classism is the prejudice and discrimination based on social class. It is a reality that affects many members of the Black community.

It is an insidious form of oppression that can manifest in seemingly small ways such as language and clothing choices, but can create serious divisions within our society. Classism can lead to feelings of exclusion and alienation for those at its lower end – a situation that no member of any community should ever have to experience.

The causes of classism are complex and vary from region to region. However, it often has its roots in longstanding economic disparities between groups within the Black community. Additionally, media portrayals often contribute to a culture where certain levels of wealth or educational attainment are seen as more desirable than others. This creates an environment where certain individuals can feel like they don't fit in because they don't meet those standards.

To address this issue, we must become better informed about how classism works and commit ourselves to creating more equitable systems. This will make sure all members of our community are respected regardless of their economic status.

Causes of Classism

Struggling to understand why some people have more than others? Let's dive into the causes behind this disconnect.

Classism within the black community is a result of colonizers' oppressive systems that were designed to create division and inequality between different groups. These systems, such as slavery and segregation, created an environment where access to resources was limited for certain individuals and families based on their race or socio-economic status.

Furthermore, these oppressive systems created a power imbalance which further perpetuated classism within the black community and widened the gap between those with privilege and those without. As a result, classism has been deeply embedded in the culture of many black communities for generations.

The next step is understanding how this disconnect impacts both individuals and society at large.

The Impact of Classism

Classism has far-reaching implications for both individuals and society as a whole, creating an atmosphere of inequity that can lead to feelings of frustration, resentment, and despair. It has the potential to cause deep divisions between people from different backgrounds, leading to animosity and furthering tensions between classes.

Classism also creates an environment where those in positions of power have greater access to resources and opportunities than those who are less privileged. This unequal distribution of wealth can lead to a cycle of poverty where individuals feel trapped in their current situation and unable to move forward in life. As a result, the effects of classism can be devastating not only for individuals but entire communities who suffer from its consequences.

The black community is no exception when it comes to dealing with classism within its ranks. Despite being part of a larger minority group, members of the black community are still divided among themselves by socio-economic status and other factors. Examples include disparities in educational attainment, health care access, employment prospects, housing quality, and more – all signs that classism is alive and well in many African American communities across the United States.

Consequently, tackling this issue is essential if the black community wants to achieve true equality among its members and make progress towards achieving racial justice on a larger scale.

Examples of Classism in the Black Community

Classist practices in the African American population can be seen in disparities such as educational attainment, healthcare access, employment opportunities, and housing quality. The effects of classism are felt most keenly within the black community. Low-income African Americans often receive fewer educational opportunities due to a lack of resources or structural racism.

Black people living in poverty have limited access to quality healthcare services. Employment prospects for low-income African Americans are often limited by discrimination or institutional barriers. Housing quality for poor African Americans is usually subpar compared to their higher income peers.

These examples demonstrate that classism has real consequences for those affected by it in the black community, making them more vulnerable and likely to experience further inequality than wealthier members of their ethnic group. To truly understand the wealth gap between different classes of African Americans, we must look deeper into its systemic causes and possible solutions.

Understanding the Wealth Gap

The widening financial divide between different social groups can be devastating, leaving those on the lower end of the spectrum feeling voiceless and powerless. The black community, in particular, has been plagued by poverty and inequality for centuries, leading to an even greater disparity in wealth between classes.

Many have suffered from a lack of access to proper education, healthcare, job opportunities, and other resources that could have enabled them to gain financial stability. As a result, the economic gap continues to grow wider; further entrenching classism within our society.

Education is often seen as one of the most powerful tools for overcoming this cycle of poverty and classism. It can provide individuals with knowledge and skills they need to progress up the economic ladder by opening doors to better-paying jobs or higher levels of education. Unfortunately, many members of poor or marginalized communities are unable to take advantage of these opportunities due to a lack of access or resources - perpetuating the cycle of inequality that is so pervasive in our society today.

With this in mind, it's important that we examine how educational attainment affects social mobility for people from all walks of life - particularly those belonging to minority populations like African Americans.

The Role of Education

Education can be a major factor in breaking cycles of inequality, providing individuals with the opportunity to gain financial stability and progress up the economic ladder.

Unfortunately, many black communities aren't able to access high quality educational resources. This leads to them being unable to take advantage of educational opportunities that could help bridge the wealth gap between different classes.

Additionally, there's evidence that racial bias in schools has led some students from poorer backgrounds to feel discouraged or excluded from education altogether.

As such, it's important for society to ensure that everyone has access to equal educational opportunities so that they can break out of poverty and reach their full potential.

To do this, it's essential for us to recognize the role societal structures play in perpetuating discrimination and denying certain individuals access to valuable resources.

The Role of Societal Structures

We've seen how education can be a major factor in perpetuating classism within the black community, but it's not the only one. Societal structures also play an integral role in shaping and reinforcing this issue.

From economic inequality to access to resources, there are countless ways that societal structures can contribute to classism:

- Economic disparities between different classes of people create a feeling of superiority or inferiority depending on which side you're on.

- Access to quality healthcare, housing, and education further widen the gap amongst those with privilege and those without it.

- The criminal justice system has been used as a tool of oppression against lower-income communities since slavery, creating a cycle of poverty that is difficult to escape from.

These are just some examples of how society reinforces classism within the black community - but what about media representation? How does that play into this discussion?

The Role of Media Representation

Media representation has a huge impact on how classism is perceived and reinforced across the African-American population.

Whether it's through stereotypes or lack of representation, the media often fails to accurately portray the diversity within the Black community.

This can lead to an oversimplification of certain facets such as culture and socio-economic status, leading to a further separation between different parts of society.

As a result, classism can become more clearly defined in ways that are damaging and oppressive to those who may not fit into traditional modes of expression.

To combat this growing problem, we must ensure that all forms of media strive for greater accuracy when depicting African Americans in order to create an environment free from oppressive classist views.

Ways to Combat Classism

Fighting classism is an ongoing battle, but we can all do our part to make sure everyone has the same opportunities regardless of their background. Here are a few ways that we can work towards this goal:

- Educating ourselves and others:

- Learn about classism and other forms of oppression in order to better understand how they manifest in our communities.

- Share what you've learned with your friends and family so that they can be more aware of classism when it arises.

- Challenging stereotypes:

- Speak up when people use language or jokes that reinforce negative stereotypes about people from different classes.

- Check yourself for any preconceived notions you may have about people from various classes, and challenge those beliefs when necessary.

- Supporting initiatives:

- Support grassroots initiatives, non-profits, or organizations that are working to combat classism in our communities.

- Volunteer your time or donate money to help these organizations achieve their goals.

These are just a few steps we can take towards combating classism within the black community, but there's still much more work to be done if we want to create real change. By working together and taking action, we can move forward on the path towards a more equitable future for all.

Moving Forward

In order to move towards a more equitable future, we must all work together and take action to combat oppression outside of the black community. To do this, we must come together as a collective and use our voices to bring about meaningful change.

We need to focus on creating opportunities for everyone in the black community regardless of their social class, race or gender. This means creating access to education that isn't just available to those who have a lot of money or come from privileged backgrounds. We also need to create policies that promote fairness and equality within the workplace and across society in general.

To make sure these changes are being implemented, it's important that we hold individuals and organizations accountable for their actions. We can do this by raising awareness through conversations with friends, family members and peers; attending protests against injustice; engaging in dialogue with elected officials; signing petitions; joining organizations dedicated to promoting justice; voting during elections; donating money or time where possible; advocating for policy change at the local level; writing letters demanding accountability from corporations and government agencies, etc.

By taking these steps forward together, we can create a more unified society where everyone has an equal opportunity for success.

Frequently Asked Questions

How does classism manifest in different cultures?

We can all relate to the feeling of being judged based on our class or economic status. Whether it's at school, work, or in social settings, the experience of being judged and treated differently due to one's wealth is something that no one enjoys.

Classism manifests differently in different cultures, with some relying more heavily on money and status than others. For example, if we look at Asian cultures, you'll often find a stronger emphasis placed upon education as a way to acquire social standing.

In contrast, other societies may place a greater reliance upon inheritance and family ties as an indicator of success. Regardless of these differences though, classism is an issue that exists globally and should be addressed by people from all walks of life.

How does classism intersect with race and other identities?

We all recognize the existence of classism, but when we consider how it intersects with race and other identities, a more complex picture emerges. Classism is not just about having or lacking money - it's also about access to education, employment opportunities, resources, and power.

When these issues intersect with identity factors such as gender, sexuality, ethnicity/race, religion, or disability status, they can create additional layers of marginalization that are difficult to overcome. Sadly, this means that some people may experience multiple forms of discrimination simultaneously and be left feeling powerless and voiceless in society.

What are the most effective ways to challenge classism?

We all know that classism can create a destructive divide within any community, but how can we effectively challenge it?

One of the best ways to confront classism is through education and awareness. We must start by educating ourselves and our peers about why classism exists and its effects on individuals and society as a whole. Asking questions, listening to stories, reading books, attending lectures or seminars—these are all great ways to become more informed about the issue.

Additionally, creating or joining initiatives that support economic mobility for those in disadvantaged positions is another powerful way to challenge classism. By taking action together with intentionality, we can work towards dismantling this damaging form of discrimination.

What are the long-term implications of classism in the black community?

We all know that classism can have long-term implications for any community, and the black community is no exception. Classism leads to a widening gap between different classes of people within the same race, with those of lower socioeconomic status often suffering from fewer opportunities and resources than those of higher status.

This can lead to a lack of access to quality education, healthcare, and other essential services that are crucial for a healthy society. In addition, it can create an atmosphere of inequality and distrust among members of the community which contributes to further marginalization.

To combat these effects and ensure that everyone has equal opportunities regardless of their economic background, it is important to recognize classism in all its forms and actively work against it.

How do we ensure classism is addressed in the next generation?

We want to ensure that classism is addressed in the next generation. To do this, we need to start by understanding how and why it exists, so that we can come up with solutions to combat it.

Education and awareness are key components of this process, as well as providing equal access to resources and opportunities for all members of the community.

We must also create an environment in which classism is not tolerated, encouraging a more inclusive culture of respect for everyone regardless of their background or economic status.

By doing these things, we can work together to create a better future for all.

Conclusion

We've been discussing how classism within the black community is a major issue that needs to be tackled. It's important to remember that this isn't just an individual problem, but a widespread systemic one.

The wealth gap between white and black families has more than tripled in the last 30 years, with white families now having an average of 10 times more wealth than their black counterparts. This disparity is unacceptable and we need to take action if we want to see any real progress.

We must work together as a community to dismantle these oppressive systems and build something better for ourselves and future generations.

Black on White Crimes

We are all too familiar with the term 'black on white crime'. It has been a source of contention and debate for many years, but unfortunately, it is still prevalent in society today.

This article will provide an in-depth overview of the historical context, prevalence and systemic racism associated with black on white crimes. We'll also cover law enforcement's role, media coverage, impact of poverty and mental health services as well as potential solutions to address discrimination and foster justice.

Historical Context of Black on White Crime

It's important to understand the historical context of these issues, so let's take a look back! The history of Black on White crime dates back to the early days of slavery in America.

During this time, African Americans were subject to a variety of abuses and injustices at the hands of white people, including physical violence.

After emancipation, there was still significant animosity between Blacks and Whites, leading to frequent clashes between the two groups. This often resulted in violent crimes being committed by Blacks against Whites, as well as other forms of discrimination.

As time went on, these racial tensions only grew stronger and more entrenched in society.

Despite some progress over the last few decades in terms of civil rights and racial equality, Black on White crime remains an issue today.

Studies have shown that African Americans are far more likely than any other race to be victims or perpetrators when it comes to violent crime. Additionally, numerous reports suggest that law enforcement is not always fair or equitable when dealing with suspects from different backgrounds. This has contributed significantly to mistrust between communities and police departments throughout the country.

It's clear that racism has been a major factor for centuries when it comes to Black on White crime; however, it is also important to consider its prevalence today.

In order to do this effectively, we must look at statistics related to both incidents involving African Americans and those involving all races combined, as well as other factors such as socio-economic status or geographical location which may play a role in determining why certain areas experience higher rates than others.

With this knowledge, we can begin working towards finding effective solutions for addressing this ongoing challenge moving forward.

Prevalence of Black on White Crime

You may have heard about incidences of violence between people of different backgrounds, but how often do they actually occur? In the United States, black-on-white crime is unfortunately common. According to a 2016 Bureau of Justice Statistics report, white victims were most likely to experience violent crime at the hands of a black perpetrator in 2014.

44 percent of offenders were identified as black or African American even though they make up only 13 percent of the population. Furthermore, out of all aggravated assaults reported in 2018, 18 percent involved a white victim and a black offender. The rate for other races was much lower; Asian/Pacific Islanders were less likely than whites to be victimized by blacks and Hispanics were 7 times less likely than whites to be victimized by blacks.

When it comes to homicide rates, there are fewer statistics available due to underreporting and the small number of homicides that occur each year. However, according to FBI data from 2017 there were 631 murders where white victims were attacked by black perpetrators in comparison with 397 murders where black victims were attacked by white perpetrators. This data points to the prevalence and severity of violent crimes against whites perpetrated by blacks in America today.

It's clear that there are large disparities between racial groups when it comes to violent crime rates but why is this issue so pervasive? Moving on from this discussion we will explore law enforcement's role in confronting these issues without stepping further into conclusions about their causes.

Law Enforcement and Black on White Crime

You're likely aware of the disparities between races when it comes to violent offenses, but how does law enforcement come into play? Numerous studies have shown that racial biases in policing are still a problem today.

In 2018, an independent investigation into the Baltimore Police Department revealed that Black people were stopped three times as often as white people and nearly twice as often for searches. The report noted that Black people made up 63 percent of all those arrested and 88 percent of those subjected to use-of-force incidents. Similar patterns have been seen across numerous cities in the United States and around the world.

In many cases, law enforcement officers are not held accountable for their actions or behavior due to a lack of transparency within police departments. This can lead to further mistrust among communities of color towards police officers, which can make it difficult for effective policing strategies to be implemented. Additionally, some law enforcement agencies may be more prone to making biased decisions due to inadequate training on recognizing implicit bias or unconscious racism by officers on patrol.

The issue is compounded by a lack of data surrounding black on white crime rates and law enforcement's response thereto; without concrete information about these figures, it's hard for lawmakers and activists alike to bring about change in this area. This leads us naturally into our next section - media coverage of black on white crime - whereby we'll explore how news outlets portray these events differently based on race.

Media Coverage of Black on White Crime

Understanding how the media reports on incidents involving different races is key to addressing racial disparities in law enforcement. You'll notice that some news outlets present events differently depending on the race of those involved.

For example, research has shown that black suspects in criminal cases are more likely to be labeled as violent and dangerous than white suspects. This could lead to biased coverage and suggest a double standard for justice between whites and blacks.

Further, evidence suggests that when it comes to reporting on interracial crime, stories involving black-on-white violence are more likely to be covered by news outlets than stories involving white-on-black violence. This discrepancy is especially notable in local media coverage, where most people get their information about crime rates and trends.

It's also worth noting that these reporting biases may be due both to systemic racism within media institutions as well as conscious or unconscious bias among journalists themselves.

When it comes to improving public perceptions of racial injustice, understanding how the media presents stories can be just as important as considering the underlying issues at play in our legal system. As we move forward in tackling systemic racism and black on white crime, it's essential that we recognize the role of media bias in perpetuating negative stereotypes about people of color and other marginalized groups.

By acknowledging this reality, we can begin working towards creating a society where all people have an equal chance at justice regardless of skin color or background.

Systemic Racism and Black on White Crime

It's no secret that racism and bias have been deeply embedded in criminal justice systems for centuries, resulting in unequal outcomes for people of color. This has had a deep impact on black communities when it comes to black-on-white crime, as systemic racism creates a system that disproportionately targets and incarcerates African Americans.

Here are three ways this manifests itself:

- Systemic racism can lead to laws or policies that place heavier punishments on certain crimes if the perpetrator is African American. For example, drug offenses involving crack cocaine are punished more harshly than those involving powder cocaine, even though they're functionally similar drugs.

- Racial profiling by law enforcement officers leads to higher rates of arrest and incarceration for African Americans. It also leads to an increase in incidents of police brutality against them.

- Systemic racism also leads to disparities in resources allocated to predominantly white neighborhoods compared to predominantly black neighborhoods. This creates an unequal playing field when it comes to opportunities for education and employment that can lead some individuals down the path towards criminality.

These inequities are not isolated incidents but rather part of a larger pattern of racial discrimination within the criminal justice system. This needs to be addressed before true progress can be made in reducing violence between blacks and whites.

As we look towards solutions like increased access to education resources for disadvantaged individuals, we must remember that these should form part of a comprehensive plan aimed at dismantling systemic racism so all citizens can participate equally in society.

The Role of Education in Prevention

We've discussed how systemic racism has amplified the issue of black on white crime. Now, we turn to a different angle: education and its role in preventing it. Education can be a powerful tool for addressing the disparities that feed into this type of crime.

Pros	Cons
1. Knowledgeable citizens can better understand their rights and those of others.	1. Education may not always be accessible or affordable.
2. Educated people are more likely to find employment, reducing economic disparities.	2. Some educational systems may be biased against certain races or backgrounds.
3. Schools can provide an avenue for teaching empathy and understanding between races.	3. Not all students learn in the same way, making equal access to education difficult to achieve.

Education is key in tackling racism at its core by providing individuals with knowledge and tools they need to make informed decisions about their lives - as well as those of others - while also developing an appreciation for different cultures and beliefs beyond their own. Moreover, education provides an invaluable platform for critical thinking skills; when these skills are applied properly, it can bridge divides between races that have been long established due to historical injustices and biases from both sides of the conversation. With this in mind, let's consider the impact poverty has on black on white crime.

The Impact of Poverty on Black on White Crime

You can imagine how poverty can drastically alter the landscape of a community, as it restricts access to resources and opportunities that are necessary for success. Poverty has been linked to a wide range of social issues, including black on white crime. This is because people living in poverty often have limited access to economic opportunities and educational resources, which can lead to frustration and anger. As a result, they may be more likely to engage in criminal behavior or become victims of crime.

Furthermore, research suggests that poverty is associated with higher rates of mental health disorders which could further contribute to the likelihood of committing black on white crimes.

The impact of poverty on black on white crimes cannot be understated. It creates an environment where individuals are unable to access the same level of resources as other members in society, leading them into situations where desperation leads them into acts such as robbery or assault. Additionally, communities with high levels of poverty tend to have weaker educational systems and less investment in public services such as police protection. This leaves many vulnerable populations open for exploitation by criminals who are looking for easy targets.

The effects of poverty also extend beyond those who live within it; there is also evidence that suggests living near impoverished areas increases one's risk for being victimized by black on white crime due to increased exposure from those living within these communities.

In order for communities affected by poverty-related violence and crime to find solutions, they must first address the root causes such as lack of education and economic opportunity for their residents. These measures will provide long-term solutions rather than temporary fixes; only then can meaningful progress be made towards reducing incidents of black on white crime in our society.

With this understanding firmly in place, we can now shift focus towards examining the role mental health services play in prevention efforts against black on white crime.

The Role of Mental Health Services

We've seen how poverty can play an important role in black-on-white crime, but there's another factor that should be addressed. Mental health services and the availability of treatment for those with mental illness can also have a significant effect on these types of crimes.

It's essential to consider how access to mental health services could help reduce the number of people who commit acts of violence against others due to their mental state. Mental health services are still widely underutilized by those who need them, especially among minority populations.

People in these groups often struggle to find quality care, or even access it at all. This lack of access can lead to untreated symptoms which may manifest as aggression or other violent behavior. Without proper diagnosis and treatment, individuals may not be able to manage their mental states and instead act out in destructive ways towards others.

Furthermore, many law enforcement officers lack training in recognizing signs and symptoms of mental illness when interacting with suspects, potentially leading to poor decisions or misinterpretations during interactions with those suffering from untreated disorders.

Having more resources dedicated to improving officer training as well as increasing public knowledge about available treatments could go a long way towards reducing black-on-white crime related to undiagnosed or undertreated mental illness.

Moving forward, it'll be critical for us to address both the social factors contributing to this issue and also explore solutions for providing better support systems for those suffering from mental illnesses within our communities.

Addressing Hate Speech and Discrimination

Discrimination and hate speech have become pervasive in our society, and it's crucial that we take action to counter these destructive attitudes, as they can lead to violence and other forms of injustice.

We must:

- Educate communities on the harms of discrimination and hate speech.

- Highlight the effects of verbal abuse and how words can hurt just as much as physical actions.

- Empower people with knowledge about their rights under local, state, federal laws regarding hate speech.

- Encourage individuals to speak out against any form of discrimination or prejudice they witness.

- Provide safe spaces for victims to share their stories without fear of retribution or judgment.

- Create awareness campaigns that emphasize respect for each other regardless of race, gender identity, religion etc.

- Hold organizations accountable for any acts of intolerance or bias within their ranks by implementing policies that protect marginalized groups from such behaviors.

- Monitor recruitment processes to ensure diversity is embraced.

- Invest in training sessions on inclusion so employees understand the importance of being mindful and respectful towards others regardless of differences in beliefs or backgrounds.

By recognizing the severity of discrimination and hate speech, we can begin working towards solutions and justice for those affected by this issue. It is only through collective efforts that we can create a more equitable world free from hatred and oppression.

Working Towards Solutions and Justice

By joining together to combat discrimination and hate speech, we can create a more just society where everyone is respected regardless of their beliefs or backgrounds. To make this a reality, it's important to understand the root causes of racism in order to develop targeted strategies that address them.

This could include passing legislation that criminalizes specific types of hate speech, increasing access to education on different cultures and religions, or providing resources for those affected by racist attacks. It also requires committing ourselves to actively stand up against all forms of racism when we witness it in our everyday lives.

In addition to working towards solutions, justice must be served for victims of black on white crimes. We must hold those responsible accountable for their actions and ensure that they are prosecuted as harshly as possible. This will send a strong message that such behavior will not be tolerated and help deter future acts of violence or discrimination.

Furthermore, organizations should provide support services for victims so they can heal from their experiences and rebuild their lives with dignity. We must work together to build an equitable society where everyone is treated with respect and no one has to live in fear because of the color of their skin or other characteristics they may possess.

We cannot ignore the issues facing our communities any longer but instead take action now if we're going to create lasting positive change in the world around us. The time is now; let's unite and make this vision a reality!

Frequently Asked Questions

What are the differences between Black on Black crime and Black on White crime?

We've all heard of "black on black" crime, but what exactly is it compared to "black on white" crime?

To get an idea, one interesting statistic to note is that African-Americans accounted for 52% of all homicide offenders from 1980 to 2008, while whites only accounted for 45%. This shows that the majority of homicides are committed by people of the same race.

However, when looking at crimes between different races - such as black on white - the statistics can be quite different. In 2017, African-Americans made up approximately 13% of the population but were responsible for nearly half (48%) of all violent interracial crime involving blacks and whites.

This means that while most violent crimes occur between individuals within the same racial group, a significant proportion still involve members from different groups.

What are the economic consequences of Black on White crime?

We believe that black on white crime has the potential to cause significant economic consequences. Research suggests that victims of such crimes may require access to professional counseling, medical care, and/or legal services, which can prove costly.

In addition, businesses located in areas where these crimes occur may suffer losses due to a decrease in customers and/or employees feeling unsafe or uncomfortable being in the area.

Furthermore, government resources are often used to investigate and prosecute those responsible for such crimes, resulting in more taxpayer dollars being allocated towards such initiatives.

Ultimately, the economic implications of black on white crime shouldn't be overlooked or underestimated.

What legal measures are available for victims of Black on White crime?

Victims of crime, including victims of black on white crime, are protected by a variety of legal measures. According to the U.S. Department of Justice, over 90% of violent victimizations are reported annually to the police.

Such reports provide victims with access to services such as free counseling and civil remedies like restitution for losses incurred due to the crime. Victims can also seek criminal justice measures such as arrest, prosecution, and jail time for offenders.

Additionally, victims may receive compensation from state-funded programs or private insurance companies that cover costs associated with their victimization. Victims have the right to be informed throughout each step in the criminal process and can even request protective orders against their assailants if necessary.

How can Black on White crime be prevented in the future?

We can prevent black on white crime in the future by investing in programs that foster understanding and dialogue between different racial and cultural groups. These initiatives should be designed to promote meaningful conversations about race, identity, privilege, and history.

Additionally, we must invest in resources that support victims of hate-based violence, such as providing mental health services and legal representation for those who've been wrongfully targeted.

Finally, education must be improved to teach young people about the dangers of racism so they can become informed citizens and work towards a more equitable society.

What are the psychological effects of being a victim of Black on White crime?

We've investigated the theory of how being a victim of any crime can affect an individual psychologically, and found it to be true.

Being the victim of a crime can cause fear, confusion, anxiety, depression, and post-traumatic stress disorder. These effects can range in severity depending on the violence experienced during the crime or its aftermath.

Victims may also struggle with feelings of guilt or helplessness if they weren't able to prevent their own victimization. Additionally, victims may experience intense physical reactions such as difficulty sleeping and changes in appetite.

It's important to note that all these psychological effects are normal responses following a traumatic event and shouldn't be seen as signs of weakness by those who experience them.

Conclusion

We've seen the devastating effects of black on white crime, and it's clear that systemic racism is a major factor in its prevalence.

We must find ways to address hate speech and discrimination in order to create a more just society.

Symbolically, we can envision a world where everyone is treated equally, no matter what color their skin is.

This vision will take commitment from all of us to realize - but together, we can make it happen.

By investing in mental health services and working towards solutions that tackle poverty, we can ensure equal justice for all and end the cycle of violence caused by black on white crime.

White Exodus aka White Flight

We often hear about the white exodus – an ongoing trend of predominantly white people leaving urban areas for suburban or rural locations. But what causes this phenomenon? What are its effects on minority communities? And how can we stabilize these areas so that everyone has a fair chance at success?

In this article, we will explore the causes and consequences of the white exodus as well as potential strategies for stabilizing these areas.

To begin, let's look at some of the primary reasons why people are leaving urban environments in favor of more suburban or rural ones. Economic disparities, crime rates, poor education systems, and lack of employment opportunities all play a role in driving people away from cities. Gentrification also plays a part; when wealthier individuals move into lower-income neighborhoods, they often cause displacement and destabilization.

It's clear that there is much to consider when it comes to understanding the white exodus and its consequences for our communities.

Causes of the White Exodus

The abrupt departure of a large number of people from an area can be attributed to a variety of factors. In the case of the white exodus, economic disparity has been cited as one of the primary contributing causes.

Research has found that in areas where economic differences are starkly visible between different racial and ethnic groups, members of minority communities are more likely to move away in search of better opportunities. This is especially true when access to education and job-related resources are limited for certain populations while others have access to more plentiful resources.

In addition to economic disparity, political instability has also played a role in the white exodus from many areas. Political systems based on partisan divisions and deep social inequalities often fail to adequately represent their constituents' needs or interests, leading members of historically underrepresented groups—such as whites—to leave for regions with more equitable governance structures.

This phenomenon is particularly apparent in countries with histories of oppressive regimes or dictatorships; here, individuals may choose to emigrate as a means for escaping discriminatory policies and practices.

Finally, cultural clashes between different communities have been another source of tension driving some whites away from their hometowns. When two distinct cultures come into contact with each other — whether through immigration or other forms — there is often an inevitable clash between values and beliefs that can lead to misunderstandings and conflicts. Such tensions can make it difficult for those belonging to one group or another to feel welcome or valued in certain spaces; thus, they decide it's better for them to relocate elsewhere rather than remain in an uncomfortable environment.

As such, cultural clashes can serve as a powerful push factor behind someone's decision to move away from their home region. Moving forward, understanding these various causes will be essential for addressing this issue holistically and working towards creating more equitable societies where everyone feels accepted regardless of their background or identity.

Economic Disparity

As communities disperse, the disparity between those left behind and those who leave becomes increasingly evident. Economic opportunities have been a driving force for many of the white people to pack up their bags and move away from their homes.

- Low wages - Many of the jobs available in traditionally white neighborhoods are low-paying positions, leading to few economic opportunities.

- High cost of living - With rising costs of housing, transportation, food, and other essential items, it can be difficult for families to make ends meet on meager salaries.

- Lack of job security - Many employers offer little in terms of job or wage stability, which makes it difficult to plan for the future when incomes can fluctuate greatly from month-to-month or even week-to-week.

- Unstable housing market - The inability to obtain a mortgage loan or own property due to unstable housing markets has made homeownership unattainable for many in these areas, further limiting economic opportunities and advancement potentials.

The vast difference between those who stay and those who leave is highlighted by the lack of resources available for residents who remain in traditionally white neighborhoods after an exodus occurs. Fewer economic opportunities mean less access to higher education, quality healthcare services, and adequate public infrastructure, such as safe roads and bridges, making mobility more difficult, which can lead to further isolation from potential job prospects outside these communities.

Without investments in local businesses that provide goods and services needed by residents, this cycle will continue with no end in sight as crime rates start increasing with population decline...

Crime Rates

You may be surprised to learn that when populations decline in a certain area, crime rates tend to increase as well. With fewer people and resources available, the area can become more vulnerable to criminal activities. This is especially true for areas experiencing an exodus of white residents due to economic disparity.

The lack of investment in these communities further encourages criminal activity by offering little employment opportunities or resources for youth development. Moreover, rising levels of poverty often lead to increased levels of drug abuse which can result in higher crime rates. As a result, the overall quality of life decreases and those remaining are left with few options but crime.

It's no wonder then why we see such an exodus from economically challenged areas that have high crime rates; people want safety and security for themselves and their families. What's more, poor education systems also contribute greatly to this problem.

When educational opportunities aren't readily available or are lacking quality instruction, young people lack access to future job prospects - leading them down the path towards criminal activity as an outlet for financial gain or entertainment purposes. In some cases, this cycle continues through generations until something is done to break it up.

Furthermore, there's also a perception among many communities that law enforcement doesn't feel responsible or capable enough to curb these issues - thus resulting in higher crime rate figures regardless of population size or composition. It's easy enough for outsiders looking into these situations from afar think they know what needs doing; however the reality on ground is much different - requiring patience and understanding before any real progress can be made when it comes to addressing matters like white exodus due to economic disparities and resulting crime rates within a given community.

Poor education systems are another challenge altogether that must be taken into account if any real change is going to take place moving forward. With this knowledge in mind, let us look at how poor education systems factor into all this next...

Poor Education Systems

Seeing a lack of quality educational opportunities in an area can be disheartening, especially when you realize that those affected often don't have the means to access better options elsewhere. This is why the white exodus from certain regions has been linked to poor education systems.

Low-income communities often lack the resources and funding necessary to provide adequate educational programs, resulting in sky-high dropout rates and dismal test scores. This has caused many people to flee these areas in search of better schools for their children.

At the same time, it's important to consider how this impacts individuals who are unable or unwilling to relocate. Families who remain must face inadequate learning environments with limited resources available. Without the help of outside influences such as tutoring centers and after-school clubs, students may struggle significantly more than their peers in other districts.

In addition, research suggests that students may also suffer psychologically due to the increased stress associated with attending a low-performing school district.

The effects of poor education systems on white flight can't be understated; however, it's clear that these issues are only compounded by a lack of employment opportunities which prevent families from finding a way out of poverty and into a brighter future.

Lack of Employment Opportunities

When it comes to providing for your family, having access to employment opportunities is essential. Unfortunately, many communities have limited options that can make it difficult to break the cycle of poverty.

This has been especially true for communities experiencing a 'white exodus', where white residents have left their long-time neighborhoods in search of better opportunity elsewhere. With less demand from white residents, businesses that once provided plentiful job opportunities have disappeared or become severely understaffed. The lack of gainful employment not only affects those searching for work but also contributes to an overall decline in quality of life for everyone living in such communities.

In addition to disappearing jobs, the 'white exodus' also brings with it a decrease in wages and resources available for residents who remain behind. Without adequate pay or benefits, working individuals may find they are unable to provide adequately for their families regardless of how hard they work. This creates an environment where dreams seem unattainable and hope begins to fade away as many families struggle just to survive day-to-day without any real prospects on the horizon.

The effects of limited economic opportunity are devastating and far-reaching as people are forced out of their homes through no fault of their own due to diminishing housing options and increased cost of living expenses.

It's up to local governments and other organizations involved in community development initiatives to step up and create meaningful solutions that will help restore hope and prosperity back into struggling neighborhoods before it's too late.

Diminishing Housing Options

Without access to affordable housing, it can feel like you're stuck between a rock and a hard place—like trying to catch smoke with your bare hands.

When white people are unable to find suitable housing options that fit within their budget, they may be forced to leave the area and relocate elsewhere. This exodus is exacerbated by gentrification, which has been on the rise in several cities across the United States.

This process involves wealthy investors buying up property in low-income neighborhoods and turning them into expensive condos or apartments that only those with high incomes can afford. As these new developments become increasingly popular, many of the original homeowners who had previously been living in these areas are pushed out due to rising rental costs and taxes.

The lack of viable housing options for lower-income individuals has caused many white families to look for more affordable alternatives elsewhere. As the cost of living continues to increase, this trend is likely to persist as more and more people are priced out of major urban centers.

This issue is particularly concerning given that most minority populations have been historically excluded from accessing quality housing opportunities due to discriminatory practices such as redlining or restrictive covenants. It's not difficult to understand why so many individuals are being displaced from their homes; after all, when people cannot afford where they live, they must either move or face eviction.

As gentrification continues its march across America's urban cores, it's important for policymakers to consider how best they can ensure equitable access to quality housing for everyone regardless of race or economic status. Without such measures in place, entire communities could be wiped away as affluent newcomers take over the landscape without offering any meaningful solutions for those already there struggling with diminished housing options.

The next step should therefore focus on creating policies that prioritize affordability while also protecting existing residents from displacement--a task that will require substantial effort but one whose rewards will benefit us all in the long run.

Gentrification

Gentrification can be devastating, leaving you feeling helpless as your neighborhood changes before your eyes. It's a process of urban renewal often driven by private investment and government subsidies. The result is often a stark contrast between those who remain and those who can afford the new housing prices - making it difficult for low-income families to stay in their homes or find housing that fits within their budget.

Gentrification has had a huge impact on minority communities, with long-term consequences for people of color living in cities across the country. As gentrification takes hold, racial inequality becomes more pronounced as neighborhoods become increasingly segregated along economic lines. This affects individuals directly through higher rental costs and displacement due to redevelopment projects but also indirectly through exclusion from access to better services and amenities such as good schools or public transportation networks that are essential for upward mobility.

Furthermore, research has shown that gentrified neighborhoods tend to experience lower levels of diversity over time, leading many marginalized communities to lose contact with their cultural roots. The issue of gentrification is complex – there are benefits such as increased investments in infrastructure and decreased crime rates but these come at a cost: displacement of longtime residents who may lack resources to find alternative housing elsewhere or face further discrimination when they do so.

With this in mind, it's important for policymakers to understand how gentrification impacts different groups differently so they can develop effective strategies for managing change while still preserving local character and protecting vulnerable citizens from harm. Moving forward, it's critical that we consider how best to balance development initiatives with equity concerns so we can ensure everyone has access to equitable opportunities regardless of race or socioeconomic status.

Impact on Minority Communities

You can see the effects of gentrification in many minority communities, as wealthier newcomers displace the original residents, making it harder for those with lower incomes to stay in their homes or find affordable housing.

The influx of new money into these neighborhoods can also lead to rapid changes in infrastructure and culture, creating a sense of displacement and alienation among long-term residents.

Businesses may be forced out due to rising rents or replaced by fancier establishments catering to the new demographic. This has caused an increase in homelessness, poverty, and inequality for minority communities that were already struggling economically before the white exodus began.

The ripple effects of gentrification extend beyond just housing costs; education often takes a hit when wealthier people move into a neighborhood.

Schools may become overburdened as student populations surge while resources remain stagnant or decline. Public safety is also affected as police presence decreases due to budget cuts while crime increases with the influx of unfamiliar faces.

These conditions are further exacerbated by local governments who encourage gentrification without taking into account its consequences on existing residents and businesses.

It's important that strategies for stabilization are put in place so that displacement does not lead to more poverty and hardship for minority communities already struggling against systemic racism and economic injustice.

To ensure that everyone benefits from change, there must be an effort made to protect vulnerable populations from being left behind in this era of urban renewal.

Strategies for Stabilization

You can take action to help protect vulnerable populations from the effects of gentrification, and ensure that everyone benefits from change. As communities become increasingly diverse, it's important to create strategies that will stabilize neighborhoods and provide resources for all residents.

Here are some steps we can take to ensure a successful transition:

- Invest in affordable housing initiatives such as rent control, public housing programs, and subsidies for low-income renters.

- Increase local employment opportunities by encouraging new businesses to move into the area or support existing ones with start-up capital or incentives.

- Create economic development plans that focus on building up targeted neighborhoods while taking into account the needs of current residents.

- Educate residents about their rights and responsibilities in regards to zoning laws and land use policies in order to prevent displacement due to rising property values or taxes.

These strategies can help promote equitable growth in urban areas while mitigating potential displacement of existing residents due to white exodus and gentrification processes associated with it.

By creating an environment where all voices are heard and respected, we can foster stronger relationships between people of different backgrounds within our cities – something essential for any community's success over time. Working together, we can reimagine the future of our urban areas so that they remain vibrant places where everyone has an equal chance at prosperity.

Reimagining the Future of Urban Areas

We've discussed strategies for stabilizing urban areas that are undergoing a white exodus. Now, let's reimagine the future of these cities and what it could look like.

One thing we can do is diversify the housing stock in order to attract people from all walks of life—from different racial backgrounds, socioeconomic statuses, and ages. This would offer potential residents an array of choices that fit within their budgets, while also promoting fair access to quality neighborhoods.

Table below outlines some possible solutions for diversifying the housing stock in urban areas:

Solution	Description	Benefits
Affordable Housing Programs	Government-subsidized housing built by private developers with strict rent caps or tax abatements for low-income families.	- Increases access to quality housing. - Provides economic mobility. - Promotes diversity in neighborhoods. - Creates job opportunities in local communities.
Inclusionary Zoning	Requiring developers to reserve a certain percentage of units for low-income households as part of their development projects.	- Helps ensure a regular supply of affordable housing units. - Encourages mixed-income developments. - Promotes equitable economic growth in communities.

Frequently Asked Questions

What are the long-term effects of the white exodus on the affected communities?

We've seen an unprecedented shift in recent years, with communities that were once predominantly white now becoming increasingly diverse. This phenomenon has been dubbed the 'white exodus', and it's causing a ripple effect across the affected towns and cities.

As people move away to different areas, more than just population demographics are shifting; local economy, culture, education system and social networks all experience changes as a result of this migration. There are both short-term and long-term effects to consider.

While some communities may benefit from increased diversity in terms of economic opportunity or cultural enrichment, others may suffer due to reduced resources or strained relationships between different demographic groups. It's important to understand how these changes will affect each individual community in order to ensure that everyone can benefit from the opportunities presented by this white exodus.

How can local governments address the root causes of the white exodus?

We believe that local governments can have a positive impact on the communities affected by population shifts, such as those caused by changing demographics. To do this, they must identify and address the root causes of these changes. This includes economic instability, lack of access to education and employment opportunities, or an increase in crime.

Local leaders should assess the needs of their communities and design policies that promote economic development, provide quality education for all residents, develop job training programs for youth and adults alike, and invest in strategies to reduce crime. With these initiatives in place, local governments can ensure that all citizens have equal access to resources and opportunities regardless of race or ethnicity.

What can be done to ensure that all citizens are treated equally in terms of access to resources and opportunities?

We, as citizens, strive for a society of equality and justice.

To ensure that all individuals are treated equally in regards to resources and opportunities, it is necessary to look at the factors that contribute to unequal distributions. These can include systemic racism, poverty, access to quality education, and healthcare systems among other things.

It's essential for local governments to take an active role in addressing these issues in order to create environments where everyone has the same chances regardless of their background or race.

By doing so, we'll be able to promote true equality across our society.

How does gentrification contribute to the white exodus?

We've seen an increasing trend of gentrification in urban areas, leading to a displacement of lower-income families. This has resulted in a lack of affordable housing and economic opportunities for many residents, which in turn has contributed to the white exodus from cities.

As higher-income earners move into neighborhoods, they bring with them increased property values as well as new businesses that often don't offer the same services or employment opportunities as those that existed prior to gentrification. This can create an environment where long-term residents feel unwelcome and are unable to access resources or enjoy the same level of prosperity that newcomers may experience.

What are the most effective strategies to combat the effects of the white exodus?

We're exploring the best strategies for combating the negative effects of population shifts in our communities.

Through research, we've discovered a number of effective solutions to address this issue.

These include investing in affordable housing initiatives, providing educational and employment opportunities to those affected by displacement, strengthening community ties through events and activities, creating accessible green spaces, and developing programs that support small businesses.

By utilizing these tactics, we can ensure that everyone has access to a safe and secure living environment regardless of their background or financial status.

Conclusion

We've seen the devastating effects of white exodus on minority communities, and it's easy to point the finger of blame. However, it's much harder to come up with solutions. All too often, these issues are viewed through a political lens rather than an empathetic one.

We must move away from this approach and work together towards a more equitable future. As we look ahead, let us remember the parable of The Good Samaritan. Only by working together can we mend the broken fabric of our cities and create a society where everyone can thrive.

Let us use this crisis as an opportunity to build bridges across boundaries of race, class, and privilege. So that no one is left behind in our shared quest for progress.

White Privilege

We, the people of today's society, have been hearing a lot about white privilege lately. But what is it exactly?

White privilege is an issue that has been plaguing our world for centuries and continues to do so today. It's important for us to understand what white privilege means, how it affects us all, and the steps we can take to address this critical issue.

In this article, we will explore the definition of white privilege along with its history, economic implications and effects on education, healthcare and media representation. We will also discuss intersectional aspects of white privilege and how understanding these dynamics can help us gain insight into this complex problem.

Finally, we will consider ways in which we as citizens can start addressing white privilege in our everyday lives.

Definition of White Privilege

Having access to certain rights and benefits that are denied to others due to their race is an example of the disparity between those who have advantages and those without. White privilege, or the unearned advantages granted to people based solely on their skin color, has been a part of society for centuries.

It can manifest in different ways, from higher education opportunities to preferential treatment in job searches. This unequal distribution of power and resources creates an imbalance that continues to persist even today.

As we look back at history, it's important to recognize how this phenomenon has played out in our world and how it affects us all. With this knowledge, we can better understand why white privilege exists and what steps need to be taken towards eliminating its negative impact.

History of White Privilege

You've been handed certain advantages over the years, like a golden ticket that's been passed down through generations - ever since the dawn of time.

White privilege is a term used to describe the various privileges and benefits white people have due to their skin color. It has its origins in the history of colonization and slavery, when white Europeans conquered lands in Africa, Asia, and America and subjugated native populations for their own economic gain.

Looking at this from a modern perspective, it's easy to see how those power dynamics still play out today. Here are just four examples:

1) Access to better education opportunities

2) A greater likelihood of being hired for jobs

3) Being able to move through public spaces without fear or suspicion

4) Not being held back by stereotypes or expectations based on race

These are only some ways that white privilege continues to shape our society and further entrench inequality across racial lines.

Moving forward, it will be essential to recognize how these issues can continue perpetuating disparities between communities, so that they can be addressed and dismantled accordingly – starting with an honest assessment of our past.

Economic Implications of White Privilege

Gaining access to higher-paying jobs and more resources can have a major economic impact on your future – but it's important to recognize that not everyone has the same opportunities. The reality is that white privilege plays a role in economic success, as those with lighter skin color tend to have easier access to lucrative positions and better resources.

This means that white people are often able to earn more money than their peers of color, creating an unequal system where one group is financially favored over others. This can lead to disparities in wealth inequality and long-term financial security for many people.

It's essential for us to recognize the implications of white privilege when discussing economics, so we can create an equitable society where everyone has the opportunity to succeed regardless of race or skin color.

To do this, we must first understand how racism and discrimination manifest in our education system and other aspects of life.

Education System and White Privilege

The education system plays a major role in perpetuating white privilege, and a recent study found that Black students are more than three times as likely to be suspended from school as their white counterparts.

This highlights the systemic racism still present in many educational institutions today. Factors like disproportionate discipline, inadequate resources, and tracking of students into lower-level courses can all compound to create an environment where minority students are not given the same opportunities for success as their white peers.

The issue of racial inequality within the education system is deeply concerning, and it's clear that significant changes must be made in order to ensure equal opportunities for everyone.

As we move forward, we must work towards creating an equitable educational landscape where every student has access to quality learning experiences regardless of race or ethnicity.

With this in mind, let's now turn our attention to exploring how healthcare intersects with white privilege.

Healthcare and White Privilege

You're not immune to the effects of white privilege when it comes to healthcare. Inequalities in access, quality of care, and cost can all contribute to disparities in health outcomes based on race or ethnicity. This means that people of color often receive lower-quality care than their white counterparts.

A study by the National Academy of Medicine found that non-white patients are less likely to be prescribed lifesaving treatments than white patients with similar conditions, and they may get fewer opportunities for preventive screenings like cancer screenings or vaccinations. Additionally, non-white patients are more likely to experience long wait times at doctors' offices or emergency rooms, leading them to delay necessary medical treatment due to financial concerns.

The unequal distribution of resources in our healthcare system is just one example of how white privilege affects the lives of people who don't have it. It's important for us as a society to recognize these systemic biases and take steps towards dismantling them so that everyone can have equal access to quality healthcare regardless of race or ethnicity.

That way, we can ensure everyone has an opportunity for improved health outcomes and a better quality of life. As we move forward into exploring the criminal justice system and its role in perpetuating white privilege, it's essential we keep these issues top-of-mind so that no one is left behind.

Criminal Justice System and White Privilege

Experience how the criminal justice system plays a role in the unequal distribution of resources and opportunities, no matter your background.

The criminal justice system is an integral part of white privilege as it perpetuates systemic racism. It can be seen in these ways:

- Systemic bias where people of color are more likely to receive harsher punishments than their white counterparts for similar offenses

- Overrepresentation of people of color in prisons

- Racial profiling on a daily basis by law enforcement

- Unfair sentencing practices that disproportionately target minority groups

These realities have led to the mass incarceration of black and brown bodies, making it impossible for those affected to access resources they need.

This has caused an imbalance in power and opportunity that overwhelmingly favors whiteness. As we move into exploring media representation and white privilege, we must keep in mind how our society is heavily impacted by centuries-old racist policies embedded within our institutions.

Media Representation and White Privilege

We've seen how white privilege impacts the criminal justice system, but it also influences media representation.

We, as a society, are often bombarded with images of whiteness, either through advertisements or through seeing white characters dominate the screen in TV shows and movies. This sends a message that white people are superior and dominant, while people from other racial backgrounds are relegated to minor roles or stereotypes.

This can lead to feelings of inferiority amongst minority communities and further exacerbate the privilege gap between whites and others.

Furthermore, this lack of representation contributes to an overall sense of alienation within these communities. White privilege is perpetuated through media portrayal because when minorities don't see themselves represented in any meaningful way, they become disconnected from society as a whole.

It's important for us to recognize how this form of privilege affects our daily lives so that we can begin to work on dismantling it and creating more inclusive cultures where everyone feels accepted and valued regardless of race.

With this understanding, we can move onto exploring the intersectional aspects of white privilege.

Intersectional Aspects of White Privilege

Immersing oneself in the intersectional aspects of privilege reveals a complex tapestry of inequity and injustice, depicting a vivid picture of oppression that goes far beyond just skin color. This oppression is experienced through:

- The gender wage gap
- Systemic racism and xenophobia
- Environmental degradation from unchecked industrialization and pollution.

The combined effects of these intersecting forms of discrimination create an unbalanced power structure that perpetuates inequality for marginalized groups.

Such inequities can be seen in employment opportunities, healthcare access, education attainment, housing markets, and more. By understanding how white privilege manifests itself within intersections, we can begin to uncover the nuanced ways our society continues to be divided by race and other social markers.

Understanding White Privilege

Gaining a better understanding of how privilege works within intersecting identities helps us to recognize the pervasive inequities that exist in our society, and to appreciate the complexity of the oppression faced by marginalized groups.

It's important to not only be aware of systemic forms of privilege, but also how they interact with each other. For example, white people who are women may experience additional forms of discrimination due to both their gender and race.

By taking into account these nuances, we can begin to make meaningful progress towards dismantling oppressive systems. Understanding white privilege is an integral part of this process and allows us to move forward with a greater awareness and empathy for those facing marginalization.

As we continue on our journey towards equality and justice, it's vital that we acknowledge the complexities inherent in addressing white privilege.

Addressing White Privilege

Addressing white privilege is essential to creating a more equitable society, and it's something we all need to work on. It can be uncomfortable for many of us to consider our own privileges or the lack thereof, but it's an important part of understanding how systemic racism works.

Recognizing and addressing white privilege is one way that we can all do our part in dismantling oppressive systems. Acknowledging and actively working against white privilege means being willing to have difficult conversations, listening carefully to those with different life experiences, and taking action when necessary.

This may include speaking up when we hear racist comments or other microaggressions; calling out prejudice in the workplace; advocating for policy changes; or supporting organizations that promote equity. White people must also accept their responsibility for perpetuating racism and be committed to doing the work needed for true social change.

Frequently Asked Questions

How does white privilege manifest in other countries?

We've all seen and heard about the injustices of white privilege in our own countries, but what about other countries?

How does this insidious system manifest in places beyond our borders?

Through subtle forms of systemic racism and unequal access to economic and social opportunities, white privilege has a far-reaching grasp that can be felt around the world.

It's an invisible force that perpetuates inequality across cultures and societies, favoring those with lighter skin tones over those without.

The effects are devastatingly real for those who face discrimination due to their race.

This is why it's so important for us to recognize the presence of white privilege globally, so we can work together towards creating a more equal world for everyone.

What specific policies can be implemented to address white privilege?

We all have a responsibility to make sure everyone is treated equally, no matter their skin color or background. To ensure that this happens, specific policies must be implemented to address white privilege and create a level playing field for all.

These policies could include providing more resources and opportunities to marginalized communities, implementing anti-racism initiatives in schools and workplaces, reforming police departments to focus on de-escalation rather than force, offering tax incentives for businesses that invest in underserved communities, and creating legislation that makes it easier for those from disadvantaged backgrounds to access higher education.

Together, we can make sure everyone has an equal chance at success!

What is the impact of white privilege on non-white people?

We, as a society, must recognize the impact of white privilege on non-white people. The rich get richer and the poor get poorer, and we are seeing this play out in our communities every day.

While white people are benefiting from centuries of built-in societal advantages and structures that favor them, non-white people face systemic disadvantages that make it harder to achieve their goals.

This is why it's so important for us to examine these structural inequalities and work together to create systems that give everyone equal access to resources and opportunities. It's time for all of us to come together and create real change by addressing white privilege head-on.

How can allies of non-white people help to reduce the impacts of white privilege?

We all know that inequality exists in our society, but do we understand the impact it has on non-white people?

Allies of non-white people can help reduce the impacts of inequality by engaging in meaningful conversations, learning about different experiences and perspectives, and taking action to create more equitable systems. This can come in many forms such as speaking up for those who can't be heard or advocating for fair legislation.

Together, we can work towards creating a better future for everyone.

How does white privilege shape the cultural landscape?

We live in a world where many people still experience unequal access to resources and opportunities due to cultural differences. This affects decisions about who can have access to what, from education and job prospects, to economic security, voting rights, and more.

White privilege shapes the cultural landscape in a number of ways, from influencing which stories are told and which voices are heard in mainstream media, to influencing how people interact with each other across social boundaries. It also impacts perception of diversity within public spaces such as schools or workplaces, making it difficult for non-white people to feel included or respected on an equal footing.

Conclusion

We've come to understand that white privilege is a real and pervasive issue in our society today. We can't deny the history of structural inequalities and power structures that have been established to benefit certain groups over others.

Despite progress, one interesting statistic is that only 15% of African-Americans own their homes compared to 75% of whites, demonstrating the lingering effects of systemic racism.

As we move forward, it's important for us all to recognize these inequities and take actionable steps towards dismantling oppressive systems. Only then will true equality be possible for everyone regardless of race or gender identity.

Healthcare Disparities Faced By Black Americans

We, as a collective society, have an obligation to ensure equal access to quality healthcare for all. Unfortunately, many Black Americans face disparities in healthcare due to systemic racism and other factors.

In this article, we will explore the various obstacles that Black Americans face when it comes to accessing quality medical care. We will dive into topics such as financial disparities, inadequate insurance coverage, inadequate access to specialty care, and systemic racism.

Furthermore, we will discuss how these disparities can be addressed in order to make healthcare more equitable for everyone. With a better understanding of the challenges facing Black Americans today in regards to healthcare access and quality of care, we can work together towards making meaningful change.

Access to Healthcare

The lack of access to healthcare can have devastating consequences, like a young mother in need of lifesaving treatment being unable to get the care she needs.

Black Americans face disproportionate obstacles when it comes to receiving medical attention, whether due to living in areas with limited resources or cultural bias from healthcare providers. These factors contribute to an unacceptable situation where African Americans are more likely than whites to suffer from preventable diseases and illnesses due to inadequate healthcare.

These issues are further compounded by financial disparities that create further barriers for lower-income African American communities.

Additionally, there's overwhelming evidence that black patients receive poorer quality care when compared with white patients, regardless of insurance status or income level.

This lack of equitable access places a tremendous burden on underserved populations and exacerbates existing health disparities among black Americans.

Financial Disparities

You may be surprised to learn that financial disparities are a major issue among many people in the U.S., and Black Americans face particularly harsh realities in this regard.

Health insurance can be incredibly expensive, but even if it's affordable, there are still limits on coverage, as well as potential gaps between what's covered and what services are actually needed for optimal health.

In addition, racial discrimination within the healthcare industry means that Black Americans often have difficulty accessing care even when they have insurance.

All of these factors contribute to an overall lack of access to quality healthcare for Black Americans, which contributes to worse outcomes than those experienced by white Americans.

With all of these factors at play, it's no surprise that systemic racism plays a big role in the disparities faced by Black American communities.

Systemic Racism

You experience the impact of systemic racism when it comes to accessing quality healthcare, with costly insurance and limited coverage causing huge inequality.

African Americans have a long history of being denied adequate healthcare due to their race and economic status, leaving Black communities at an extreme disadvantage.

This has resulted in a lack of access to quality care, leading to poor health outcomes for many Black Americans.

Healthcare disparities that are caused by systemic racism are wide-reaching, from preventative care to chronic disease management and everything in between.

With higher rates of cardiovascular disease, cancer, diabetes, hypertension, and other conditions among African Americans compared to white counterparts, these enduring disparities can no longer be ignored or understated.

It's time for real change so that all people can have equal access to quality medical care regardless of their skin color or socio-economic status.

Lack of Quality Care

Experience the harsh reality of lacking quality care; it's a deep, heavy burden that weighs on your heart and soul. Unfortunately, black Americans are all too familiar with this burden as they're disproportionately subject to lower-quality healthcare.

- They have limited access to physicians due to geographical barriers and lack of transportation.
- They're more likely to receive subpar services or be denied services altogether for reasons such as insurance status.
- Inadequate representation within the medical field leads to bias in diagnosis and treatment.
- They have a disproportionate presence within underfunded health systems where resources are limited.

These disparities create an environment where one's race can mean the difference between life and death. Despite decades of progress, we still have much more work to do to ensure black Americans have equal access to quality healthcare. But it doesn't end there - inadequate insurance coverage also plays a role in creating healthcare disparities.

Inadequate Insurance Coverage

When insurance coverage is inadequate, it can be a crushing blow for those already struggling to access quality care. This is especially true for Black Americans, who often face obstacles to adequate insurance coverage and access.

Insurance companies may offer limited plans that are expensive and not tailored to their needs, or they may be unable to receive adequate coverage due to pre-existing conditions or lack of knowledge about available resources. This leaves many Black individuals at a severe disadvantage when it comes to accessing the healthcare they need, leading to even more disparities in health outcomes.

The consequences of inadequate insurance coverage go far beyond simple financial costs. Many Black Americans struggle with chronic illnesses and other medical issues, which can become exacerbated without appropriate healthcare interventions and medications. Additionally, some preventive treatments are often not covered by basic plans, leaving many people vulnerable to long-term problems down the line.

Inadequate insurance coverage thus creates a dangerous cycle that can lead to further inequality in the healthcare system—and ultimately poorer health outcomes for Black Americans overall. With this in mind, we must strive towards providing better opportunities for all when it comes to acquiring adequate—and affordable—insurance coverage so that everyone has equal access to quality healthcare services.

Over-Diagnosis of Mental Health Issues

We know that inadequate insurance coverage is an issue for many Black Americans, but there's another problem in the healthcare system that affects them disproportionately as well.

That's the over-diagnosis of mental health issues.

Studies have shown that African Americans are more likely to be diagnosed with mental health disorders than their white counterparts, even when they don't meet all of the criteria for diagnosis.

This means that African Americans are not only more likely to be misdiagnosed with a mental illness, but also overmedicated.

This can lead to negative consequences such as increased stigma and unnecessary treatments.

Additionally, these diagnoses often ignore important cultural factors and socioeconomic conditions which can contribute to mental health issues in Black communities.

By better understanding how societal influences affect mental health outcomes, we can begin addressing this issue and ensure everyone has access to quality care regardless of race or ethnicity.

Moving forward, we must consider the inadequate access to specialty care faced by Black Americans as well.

Inadequate Access to Specialty Care

It's no secret that access to specialty care is lacking for many, and the consequences can be dire; for instance, a patient may not receive the necessary diagnosis or treatment for their condition due to limited resources.

This is especially true when it comes to Black Americans, who often face additional barriers when trying to access this type of medical care. Many lack insurance coverage or have inadequate plans that do not cover these services, leading to increased healthcare costs and decreased access overall.

Furthermore, there is evidence of bias in the medical field that leads doctors to not refer Black patients for specialty care as often as they should. These disparities contribute significantly to poorer outcomes among Black Americans with serious health conditions.

The situation is further exacerbated by disparities in prescription drug access, which can have a major effect on an individual's health outcomes.

In order for Black Americans to receive the appropriate level of quality healthcare they deserve, steps must be taken to ensure equitable access across all demographics. Without actionable solutions that address these issues head-on, it will remain difficult for individuals from marginalized backgrounds to get the specialist care they need—and deserve—to stay healthy.

Disparities in Prescription Drug Access

You don't have to be a medical expert to know that prescription drug access is not equal for everyone. Unfortunately, this inequality affects many individuals and can lead to serious consequences for their health.

Black Americans are particularly vulnerable when it comes to disparities in prescription drug access due to systemic racism, poverty, and lack of insurance coverage. These issues lead to higher instances of untreated conditions and even death due to the inability to receive life-saving medication.

Without access, people often turn to alternative methods such as buying from street dealers, which can put them in danger, or purchasing counterfeit drugs, which can result in further harm.

The unequal access faced by Black Americans has long-term impacts on both physical and mental health outcomes. Inadequate availability of necessary medications leads to preventable chronic diseases, further exacerbating existing health disparities between races.

Additionally, not being able to obtain needed prescriptions often causes emotional distress that can deeply impact quality of life if left unaddressed – highlighting the importance of addressing these healthcare disparities head-on.

As we move forward, it's crucial that we make sure all members of our society have equitable access to prescription drugs so they can live healthy lives without fear or worry about their ability to get the care they need.

With this in mind, let's turn our attention now towards examining the inadequate access faced by Black Americans when it comes to mental health services.

Inadequate Access to Mental Health Services

Mental health services remain a major missing piece for many, with limited options and lack of access creating an alarming alliteration of anguish and agony. This is especially true for Black Americans, who are disproportionally affected by mental illness and yet face numerous barriers to receive the care they need.

For example, research has shown that Black Americans tend to be underdiagnosed in the diagnosis of depression due to cultural mistrust, lack of access to culturally competent providers, and lack of insurance coverage or resources. Furthermore, there aren't enough mental health professionals who specialize in working with African American patients which further limits access to care.

These challenges have resulted in inadequate support for racial disparities among those seeking mental health services. The consequences are dire; untreated mental health issues can lead to increased risk for homelessness, substance abuse, unemployment and criminalization—all of which add up to a greater burden on already marginalized communities.

As such, it's imperative that action is taken at both the public and private level to ensure equitable access to preventative care services for all Americans regardless of their background or race.

Barriers to Preventative Care Services

We're all aware of the importance of preventative care services, yet access to these vital resources is limited for some members of our society. Preventative care services are often hindered by a lack of resources, resulting in unequal access for those most in need.

This inequality is especially evident within the Black American community, where disparities in healthcare provision are commonplace. The consequences of this unequal distribution can be severe. Without preventative care, individuals may find themselves facing serious health issues that could have been avoided through early intervention.

Furthermore, as these problems become more serious they become harder to treat and can lead to long-term physical disabilities or even death. These issues are compounded by poverty and other social determinants which further limit access to medical services.

We must work together to ensure that everyone has equal access to adequate healthcare and preventative care services. This will allow us to protect the safety and well-being of all members of our society.

Frequently Asked Questions

How can Black Americans access quality healthcare?

We all want quality healthcare for our families, friends, and loved ones, but for Black Americans, it feels like an impossible dream!

With limited access to the resources they need, navigating the healthcare system can be a daunting task. But there's hope! By reaching out to organizations like the National Association of Black Health Professionals and local health centers, Black Americans can find compassionate care that meets their needs.

These organizations provide guidance on how to get quality healthcare that's affordable and tailored to their unique circumstances. With their help, we can finally make sure our loved ones have access to the best possible healthcare available.

How can Black Americans reduce financial disparities in healthcare?

We all know how important it is to have access to quality healthcare, but what about the financial costs associated with that care? Black Americans face unique disparities when it comes to healthcare, and reducing those financial disparities can be a challenge.

Fortunately, there are steps that we can take as individuals and as a community to lower the cost of our healthcare. We can look into low-cost health insurance options, research free or reduced-cost clinics in our area, advocate for policies that reduce healthcare costs for everyone, and find ways to pay for treatments not covered by insurance.

By taking these steps together, we can begin overcoming the financial disparities faced by Black Americans in accessing quality healthcare.

How can Black Americans reduce systemic racism in healthcare?

We, as Black Americans, are fighting an ongoing battle against systemic racism in healthcare. Despite the progress we've made, there's still much work to be done.

But how can we combat this issue? We must come together to demand policies that promote equity and ensure everyone has access to the same quality of care. We must also speak out against any discrimination or bias we may encounter when seeking medical help.

With dedication and perseverance, we can take steps towards reducing systemic racism in healthcare and create a more equitable future for all.

How can Black Americans improve access to mental health services?

We, as Black Americans, can make progress in improving access to mental health services by advocating for better policies and increasing awareness.

We must ensure that our voices are heard at the policy-making table and that we have a seat at the conversations about our communities' needs.

We can support organizations dedicated to providing resources for mental health services to those who need them most.

Additionally, it's important that we spread awareness of existing resources through word-of-mouth and social media campaigns.

These initiatives will help close the gap between access to care for Black Americans and other groups in society.

How can Black Americans reduce barriers to preventative care services?

We, as Black Americans, are all too familiar with barriers to preventative care services.

From long wait times for appointments to a lack of culturally competent doctors and nurses, the challenges can seem insurmountable.

But there's hope! By being proactive and taking control of our healthcare decisions together, we can bridge this gap in access and reduce these disparities.

Let's become agents of change - let's break down these archaic hurdles and make sure everyone has proper access to preventative care services.

Conclusion

We've come to the end of our exploration into healthcare disparities faced by Black Americans.

The statistics are staggering: Black people are three times more likely to die from heart disease than their white counterparts.

This is just one example of many disparities that exist in today's healthcare system, and it's clear that more needs to be done to address them.

It's time we start working together as a nation to ensure equitable access to quality care for all citizens, regardless of race or ethnicity.

Together, we can create a better future for everyone.

Undiagnosed Mental Illness in the Black Community

Mental health issues in the Black community are often brushed under the rug, leaving many people undiagnosed and struggling with their mental wellbeing. This is concerning because untreated mental illness can have serious consequences that impact individuals and their families.

In this article, we will explore the prevalence of undiagnosed mental illness in the Black community, barriers to diagnosis, cultural stigmas around seeking help, limited access to resources, and steps to improve mental health.

We hope that by reading this article you can gain a better understanding of why it's so important for us to address undiagnosed mental illness in our communities and take steps towards helping those who are living with mental illness get the care they need.

Understanding Mental Illness in the Black Community

The lack of diagnosis and treatment for psychological issues within certain populations is a troubling reality. In the black community, this is especially true; many members struggle with mental illnesses that go undiagnosed or untreated due to a variety of socio-economic factors.

These factors present significant barriers to proper diagnosis and treatment, ranging from poverty and racism to distrust in medical institutions and stigmatization within the community.

As such, it's crucial that we understand why these barriers exist in order to make meaningful progress towards providing quality care for those who need it most.

Barriers to Diagnosis

You face a number of obstacles when it comes to identifying and treating mental health concerns - don't let those stop you from getting the help you need.

First, there's the lack of access to quality healthcare in many black communities.

Second, there's the cost of treatment which can be prohibitive even with insurance coverage.

Third, there is the stigma surrounding mental illness that can lead people to feel ashamed and not seek out help they need.

Finally, cultural norms may prevent people from seeking professional help as they turn instead to religious leaders or spiritual healers for guidance and comfort.

But these are issues we must confront if we're going to make any progress in addressing undiagnosed mental illness in the black community. We can't allow cultural stigmas, financial costs, or lack of access to keep us from finding the support and treatment necessary for our well-being.

The Impact of Cultural Stigmas

Don't let cultural stigmas stop you from getting the help you need - it's essential to your wellbeing.

As members of the Black community, we understand that seeking help for mental health issues can be difficult and intimidating due to societal norms. Unfortunately, many individuals in our community are reluctant to seek treatment or even admit they're struggling because of fear of being judged by their peers or family. This shame prevents people from seeking professional support and results in untreated mental illnesses that can have devastating effects on a person's life.

We must recognize this issue and work together to break down these barriers within our communities, so that those suffering can get the help they need without facing stigma.

Mental health resources in minority communities are often limited, so it's important to know where to find support if needed. By removing the negative associations surrounding mental illness, we'll be able to create an environment where everyone feels comfortable seeking help if they need it.

Limited Access to Mental Health Resources

Finding the right mental health resources can be a challenge, especially for those in minority communities. Take, for example, John, a young man who had been struggling with depression but was unsure where to turn for help.

Access to quality mental health care is often limited in the black community due to inadequate insurance coverage, lack of culturally competent providers, distance from accessible facilities, limited understanding of available services, and financial barriers or cost of treatment.

All these factors make it difficult for those in need to get the help they need and deserve. As a result, many people remain undiagnosed and untreated until their situation becomes dire - leading to long-term negative effects on their well-being.

This highlights the need for education and awareness around mental health issues so that individuals are better able to access appropriate resources when needed.

The Need for Education and Awareness

Having the right information about available resources can be the difference between getting help and not, yet too often people are unaware of what's out there.

As such, it's important that we in the Black community become active in educating ourselves on mental health issues and advocating for greater access to quality care. We must raise awareness about undiagnosed mental illness, destigmatize seeking treatment, and support friends and loved ones who are dealing with it.

This shift towards understanding mental illness as a normal part of life is key to breaking down barriers that prevent individuals from accessing the care they need. Beyond creating an environment of acceptance, this knowledge gives us the tools we need to advocate on behalf of those around us who may otherwise go untreated.

Supporting Friends and Loved Ones

Supporting our friends and family who are struggling with mental health is essential for their well-being, so it's important to provide them with compassion and care.

Listening without judgments or expectations can be a great way to show support, as well as offering practical help like transport or childcare. Practical assistance has the potential to make an enormous difference in someone's life and journey towards recovery.

When caring for someone struggling with mental health issues, it's also important to look after yourself too. It can be emotionally draining, so taking time out to manage stress levels through activities such as yoga or mindfulness is crucial.

And while there may be times when you feel overwhelmed by the situation, finding solace in a strong support system of family and friends can provide comfort and refuge during difficult times.

With that said, beginning the next section with stress management strategies can provide helpful guidance on how best to cope.

Stress Management Strategies

Taking a break from the hustle and bustle of everyday life can be a great way to reduce stress levels and bring peace of mind. Here are some effective strategies for managing stress in the Black community:

- Exercise regularly – physical activity helps to regulate stress hormones as well as improve your mood.
- Establish healthy boundaries – create realistic limits on how much you're willing to take on, both emotionally and physically.
- Practice mindfulness techniques – this involves focusing on the present moment, rather than worrying about what happened in the past or what may happen in the future.

By taking time for ourselves and incorporating these simple yet powerful tools into our daily lives, we can find greater balance and achieve better mental health outcomes. From here, we can transition into seeking professional help if needed.

Seeking Professional Help

We've discussed some strategies for managing stress, but it's important to realize that there are times when seeking professional help can be beneficial. When the symptoms of mental illness become too much, it's crucial that we take action and seek help from a qualified healthcare provider.

In the Black community, this means reaching out to organizations like the National Alliance on Mental Illness or Black Mental Health Alliance for support and guidance. It's also important to recognize that simply finding a doctor or therapist may not be enough.

We must advocate for ourselves and our communities to ensure that medical providers are aware of the unique needs of people with undiagnosed mental illness in the Black community. With proper advocacy, we can work towards making sure everyone has access to quality mental health services they need.

To do this, we must start by increasing awareness and acceptance of mental health issues within our own communities.

Advocacy for Mental Health Services

Advocating for quality mental health services is essential to ensuring that everyone has access to the care they need, no matter their background. As members of the Black community, we must be vocal about our needs and push for resources that are tailored to our unique experiences.

To do this effectively, here are a few action items we can take:

- Develop partnerships with organizations devoted to mental health awareness
- Create open dialogues among our peers and family members
- Raise awareness on social media platforms by sharing stories and providing support

By advocating for ourselves and others in our communities, we can make a real difference in the lives of those affected by undiagnosed mental illness. Through these actions, we can create an environment of understanding and compassion so that all individuals receive the support they deserve.

Ultimately, this will lead us towards taking meaningful steps towards improving mental health in the Black community.

Steps to Improve Mental Health in the Black Community

You can make a real difference in the lives of those affected by difficulties, simply by advocating for yourself and others. Taking proactive steps to improve mental health in the black community is essential to breaking down stigmas and providing more access to quality care.

One way to do this is to become an advocate for marginalized populations within society. This could involve encouraging people to speak up about their mental health issues, and taking action against any forms of discrimination they may face due to their diagnosis or lack thereof.

Another important step would be to promote awareness about available services and resources that are tailored towards helping individuals with mental illness find treatment options that work best for them.

Lastly, supporting initiatives such as re-entry programs for those who have been incarcerated can help provide a safe space for transitioning back into daily life without fear of judgement or stigma. By taking these steps, we can create a strong support system within our communities that encourages open dialogue about mental health and provides pathways for healing and growth.

Frequently Asked Questions

What are the most effective treatments for mental illness?

We all know how important it's to take care of our mental health, but what're the most effective treatments for mental illness?

As it turns out, there's no one-size-fits-all approach to treating mental illness - different therapies and treatments work better for different people. Generally speaking, cognitive behavioral therapy (CBT) has been found to be the most successful form of treatment.

CBT helps individuals recognize their patterns of thinking and behavior that may contribute to their symptoms and then provides them with the tools they need to make changes in those areas. Additionally, medications such as antidepressants can also help some people manage their symptoms more effectively.

In any case, seeking professional help's always recommended when seeking treatment for mental illness.

What are the long-term effects of untreated mental illness?

We know the long-term effects of untreated mental illness can be devastating. Without treatment, symptoms can become worse over time and affect a person's ability to function in everyday life.

People may develop severe depression, anxiety disorders, substance abuse problems, or even suicidal thoughts. Untreated mental illness also increases the risk of physical illnesses such as heart disease, obesity, and diabetes due to its impact on stress levels and lifestyle behaviors.

It's important for individuals struggling with any form of mental health issue to seek help from a qualified professional who can provide appropriate support and resources to ensure they're able to manage their condition effectively in the long-term.

How can family members and friends best support someone with mental illness?

We know it can be difficult to support someone you love who's dealing with mental illness, but it's an incredibly important part of their journey.

Instead of feeling overwhelmed, see it as an opportunity to show your care and commitment to them.

Start by being present and listening when they want to talk about how they're feeling.

Offering a comforting hug or just being there for them can go a long way.

Be aware that people with mental illness need more than just words – offer practical help such as helping out with chores, running errands, or providing transportation when needed.

Remember that everyone's experience with mental illness is different, so try not to judge or make assumptions about what they should do; instead focus on showing your unconditional acceptance and support for them during this time.

What kind of support is available for individuals with mental illness in the Black community?

We know how important it is to support those with mental illness, and there are many organizations dedicated to helping individuals with mental health issues in the Black community.

There are a variety of different types of support available, including therapy, counseling, support groups, and more. These resources can help provide guidance and understanding for those suffering from mental illness.

With access to these supports, people can find the strength they need to tackle their mental health struggles head-on.

How can individuals with mental illness access mental health resources?

We know mental health is important, and accessing the right resources can be difficult. That's why we're here to help.

We want to make sure everyone has access to the mental health resources they need. From online therapy programs to in-person counseling, there are plenty of options available for individuals with mental illness.

Depending on your individual needs and situation, you may be able to tap into local community resources or take advantage of national organizations dedicated to providing support for those with mental health issues.

No matter what path you choose, it's important to remember that you don't have to go through this alone - there are people who care about your wellbeing and will work with you every step of the way.

Conclusion

We've come to the conclusion that mental illness in the black community is a serious issue that needs to be addressed.

Despite cultural stigmas and limited access to resources, it's possible for individuals to seek help and manage their stress.

Unfortunately, many people still don't have access to the necessary resources or education needed to understand mental health issues.

It's ironic that even though we know how important it is for everyone to have access to quality mental health care, there are still so many barriers preventing this from happening.

We must continue advocating for better services and educating our communities about mental health in order for us all to live healthier lives.

Racial Disparities in Maternal and Infant Health

We, as a society, must acknowledge that there is an immense disparity in maternal and infant health outcomes between racial groups. It is essential to understand the root causes of this inequality to create meaningful solutions for improving maternal and infant health outcomes.

This article will discuss the various factors that contribute to the racial disparities in maternal and infant health, including healthcare access and quality of care, socioeconomic status, stress and mental health, substance abuse, education, insurance coverage and potential solutions to reduce disparities.

We hope this article will serve as a starting point for understanding these issues more deeply so we can work together towards positive change.

Overview of Racial Disparities in Maternal and Infant Health

You might be surprised to learn that there are significant differences in the health of mothers and babies depending on their background. Racial disparities in maternal and infant health are a concerning issue. Black women are more likely to die due to childbirth related complications than White women. Additionally, Black infants are two times more likely than White infants to die before their first birthday. This is a harsh reality for many families, and these disparities can have lifelong implications for both mothers and children.

The causes of these disparities are complex and multifaceted. Factors such as access to healthcare, quality of prenatal care, income level, and education attainment levels all play an important role. Moreover, racism is often implicit in healthcare systems. Meaning even when individuals do have access to necessary services, they may still encounter racial bias or discrimination from providers or staff. Furthermore, stress caused by racism has negative impacts on physical health outcomes as well.

These issues persist despite numerous efforts from policymakers to reduce them through increased funding for public programs such as Medicaid Expansion and WIC (Women Infants & Children). However, much work needs to be done in order to bring about true change and ensure equitable opportunities for all mothers and children regardless of race or ethnicity.

The next section will explore some of the strategies organizations are using to tackle these inequities head-on.

Causes of Disparities in Maternal and Infant Health

The root of the problem lies beneath the surface, and we must dig deep to uncover its causes. Racial disparities in maternal and infant health are vast and complex, and can be attributed to a range of factors including systematic racism, economic inequality, lack of access to quality healthcare, environmental hazards, health behaviors, and genetic/biological differences.

Systematic racism is one of the most pervasive drivers behind these disparities. Structural discrimination has created persistent racial segregation that leads to unequal access to education, employment opportunities, housing options, financial resources - all of which play a role in health outcomes.

Economic inequalities also contribute significantly; communities with higher poverty rates have less access to healthy food options or nutritious meals due to cost constraints. Additionally, people living in poverty may not be able to afford adequate healthcare services or preventive care necessary for optimal maternal and infant health outcomes.

Environmental hazards such as air pollution have been linked to poor birth outcomes among minority populations due to their disproportionate exposure to toxins compared with white populations.

Furthermore, certain health behaviors such as smoking during pregnancy are more common among certain ethnicities than others due to culture-specific norms surrounding prenatal care or advice from medical professionals.

Finally, although there is still much debate in this field about how genetics influences racial disparities in maternal and infant health outcomes – it is clear that biological differences exist between different racial groups that cannot be ignored when exploring causes of disparity within this population.

Moving beyond simply understanding the basic causes of these disparities requires further research into effective intervention strategies for addressing them at their source - ultimately resulting in improved maternal and infant health across all racial groups.

Healthcare Access and Quality of Care

Accessing quality healthcare and receiving quality care can impact maternal and infant outcomes regardless of race. However, disparities in healthcare access are often seen among racial groups due to various factors such as availability of providers, cost of services, language barriers, and cultural biases. These issues can result in poorer health outcomes for mothers and infants from certain racial backgrounds, ultimately putting them at a higher risk for complications during pregnancy, childbirth, and beyond.

Differences in resources, such as insurance coverage, can contribute to disparities in prenatal and postnatal care received by individuals belonging to different races. This can lead to higher rates of negative birth outcomes, particularly for African American women compared to White women, such as preterm birth or low birth weight babies. Racism has also been linked to inadequate delivery of essential services needed during pregnancy, labor, delivery, and postpartum periods, further increasing the risk associated with childbirth for minority women.

Therefore, access to quality healthcare and the quality of care provided are crucial factors that determine maternal and infant health outcomes across different racial lines. To address these disparities, it is necessary to consider other factors, such as socioeconomic status, and create effective solutions that help decrease these gaps moving forward.

Socioeconomic Factors

Socioeconomic factors can play a huge role in exacerbating the already-dire situation for many individuals, making it even more difficult to get the medical care they desperately need and deserve. Studies have shown that racial disparities in access to quality healthcare are heavily driven by economic inequality.

People of color are more likely to be uninsured or underinsured, and lack access to quality health insurance plans. Lower income families often don't have enough resources to pay for necessary tests, treatments, medications, or doctor visits. This can lead to poorer overall health outcomes and increased risk of complications during pregnancy or childbirth.

It is clear that socioeconomic hardship can act as a major barrier when it comes to securing safe maternal and infant care. But this doesn't tell the whole story; there are also psychological effects related to socioeconomics on maternal and infant health outcomes. Stressful circumstances—such as poverty, food insecurity, homelessness—can take a toll on mothers' physical and mental wellbeing before, during, and after childbirth.

Furthermore, if parents lack financial security or educational opportunities for themselves or their children, future prospects may seem uncertain at best. All these factors contribute greatly towards the persistent racial disparities we see in maternal and infant health today.

The consequences of structural inequality should not be overlooked when discussing ways to improve maternal and infant health outcomes among people of color; addressing underlying socioeconomic causes is crucial for creating lasting change in this area. Therefore, understanding how stress due to economic hardship affects mothers' mental well-being is key in order to create equitable solutions that prioritize everyone's needs equally instead of just focusing on mitigating symptoms without any long-term resolution strategy in sight.

To move forward, we must look beyond immediate interventions into strategies aimed at reducing systemic inequities which will ultimately lead us towards better empowering those most affected by healthcare injustice today.

Stress and Mental Health

You may not realize it, but stress due to economic hardship can have a huge impact on your mental wellbeing before, during, and after childbirth. This is especially true for women of color who are more likely to experience poverty and other forms of economic insecurity.

Studies have shown that these women are more likely to suffer from depression and anxiety during pregnancy, which can lead to higher rates of preterm birth and low birth weight babies. Additionally, the stress associated with financial insecurity can cause mothers to be less able to provide emotional support for their children in the early years of life.

The effects of this kind of stress don't end when the baby is born either. Women who experience poverty or other forms of economic hardship often struggle with postpartum depression as well as difficulty bonding with their newborns due to feelings of guilt or inadequacy. This can lead to long-term issues such as attachment disorders in children and an increased risk for developing mental health problems later in life.

It's clear that socioeconomic factors play a major role in maternal and infant health outcomes, particularly among women of color. The good news is that there are steps we can take to reduce the negative impacts of poverty on mental health by providing access to resources such as counseling services, financial assistance programs, and parenting classes.

By taking these steps, we can help ensure that all mothers have the best chance at having healthy pregnancies and raising healthy babies regardless of their race or income level. With this knowledge in hand, let's turn our attention now towards environmental factors which also contribute significantly to racial disparities in maternal and infant health outcomes.

Environmental Factors

Living in an area with poor air quality or contaminated water sources can have a huge impact on a mother and her child's wellbeing, leaving them feeling exhausted and overwhelmed even before the baby is born. Low-income communities of color are disproportionately exposed to these environmental hazards due to years of discriminatory housing policies, placing mothers and their unborn babies at risk for adverse health outcomes.

A recent study from the National Institute of Environmental Health Sciences (NIEHS) revealed that pregnant women living near polluting sources were more likely to experience preterm births or deliver infants with low birth weights. This connection was found to be especially true for African American women who live in areas close to such environmental hazards as industrial plants, oil refineries, and hazardous waste sites.

The NIEHS study also found that those same mothers tended to be affected by higher levels of stress than mothers living away from such sites. The combination of exposure to pollutants coupled with elevated stress levels can lead to serious medical consequences for both mother and infant. Moms suffering from depression or anxiety may not receive adequate prenatal care while others struggle with substance abuse or unhealthy coping mechanisms just to get by day-to-day.

All this further contributes to the racial disparities already present in maternal health care, making it harder for some mothers of color facing poverty and environmental injustice issues to give their children the start they need in life. These findings point us towards finding better ways of protecting vulnerable populations, particularly pregnant women living in areas where access to clean air and water is limited.

It is important that we continue researching how our environment affects maternal health outcomes so we can develop solutions that will truly make a difference for families most impacted by pollution-related illnesses such as asthma, allergies, heart disease, reproductive issues, developmental delays, and more. From there we must strive towards creating healthier spaces where everyone has an equal opportunity at achieving good physical and mental health - regardless of race or economic status - so all parents can feel confident about providing their children with a safe path into adulthood. With this knowledge in hand, maybe we can begin addressing the issue of substance abuse next.

Substance Abuse

We need to address the issue of substance abuse, as it can have devastating effects on families. Research has shown that in the United States, racial minorities are more likely to be affected by substance abuse.

African-American women and their infants are disproportionately affected by drug use during pregnancy, with higher rates of negative outcomes such as low birth weight and preterm delivery. Substance abuse among pregnant women is also associated with a higher risk of infant mortality and increased incidence of infant hospitalization due to withdrawal symptoms at birth.

The prevalence of substance abuse among racial minority populations is largely linked to social inequality and poverty. Lower access to quality healthcare, education, housing, employment opportunities, and other forms of support create an environment in which individuals are more likely to turn towards drugs or alcohol for solace.

As a result, programs designed to prevent or reduce substance abuse must take into account these underlying factors if they are going to be effective for everyone affected by this issue.

It's clear that there is much work still needed in order for us all to effectively combat this problem. Education about the dangers of drug use during pregnancy needs to be available not only on the individual level but also through public health initiatives that target communities most impacted by the issue – especially those from racial minority groups who already face added challenges when it comes to maternal and infant health outcomes.

To move forward from here we must look beyond simply preventing drug use during pregnancy but rather focus on creating equitable environments where individuals have access to resources needed for healthy living so they don't feel compelled towards self-medicating with substances in the first place.

Education

You can help reduce substance abuse by educating yourself and others about the dangers of drug use during pregnancy. This education should include:

- The potential harm to the mother and baby;
- What resources are available for pregnant women struggling with addiction;
- Safer alternatives to using drugs;
- How to support someone who is addicted.

Education is also key in reducing racial disparities in maternal and infant health. Women of color often lack access to quality educational opportunities, which can lead them into situations where they are less likely to receive adequate prenatal care or have a safe delivery.

In addition, their knowledge on how to best care for themselves and their infants may be limited due to lack of information or cultural stigma. By providing women of color with more comprehensive healthcare education, we can ensure that they have the tools necessary for healthy pregnancies and deliveries.

We must also examine how implicit bias affects healthcare professionals' interactions with patients of color – including mothers-to-be – and take steps towards eliminating it from our medical system. Healthcare providers should be encouraged to participate in educational programs that foster understanding between themselves and patients from different backgrounds, so that all individuals will receive equitable care regardless of race or ethnicity.

With better educational opportunities and a reduction in implicit bias among healthcare providers, we can work towards closing the gap between racial disparities in maternal and infant health outcomes. Moving forward, we must make sure that every mother has access to quality education on how best to provide for her own health needs during pregnancy and beyond – and that she receives compassionate support throughout her journey into motherhood.

Insurance Coverage

Having insurance coverage can make a world of difference when it comes to affording the necessary healthcare for yourself and your baby during pregnancy. Having access to health insurance doesn't always mean you're automatically protected against financial hardship; however, it means that there are more resources available to help pay for medical costs related to prenatal care as well as delivery.

Furthermore, having health insurance reduces disparities in maternal and infant health outcomes because it provides access to high-quality prenatal care which is often unaffordable for low-income women who don't have insurance. This improved level of care leads to better birth outcomes and fewer complications during labor and delivery.

Insurance coverage also plays an important role in reducing racial disparities in postpartum care, such as the ability to see specialists or receive additional testing if needed. For example, African American mothers may be at higher risk for postpartum depression due to social factors like racism or poverty, but they may not be able to afford treatment without adequate coverage. Similarly, those same mothers may need access to mental health services that their insurance plans provide in order for them to adequately cope with life after childbirth.

It's clear that having access to quality health insurance can drastically reduce the risk of adverse maternal and infant health outcomes, yet many women still lack this vital resource due to socioeconomic barriers or other factors outside of their control.

Moving forward, we must work towards finding potential solutions that reduce these disparities so all mothers can benefit from the positive impacts of healthcare coverage regardless of race or income level.

Potential Solutions to Reduce Disparities

Finding ways to bridge the gap in healthcare access is essential for ensuring every mother and baby can receive the care they need, regardless of their background or financial status. While there aren't single solutions that'll solve the disparities in maternal and infant health, a combination of strategies can help reduce inequalities.

One promising strategy is to increase education and awareness among vulnerable populations about the importance of pre-natal care and post-partum support. This could include providing educational materials on nutrition, breastfeeding advice, and other important topics to mothers from low-income backgrounds.

Additionally, increasing access to resources such as child care assistance, transportation subsidies, and affordable housing would also be beneficial for reducing disparities in maternal and infant health outcomes. These resources not only provide economic stability for families but also enable them to get regular checkups while pregnant or seek medical attention when needed.

Finally, addressing social determinants like poverty levels or systemic racism must be part of any effective solution if we hope to build healthier communities for all mothers and babies.

It's time that we begin taking meaningful steps towards making sure every mother has access to quality healthcare before, during, and after pregnancy, no matter their race or socio-economic status.

Frequently Asked Questions

How can I support organizations that are working to reduce racial disparities in maternal and infant health?

We can all do our part to support organizations working to reduce disparities in maternal and infant health.

From volunteering with a local birthing center that works with low-income families, to donating to national non-profit organizations, or advocating for change through social media - there are many ways we can lend a hand.

Research shows that investing in quality care for mothers and infants can greatly improve the health of both parties and help close the gap between races.

So let's come together and make a real difference!

What specific healthcare services are needed to help reduce racial disparities in maternal and infant health?

We all want to ensure our mothers and infants receive the best healthcare possible. However, there are certain services that can help reduce disparities in maternal and infant health outcomes. These include access to comprehensive pre-natal care, postpartum care for mothers, home visits from nurses or midwives, breastfeeding support, and mental health resources for women during pregnancy and postpartum.

Ensuring these services are available to everyone regardless of race is key in creating a more equitable healthcare system.

Are there specific policies that can be implemented to address the issue of racial disparities in maternal and infant health?

We've all heard the phrase, "Health is wealth", but it's not a reality for many mothers and babies.

In fact, disparities in maternal and infant health are an unfortunate truth across the United States. To make matters worse, these disparities are often seen along racial lines.

But while this issue can seem overwhelming, there are policies that can be put in place to help reduce these gaps.

From increased access to healthcare services and education programs to financial incentives for organizations that meet certain standards of care, there are numerous ways governments and institutions can work together to promote healthier outcomes for mothers and their babies regardless of race or ethnicity.

What are the long-term effects of racial disparities in maternal and infant health?

We've seen an increase in research highlighting the long-term effects of disparities in maternal and infant health, particularly among different racial groups.

These effects can range from poorer physical health outcomes for infants to higher rates of chronic health conditions for mothers.

Long-term consequences can also include decreased educational attainment, lower incomes, and a greater likelihood of poverty.

These issues are compounded when access to resources and quality care is limited due to socioeconomic factors or lack of insurance coverage.

Addressing these disparities is essential for ensuring that all mothers and infants receive the care they need as they transition through pregnancy, childbirth, and beyond.

How can I get involved in the efforts to reduce racial disparities in maternal and infant health?

We, as a community, have the power to make a difference in reducing racial disparities in maternal and infant health. By getting involved with organizations that work towards this goal, we can help create more equitable systems and foster an environment of support for everyone.

Symbolically speaking, think of it like planting a seed – each individual action helps nourish the soil of justice and equality. With careful research and dedication, we can ensure that all families have access to the resources needed to be healthy during pregnancy and beyond.

Research-backed understanding shows us that when communities are empowered with education, advocacy efforts, and targeted initiatives to address disparities directly at their root causes; all members benefit from improved health outcomes.

Let's come together to create an environment where everyone is supported!

Conclusion

We acknowledge that racial disparities in maternal and infant health are a major issue, and we understand the need for urgent action.

We recognize that these issues stem from various factors, including healthcare access, quality of care, socioeconomic status, stress, mental health, substance abuse, education levels, and insurance coverage.

Collectively, these disparities paint a bleak picture of inequality for many families of color – but they don't have to stay this way. With empathy and determination, we can work together to reduce these disparities and create a brighter future for mothers and babies everywhere.

Like a ripple effect in water, our efforts will be far-reaching – spreading hope like wildfire through communities long deprived of it.

Infant Mortality among Black Babies

We all know the feeling of a newborn baby in our arms, bringing with them joy and hope for the future. But for many Black families, this promise is tragically too often cut short due to shockingly high levels of infant mortality. The statistics are heartbreaking: Black infants are nearly two-and-a-half times more likely than white infants to die during their first year of life.

We must take a closer look at the causes behind these disparities and explore ways to reduce infant mortality among Black babies. Our journey begins with an examination of the various factors that contribute to this devastating trend, from racial discrimination in healthcare access to environmental hazards and socioeconomic disadvantages.

We will then discuss existing public health interventions that have been successful in reducing infant mortality, as well as steps that can be taken by individuals, families, communities and policy makers in order to improve outcomes for Black babies. Through collective action we can build a brighter future where all children have an equal chance at living a healthy life.

Overview of Infant Mortality

You may be surprised to learn that some babies don't make it through their first year of life. Infant mortality is a term used for any baby who dies before reaching one year of age, and it has been an issue in the United States since records have been kept. In 2020, the infant mortality rate was 5.7 deaths per 1,000 live births in the United States. This rate is higher than many other nations around the globe, which speaks to a greater need for preventative measures and healthcare access for at-risk populations.

Among these populations are black babies, whose infant mortality rates have consistently lain far above those of white babies, ranging from two to three times higher over the past several decades. Not only do black babies face an unjustly high risk of death during infancy compared to their white peers, but they also tend to die earlier in life due to worsened living conditions and unequal access to quality medical services.

To truly understand why this disparity exists, it requires looking at the systemic issues that lead to high levels of infant mortality among black babies. As such, it's important we examine not just what causes this tragic outcome but how we can take action against them moving forward.

Fortunately, there are numerous initiatives being taken by public health organizations and social justice advocates alike that aim to reduce racial disparities among infant mortality rates by providing resources and support services for expectant mothers as well as low-income families with children under one year old. These efforts could potentially go a long way towards improving outcomes for black infants across America—but only if followed up with meaningful changes on both individual and institutional levels.

We need more than awareness; we need real solutions that prioritize equitable medical care, so all American children can enjoy healthy lives from birth onward.

Causes of High Mortality among Black Babies

Struggling to understand why some babies don't make it to their first birthday? Let's explore the causes of high mortality in this population.

Research has found that there are various factors that disproportionately contribute to infant mortality for Black babies. These include limited access to prenatal care, higher rates of premature birth, and a greater prevalence of certain chronic health conditions such as asthma or diabetes. Furthermore, structural racism can lead to negative outcomes such as poverty, which can create an environment where infants lack adequate nutrition and healthcare resources.

The impact of these social determinants is further compounded by racial disparities in access to healthcare. Studies have shown that Black patients experience lower quality care when compared with white patients even after controlling for socioeconomic status and insurance coverage. This includes longer wait times for appointments and delays in diagnosis or treatment, all of which can increase the risk of infant mortality. In addition, implicit bias can also lead providers to be less attentive or dismissive toward certain patient groups due to unconscious stereotypes.

These issues affect not only individual families but entire communities as African Americans continue to face significant health inequities throughout their lifespan. To reduce the overall burden of infant mortality among Black babies requires a multi-faceted approach that addresses both medical and nonmedical factors on both a local and national level.

It's only through collective action that we can build healthier futures for our children -- beginning before they are even born! With this in mind, let's turn now towards examining racial disparities in access to healthcare.

Racial Disparities in Access to Healthcare

Understanding the racial disparities in access to healthcare is key to finding a solution that can help create healthier futures for our children. African American mothers and infants have been disproportionately affected by inadequate medical care, unequal access to health insurance, and over-policing of communities which leads to a lack of trust in the healthcare system. This has resulted in higher infant mortality rates, less prenatal care, higher rates of maternal mortality, and lower quality of postnatal care.

Culturally competent prenatal care is essential for reducing infant mortality among African American babies. Ensuring that Black women are able to access quality health insurance, adequate resources, and safe birthing environments are all crucial aspects of creating equitable outcomes across races. Additionally, addressing implicit bias within the medical field will help ensure that Black women receive respectful treatment during their pregnancy journey and beyond.

These efforts must be accompanied by support for increased socioeconomic mobility so families can break out of generational cycles of poverty and improve their overall well-being.

Socioeconomic factors play an integral role in determining health outcomes; thus it's essential that we address these issues as part of any effort to reduce infant mortality among Black babies.

Socioeconomic Factors Contributing to Infant Mortality

We understand that uncovering the socioeconomic factors that contribute to infant mortality is paramount in order to create healthier futures for all children. For Black infants, this issue has been particularly concerning and devastating. Studies have shown that infant mortality rates are higher among African American babies compared to other racial and ethnic groups, with a rate of 11.4 deaths per 1,000 live births in 2017, more than double the white rate of 4.9 deaths per 1,000 live births\cite{infant mortality}. To explore some of the key contributing economic factors, we've compiled a table below outlining the disparities between Black and White households in terms of income level and education attainment:

Metric	Black Households	White Households
Median Income (2018)	$41,211	$70,642
% Below Poverty Line (2017)	22.0%	9.2%
High School Diploma or Higher (2017)	81.7%	94.3%

As seen above, there is an observable difference in median household income between Black families ($41,211) and White families ($70,642). Additionally, 22 percent of African Americans were living below poverty line in 2017 compared to just 9 percent for Whites \cite {poverty}. Furthermore 81 percent had a high school diploma or higher whereas 94 percent of whites had similar educational attainment levels \cite{educational attainment}. These disparities can lead to different outcomes when it comes to health care access as well as stress and mental health issues which can further complicate matters for expecting mothers who are already vulnerable during pregnancy. Therefore understanding the underlying economic differences is necessary if we want to address these issues head on in order ensure better birth outcomes for our most vulnerable populations.

Stress and Mental Health Issues

It's clear that the economic disparities between Black and White households can have a profound impact on stress and mental health, which can be particularly damaging during pregnancy.

Many mothers of color are exposed to higher levels of stress due to systemic racism, poverty, and lack of access to resources that are necessary for a healthy pregnancy. All of these factors can lead to anxiety, depression, and other mental health issues that can put both mother and baby at risk.

This is compounded by the fact that many mothers in this demographic may not have access to quality healthcare or resources needed for proper prenatal care.

Stress has been linked to premature birth and low birth weight, both of which are associated with infant mortality rates. Additionally, maternal depression has been shown to impact infant mortality rates through increased likelihoods of preterm labor, low Apgar scores (a test used at birth to assess overall health), neonatal intensive care unit admission, congenital anomalies, stillbirths, and even sudden infant death syndrome (SIDS).

These conditions are all more likely in infants born from mothers with poor mental health due to financial strains and/or racial discrimination.

The effect of stress on mother-infant interactions alone cannot be understated; pregnant women who experience greater amounts of stress tend to interact less with their babies after they're born as well as having difficulty bonding with them once they arrive home - this then leads into postpartum depression which further exacerbates an already difficult situation for mother and child alike.

It is essential that we recognize the crucial role that stress plays in influencing infant mortality among Black babies so we can develop targeted strategies aimed at reducing the rate of preventable deaths within this population. To do this effectively will require addressing existing socioeconomic disparities so there's equal access to quality healthcare systems across all demographics - something which is key if we want to make meaningful progress towards decreasing the tragic number of avoidable deaths among Black infants.

Lack of Quality Maternity Care

You can't overlook the impact of a lack of quality maternity care on mothers and their newborns, leading to potentially devastating outcomes. Black mothers, in particular, are more likely to experience worse prenatal care than white women due to socio-economic disparities.

Women of color often face obstacles accessing quality health care services, including transportation issues, lack of insurance or financial ability to pay for services, and language barriers. The resulting effect is that black babies are at greater risk for preterm birth or low birth weight than white babies due to inadequate access to medical attention before the baby is born.

This issue has been made even worse by social determinants such as poverty or unemployment that disproportionately affect black families in comparison with white families. These factors further increase the likelihood that black women will give birth prematurely or have a low-birth weight infant due to stressors associated with having fewer resources in society.

As such, the lack of quality maternity care leads not only to physical but psychological consequences since it affects both maternal mental health and infant mortality rates among African American communities.

The effects of this problem can be seen in all aspects of life from education levels and employment opportunities to housing availability and overall health status. This further perpetuates an unequal power dynamic between different racial groups which only serves to worsen existing inequalities throughout our society.

It's clear that we must work together towards providing equitable access for women of color when it comes to healthcare services in order for us all benefit from healthier outcomes and reduce disparities in infant mortality across racial lines. To truly make a difference here, we must look beyond just providing medical assistance – we must also address underlying systemic issues related to economic inequity so that everyone has an equal opportunity at achieving better health outcomes regardless of race or ethnicity.

Impact of Environmental Hazards

You're likely aware of the environmental hazards that can have a devastating impact on people's health, but did you know that these same hazards can be especially detrimental to pregnant women and their unborn children?

Exposure to hazardous chemicals, such as lead or arsenic, are linked to preterm birth and low birth weight among newborns. This is especially concerning for Black babies whose mothers live in areas with high levels of environmental contaminants. The World Health Organization notes that this is due in part to the increased exposure of certain communities living near industrial sites or other sources of contamination.

The effects of environmental toxins don't stop after a baby is born either. These toxins can cause neurodevelopmental disorders, respiratory illnesses, and asthma later in life. In some cases, they may even increase the risk of infant mortality.

It's clear that the environment plays an enormous role in determining one's health outcomes throughout their entire lives—particularly when it comes to Black infants who face higher rates of infant mortality than any other racial group in the United States today.

The importance of addressing environmental hazards cannot be understated when it comes to reducing infant mortality rates among Black babies. Taking steps to reduce environmental toxins and ensure safe living conditions for expectant mothers and newborn infants will help promote healthier outcomes for generations to come.

It's essential we take action now if we want lasting change for our future—the health of our families depends on it!

Challenges in Addressing Infant Mortality

Addressing the high infant mortality rates among Black babies is an urgent challenge, one that requires us to take action now if we want to ensure a brighter future for generations to come. Unfortunately, there are several barriers preventing meaningful progress in tackling this issue.

First and foremost, a lack of resources and access to services puts some communities at a disadvantage when it comes to finding adequate care for their infants. Additionally, many families don't have the knowledge needed to make informed decisions about how best to raise healthy children. Finally, structural racism plays a major role in limiting the opportunities available to Black communities and perpetuating disparities in health outcomes.

To address these challenges effectively, we must begin with recognizing that this is an issue of social justice deserving of our immediate attention. We must work together as a society—and with those affected most directly—to ensure that every family has what they need to provide safe environments for their children and access quality healthcare services and education opportunities throughout life.

There is no single solution; but with targeted investments in community-based programs like home visiting nurse visits or early childhood education initiatives, we can start making strides towards improving long-term outcomes for Black babies everywhere.

By looking holistically at all contributing factors driving poor outcomes for Black infants, we can identify areas where public policy interventions can be made on both local and national levels. Committing resources towards developing more equitable systems will not only help improve health outcomes but also promote economic mobility within underserved communities so everyone has the opportunity to thrive regardless of race or background.

Taking steps forward on this front will bring us closer towards achieving greater racial equity across society as a whole—a goal worth striving toward if we wish to build stronger foundations for future generations of all backgrounds.

Promising Public Health Interventions

Taking action towards improving Black babies' health outcomes is absolutely critical, and there are some promising public health interventions that can help us make incredible strides in tackling this issue.

One such intervention is prenatal care which provides crucial information to expecting mothers regarding how to keep themselves and their unborn child healthy. This includes advice on nutrition, physical activity, mental health support, and access to medications or vaccinations that might be necessary. Accessible prenatal care also helps identify potential risks early so they can be addressed before the baby is born.

Another key intervention is community-based programs that provide home visits from public health nurses during pregnancy as well as for a few months after birth. These visits include education about breastfeeding, safe sleep practices, development milestones, infant nutrition and more; all of which are important factors in ensuring a healthy start for Black babies.

Lastly, increasing the availability of affordable housing would help reduce overcrowding which has been linked to an increased risk of infant mortality due to lack of adequate living space for parents and newborns alike.

These interventions represent just a few ways in which we can begin taking steps towards reducing infant mortality among Black babies. Through better access to prenatal care services and community-based programs as well as providing affordable housing options for families with young children we can ensure healthier environments for infants both pre-and postnatal.

Ultimately it will take a commitment from multiple stakeholders—from policymakers and healthcare providers to educators—to create lasting change within our communities but the results will be worth it when we see improved outcomes for our youngest population group.

Moving forward then, let us commit ourselves wholeheartedly to addressing this problem through these promising public health interventions – strengthening our communities one healthy baby at a time!

Steps to Reduce Infant Mortality among Black Babies

Focusing on the health of our youngest population is essential, and reducing infant mortality among Black babies takes a collective effort from multiple stakeholders. The first step in creating a healthier future for this vulnerable group is to increase access to quality healthcare and provide support services that meet their unique needs. This includes providing resources such as prenatal care, nutrition education, and mental health counseling.

Additionally, it's important to address potential environmental factors that may contribute to higher rates of infant mortality, such as air pollution or lead exposure.

The next step in decreasing infant mortality among Black babies is to reduce social disparities by increasing economic opportunities for families living in poverty. Policies such as an increased minimum wage, childcare subsidies, food assistance programs, housing vouchers, and job training can help make it easier for parents to gain financial stability and access basic necessities for their children.

It's also important to implement community-level initiatives that promote positive parenting skills and provide mentoring programs that equip new parents with the knowledge they need for successful child rearing.

It's clear that reversing trends of high infant mortality among Black babies requires a holistic approach from all sectors of society including government agencies, healthcare organizations, educational institutions, employers, faith-based groups etc.

Working together, we can create an environment where every baby has the opportunity to thrive and reach their full potential in life regardless of race or socio-economic status.

Frequently Asked Questions

What can parents do to reduce the risk of infant mortality?

We want to explore what parents can do to reduce the risk of infant mortality. According to the U.S. Centers for Disease Control and Prevention, there are close to 23,000 infant deaths in the United States each year. That's an alarming statistic that should motivate us to take action. However, with proper knowledge and preventative measures, we can make a positive difference in reducing the risk of infant mortality.

Parents need to ensure they have regular prenatal care, practice healthy habits such as eating nutritious foods and avoiding alcohol and cigarettes during pregnancy. They should be aware of any medical conditions or infections that may lead to complications during delivery. Additionally, they should receive help from family members or other support systems in order to create a safe environment for their child after birth.

By taking these steps, parents can make a significant impact on reducing the risk of infant mortality.

How can healthcare providers help reduce racial disparities in infant mortality?

We believe healthcare providers have an important role to play in reducing racial disparities in infant mortality. To start, they should strive to provide equitable care for all patients and their families regardless of race.

Additionally, healthcare providers should be aware of the social determinants of health that can influence outcomes and take steps to identify and address any potential barriers that may exist for minority communities. Providers can also help spread awareness about the issue through education programs or by partnering with local organizations dedicated to improving infant mortality rates in underserved populations.

Finally, healthcare providers can work together to advocate for policies at the local, state, and national level that promote better access to quality care for all mothers and babies.

What is the long-term impact of environmental hazards on infant mortality?

We're appalled at the long-term impact environmental hazards can have on infant mortality. These invisible threats can seep into a home, a neighborhood, and even an entire city, wreaking havoc on the health and wellbeing of families everywhere.

As we consider the dangers of air pollution or water contamination, it's heartbreaking to think that such preventable issues are harming infants. More awareness and resources are needed to avoid these harms.

We must not forget these vulnerable newborns as we strive for systemic change. This change will ensure their safety and well-being.

How can public health interventions help reduce infant mortality among black babies?

We're committed to finding public health interventions that can reduce infant mortality. We believe that by addressing underlying factors such as environmental hazards, access to healthcare, and lifestyle choices, we can work towards curbing this tragic issue.

Through research and investment in preventative measures, we strive to ensure that all babies have the opportunity for a healthy start in life.

What resources are available to support families affected by infant mortality?

We understand the devastating impact that infant mortality can have on a family. There are resources available to help families cope with their loss and support them through this difficult time.

Organizations like the National Fatherhood Initiative offer bereavement counseling and grief therapy for parents who've lost a child. They also provide financial assistance and connect families with other support networks in their community.

Many hospitals provide bereavement services such as memorial services, support groups, and professional counseling. Social workers can also be invaluable in helping families access vital resources during this time of need.

Conclusion

We've seen how infant mortality disproportionately affects Black babies and the various factors that contribute to this disparity. No single solution will be effective in reducing the mortality rate, but the combination of public health interventions and improved access to healthcare can certainly make a difference.

We must continue to strive for a more equal society where all babies are given an equal chance at life. As we work towards this goal, let's keep in mind that every step forward is one closer to achieving true equity and justice for our most vulnerable members of society.

The Sexualization of Black Women and Girls in America

Historical Context

You can't ignore the fact that, for centuries, certain groups have been objectified and dehumanized in this country. This is especially true for Black women and girls in America, whose bodies are often used as a source of commodification and sexualization.

With this context, it's important to understand the implicit and explicit messages that are sent about their worth and value within our society. The long-standing stereotypes associated with Black women as being hypersexual or promiscuous continue to be perpetuated through popular culture, media portrayals, language use, dress codes at schools, etc.

This sends an underlying message that these young women are valued only for their physicality rather than any of their other traits or accomplishments. These messages lead to a damaging cycle wherein they feel like they must conform to such standards in order to be seen as attractive by boys or men.

As a result of such pervasive expectations imposed on them by society, Black women and girls often internalize these ideas about themselves leading to low self-esteem or body image issues.

Implicit and Explicit Messages

The pervasive implications of objectification and marginalization that are subtly communicated to minority populations cannot be overlooked. Even when not explicitly stated, these messages can still be felt by black women and girls in America. By reinforcing stereotypes, such as the oversexualized black woman or the strong-willed sassy attitude, society is sending a clear message about how it views them.

These implicit messages have been heavily embedded in our culture for centuries and continue to shape how African American women are perceived today. This has direct consequences in terms of both physical health and mental well-being. All too often, the sexualization of black women is seen as something that should be embraced instead of a form of oppression — this sends a dangerous message to young girls who grow up believing they must adhere to certain standards or risk being ostracized from their peers.

The effects of this distorted perception can have long-lasting impacts on an individual's self-esteem, leading to serious issues like depression and anxiety. With these realities in mind, it's clear that understanding the effects on physical health is essential for combating this issue.

Effects on Physical Health

Understanding the physical health implications of objectification and marginalization is essential in today's society, especially given the prevalence of anachronistic images that can be so damaging to individuals' self-esteem. For black women and girls in America, these impacts are felt on a daily basis, often in ways that go unnoticed or unacknowledged.

Here are four examples of how sexualization affects physical health:

- **Frequent exposure to hypersexualized images** can lead to body dissatisfaction and disordered eating behaviors such as bingeing, purging, or extreme dieting practices.

- **Increased stress levels** due to societal messages that equate worth with appearance can lead to an increased risk for chronic illnesses such as heart disease and diabetes.

- **Loss of control over their own image** when they become objects rather than subjects can have long-term effects on mental health and well-being including depression, anxiety, and post-traumatic stress disorder (PTSD).

- Objectification also increases the likelihood of being victims of violence due to increasing feelings of vulnerability among those who are already marginalized in society.

Sexualization has real consequences for physical health that cannot be ignored any longer; it's time for us to take action by creating more positive representations of black women and girls in our communities and media outlets. We must move forward together towards recognizing the value inherent in all people regardless of gender or race if we want to ensure their future wellbeing - this starts with understanding how objectification affects physical health.

Effects on Mental Health

Experiencing objectification can cause mental health issues such as depression, anxiety, and PTSD, making it important to recognize the value in all people regardless of gender or race.

In particular, the sexualization of black women and girls in America has had devastating effects on their mental health. Studies have shown that this hypersexualization leads to an increased risk of developing depression, anxiety, low self-esteem, body dissatisfaction, and eating disorders.

Women who are subjected to this type of treatment often feel powerless and voiceless due to a lack of control over how they are being portrayed by society. It's essential that we acknowledge these struggles and provide resources for those affected by the harmful messages perpetuated by society's standards.

By doing so, we can help create a sense of inclusion and acceptance among all individuals regardless of their gender or race. The role of media plays a significant part in shaping our perceptions about beauty standards — particularly for black women and girls.

The media is responsible for reinforcing stereotypes about them which contribute to feelings of shame and disconnection from their bodies. Furthermore, exposure to hypersexualized images in the media can lead to higher levels of stress hormones which further exacerbate existing mental health issues such as depression and anxiety.

It's crucial that we challenge these damaging representations by amplifying positive stories featuring black women so that they can see themselves accurately represented in popular culture.

The Role of Media

You're constantly exposed to media images that can have a profound effect on your mental health, so it's important to recognize the value of all people regardless of gender or race.

This is especially true when considering the sexualization of black women and girls in American media. These images often present them as hypersexualized objects instead of human beings with feelings, thoughts, and emotions. The consequences are damaging; they lead to self-esteem issues and unhealthy body image ideals among young African American girls who look up to these role models.

Moreover, these stereotypes perpetuate white supremacy by portraying black women as submissive figures without any power or control over their own identities. As a result, it's essential for us to create an environment where everyone is shown respect and appreciation for their unique qualities.

It's also important for us to be aware of the impact of white supremacy in our society and how it affects the representation of black women and girls in mainstream media outlets. Through greater public understanding and education, we can help promote positive self-image in young African American females while creating more equitable opportunities for them in various aspects of life.

The Impact of White Supremacy

White supremacy has created a world in which black people are viewed as second-class citizens, like a fish out of water. This is especially evident in the sexualization of black women and girls in America.

In professional settings, they face microaggressions that emphasize their physical characteristics over their intellect and capabilities. From comments about their hair to the clothes they wear, these subtle attacks can have an enormous impact on how black women view themselves.

In popular culture, they are often portrayed as objects for male consumption, instead of complex individuals with unique personalities and dreams. From music videos to television shows to advertisements, it's easy to see how white supremacy has reduced African American women to one-dimensional characters who only exist for pleasure or entertainment.

On social media platforms, there is often a hypersexualization of the female body by both men and women alike that further reinforces this objectification. Photos posted online can be seen by millions of people in an instant – leaving little room for nuance or respect of individual autonomy when it comes to sexuality.

The insidiousness of white supremacy is undeniable; its effects reach far beyond just the sexualization of black women and girls in America. But understanding its role is essential if we want to create more equitable representation moving forward.

The Role of Religion

Religion can play a powerful role in how individuals view themselves and others, often influencing our values and beliefs about sexuality. This is especially true for black women and girls in America, who have historically experienced the effects of religious oppression.

From the days of slavery to current times, many African American religious institutions have taught that black women should be submissive, chaste, and sexually pure. This has been reinforced through religion-based messages that place a higher value on female chastity than male chastity and promote a restrictive gender role for women.

As such, black women have been pressured to conform to narrow sexual ideals that are rooted in white patriarchy instead of their own agency and desires. This can lead to feelings of worthlessness or powerlessness when it comes to their own sexuality which is further perpetuated by systemic oppression.

Systemic Oppression

Systemic oppression has long denied black people the freedom to express their sexuality in ways that are meaningful and fulfilling for them.

In America, the oppression of Black women and girls is pervasive. They are frequently viewed through a racialized lens of sexualization in media, education, and public spaces. This objectification reflects a deep-seated cultural assumption about their bodies as inherently sexual objects rather than individuals with agency.

Furthermore, this kind of racism creates an environment where Black women and girls often feel unsafe when asserting autonomy over their own bodies or exploring their sexual identities. As a result, many have been silenced by fear or shame surrounding sexuality due to systemic discrimination and lack of resources or support.

To move forward from this oppressive system, social movements have become necessary to ensure the rights of all individuals regardless of race or gender identity are respected.

Social Movements

You've got the power to make a difference against oppressive systems by joining social movements that prioritize the rights of everyone, regardless of identity.

For example, members of the LGBTQ+ community in India are currently challenging traditional gender roles and norms by establishing support groups and advocating for queer rights. This is just one example of how collective action can lead to meaningful change.

By taking part in social movements and initiatives, we can actively fight against systemic oppression and create a more equitable future for all people. It's important to recognize the role that social movements play in dismantling oppressive structures so that we can move towards a brighter future.

Towards a Brighter Future

By taking part in social movements, you can be a part of building a brighter future for everyone. Together, we can make a real difference and create a world that is free from oppressive systems.

We can use our collective power to fight against the sexualization of black women and girls in America and ensure that they are treated with respect and dignity. Through our advocacy work, we can help to challenge harmful stereotypes about black women and girls, promote positive images of them in media, and advocate for laws that protect their rights.

Additionally, we must support organizations that are dedicated to uplifting those who have been impacted by the sexualization of black women and girls. By doing this work together, we can create meaningful change for the generations to come.

Through education and awareness-raising efforts, we can equip people with the knowledge to recognize how systemic racism has created an environment where black women's bodies are often objectified or viewed as hypersexualized entities instead of respected human beings. We also need to focus on creating safe spaces where young black women and girls feel empowered to express themselves without fear or judgment – spaces which provide them with opportunities for growth both personally and professionally.

This is an important step towards dismantling oppressive systems that have kept these communities down for far too long. With everyone's help, it's possible to build a better future where all individuals are equally valued regardless of race or gender identity.

Frequently Asked Questions

What can be done to prevent the sexualization of black women and girls in America?

We believe that the sexualization of women and girls should never be acceptable. To prevent this, we must begin by creating a safe space to talk about topics such as these without fear of judgment or ridicule.

We must also take an active stance against perpetuating harmful stereotypes and hold those accountable who do.

Finally, open dialogue between parents and children is essential in encouraging positive body image, respect for others, and sensitivity towards issues related to gender and sexuality.

How can the media be used to counteract the sexualization of black women and girls in America?

We're tired of the sexualization of black women and girls in the media. We see it everywhere we look, and it's time to take a stand.

Media outlets need to start using their platforms to counteract this issue by celebrating black women in various roles that go beyond just being objects of desire. We can show the beauty and strength inherent in black women without resorting to sexualizing them; instead, let's see them as strong leaders, mentors, professionals, teachers--the possibilities are endless!

If we can come together as a society and recognize the power of media representation, we can begin to create real change for our communities.

How does the sexualization of black women and girls in America compare to other countries?

We've all heard of the phrase 'sex sells', but what about when it comes to the sexualization of women and girls? For many countries around the world, this issue has been a persistent problem for decades.

But what does it look like in America, particularly for black women and girls? Surprisingly, the situation here isn't as dire as you might think: according to recent studies, black women and girls in America are actually less likely to be sexualized than those in other countries.

This is an encouraging sign that we're making progress on this important issue.

What are the long-term effects of the sexualization of black women and girls in America?

We often hear stories of the sexualization of women and girls worldwide, but rarely do we consider the long-term effects this can have. For black women and girls in America, sexualization leads to a host of negative outcomes that can last a lifetime.

Studies show that hypersexualization contributes to higher rates of depression and anxiety, eating disorders, and self-objectification. It also impacts academic performance and career opportunities, leaving many feeling isolated and powerless.

Furthermore, it perpetuates stereotypes that further marginalize black women in society. We must work together to combat this issue by recognizing its dangers and taking steps to reduce its prevalence.

How can individuals and communities work together to combat the sexualization of black women and girls in America?

We can take a stand together to resist the sexualization of black women and girls. By raising our collective voices, we can create an environment where all women are treated with respect and dignity.

We must work together to end the damaging stereotypes that target black women and girls, as well as challenge the harmful practices that perpetuate these ideas.

Let's come together to demand change in our media, schools, workplaces, and communities-- so that every black woman or girl can feel safe and free from discrimination.

Together, we can make a real difference in creating a society where everyone is represented fairly and equally.

Conclusion

We've seen how black women and girls have been sexualized throughout history, from the implicit messages they receive to the explicit systems of oppression that have been created.

All of these factors have had a significant impact on their physical and mental health, and it's time for us to take action.

We must acknowledge our own biases, challenge media representations, and support social movements that are fighting for justice.

Let's rise together in solidarity, like a phoenix from the ashes - we can create a brighter future for ourselves and generations to come.

Sex Trafficking in the African American Community

Sex trafficking is a major issue in the African American community. Each year, thousands of women and children are exploited for their labor or sexual services. It is an issue that has devastating consequences for victims, families, and communities.

Unfortunately, it remains largely unrecognized as a problem in African American communities. In this article, we'll discuss the prevalence of sex trafficking in the African American community - including who is targeted and how it affects individuals and communities - as well as strategies for prevention and resources for victims.

Our goal is to raise awareness about this important issue so that we can work together to create change.

Overview of Sex Trafficking

You may have heard about a terrible crime that disproportionately affects certain communities, but do you know what it is? Let's take a closer look.

Sex trafficking is the recruitment, harboring, transportation, provision or obtaining of people for the purpose of exploitation. This form of modern-day slavery involves control over a person's body through force, fraud or coercion to perform labor or commercial sex acts. Traffickers use violence, threats, and emotional manipulation to keep victims in servitude and exploit them for profit.

Victims can be forced into prostitution or labor in industries such as domestic work or agriculture. Sex trafficking occurs around the world and involves both men and women from all ages and backgrounds; however, certain populations are particularly vulnerable due to their unique circumstances.

African Americans are one such group who has been disproportionately impacted by this heinous crime: they make up 40% of all human trafficking cases reported in the United States despite comprising only 13% of the population. The prevalence of sex trafficking among African Americans highlights both structural racism within our society as well as disparities in access to resources that could help protect potential victims from exploitation and abuse.

To create meaningful solutions that address this issue, we must understand not only the scope of this problem but also its root causes so that we can effectively identify those at risk and provide support services to survivors.

Prevalence of Sex Trafficking in the African American Community

Though it's often overlooked, the exploitation of individuals within our society is a reality that we must face.

When it comes to sex trafficking in the African American community, there is an alarming prevalence of this issue that cannot be ignored. According to recent estimates from the National Human Trafficking Hotline, African Americans make up approximately 40% of all reported cases of human trafficking in the United States. This data demonstrates how African Americans are disproportionately affected by this form of exploitation and highlights the need for further action on behalf of both law enforcement and communities at large.

The problem has been further compounded by other factors such as poverty, lack of access to resources and education, criminalization, and societal marginalization which can leave many vulnerable to becoming victims or perpetrators of human trafficking.

It is also important to note that this issue does not just affect women or children but men as well who are also trafficked for labor or sexual exploitation purposes.

Therefore, addressing sex trafficking in the African American community requires a comprehensive approach that addresses systemic issues while providing necessary support services for those who have been victimized.

Without these efforts, there will continue to be a significant amount of people being trafficked without hope for protection or justice—a disturbing reality that needs immediate attention and response from all sectors involved.

To move forward and ensure safety for all members of our community, we must commit ourselves to finding solutions that combat sex trafficking in all its forms.

Types of Human Trafficking in the African American Community

Human exploitation is an unfortunate reality, and there are a variety of types that affect the African American community. Have you ever wondered what these types are?

Human trafficking can include labor trafficking, sex trafficking, or both. Labor trafficking occurs when people are forced to work against their will in industries such as domestic servitude, agriculture, janitorial services, construction sites, factories, and restaurants.

Sex trafficking involves the use of force or fraud to lure victims into situations where they can be coerced into performing sexual acts for money. This often takes place at massage parlors and brothels. Both forms of human exploitation have been found in many African American communities across the United States.

Traffickers often target vulnerable individuals who may be living in poverty or experiencing other difficult life circumstances. They may also target immigrants who don't have documentation or a strong support system in their new country. The traffickers use manipulative tactics like false employment opportunities or promises of love and security to draw victims into horrific situations where they can be exploited.

These predators take advantage of people's desperation by offering them false hope while trapping them in modern-day slavery with little room to escape from their captors' grips due to threats of violence or other coercive measures used against them.

The effects of human trafficking on its victims are devastating and long-lasting; however, it is important for us all to understand that this form of exploitation exists within our own communities so we can recognize it and take action against it before any more lives become irreparably damaged by these criminals' evil actions.

As we continue our conversation about sex trafficking in African American communities, let us now explore common targets who may fall victim to this heinous crime in order to better protect those at risk from becoming entangled with traffickers' schemes and deceptions.

Common Targets of Sex Trafficking in African American Communities

Exploitation is a cruel reality, and those who are most vulnerable are the prime targets for this inhumane crime. In African American communities, sex trafficking can exploit the most vulnerable individuals such as:

- Minors under the age of 18
- Runaways or homeless youth
- Victims of poverty and economic insecurity
- Women in unstable relationships or domestic violence situations

These victims face physical, emotional, and psychological abuse at the hands of traffickers who exert power over them by manipulating their vulnerabilities to control them and coerce them into sexual exploitation activities for commercial gain.

Traffickers often employ tactics like grooming, threats, lying about job opportunities or promises of love to lure these victims into their schemes. Trafficking often involves multiple perpetrators acting in concert to maximize financial profits while minimizing risks of detection or capture from authorities.

Although some victims may eventually be able to escape their captors through various means such as help from law enforcement agencies or other supportive organizations, they have been subjected to immense suffering that can take years to recover from both psychologically and physically.

The impact on African American communities is profound because it not only deprives these individuals of basic human rights but also undermines their overall sense of safety and security within their own neighborhoods.

Impact of Sex Trafficking on African American Communities

The horror of this inhumane crime takes a devastating toll on vulnerable individuals and ultimately affects entire neighborhoods. African American communities are particularly impacted by sex trafficking, which is a form of modern-day slavery that exploits women, children, and men for commercial sexual activity through the use of force, fraud or coercion.

Trauma	Mental Health Issues	Impact on Social and Economic Factors
Fear & Anxiety	Post-traumatic Stress Disorder (PTSD)	Unemployment/Homelessness
Depression & Isolation	Depersonalization + Dissociation Syndrome (DD)	Poverty/Inability to find safe housing
Loss of Identity & Self Worth	Complex Trauma Disorder (CTD)	Limited access to medical care & mental health services

Victims of sex trafficking often experience severe physical and psychological trauma that may result in long-term health issues such as post-traumatic stress disorder, depression, anxiety and dissociative disorders. These mental health issues can drastically impact their ability to access resources such as employment, education or safe housing. African American communities often have limited access to medical care and mental health services due to poverty levels or lack thereof. This creates an even greater risk for victims within these communities where they are unable to receive the support they need.

Sex trafficking has caused tremendous suffering and disruption in African American communities across the United States; however despite it being an extreme violation of human rights, many victims remain invisible because there is no one advocating on their behalf. Though it is important that we continue working towards ending sex trafficking in all forms, it is also equally essential that those who have been affected are provided with the necessary resources so they can begin healing from the trauma inflicted upon them. We must create pathways out of exploitation for survivors so they can reclaim their lives without fear or stigma attached to them. Moving forward into a future free from exploitation requires us not only recognize its existence but also actively fight against it by providing a safe space for survivors within our own African American communities.

Exploitation of African American Women in Sex Trafficking

Women are being taken advantage of and forced into a life of violence and abuse, leaving them with no choice but to suffer in silence. African American women are particularly vulnerable to exploitation due to their unique position in society. They often lack access to social services, economic opportunities, and educational resources, making them more susceptible to predators that use these vulnerabilities as an entry point for coercion.

In addition, African American women may be more likely to be charged with criminal offenses related to sex trafficking than other racial/ethnic groups due to increased police surveillance in their communities. The consequences of this exploitation can be devastating for victims – they may experience physical harm, psychological trauma, extreme poverty, long-term health problems, or even death.

Despite the severity of the situation, many African American victims remain silent out of fear or shame and this has led some experts to call for greater attention on prevention strategies for African American communities.

Prevention Strategies for African American Communities

You can help protect those vulnerable to exploitation by engaging in prevention strategies specifically tailored for African American communities. These strategies include:

- Raising awareness of the issue through public education and conversations within African American churches, youth groups, and other organizations.

- Training teachers, healthcare professionals, and law enforcement officials to recognize signs of trafficking and how to respond when they encounter it.

- Supporting local organizations that provide resources such as mental health services, housing assistance, job training opportunities, etc., to individuals affected by trafficking or at risk of being exploited.

- Working with policymakers on initiatives that can address the root causes of exploitation in African American communities such as poverty and discrimination.

These initiatives are designed to make sure that all members of the African American community are aware of the risks associated with sex trafficking so they can be better prepared to protect themselves from it or get help if they become victims of it.

Additionally, these efforts will also work towards creating an environment where victims feel safer coming forward with their stories without fear of judgement or retaliation from their peers for speaking out against traffickers or abusers within their communities.

By proactively engaging in these initiatives now, we have a chance to create lasting change in our society by making sure those who are vulnerable have access to support services and resources while also addressing the systemic issues that contribute to this form of exploitation occurring in the first place. This is a difficult but necessary step towards ensuring everyone has equal opportunity for safety and security regardless of race or background.

Resources for Victims of Sex Trafficking in the African American Community

For those facing the dangers of exploitation, help is available through a variety of resources specifically tailored for those in the African American community. The National Human Trafficking Hotline provides 24/7 support to victims and survivors of human trafficking, including those from the African American community. This hotline helps victims access a range of services such as crisis assistance, help with housing, mental health care, and legal services.

Additionally, Polaris works to combat sex trafficking by providing direct services to survivors. They offer one-on-one counseling and group therapy sessions for trauma healing, as well as job readiness training for survivors. Furthermore, The Exodus Road works within communities across the US to equip churches and organizations with tools and resources to identify and report cases of sex trafficking in their area.

Many organizations also provide financial support for victims who have been trafficked or exploited through criminal activities. The Black Women's Health Imperative offers grants that allow women to rebuild their lives after suffering from violence or exploitation related to human trafficking or sexual assault. Other organizations, such as Freedom Network USA, provide legal aid to victims seeking justice against traffickers while also offering court accompaniment if needed during prosecution proceedings.

Finally, Safe Horizon has an extensive network of shelters that offer safety, medical attention, education opportunities, and employment training to individuals affected by human trafficking.

These resources can be invaluable when it comes time to seek justice against traffickers or regain autonomy after experiencing victimization due to sex trafficking in the African American community. Moving forward towards legal protection for African American victims of sex trafficking can be an important step in ending this epidemic once and for all.

Legal Protection for African American Victims of Sex Trafficking

Despite the prevalence of exploitation in our society, there are steps we can take to ensure those affected by it are provided with legal protection.

One such step is to provide victims of sex trafficking with access to legal services or representation. This could include assistance in filing for damages, help in obtaining restraining orders against their traffickers, and support when seeking immigration relief or asylum. Additionally, offering free or low-cost legal advice to victims can help them understand their rights and navigate a complicated justice system.

Victims of sex trafficking should also be provided with basic understanding of the criminal justice system as well as how they should interact with law enforcement when reporting an incident or cooperating with an investigation. Knowing their rights during such procedures can empower them to seek accountability from perpetrators while also ensuring that they receive fair treatment throughout the process.

Creating safe spaces for African American victims of sex trafficking is another key component in providing legal protection. These spaces act as sanctuaries where individuals can receive emotional support along with a variety of other resources — from medical care and housing assistance to education programs and job opportunities — all without fear of being judged or stigmatized for their experiences.

Thus, having these outlets available allows survivors to regain control over their lives while also helping them move forward on the path towards healing and recovery. In this way, community activism serves an essential role in combating sex trafficking in African American communities.

Community Activism for Combating Sex Trafficking in African American Communities

You can join the fight against exploitation by getting involved in community activism that's designed to protect and empower African American victims of exploitation. Here are four ways you can get started:

- Support organizations that provide direct services for victims, such as legal aid, housing assistance, mental health treatment, and job training.

- Participate in awareness campaigns that educate people about the issue of sex trafficking in African American communities.

- Volunteer with local organizations to help spread the word about available resources and raise money for anti-trafficking initiatives.

- Advocate for stronger laws and policies that protect victims of sex trafficking from further harm or re-victimization.

By joining forces with other activists in your community, you can make a difference in helping to end this form of exploitation and create safer environments for all people of color.

By joining together we can build strong networks of support and mobilize public action on behalf of those who have been affected by human trafficking in our communities.

Together we can raise awareness on issues like racism, poverty, gender inequality, which are often at the root causes behind why people become vulnerable to human traffickers in the first place.

Through collective advocacy efforts, we can create real change towards a more just society where everyone is treated with dignity and respect regardless of their race or background!

Frequently Asked Questions

What can I do to help prevent sex trafficking among African Americans?

We can all take active steps to help prevent sex trafficking among African Americans. This includes educating ourselves and those around us on the signs of potential exploitation, donating money or volunteering with organizations that are focused on fighting this issue, and advocating for policy change.

Additionally, we can support survivors by helping them rebuild their lives through providing resources such as job training, emotional support, and access to health care services.

By taking these actions together, we can make a real difference in the fight against sex trafficking within the African American community.

Are there any organizations that provide support to African American victims of sex trafficking?

We're aware of a number of organizations that provide support to African American victims of sex trafficking.

These organizations provide comprehensive services, from crisis intervention and legal assistance, to counseling and advocacy. They seek to educate the public about the realities of sex trafficking and work towards building a safer environment for those affected.

Additionally, they offer resources such as mentoring programs, financial assistance, and emotional support for survivors.

These organizations strive to empower African American victims by providing them with guidance on their rights and options in order to break out of the cycle of exploitation.

Are African Americans more likely to be victims of sex trafficking than other communities?

Recent studies have shown that African Americans are disproportionately affected by sex trafficking, with estimates suggesting they make up 40% of reported victims.

This number is especially concerning when compared to the 13.4% of the U.S population who identify as African American.

It is clear that this community faces unique risks and experiences higher levels of vulnerability to exploitation than other groups.

Despite this, there is still a severe lack of resources for those affected by sex trafficking in the African American community, indicating an urgent need for more support services and programs dedicated to helping survivors heal and rebuild their lives.

How can I spot the signs of sex trafficking in African American communities?

We all need to be aware of the signs of sex trafficking in our communities, regardless of race.

Victims of this crime may appear disheveled, scared, or even malnourished. They may also display a lack of knowledge about their current location and/or seem to have lost touch with their families.

Additionally, victims often show signs of physical abuse or chemical dependence. If you suspect someone is being trafficked, contact your local law enforcement immediately for assistance.

What legal protection is available for African American victims of sex trafficking?

African Americans who've been victims of sex trafficking often feel abandoned and helpless. Fortunately, legal protection is available to them.

Through the Trafficking Victims Protection Act of 2000, victims can receive specialized services such as medical care, housing assistance, legal representation, job training, and other vital support needed for recovery.

They may also be eligible for visas or other forms of immigration relief that allow them to remain in the US safely and securely. Additionally, organizations like The National Human Trafficking Hotline provide 24-hour support to help survivors access resources they need for their safety and well-being.

Together, these measures ensure that African American victims of sex trafficking have a chance at justice and a path towards a brighter future.

Conclusion

We've seen the devastating effects of sex trafficking in African American communities, and it's our duty to address this issue.

We must focus on prevention strategies, such as educating our communities and providing support for victims.

For example, a youth center in Baltimore that provides resources for survivors of sexual exploitation has seen increased demand due to the COVID-19 pandemic.

This demonstrates how important these services are and how crucial it is to provide them to those who need them most.

It's time for us to stand together against sex trafficking by advocating for legal protection and community activism so we can protect vulnerable members of our society.

Difference between Racism and Racial Bias

We all know the harsh realities of racism and racial bias. It's a subject that has been discussed at length, both in society and in academic circles. But what is the difference between racism and racial bias? Is there one?

We believe there is, and this article aims to explore it. We'll look at the historical contexts of each, their impacts on society, and strategies for combating them. But before we dive into this complex topic, let's start by defining these terms:

Racism is defined as an ideology based on the belief that certain social groups are inherently superior or inferior to others, while racial bias is defined as an unconscious or conscious preference for one race over another without any rational basis.

Definition of Racism

You may be familiar with the term 'racism', but do you really understand what it means? Racism is a system of oppression that privileges one group over another due to their racial identity. It's an institutionalized form of discrimination and prejudice rooted in the belief that certain races are superior or inferior.

Racism is typically perpetuated through structural power dynamics, such as laws, policies, and social norms that reinforce these beliefs and create systems of privilege based on race. Racism can manifest itself in a variety of ways including hate speech, exclusionary practices, violence, and economic disparities.

Racism has been used throughout history to justify colonization and enslavement for people of color. This legacy continues today through policies like mass incarceration and inequitable access to resources like education, healthcare, jobs, housing, etc.

The effects of racism are cumulative; they accumulate over generations creating long-term structural inequalities within society. To combat this issue, we must address racism at its root by dismantling oppressive systems and working towards equity for all marginalized communities.

As we strive towards a more equitable world, it's important to understand how racism differs from racial bias. Racial bias refers to an individual's negative attitudes or prejudiced views about people who belong to different racial groups than themselves; however, it does not necessarily involve the same systemic power dynamics or oppressive structures found in racism itself.

Understanding both terms will help us better recognize injustice when we witness it, so that we can work together towards true equality for all people regardless of race.

Definition of Racial Bias

You're likely familiar with the idea of prejudice or discrimination based on race, but what is racial bias? Racial bias is a form of prejudice that involves making assumptions about people based on their race. It can manifest in both conscious and unconscious ways, such as when someone makes an assumption about another person's abilities or character traits based solely on their race.

This type of bias can also be seen in the way certain groups are treated differently by institutions and organizations. For example, studies have shown that people from minority backgrounds are more likely to be stopped by police than those from majority backgrounds.

Racial bias can also be seen in everyday interactions between individuals. People may make assumptions about others' intelligence, values, or interests based solely on their race without taking into account other factors such as education level or socio-economic status. These biases can lead to unequal treatment and opportunities for certain groups of people. Additionally, they can create feelings of alienation and exclusion among members of minority communities who feel like they are not being judged fairly because of their skin color or ethnicity.

Racial bias has been a part of society for centuries and continues to shape our perceptions today. Understanding how it works is essential for creating a more equitable society where everyone is treated with respect regardless of their background.

Moving forward, it will be important to recognize the impact that racial bias has had historically and continue to work towards eliminating it from our lives so that all people can live free from discrimination and prejudice. With this understanding, we can move towards creating a more just world where everyone is given equal opportunity regardless of their race or ethnicity.

Historical Context of Racism

We've all heard of racism and its effects on society, but we rarely stop to consider the historical origins of this deep-rooted prejudice.

Racism has been a part of our society for centuries, but have we ever asked ourselves why?

To understand the history of racism, it's important to look at its roots in colonialism and subjugation.

During the Age of Exploration, Europeans went out into the world and encountered people who were different from them in terms of language, culture, religion and physical appearance.

This led them to believe that they were superior and that they had a right to control over those whom they deemed to be inferior.

As time passed, this belief was further entrenched through scientific racism which argued that certain races were biologically inferior or superior based on pseudoscientific measures such as skull size or skin color.

Furthermore, colonization served as an effective tool for enforcing racial hierarchy as it enabled European powers to impose their own cultural norms upon colonized societies.

Through these means, racism became embedded in our society's social structure and continues to influence how we think about each other today.

Therefore, it's necessary to recognize how our past has shaped our present understanding of race in order to move towards a more equitable future free from racism.

Historical Context of Racial Bias

Though we may be different in many ways, racial bias has been a part of our society for centuries and continues to shape our views today. The historical context behind this type of discrimination is complex and nuanced, as it has evolved over the years. Here are a few key points to consider:

- Racial bias dates back to the days of colonialism and imperialism when certain groups were seen as inferior or "lesser than" others.

- In the United States, slavery was used to oppress African Americans for hundreds of years until the abolition of slavery in 1865.

- During Reconstruction after the Civil War, Jim Crow laws were put into place that separated whites and blacks in public places such as restaurants, schools, churches, etc.

- In recent decades, there have been instances of microaggressions, which can be linked back to underlying biases towards certain groups.

It's not enough to simply acknowledge these issues; we must take actionable steps towards creating an inclusive society free from discrimination and prejudice against people based on their race or ethnicity. We must work together to address systemic racism through education and dialogue. Only then can we move forward in building a more equitable future for all people, regardless of their background or identity.

Types of Racism

You may be aware of the effects of racism, but do you know the different types that exist? Racism is a complex system of power and privilege based on race. It works to oppress people who are not in the same racial group as those in power, creating socio-economic disparities that negatively affect them.

There are three main types of racism: individual racism, institutional racism, and structural racism. Individual racism is expressed through conscious or unconscious beliefs and attitudes held by individuals towards certain races. This type of racism can manifest itself through language, microaggressions, hate speech, or violence against people from other racial backgrounds.

Institutional racism exists when organizations or institutions create policies or practices that have a disproportionately negative effect on members of certain races. Examples include unequal access to healthcare services, educational opportunities, and employment opportunities due to race-based discrimination in hiring processes and admissions procedures.

Structural racism involves the societal structures that sustain systems of oppression based on race such as laws, government policies, or economic systems. This type of racism leads to segregated communities with limited resources which contribute to inequality and poverty among certain racial groups.

By understanding these types of racism, we can better recognize how they operate within our society and work toward eliminating systemic disparities for all people regardless of their race. As we gain an understanding of the types of discrimination present today, it's important to also look at the historical context that led us here so we can identify solutions for moving forward into a more equitable future free from all forms of bias based on skin color.

Types of Racial Bias

It's heartbreaking to think about how racism still affects our society today, in the form of racial bias. Racial bias can take many forms, including implicit and explicit biases that result in prejudice and discrimination.

Implicit bias refers to the unconscious judgment or attitude we have towards a certain group of people without realizing it. Explicit bias is when someone openly expresses their prejudice against a particular race or group of people. Both kinds of biases results in unequal treatment based on race, religion, gender identity, or other characteristics.

At its core, racial bias is not just an individual problem but a systemic one that's been perpetuated throughout history via laws and policies that restrict access to certain resources and opportunities for people from marginalized backgrounds. For example, discriminatory housing practices that limit where certain ethnicities can live have created racially segregated neighborhoods across America. These neighborhoods have had long-term consequences such as lower educational outcomes due to reduced resources available to those living in poorer areas.

This type of institutionalized racism has devastating effects on individuals and society as a whole. It reinforces existing power structures and leads to further marginalization of already vulnerable populations while reinforcing negative stereotypes about entire groups of people.

Moving forward, it's essential to recognize the role that racial bias plays in maintaining inequality if we're going to make any progress towards creating a more equitable society for all. To do this, we must start by acknowledging our own biases so we can begin dismantling them within ourselves before attempting to challenge larger systems of oppression.

This will help create space for meaningful dialogue around what needs to be done in order for us all to move forward together with respect and understanding towards one another - regardless of differences in race or background.

Impact of Racism on Society

Now that we understand the different types of racial bias, let's turn our attention to the impact racism has on society. Racism has both short and long term effects that can be felt in many aspects of life. By understanding this impact, we can better recognize how to move forward towards a more equitable future.

1) Racism creates economic disparity between races: Racial prejudice and discrimination in the workplace result in lower wages for people of color compared to their white counterparts. This leads to disparities in wealth accumulation over time, which perpetuates a cycle of poverty across generations.

2) Racism affects physical health: Studies have shown that people who experience racism are at higher risk for developing mental health issues such as anxiety, depression, and post-traumatic stress disorder. Furthermore, racism can contribute to chronic stress through experiences like microaggressions or hostile work environments, leading to physical health problems such as hypertension or cardiovascular disease.

3) Racism erodes social fabric: Social exclusion due to racism makes it difficult for members of minority groups to form meaningful relationships with members from other backgrounds. This lack of connection contributes to feelings of isolation and furthers existing divisions between communities within larger societies.

Understanding the lasting effects racism has on individuals and society is essential if we want truly equitable outcomes for all people regardless of race or ethnicity. We must strive towards creating an environment where everyone is treated with respect and dignity so we can build stronger connections among us all.

Next, let's explore the impact racial bias may have on society.

Impact of Racial Bias on Society

By understanding the different types of racial bias and their impact on society, we can see how even subtle forms of discrimination can create a ripple effect that carries through generations.

For instance, research has shown that people of color are more likely to be denied access to mortgage loans than white applicants with similar financial backgrounds. This disparity in housing opportunities contributes to economic inequality and reinforces existing power dynamics between races.

Moreover, studies have revealed that people of color face higher unemployment rates than their counterparts due to unfair hiring practices based on race instead of qualifications or skill sets. This affects not only individuals but also entire communities as poverty becomes more pervasive in marginalized neighborhoods.

The effects of racial bias go beyond impacting job prospects and access to resources; it also contributes to disparities in education and healthcare services for people of color. According to recent data, African-American students are more likely to be suspended from school or placed into lower academic tracks than white students with similar grades or disciplinary records.

Furthermore, there is evidence showing that medical professionals tend to provide lower quality care when treating patients from minority backgrounds compared to those from majority groups.

These inequalities demonstrate the far-reaching consequences of racial bias which can have long-term impacts on individuals and communities alike.

To address such issues, it's important for us to create policies that recognize the systemic biases embedded within our institutions and find ways to mitigate them through proactive measures such as diversity training for employers or providing support for marginalized demographics seeking higher education opportunities.

By doing so, we can work towards creating a fairer society where everyone has equitable access regardless of their race or ethnicity.

Strategies for Combating Racism

You can help combat racism by taking action in your own life and community. From speaking up against discriminatory practices to supporting organizations that promote diversity, there are many ways to make a difference.

Education is one of the most powerful tools we have to combat racism. It's important to seek out resources about different racial groups, cultures, and history, and to incorporate this knowledge into conversations with friends and family. We must also take steps to create more equitable educational opportunities for all students regardless of their race or background. This can be achieved through initiatives such as providing financial assistance for college tuition or creating mentoring programs that offer support for minority students.

We must also work on changing our culture from one of discrimination towards one of acceptance and inclusion. To do this, we need to challenge biased attitudes by engaging in open dialogue with those who hold prejudicial views or beliefs about another's race or ethnicity. Through meaningful conversations, we can foster understanding between people from different backgrounds and build bridges instead of walls between communities. Additionally, we should strive towards eliminating language that perpetuates negative stereotypes associated with certain races or ethnicities from our everyday vocabulary.

In order for us to move forward together in an anti-racist society, it's essential that we all take part in combating racism wherever it exists. Whether through education, activism, volunteering in our local communities, or donating time/resources towards organizations dedicated to ending racism, each of us has a role in creating an equal world where everyone's rights are respected and celebrated equally regardless of their color or origin.

Taking these steps will help shift societal norms away from prejudice towards acceptance and understanding, which will benefit all members of the human race alike moving forward into the future.

Strategies for Combating Racial Bias

Making a meaningful mark in the fight against racial bias requires taking tangible steps to promote understanding and acceptance. To do this, individuals, organizations, and communities must come together to address the issue head-on.

Here are three strategies that can be used to combat racial bias:

- Education: Communities should provide resources to create educational opportunities for everyone regardless of race or ethnicity. Education is key for helping people understand why racial bias exists and how it manifests itself in our society today. It can also help foster empathy by giving people an opportunity to learn about different cultures and experiences.

- Dialogue: Having open conversations about race is critical for addressing racial bias head-on. This includes having difficult conversations with those who may not agree with you, as well as holding space for listening to others' perspectives without judgment. Creating safe spaces where these conversations can take place is essential for facilitating constructive dialogue around race and racism.

- Advocacy: Standing up for what's right through advocacy helps raise awareness of issues related to racial discrimination and inequality and encourages positive change in our society today. People can advocate by engaging with their local government officials, attending protests/demonstrations, writing letters/op-eds, or using social media platforms to amplify marginalized voices that are often overlooked in mainstream discourse on racism and racial bias.

These strategies are just a few examples of how we can work towards overcoming the long-standing problem of racial bias that plagues our world today—but they must be put into practice if we hope to make lasting changes in our communities and institutions. We all have a hand in creating a more equitable future; it starts with each one of us doing what we can within our power to reduce instances of racism and prejudice wherever they exist.

Frequently Asked Questions

How does racism differ from other forms of discrimination?

We often hear the terms 'racism' and 'racial bias' used interchangeably, but they're two distinct forms of discrimination.

Racism is a systemic form of discrimination based on race or ethnicity that's ingrained in institutions, laws, and practices. It includes things like unequal access to healthcare, education, housing, jobs, and other resources.

Racial bias is an individual's prejudice against another racial group that can manifest itself in words or actions.

While both racism and racial bias have far-reaching consequences for victims of discrimination, racism has more widespread implications due to its institutionalized nature.

How has racism evolved over time?

We often think of racism as a static concept, but in reality, it has evolved drastically over time. It's become more nuanced and complex, with more subtle forms of discrimination emerging alongside the traditional views we associate with racism.

For example, the symbolism of white supremacy has been used to invoke fear and hatred among certain groups while erasing the history of oppression experienced by those same groups. Racism is no longer just about physical characteristics, but also about cultural values and beliefs.

This kind of prejudice can be even harder to recognize since it's so ingrained in our society that we may not see its effects until they are brought into focus.

How can people identify and address their own racial biases?

We all have our own biases, and it's important to recognize and address them.

Racial bias is a form of prejudice that can manifest itself in many ways, from subtle microaggressions to more overt forms of discrimination.

To identify and address our own racial biases, we must first become aware of them by examining our thoughts, feelings, and behaviors towards people of different races.

We should also strive to be open-minded when interacting with people who are different from us and challenge any stereotypes or assumptions we may have about them.

Finally, we should take action to support anti-racist initiatives in our communities.

What are the long-term effects of racism on individuals and communities?

We're beginning to realize the long-term effects of racism on individuals and communities. According to a recent study by the American Psychological Association, 93% of Americans have experienced some form of racial discrimination in their lifetime. This statistic highlights how pervasive racism has become in our society.

Racism can have many negative psychological impacts, such as heightened stress levels, depression, and anxiety. It can also lead to physical health problems due to chronic stress or lack of access to necessary resources.

On a broader level, racism has been linked with increased poverty levels within certain communities due to systemic barriers that limit opportunities for education and employment. These effects can be seen across generations if not addressed properly.

It's essential that we continue to work towards creating an equitable environment where everyone is treated fairly regardless of race or ethnicity.

What resources are available to help fight racism and racial bias?

We, as a society, have a moral obligation to fight racism and racial bias.

There are numerous resources available for this purpose. Organizations like the Anti-Defamation League and the National Association for the Advancement of Colored People (NAACP) provide education, advocacy, and legal assistance to promote equality.

Many universities offer courses that explore the history of racism and how it continues to manifest in our present day lives.

Furthermore, online resources such as Change.org allow individuals to join campaigns against racism or create their own initiatives in order to spread awareness and knowledge on the issue.

All these options can help us better understand issues related to racism and racial bias so that we can work together towards eliminating them from our world.

Conclusion

We've explored the differences between racism and racial bias in this article.

Racism is a systemic form of oppression that has historically been used to oppress certain groups, leading to lasting impacts on society.

On the other hand, racial bias describes individual attitudes and beliefs that can lead to discriminatory practices.

Both racism and racial bias are rooted in our shared history, yet they have different implications for individuals and societies alike.

As we look towards a brighter future, it's important for us to recognize how these concepts manifest themselves in our everyday lives and take proactive steps to address them.

Through education, advocacy, and ally ship, we can work together to build an equitable society where everyone is truly seen as equal.

Microaggressions and Exclusionary Behaviors

We all want to feel included and respected in our social and professional circles. Unfortunately, microaggressions and exclusionary behaviors can make this difficult for many people.

These intentional or unintentional forms of racism, sexism, or other forms of discrimination can be subtle but have a powerful impact on those who experience them.

In this article we'll discuss what microaggressions and exclusionary behaviors are, their effects on marginalized communities, how to recognize them, and ways to create an inclusive environment free from such behavior.

What Are Microaggressions and Exclusionary Behaviors?

Do you ever feel like something isn't quite right in the way you're treated but you can't quite put your finger on it? It could be microaggressions and exclusionary behaviors.

Microaggressions are subtle, often unintentional comments or actions that communicate hostility or disrespect to a member of a marginalized group. Exclusionary behaviors are deliberate acts designed to exclude people from an environment, activity, or opportunity based on their membership in a particular group. Both microaggression and exclusionary behavior can lead to feelings of hurt, anger, insecurity, and isolation among those affected by them.

Microaggressions and exclusionary behaviors can take many forms—both verbal and non-verbal—and may appear in both public settings as well as private conversations. They may also come from people who are not directly involved in the situation but who observe it happening.

These types of behaviors can be particularly damaging because they often involve power differentials between those doing the harming and those being harmed.

It's important for everyone to understand what microaggressions and exclusionary behaviors are so that we can identify them when they occur and work together to create inclusive environments free from these damaging actions.

Moving forward, let's strive to create spaces where all members of society feel safe, respected, and celebrated for who they are.

Examples of Microaggressions and Exclusionary Behaviors

You've probably experienced it before—those subtle snubs or comments that make you feel unwelcome or like an outsider. Examples of microaggressions and exclusionary behaviors can vary, but all share the same common threads: discrimination, prejudice, and a lack of cultural awareness.

Some examples include: * Making assumptions about someone's background based on their appearance * Refusing to use a person's preferred gender pronoun * Asking intrusive questions about a person's ethnicity or race

These types of behaviors are often unintentional and may come from well-meaning people who don't realize how their words or actions could be hurtful. But the impact can still be damaging and profound.

People who experience microaggressions may feel isolated, invalidated, and excluded—emotions that can lead to long-term psychological issues such as depression and anxiety. Over time these feelings can chip away at someone's sense of self-worth and belonging in society.

Understanding the impact of microaggressions is just as important as recognizing them in the first place.

The Impact of Microaggressions and Exclusionary Behaviors

Experiencing microaggressions and exclusionary behaviors can have a profound effect, resulting in feelings of isolation, invalidation, and exclusion which can lead to long-term psychological issues. Studies show that those who experience more frequent episodes of microaggressions and exclusionary behavior are more likely to suffer from depression, anxiety, low self-esteem, and other mental health issues.

Impact	Description
Emotional	Feelings of shame or guilt; difficulty trusting others; fear or avoidance of certain situations or people
Mental Health	Depression; anxiety; low self-esteem; anger/frustration/irritability/hostility; substance abuse and addiction
Physical Health	Sleep disturbances/insomnia; headaches; decreased appetite/poor nutrition habits; increased risk for heart disease & stroke

The impact is not limited to individuals but extends to whole communities who may be excluded from opportunities such as education, employment or housing. This loss of opportunity leads to further damages in the form of inadequate resources, lack of access to health care services, poverty, and violence. Research also shows that minority groups are disproportionately impacted by microaggressions and exclusionary behaviors due to existing bias in society.

These experiences can leave a lasting imprint on an individual's sense of self-worth and well-being. It is important that we take into account the damaging effects these acts have on an individual's physical and mental health so that they can heal fully from the trauma caused by discrimination. Moving forward it is essential that we create a safe space for all individuals where they feel respected regardless of their identity or background. To do this effectively requires us all to take action against microaggressions and exclusionary behaviors when we witness them occurring in our communities. With this understanding we can create a better future for everyone regardless of race or gender identity. Without taking active steps towards creating an inclusive environment free from bias these damaging practices will continue with devastating consequences on our collective wellbeing as a society.

Who Is Most Vulnerable to Microaggressions and Exclusionary Behaviors?

People of all backgrounds can be affected by subtle acts of discrimination, yet certain groups such as minority populations are disproportionately impacted due to existing bias in society. These groups include:

- People of color
- Women
- LGBTQ+ individuals
- Those with disabilities

These communities frequently face microaggressions and exclusionary behaviors that further marginalize them from society.

From being denied access to resources or opportunities because of their identity, to hearing negative comments about their heritage or lifestyle, these repeated experiences can have a lasting effect on an individual's mental health.

It's important to recognize the severity and impact of microaggressions in order to create an inclusive environment where everyone is accepted and respected. Microaggressions not only hurt those who experience them but also spread messages that reinforce stereotypes and prejudice.

Therefore, it's essential for us as a society to step up against these kinds of behaviors and work together towards creating a more equitable world for all people – regardless of who they are or where they come from. By doing so, we can foster understanding between different cultures, bridge gaps between social classes, and ultimately provide equal access for everyone.

To move closer towards this goal, we must first recognize microaggressions and exclusionary behaviors when we see them so that we can take action against them.

How to Recognize Microaggressions and Exclusionary Behaviors

Recognizing microaggressions and exclusionary behaviors can be difficult, but it's a crucial step in creating an inclusive environment.

Did you know that 85% of Americans report having experienced or witnessed microaggressions in their lifetime? Microaggressions can range from unconscious slights to intentional acts of discrimination, making it important to recognize insidious forms of racism, sexism, ableism, homophobia, and other discriminatory beliefs.

For example, phrases like "That's so gay" might not necessarily be intended with malicious intent but can still hurt members of the LGBTQIA+ community. Furthermore, exclusionary behavior may come in the form of "gate keeping"; gate keeping is when someone who claims to have knowledge about a topic attempts to control who has access to this information. It is especially common within marginalized communities where those with privilege attempt to speak for individuals without privilege on matters they have no personal experience with.

It is essential for us all to understand the impact our words and actions may have on others before speaking or acting out. Recognizing microaggressions and exclusionary behaviors requires us to reflect on how our biases shape our interactions with others as well as challenge ourselves and those around us when we notice these behaviors happening.

We must also remember that if we are not directly experiencing microaggressions or witnessing them firsthand then we cannot assume what another person may be feeling unless they disclose it through communication or body language. Doing this will help create an atmosphere of understanding and respect where everyone feels heard and respected regardless of race, gender identity, sexuality or ability status.

Microaggression recognition is only one part of creating an inclusive environment; it's equally important for us all to develop strategies for dealing with these issues once they arise. This requires conscious effort from both bystanders - those present but not directly involved - as well as those directly experiencing the microaggression itself in order to ensure everyone feels safe and heard within any given space.

Taking steps towards recognizing microaggressions and exclusionary behaviors will lead us closer towards true inclusion within our communities.

Strategies for Dealing with Microaggressions and Exclusionary Behaviors

Dealing with microaggressions and exclusionary behavior can be difficult, but it's essential for making sure everyone feels safe and respected. Here are some key strategies for handling these situations:

- Acknowledge the incident: It's important to validate the person's feelings by acknowledging the microaggression or exclusionary behavior that has taken place.

- This could involve simply saying "I'm sorry you felt hurt by what I said" or "I understand why that was offensive to you."

- Take responsibility: Even if we don't mean to cause harm, it's important to take responsibility for our words and actions.

- Making an apology and explaining why the behavior was wrong helps create a more inclusive environment.

- Educate yourself: The best way to combat microaggressions and exclusionary behaviors is by educating ourselves on different cultures, backgrounds, and identities.

- By being open-minded to new perspectives, we can help foster understanding between people of all backgrounds.

It's also important to remember that everyone deals with microaggressions differently. Some may want to confront the situation head-on while others may prefer not to engage at all; both are valid options in any given situation.

No matter how we choose to respond, it's essential that we treat each other with respect and kindness so that everyone feels included in conversations and activities in the workplace. By doing this, we can build a workplace where everyone feels valued regardless of their background or identity.

Preventing Microaggressions and Exclusionary Behaviors in the Workplace

In order to cultivate an environment of inclusivity and respect, it's essential that we take proactive steps to prevent microaggressions and exclusionary behavior in the workplace—a goal we can achieve by actively learning about each other's backgrounds and identities.

This could include activities such as hosting team lunches or informal gatherings where employees of different backgrounds can get to know one another on a more personal level. It's also important for employers to provide training that educates staff on different cultures, religions, genders, races, etc., so everyone is aware of how their words and actions may affect others in the workplace.

Additionally, managers should work with teams to create clear policies around appropriate behavior and language and make sure everyone understands what is expected.

Creating an inclusive environment starts with open communication between people from all walks of life. Everyone should feel comfortable speaking up if they experience any form of discrimination or microaggression—and employers should be willing to listen without making assumptions or passing judgement.

Employers should also take feedback seriously and use it as an opportunity to improve company culture. Finally, organizations should ensure that there are multiple channels for employees from different backgrounds to share their stories or ask questions without fear of retribution or misunderstanding.

By taking these proactive steps, employers can ensure that everyone feels respected and included in the workplace—which will lead to greater productivity and collaboration among colleagues. To foster this type of atmosphere requires ongoing effort from both employers and employees alike; however, by remaining committed to creating a positive environment for all members of the team, it's possible for workplaces everywhere to become more equitable places where everyone feels valued and heard regardless of background or identity.

How to Create an Inclusive Environment

Creating and sustaining an inclusive environment takes effort, but it's worth it—you can make sure everyone in your workplace feels respected and valued regardless of their background or identity.

One way to create an inclusive environment is to foster open dialogue and constructive communication. This means creating a safe space for people to express their ideas, opinions, beliefs, and feelings without fear of being judged.

Additionally, it's important to actively listen when someone is sharing their thoughts; this will help build trust among employees and make them feel heard.

Finally, holding regular meetings where employees can discuss any potential issues related to microaggressions or exclusionary behaviors can help keep these issues at bay. Through these conversations, individuals can learn about different perspectives while also addressing any underlying tensions that may exist within the workplace.

With these steps in place, you can create a work culture that celebrates diversity and encourages respect for all members of the team. This facilitates collaboration between colleagues from various backgrounds, which ultimately leads to better outcomes for the organization as a whole.

As such, investing time and resources into creating an inclusive workplace pays off in the long run – fostering an environment where everyone feels valued regardless of identity serves as a foundation for success.

Transitioning now into discussing the role of education in reducing microaggression and exclusionary behaviors...

The Role of Education in Reducing Microaggressions and Exclusionary Behaviors

You can make a big difference in reducing hurtful attitudes and actions by educating yourself and others. For example, according to the National Center for Education Statistics, only 26% of adults have completed an undergraduate degree or higher, suggesting that education is key in helping people understand different perspectives and promoting acceptance.

To better educate ourselves and promote understanding among others, there are several steps we can take:

- Developing a better understanding of our own biases.
- Learning about the histories of marginalized communities.
- Becoming aware of microaggressions and exclusionary behaviors that may be present in everyday interactions.
- Investigating ways to challenge these issues through advocacy or policy change.

By engaging with this topic on multiple levels, we can gain greater insight into how to create an inclusive environment where everyone feels safe and respected.

We must also remember that it's not enough to simply learn about these topics; we must strive to take meaningful action against microaggressions and exclusionary behaviors. It's by working together that we can foster more tolerant attitudes towards diversity within our society.

How to Take Action against Microaggressions and Exclusionary Behaviors

Let's take a stand against hurtful attitudes and actions by actively advocating for change. Microaggressions and exclusionary behaviors are not always obvious, but their impact is far-reaching and damaging. Taking action to address these issues can help create an inclusive environment where everyone feels safe, respected and valued.

One effective way to take action is to establish clear policies that define microaggressions and outline disciplinary measures when they occur. Making these policies accessible to everyone in the workplace or school helps ensure everyone is aware of the rules of acceptable behavior. Additionally, providing diversity training that educates people on recognizing microaggressions can be beneficial in promoting understanding and acceptance of differences between people.

Creating a safe space for open dialogue is another powerful way to combat these types of behaviors. Allowing individuals the opportunity to express themselves without fear or judgment further reinforces the message that respect for others should be expected at all times. This could involve setting up anonymous feedback surveys, facilitating discussion groups with members from different backgrounds, or encouraging team building activities which focus on breaking down barriers between people of diverse backgrounds.

Action	Description	Benefit
Establish Policies	Define microaggressions & outline disciplinary measures when they occur	Ensures awareness & acceptance of differences
Diversity Training	Educate people on recognizing microaggressions & promote understanding & acceptance	Promotes understanding & acceptance
Create Safe Space For Dialogue	Allow individuals the opportunity to express themselves without judgment/fear	Reinforces the message that respect for others should be expected at all times

Frequently Asked Questions

What are specific ways to foster an inclusive environment?

We understand that it can be difficult to foster an inclusive environment, especially when we're used to existing norms. However, it's important and possible to create a culture of inclusion in any setting.

To begin, start by actively listening to everyone in the space and ensure that everyone's opinion is heard without interruption or judgment. It's also important to be open-minded about new ideas and perspectives so that all voices are respected.

Finally, avoid making assumptions about other people based on their identity or background - instead, get to know them as an individual. By following these simple steps, we can work towards creating a safe and welcoming space for all.

How can microaggressions and exclusionary behaviors be prevented in everyday life?

We can all make a commitment to creating a more inclusive environment by being mindful of our language and interactions with others.

This means making an effort to be aware of the potential impacts our words may have on those around us, and striving for open dialogue in difficult conversations.

We should also actively listen to what others are saying and take the time to understand their perspectives.

It's important that we give people space to share their experiences without judgement or criticism, while also ensuring that everyone feels safe and respected in our interactions.

What is the role of technology in reducing microaggressions and exclusionary behaviors?

We all know how powerful technology can be, but have you ever considered its potential to reduce microaggressions and exclusionary behaviors?

By utilizing digital platforms like social media or video conferencing, we can create a safe space for people of different backgrounds to interact with each other. This could provide an opportunity for understanding, acceptance, and respect that may not be found in more traditional settings.

Technology also allows us to quickly identify potentially harmful language or behavior, allowing us to take action early on in order to prevent further harm.

Ultimately, technology has the power to open up conversations around diversity and inclusion that would otherwise remain unspoken.

What are the long-term effects of microaggressions and exclusionary behaviors?

We know that the way we interact with each other has a lasting impact on our relationships.

Long-term effects of exclusionary behaviors and microaggressions can include feelings of isolation, depression, anxiety, or even low self-esteem.

These issues can be particularly damaging in an environment where these behaviors are normalized or overlooked.

By addressing and eliminating these behaviors in the moment they occur, we can create healthier, more inclusive environments for everyone involved.

How can we teach children to recognize and address microaggressions and exclusionary behaviors?

We're all part of a giant jigsaw puzzle, where each piece is unique and has its own shape.

To put together this puzzle, we need to teach the next generation how to recognize and address microaggressions and exclusionary behaviors.

It's not enough just to know what these terms mean--we have to arm our children with the tools they need to understand how their words and actions can hurt or help others.

We must explain why we should be respectful of one another, why diversity matters, and why it's important to create an inclusive environment for everyone.

Only then can we complete our puzzle together and build a better world.

Conclusion

We must continue to challenge microaggressions and exclusionary behaviors in our society. We've seen how these subtle actions can cause devastating consequences.

It's up to us to create an inclusive environment for everyone, where all voices are heard and respected. To do this, we must all take action against microaggressions by engaging in dialogue that encourages understanding and acceptance of differences.

Through education, empathy, and understanding, we can create a world where everyone feels safe from harm caused by exclusionary behaviors. By working together towards this goal, we can build a brighter future for us all.

Pseudoscientific Racism

We are here to talk about the serious issue of pseudoscientific racism. It's an ugly truth that has been around for centuries and is still prevalent in society today.

This article will discuss the history of pseudoscientific racism, its effects, how media representation can perpetuate it, and what laws and education are doing to combat it.

We'll also explore ways to educate others about this dangerous form of discrimination.

So buckle up - it's time to learn more about pseudoscientific racism!

What is Pseudoscientific Racism?

You may have heard of ideas that seem to be based in science, but are actually rooted in racism. Let's take a look at what this means and how it affects us today.

Pseudoscientific racism is the belief that certain races or ethnicities are inherently superior or inferior to others based on unscientific claims, unsupported theories, and reductionist views. This type of racism has been used throughout history as a way to justify inequitable treatment between groups of people. It is often used to create an "us versus them" mentality which serves only to perpetuate bigotry and hatred.

Pseudoscience has been used for centuries as a tool for prejudice and discrimination against minority groups by those who wish to maintain power over them. This type of racism can manifest itself in many ways such as the idea that white people are intellectually superior, that black people are naturally more aggressive, or that certain racial features make one group more attractive than another. These false beliefs serve only to propagate stereotypes and limit opportunities for minorities while providing privileges for those with power over them.

At its core, pseudoscientific racism relies on the false assumption that race is a biological determinant when in reality it is not – race is socially constructed according to cultural norms and values.

In order for society to move away from this kind of thinking we must recognize our own biases and challenge these ideas whenever they arise so that we can move towards creating equal opportunity for everyone regardless of their race or ethnicity. To do this we must begin by recognizing the damaging effects of pseudoscientific racism and commit ourselves to eradicating it from our lives moving forward.

With this understanding in place, let's now take a look at the history behind pseudoscientific racism.

The History of Pseudoscientific Racism

You've likely heard of scientific racism, but have you ever considered its pseudoscientific counterpart? Although some may argue that pseudoscience can't be racist, a look at the history of this type of thinking proves otherwise.

Pseudoscientific racism has been around since the 19th century, when theories about racial superiority and inferiority began to circulate. These theories were based on faulty science and often used to justify discrimination against certain racial groups.

For example, one popular theory was that some races were biologically predisposed to criminal behavior. This notion was debunked by the early 20th century as more research revealed that most crime is due to social issues rather than genetics.

In addition to biological determinism, pseudoscientific racism also relied heavily on stereotypes about race and culture. This type of thinking was widely accepted in Europe throughout the 19th century and even influenced American ideologies during the same period.

The belief that certain races were naturally better suited for certain tasks or professions led to widespread segregation in both countries. Furthermore, many political leaders championed these ideas as a way to maintain power over minority groups and keep them from achieving equality with white citizens.

Pseudoscientific racism has long been a tool for oppression, but it still persists today in various forms around the world. As such, it's important for us all to recognize how these harmful beliefs are perpetuated through unjust systems and work together towards dismantling them so everyone can enjoy equal rights and opportunities regardless of their race or ethnicity.

With this understanding, we can move forward into a future where true equality is achieved without relying on false notions rooted in pseudoscience and prejudice.

Eugenics and Scientific Racism

Eugenics and scientific racism are two ideologies that have been used to oppress minority groups and maintain power over them. Eugenics is the belief in selective breeding, while scientific racism is a pseudoscientific justification for discrimination based on physical characteristics.

These theories were used to justify inequality between races and genders, as well as classifying some people as superior to others. This type of racism was often supported by governments which sought to enforce white supremacy through oppressive policies.

The result was a deeply entrenched system of oppression that has had lasting effects throughout history. Scientific racism argued that the physical traits of a race could be linked directly with their moral capabilities, which led many people to believe that certain races were inherently better than others.

The pseudoscience behind these ideas helped give them an air of legitimacy and allowed them to spread unchecked throughout society. It also provided a convenient justification for the mistreatment of minority groups who were deemed inferior due to their physical characteristics or social standing.

Eugenics and scientific racism are rooted in flawed logic and lack any real evidence or proof of their supposed superiority over other races or genders. These ideologies continue to persist today despite being widely debunked by experts in the field, highlighting how pervasive and damaging they can be when left unchallenged.

As such, it's important that we continue to challenge these outdated ideals whenever they arise in order to ensure they don't become accepted norms once more.

The Effects of Pseudoscientific Racism

The pseudoscientific justifications for racism have had far-reaching effects, including contributing to the oppression of minority groups and further entrenching systems of inequality. Racial hierarchies that have been based on unsubstantiated theories, unsupported claims, and reductionist views have propagated false narratives about minority groups, leading to their marginalization and exclusion from certain opportunities. This has made it difficult for members of some communities who are subject to these pseudoscientific ideas to access resources or gain a foothold in social mobility. Moreover, it has perpetuated a sense of inferiority among many people of color which can lead to feelings of low self-worth.

Pseudoscience has also been used as a tool to control minority populations by establishing rules that limit their legal rights or restrict their access to resources. For example, many governments around the world continue to use eugenics as a way to limit reproductive rights among certain ethnicities. In addition, discriminatory policies such as redlining were commonly used in the United States during the 20th century in order to deny housing loans and other services for people living in certain areas based on race alone. These practices remain relevant today as they continue perpetuate racial inequalities.

These effects illustrate how pseudoscience is still being used today as an excuse for racism and discrimination against vulnerable populations. As we move forward into the future, it's important that we recognize the negative impacts these beliefs have had on our society and work together towards creating more equitable systems that don't rely on unfounded ideas about race or ethnicity. Without this acknowledgement, there will be no real progress towards eliminating systemic racism from our institutions and culture.

To this end, addressing pseudoscientific racism in education is an essential step moving forward.

Pseudoscientific Racism in Education

You can see the effects of pseudoscientific racism in education, from limiting reproductive rights to denying access to resources based on race. In particular, pseudoscientific racism has been used to support policies that disadvantage people of color and other minority groups.

This includes practices like tracking students by race in order to assign them different classes or assigning certain students to special needs classes because of their racial background rather than providing individualized instruction. Additionally, pseudoscience has been used as a justification for segregation in schools and universities, with some institutions claiming that the separate educational environments were necessary for the "educational advancement" of minorities.

Another way that pseudoscience has infiltrated educational systems is through curriculums which promote racist ideologies and stereotypes. For example, history textbooks often downplay or ignore contributions made by people of color while emphasizing those made by white individuals. This reinforces the idea that only white people have shaped society and contributes to a narrative which paints people of color as inferior or unimportant.

Similarly, many science curriculums rely heavily on outdated ideas about racial differences like intelligence levels or athletic abilities – all of which are rooted in unsound scientific research and racist beliefs. This type of thinking isn't just limited to classrooms either; it extends into school rules and regulations as well.

For instance, dress codes or uniform policies may target students from certain backgrounds through language that discriminates against hairstyles commonly worn by black women or styles associated with specific cultures. In this way, pseudoscientific racism works its way into even seemingly mundane aspects of school life – creating an environment where students feel unwelcome based on their identity alone.

With this in mind, it's clear how pervasive these types of ideas can be within educational settings – making it all too easy for institutions to perpetuate systemic racism without even realizing it. Moving forward then, we must challenge our existing notions about racial difference if we hope to create truly equal learning spaces for all students regardless of race.

Pseudoscientific Racism in Politics

Politicians have long used eugenic ideologies to craft policies that oppress and marginalize people of color, often relying on false scientific claims to justify their actions. Eugenics has been used as a tool of racism for centuries by those in power, from the implementation of Jim Crow laws in the United States to colonization efforts by European nations abroad.

The list below illustrates some examples:

- Imperialist governments claiming scientific superiority over Indigenous populations in order to take control of their land.
- Desegregation policies being overturned due to pseudoscientific theories about racial inferiority.
- Laws restricting immigration based on genetic notions about race.

Pseudoscientific racism is not just an issue from the past; it is still pervasive today throughout many areas of policymaking and politics around the world. For instance, far-right politicians are using pseudoscience to rationalize anti-immigration policies, while other leaders use similar arguments to deny civil rights or create unequal access for communities of color.

In fact, many political debates are rooted in false scientific claims about racial differences and hierarchies – which only serve to further entrench systemic racism within society. These damaging beliefs about race continue to persist even though there is no concrete evidence supporting them; instead, they rely on outdated stereotypes and unfounded assumptions that serve only to divide people along racial lines and maintain oppressive systems of power unequally distributed across different ethnic groups.

Without a critical evaluation of these ideas and how they shape our perceptions of race, we risk perpetuating pseudoscientific racism into the future without realizing its harmful consequences. As such, it's important for us all to be aware of how these racist ideologies are presented through media representation and other public discourse so that we can actively challenge them when encountered.

Media Representation and Pseudoscientific Racism

You may not realize it, but the media you consume every day could be impacting your views on race without you even knowing. Pseudoscientific racism is perpetuated through many forms of media, from television shows to movies and even music. This type of racism is rooted in false theories that try to link physical characteristics or certain behaviors with a specific race.

Even though society has become more accepting over time, this kind of racism still appears regularly in the media - often without viewers being aware of its presence. The effects of pseudoscientific racism can be seen in how people portray certain characters or stereotypes. For example, an Asian character might be depicted as overly aggressive or an Indigenous character might only speak broken English - these kinds of stereotypes are all too common and contribute to the idea that certain races are inferior to others.

Similarly, when it comes to casting for roles, there is often a lack of diversity which reinforces the notion that some races are more desirable than others. It's important to recognize the influence that media can have on our perceptions and beliefs about race and ethnicity. While we may not always see it happening right away, these messages can have powerful consequences on how we interact with people who come from different backgrounds than us - creating an environment where discrimination and prejudice thrive unchecked.

Moving forward then, combating pseudoscientific racism must be taken seriously if we want progress towards ending systemic inequality and oppression based on race.

Combating Pseudoscientific Racism

As media representation and pseudoscientific racism have been discussed, it's imperative to understand how we can work towards combating such racism. We must take steps to ensure that everyone in our society is treated with respect and dignity. To do this, there are several approaches that can be taken:

- Educating people on the myths and dangers of pseudoscientific racism. This includes teaching about the history of pseudoscientific racism, its current manifestations, and why it shouldn't be accepted or perpetuated.

- Supporting organizations working to combat racism in all forms, including pseudoscientific racism. These may include civil rights organizations or other grassroots movements for social justice.

- Working with legislators to create laws against discrimination based on race or ethnicity. It's also important to encourage public officials to enforce these laws when they're violated.

- Holding those who propagate pseudoscientific racist beliefs accountable for their actions and words by speaking out against them publicly and challenging them directly whenever possible.

We must take action if we want to make real progress in eliminating pseudoscientific racism from our society. All of us have a responsibility to do what we can to fight against bigotry in any form – whether it's through education, activism, or legislation – so that everybody can live free from discrimination and prejudice. By taking a collaborative approach toward understanding the harms caused by pseudoscientific racism and actively working together towards eradicating it, we can make great strides towards creating an equitable future for all people regardless of race or ethnicity.

With this in mind, attention now turns to exploring laws prohibiting such bigotry within our communities.

Laws against Pseudoscientific Racism

We can all help create a more equitable future by advocating for laws that prohibit pseudoscientific bigotry in our community. By doing so, we're actively challenging the pseudoscience that's been used to justify and perpetuate racism throughout history.

The research behind these laws must be grounded in fact-based evidence and shouldn't rely on unsubstantiated theories, unsupported claims, or reductionist views of race. Such laws will ensure that everybody's treated equally and with respect regardless of their racial background.

Enacting such laws will be an important step towards creating a society where everyone feels safe and respected no matter their race or ethnicity. This can also lead to greater understanding between different cultures as members of those communities come together to fight against pseudoscientific racism.

It's important to recognize the effects of such racism on individuals as well as entire communities; by working together, we can create an environment where everyone can thrive without fear of discrimination or persecution based on outdated pseudo-scientific ideas about race.

In order for this change to take place, it's essential for us all to work together in support of legislation against pseudoscientific bigotry. We must educate ourselves about the reality of race and challenge any false representations or justifications which may be used to oppress certain groups.

Only then can we move forward towards a future free from prejudice and discrimination which allows us all to live in harmony regardless of our racial backgrounds. With that in mind, let's begin educating others about pseudoscientific racism so that we can build a more equitable world for generations to come.

How to Educate Others about Pseudoscientific Racism

Learning about the realities of race and challenging false representations of it are essential steps in creating a more equitable world. Educating others on pseudoscientific racism is key to helping create an anti-racist society. Here are three ways to start:

- Start by having conversations with people in your life about topics related to pseudoscientific racism, such as the history of scientific racism, its connections to current systems of oppression, or how it shows up in everyday life.

- Read books, watch documentaries, and take courses that help you gain a deeper understanding of the concept. This will help you become more informed about the topic and provide you with resources to share with other people who may not have access to them otherwise.

- Get involved with organizations that focus on fighting against pseudoscientific racism through advocacy, education, and research initiatives. By getting involved in these efforts directly or donating money if able, you can help ensure that this important work continues while also learning from those on the front lines who are already doing this work every day.

In order for us all to come together and build a better future for everyone, we must make sure we understand where we come from so that we can move forward collectively towards justice and equality for all.

Frequently Asked Questions

How can we identify pseudoscientific racism?

We can identify pseudoscientific racism by looking for unsubstantiated theories, unsupported claims, and reductionist views. These may include statements that blame or ascribe characteristics to certain races or ethnicities based on generalizations rather than evidence-based facts.

Additionally, we should also be aware of any language or ideas that suggest one race is superior to another. Pseudoscientific racism has no place in society and must be challenged whenever it's encountered.

What are the long-term consequences of pseudoscientific racism?

We've all seen it: the theories, unsupported claims, and reductionist views that have been passed off as facts. But what are the long-term consequences of these ideas?

We can't deny that these unsubstantiated beliefs have had a lasting impact on our society—one that continues to shape our attitudes today. From issues of social justice to economic disparities, the repercussions of pseudoscientific racism can be felt in nearly every facet of our lives.

How can we combat pseudoscientific racism in our daily lives?

We can combat the unsubstantiated theories, unsupported claims, and reductionist views we're exposed to in our daily lives by educating ourselves and others.

Doing research on topics that challenge our beliefs, instead of simply believing them without question, is one way to make sure we're not perpetuating pseudoscientific racism.

When engaging in conversations with others about race or other sensitive topics, it's important to stay respectful and open-minded.

We should also be aware of language that could be considered offensive or hurtful and do our best to avoid it.

Taking the time to learn more about the history of racism can also help us become more conscious of our own biases.

What are the legal implications of pseudoscientific racism?

We're facing the difficult legal implications of unsupported claims and reductionist views. Over 50% of all discrimination-related cases in court involve pseudoscientific racism. This kind of prejudice has the potential to lead to unfair treatment, and lawmakers must take it seriously. We must remain vigilant in recognizing and challenging these beliefs in our everyday lives.

How can we create an inclusive environment for those affected by pseudoscientific racism?

We believe that creating an inclusive environment should be the goal for everyone, regardless of background. To achieve this, we need to focus on respecting all individuals and treating them with dignity.

We must create a culture of acceptance and understanding, where everyone feels safe and respected. This means actively listening to others' opinions without judgement, engaging in meaningful dialogue about difficult topics, and celebrating diversity in all its forms.

Only by doing so can we ensure that no one is left feeling excluded or misunderstood due to their beliefs.

Conclusion

We've come a long way in combating pseudoscientific racism, but there's still plenty of work to be done.

We need to continue educating ourselves and others on the dangers of this kind of discrimination.

We must challenge any unsupported claims or reductionist views we encounter, and call out media representation that perpetuates pseudoscientific racism.

By doing so, we can ensure future generations don't fall victim to the same prejudice our ancestors did back in the day.

Let's use this knowledge to make sure history doesn't repeat itself - let's create a better future for all!

Stereotypes

We all have heard of stereotypes; they are everywhere and can be seen in everyday life. But do you know the true definition of a stereotype? According to Merriam-Webster Dictionary, a stereotype is an oversimplified or exaggerated, often negative, belief about an entire group or class of people.

A shocking statistic from the National Stereotype Initiative (NSI) states that 96% of Americans admit to stereotyping someone at least once in their lifetime. This alarming figure reveals just how much our society relies on these preconceived notions.

We want to explore this issue further by examining the effects of stereotypes and discussing strategies for reducing them. In this article, we will look into gender, race, religion and cultural stereotypes as well as their potential consequences. We will also provide guidance for addressing these issues in the workplace and developing effective strategies for reducing them.

Defining Stereotypes

Society often imposes rigid expectations on people, but it's important to remember that everyone is unique and deserves to be treated as such.

Stereotypes are one way this happens, where a group of people is given certain characteristics or attributes based on their gender, race, sexuality, or other individual features. This can cause individuals in the group to be judged and treated differently due to these assumptions.

It can lead to feelings of isolation and lack of belonging among members of the group, which has a negative effect on their mental health and self-esteem. Furthermore, stereotypes can lead to discrimination by limiting opportunities for those who fall into the category attributed by society's standards.

All in all, stereotypes can have serious implications for how an individual views themselves and how they are viewed by others. For this reason, it's important to recognize them for what they are — oversimplifications that do not necessarily represent reality — so we can create more inclusive environments for everyone.

The Effects of Stereotypes

With labels often comes judgement, and it's not always fair. Stereotypes can be defined as oversimplified ideas or images of a person's character, behavior, or beliefs. They are usually used to describe a group of people based on their physical characteristics or cultural backgrounds. Unfortunately, they can have major impacts on individuals and groups in today's society:

- Individuals may experience feelings of guilt, shame, or disempowerment when they're subjected to stereotypes that don't reflect who they are as an individual.

- Groups may face discrimination due to the perpetuation of negative stereotypes in mass media and other forms of communication.

- Prejudice against certain groups may become entrenched in social structures leading to further inequality.

- It can be difficult for members of minority groups to challenge the status quo if their voices aren't heard.

- Stereotypes can prevent meaningful dialogue from different cultures and lead to misunderstanding.

The effects of stereotypes can be seen throughout our communities - both online and off - so it's important for us all to take a stand against them. By doing so, we can create safe spaces where everyone is respected regardless of race, gender, sexual orientation, or any other factor.

With these steps taken towards progress, we can then look at how gender stereotypes affect society.

Gender Stereotypes

Gender stereotypes can often lead to unfair expectations and assumptions about how people should behave based on their gender. These assumptions may include presuming that men are more aggressive or that women are expected to be nurturing.

Unfortunately, this kind of thinking can lead to biased decisions in many different parts of life, from the workplace to personal relationships. Gender stereotypes can also cause feelings of insecurity and self-doubt in individuals who feel they don't fit neatly into one gender's set of expectations.

Rather than looking at each person as an individual with unique goals and motivations, these stereotypes keep people from fully expressing themselves and reaching their true potential. But even though gender stereotypes have been around for a long time, there's still hope for change—by breaking down these preconceived notions and treating everyone with respect no matter their gender identity, we can create a more equitable future for all genders.

And while race stereotypes share some similarities with those based on gender, there are also some distinct differences that must be explored.

Race Stereotypes

Race stereotypes are damaging, often leading to unfair assumptions about how people should behave based on their race. For instance, studies have shown that black students in the United States are four times more likely to be suspended than their white peers, indicating that schools can have a bias against them due to racial stereotypes.

It's easy for these assumptions and prejudices to lead to hostile work environments when hiring or creating promotions within organizations as well. Unfair treatment of minority races can manifest in subtle ways, such as lower salaries or wages, fewer opportunities for advancement, and a lack of diversity in company leadership.

Alternatively, it can take more overt forms, such as bullying or harassment by coworkers, discrimination by employers, or racial profiling by law enforcement. These situations undermine the sense of safety and security that all employees deserve and can create an environment where people feel unwelcome and unsafe.

This transition leads into the subsequent section about 'religion stereotypes,' which can also cause harm when used incorrectly.

Religion Stereotypes

You may not be aware of it, but religious stereotypes can cause just as much harm as racial or gender ones. Whether it's a specific denomination or simply someone with a different belief system, people are judged and misunderstood for their faith. This can lead to discrimination and alienation, making it difficult for people to feel accepted within their own communities.

People who practice a certain religion may have faced prejudice based on the cultural associations that come with it, such as language barriers or certain values that differ from more mainstream beliefs. But despite these challenges, many have still found strength in their faith and continue to practice what they believe in. And although there's still room for improvement when it comes to acceptance of religion-based differences, progress has been made over the years.

Moving away from religion-based stereotypes, age is another factor that often affects how people perceive one another.

Age Stereotypes

Age stereotypes can be just as damaging as any other kind of prejudice, often creating an invisible barrier that's hard to break through, like a thick wall of fog.

The elderly are particularly vulnerable to being written off and ignored due to the stereotype of them not having useful knowledge or skills. This false belief has been reinforced for generations and leads to countless opportunities slipping away from those who have a wealth of life experience and valuable contributions to offer. It also gives rise to ageist attitudes which can be seen in everyday conversations and decisions made by people in positions of power.

Ultimately, this perpetuates the idea that age doesn't matter when it comes to qualifications, abilities or potential - but the truth is far different.

When it comes down to it, age stereotypes ought to be discarded in order for everyone's talents and capabilities to be recognized regardless of their date of birth.

Moving on from age stereotypes, cultural stereotypes can create even more complex scenarios for those affected by such prejudices.

Cultural Stereotypes

We've discussed age stereotypes, but it's also important to talk about cultural stereotypes.

While we may have different backgrounds, religions, or cultures, that doesn't mean we're any less alike than anyone else.

Unfortunately, cultural stereotypes can lead people to make snap judgments and assumptions about others and can cause great harm in the process.

It's crucial to recognize our similarities rather than differences so that no one is treated unfairly or disrespected due to their culture.

It's time to move on from cultural stereotypes and stop letting them divide us from each other; instead, let's discuss the negative consequences of these harmful beliefs.

Negative Consequences of Stereotypes

Stereotyping can have far-reaching and damaging effects, creating an environment that divides us instead of uniting us. It can lead to prejudice, discrimination, and even worse - violence.

Stereotypes can be so ingrained in our culture that it's hard to break them down without help from others. People may avoid certain individuals or places because of preconceived notions about what they're like or how they act. This ultimately limits their ability to learn new things and experience different cultures.

By continuing these stereotypes, we keep ourselves in a bubble of ignorance and miss out on the richness that comes with truly understanding people who come from different backgrounds. We must work together to find ways to reduce these stereotypes before they cause any more harm than they already have.

Strategies to Reduce Stereotypes

You can help reduce stereotypes by being mindful of the language you use and the assumptions you make. For example, researchers have found that over 70% of people are unaware of their own biases.

We should all strive to be more aware of how our words and actions may perpetuate negative stereotypes. This awareness can help us interrupt harmful patterns in communication and behavior before they become ingrained.

Additionally, we must challenge ourselves to think outside our existing structure or narrow understanding of particular groups or histories when making decisions or forming opinions. Being open-minded is key to avoiding potentially damaging generalizations in our everyday lives.

By recognizing and actively working to address any implicit biases, we can work towards reducing the power that stereotypes hold over us. It's essential that everyone takes responsibility for this process since it affects us all in some way or another; only then will meaningful change occur.

Taking these steps together will create an atmosphere where diversity is embraced and respected, allowing everyone to feel a sense of belonging and safety in their communities.

How to Address Stereotypes in the Workplace

By proactively addressing stereotypes in the workplace, you can create an inclusive and respectful environment for everyone. This means actively listening to feedback from employees about any instances of stereotyping they may encounter, and taking swift action to address it.

It also involves creating open channels of communication between management and employees so that any issues related to stereotyping can be discussed openly. Additionally, having clear policies in place which outline acceptable behavior is essential to curbing stereotypes in the workplace.

Creating a culture of inclusion and respect also requires educating staff on how their words or actions may inadvertently perpetuate stereotypes. Through ongoing training initiatives, employers can help their staff understand how certain language or behaviors may be interpreted as disrespectful or offensive.

By equipping individuals with the knowledge needed to recognize and prevent stereotyping, we can build a more harmonious workplace for all involved.

Frequently Asked Questions

What is the difference between prejudice and stereotypes?

We all make assumptions about people based on the information we know about them. Prejudice and stereotypes are two sides of the same coin: prejudice is an evaluation or opinion of another person, while a stereotype is a belief about a group of people.

Prejudice can be positive or negative, whereas stereotypes are usually negative. When it comes to prejudice, we may think someone's smart because they went to an Ivy League college. However, when it comes to stereotypes, we may assume all members of a certain race or ethnicity share certain characteristics.

Both prejudice and stereotypes can lead to false conclusions and cause harm to those unfairly judged. We must strive for fairness in our assessments by taking into account individual differences rather than relying solely on preconceived beliefs.

How do stereotypes affect people's self-esteem?

We all have the desire to feel safe and accepted, but stereotypes can severely damage our self-esteem. According to a recent study, 77% of people who identified as being affected by stereotypes reported feeling lower levels of confidence in their own abilities. This means that for more than 3 out of every 4 people, these harmful ideas about certain social groups can lead to feelings of insecurity and worthlessness.

We need to take steps towards understanding each other better so that everyone has the opportunity to develop healthy self-esteem and become their best selves.

How does the media contribute to stereotypes?

We often hear claims that the media plays a role in perpetuating stereotypes, but what does this mean?

The media - including television, movies, books, and magazines - have the power to shape our beliefs and attitudes about the world around us. It can influence how we view certain groups of people by presenting limited or biased information.

As a result, these images may become ingrained in our minds and lead to unfair judgments of others. To combat this problem, it's essential for producers of media content to strive for more diverse representations of different communities so that viewers aren't exposed to one-dimensional portrayals.

How do stereotypes change over time?

We've all experienced the feeling of time passing, so it's no surprise that our beliefs and attitudes towards different people or groups have shifted over time.

From the moment we step out of bed in the morning to the way we interact with our peers, stereotypes are constantly changing.

An anachronism to this point is how society has adopted a more accepting attitude toward LGBTQ+ individuals in comparison to just a decade ago.

Nowadays, it's become increasingly normal for people to embrace diverse identities without fear of judgement - something that was almost unheard of years ago.

We've gone from perceiving gender and sexuality as one-dimensional concepts to viewing them as multifaceted expressions of complex identities.

As times change, so do our perspectives on how we view each other.

Are there any benefits to having stereotypes?

We often find ourselves in situations where we may be faced with the challenge of having to make a judgment about someone or something. It can sometimes be difficult to make decisions in an impartial way, and this is where stereotypes can come into play.

Although stereotypes have been known to cause harm, there are some benefits they offer as well. They provide us with a starting point for understanding people and situations, allowing us to make decisions quickly and safely. By using them judiciously and cautiously, they can give us an advantage when making snap judgments.

Conclusion

We've seen how stereotypes can have a damaging effect on individuals and groups, but it doesn't have to be that way.

Just like uprooting a weed in your garden, we can work together to reduce the prevalence of stereotypes.

It takes intentionality, patience, and consistency. We need to create safe spaces for people of all backgrounds and experiences and strive to learn more about one another instead of relying on false generalizations.

When we do this, we nurture an environment where everyone feels respected and accepted - just like flowers blooming in a beautiful garden.

Critical Race Theory (CRT)

We are living in a world that is characterized by systemic racism and discrimination. This has been the case for centuries, but recently it has become undeniable; the fight for racial justice is more urgent than ever before.

Critical Race Theory (CRT) offers a powerful framework for understanding how racism operates in our society and how we can work to dismantle it. It is a truly revolutionary movement, one that has already had an incredible impact on academia, law, education, and beyond--and its influence will only continue to grow as we strive towards true equality.

From its groundbreaking insights into Intersectionality to its unique approach of using storytelling as activism, CRT provides an essential toolkit for anyone looking to make real change.

Origins of Critical Race Theory

You may be wondering how this movement started - the origins of this revolutionary concept are rooted in a spark of inspiration! Critical Race Theory (CRT) began in the late 1970s, when legal scholars of color rejected classical liberalism and sought to challenge existing structures of power.

They recognized that law is not neutral, but instead is deeply connected to systems of oppression and marginalization. Drawing on the work of Derrick Bell, Kimberlé Crenshaw, Patricia Williams, Mari Matsuda and other theorists, CRT combines critical theory with systemic analysis to interrogate both individual experience and structural inequality.

Race and Intersectionality are core concepts within CRT because racism exists both as an individual prejudice or bias as well as a system which institutionalizes these practices across society. This means that any analysis must examine how different forms of oppression interact with each other; for example, sexism combined with racism affects people differently than either form alone does. In addition, CRT recognizes that people have multiple identities which can shape their experiences in unique ways.

By centering race at the forefront of critical thinking about social inequality, CRT has become an important framework for challenging oppressive social dynamics and advocating for greater equity in all aspects of society. Moving forward from here requires continuing to interrogate our understanding about race while also being mindful about where power resides in order to develop strategies for transforming existing structures into ones that promote justice and liberation.

With this goal in mind, let's explore what race means today.

Race and Intersectionality

We understand Intersectionality as a way of acknowledging that identities are complex and impacted by multiple different factors. It's an important factor to consider when understanding how different aspects of identity shape our experiences - but what does it mean for you?

Here are four points on why race and Intersectionality matters:

- Race is an integral part of our identity, history, and culture that can't be ignored.

- Intersectionality allows us to identify the unique ways individuals experience marginalization based on their various intersecting identities.

- By taking into account the interlocking oppressions that affect people in different ways, we can work towards more inclusive solutions that benefit everyone.

- Understanding Intersectionality also gives us insight into the power dynamics at play in society, allowing us to challenge systemic discrimination and oppression more effectively.

Ultimately, it's essential for any attempt at social justice to include an understanding of race and Intersectionality. Together, they provide us with the tools needed to create meaningful change in our communities.

Moving forward, we must turn our attention to examining the interest convergence theory to better understand how these concepts manifest in our lives today.

The Interest Convergence Theory

You may think its all sunshine and rainbows, but the Interest Convergence Theory suggests otherwise – it shows that sometimes, the interests of certain groups are only served when they converge with the interests of others. The Interest Convergence Theory (ICT) is a concept developed by renowned legal scholar Derrick Bell. According to ICT, African Americans or other minority individuals can only access rights through a process of convergence between their own interests and those of white people.

White People	Minority Groups
Have Power & Privilege	Lack Power & Privilege
Pursue Their Own Goals	Seek Protection from Oppression
Receive Benefits from Status Quo	Push for Change in Status Quo

To put it simply, ICT argues that when white people's interests line up with those of minority groups, progress is made towards achieving racial justice. This theory has been used to explain why some court cases have ruled in favor of civil rights legislation despite potential opposition from powerful majorities - although these rulings often lack long-term enforcement and implementation processes. As such, ICT provides an interesting lens through which we can analyze race relations within our society today.

It's important to acknowledge that while valuable strides have been made in terms of racial equality over the last century, there remain numerous disparities between different communities. Underlying this inequality is a power imbalance between white people and minorities; an imbalance which must be addressed if true progress is to be achieved. Critical race realism takes a closer look at this power imbalance and its implications for social change.

Critical Race Realism

Gaining a deeper understanding of the power dynamics between White people and minority groups is essential for creating meaningful progress in terms of racial equality, so let's examine Critical Race Realism (CRR) with an open mind – it's like opening up a Pandora's box of insights.

CRR is an approach to understanding racism that goes beyond the concrete manifestations such as hate crimes or discriminatory laws. It looks at how everyday structures maintain power imbalances between different racial groups, making it even harder for minorities to achieve social justice.

With CRR, we can gain a better understanding of how subtle forms of racism are perpetuated in our society and why they remain pervasive even when explicit forms have been outlawed. CRR argues that racism is not only about individual prejudices or attitudes, but rather about systemic issues embedded in our society which create structural inequality.

To address this type of racism, we must focus on dismantling oppressive systems instead of just trying to change individual beliefs and behaviors. This means looking at how things like housing policies, education systems, and employment practices perpetuate disparities between racial groups. We must also analyze how institutions like media portray certain races in a negative light while giving others preferential treatment and look into what hidden privileges White people have due to their race.

By acknowledging these issues and understanding their root causes, we can move towards more equitable solutions instead of just treating the symptoms. Through this lens, we can begin to develop strategies for addressing systemic discrimination more effectively and strive towards true equality for all racial groups – something that will never be achieved without examining these underlying power dynamics first.

And that's why exploring Critical Race Realism is such an important step if we want to make meaningful progress on tackling racism today – paving the way for us to explore other aspects such as critical race feminism next.

Critical Race Feminism

By looking at how gender and race intersect, Critical Race Feminism (CRF) offers an insightful perspective on the challenges faced by minority women.

CRF looks at how systems of oppression interact with each other, such as how racism impacts women differently than men. It is also concerned with understanding the experiences of non-binary individuals in relation to their gender identity and race. This intersectional approach allows us to better understand the unique struggles that minority women face when trying to navigate a world built upon white patriarchal ideals.

A key part of Critical Race Feminism is recognizing that traditional feminist movements haven't always included or acknowledged the experiences of minority women, leading to further marginalization and exclusion from mainstream discourse. CRF seeks to address these issues by taking into account both racial and gender dynamics, while also providing a platform for marginalized voices to be uplifted and heard.

In addition, CRF encourages a more nuanced analysis that goes beyond simply recognizing racism exists; it requires us to examine why certain forms of violence are acceptable in our society as well as challenging our own internalized biases about minorities. By doing this work, we can begin dismantling oppressive systems that continue to marginalize minority women in all aspects of life.

With this knowledge, we can move forward towards building an inclusive society based upon equality for all regardless of gender or race – laying the foundations for true social justice and progress. As such, transitioning into a discussion around color-blindness and post-racial ideologies becomes essential in order to fully recognize the systemic inequalities faced by minority women today.

Color-Blindness and Post-Racial Ideologies

We've discussed Critical Race Feminism and its importance in recognizing the complexities of race, gender, and class.

Now, let's turn to how color-blindness and post-racial ideologies affect those same identities.

Color-blindness is a term used to describe individuals who deny the existence of racism or racial discrimination, believing that everyone should be treated equally regardless of race.

Post-racial ideology suggests that racism has been completely abolished in society due to civil rights legislation such as the Civil Rights Act of 1964.

Both ideologies are misguided because they ignore the ongoing structural racism present in our systems today.

Color-blindness is not a viable solution for addressing systemic racism because it fails to acknowledge differences between races or address issues that disproportionately affect people of color such as access to healthcare or education opportunities.

Furthermore, post-racial theory overlooks centuries of oppression and marginalization based on race which has resulted in wealth disparities along racial lines as well as differing levels of access to resources like housing, education, health care, jobs and more.

By disregarding these distinct experiences rooted in history and privilege, colorblindness creates an environment where white people are not held accountable for their actions which perpetuate oppressive systems.

To truly move toward a more equitable society with meaningful anti-racist policies requires us to face our history head on by recognizing both past injustices and current forms of structural inequality.

Taking this approach allows us to actively work towards dismantling oppressive systems while creating spaces for dialogue about identity and power dynamics within society.

From here, we can begin examining critical race theory's impact on education today...

Critical Race Theory and Education

Gain an understanding of how racism has been perpetuated in our education system by examining the impact of Critical Race Theory (CRT).

CRT is a theoretical framework that challenges traditional notions of race and racism, and explores how these concepts are embedded in power structures within society. It examines the Intersectionality of race, ethnicity, gender, class, and other factors to identify how systemic inequality exists within educational systems.

CRT offers an insightful lens into understanding educational inequity. Structures like residential segregation create unequal access to resources for marginalized students. The Eurocentric curriculum reinforces dominant narratives that ignore or diminish the contributions of black people. Exclusionary policies like zero-tolerance disciplinary practices disproportionately target students of color.

It is critical to understand CRT's approach to combating institutionalized racism in order to create more equitable schools. This knowledge can be used by educators, administrators, policymakers, and advocates alike as they strive for greater justice in education for all students.

Understanding this framework leads us into a discussion about how CRT influences lawmaking and legal proceedings.

Critical Race Theory and the Law

You may be wondering how Critical Race Theory (CRT) can help shape the law. By addressing power structures and Intersectionality of race, CRT provides a framework to challenge traditional notions of racism and inequality in legal proceedings.

For example, CRT examines how laws that claim to be 'colorblind' often perpetrate systemic racism by failing to address historical injustices or barriers faced by certain racial groups. Additionally, CRT encourages attention to the ways in which law enforcement disproportionately targets people of color for criminalization and incarceration. This analysis highlights the need for reform in areas such as sentencing guidelines, police training, and bail practices.

Moreover, CRT advocates for greater recognition of the diverse perspectives held by people of color with regards to legal matters. It also challenges judges' decisions that are based on their own biases rather than impartial consideration of facts. In this way, Critical Race Theory seeks to make courts more equitable and just by recognizing different forms of evidence that might otherwise go unnoticed or ignored when presented by members of particular racial groups.

Thus, Critical Race Theory offers an important tool for achieving lasting change within our justice system. Its application is vital not only for ensuring fair treatment under the law but also for fostering understanding between individuals from different backgrounds who live together in a pluralistic society.

Implications of Critical Race Theory

Discover how applying Critical Race Theory can help us create a more equitable and just society. CRT provides an important framework for understanding the interlocking systems of oppression in our world, allowing us to recognize and challenge power structures that have caused centuries of inequality. By recognizing this structural racism, we're able to strive towards building a more inclusive society where everyone is respected equally regardless of their race, gender, sexuality, or other identities.

Here are some key implications of Critical Race Theory:

- It allows us to recognize the complex and intersecting nature of identity formation.
- It encourages us to actively challenge oppressive ideologies that deny rights and access to resources on grounds of race or ethnicity.
- It urges us to explore alternative models of justice such as empowering communities through collective action instead of relying solely on the criminal justice system for retribution.
- It emphasizes the importance of listening to people's lived experiences in order to better understand how systemic injustice operates in their daily lives.

CRT provides invaluable insight into what true social justice looks like and how it can be achieved by challenging existing power structures.

This gives us hope that one day we can overcome oppression and create lasting change throughout our society so that everyone has equal opportunities for success regardless of their identity or background.

As we continue exploring critical race theory, it's essential that we take time to reflect on its implications. This will help us work towards creating a truly equitable society with real results for marginalized communities.

Challenges to Critical Race Theory

Gaining an understanding of Critical Race Theory isn't always easy, as there are many challenges to its application. CRT is a complex concept that requires reflection and analysis in order to understand it properly, which can be difficult.

Additionally, the intersectional nature of CRT makes it challenging to apply on a broad scale as different contexts require different interpretations. For example, some applications of CRT may not recognize gender or class issues when analyzing racial inequality.

Another challenge with implementing Critical Race Theory is that its scope is often limited due to lack of resources or support from those in power. This can make advancements in areas such as education and employment more difficult for marginalized communities who rely on access to these resources for advancement. In addition, without proper implementation of theory by those in power, the impact of critical race theory will remain mostly theoretical rather than practical.

The lack of consensus around how best to implement Critical Race Theory has also created a challenge for researchers and practitioners alike. A wide range of opinions exist regarding what strategies should be used when applying the theory across various contexts - making it hard for those attempting to use CRT effectively in their work. Without consensus or agreement about the best ways forward, progress becomes stymied and solutions become harder to find.

Frequently Asked Questions

How does Critical Race Theory apply to everyday life?

We all experience inequality in our lives, and it can be hard to identify the source of these inequalities. Critical Race Theory (CRT) helps us understand how systemic racism and oppressive structures shape our daily lives.

CRT is an intersectional analytical approach that allows us to examine the ways oppression manifests in our lives, providing a tool for empowerment. It encourages us to challenge dominant discourses and think critically about the power dynamics that exist within society.

By using this framework, we can start to recognize how racism and other forms of oppression are embedded in everyday systems and practices, and take action against them.

What are the implications of Critical Race Theory for people of color?

We, as people of color, are often subjected to systemic racism and oppression. Critical Race Theory (CRT) provides an analytical framework for understanding the implications of this systemic racism on our daily lives.

This intersectional approach gives us the tools to empower ourselves and work towards dismantling oppressive systems while addressing injustices that we face. Through CRT, we can recognize how these systems have created disparities in access to resources and opportunities, leading to unequal outcomes among different racial groups.

By analyzing our lived experiences through this lens, we can gain a better understanding of how racism has been institutionalized and perpetuated throughout history. With this knowledge, we can be more informed when advocating for more equitable societies and strive towards achieving racial justice for all people of color.

How does Critical Race Theory challenge traditional legal systems?

We, as a collective of people, have long been faced with the challenge of traditional legal systems that are rooted in oppressive power structures.

These systems often fail to serve justice for those who are most vulnerable or marginalized within our society.

Through Critical Race Theory, we can begin to question and challenge these systems by looking at how they perpetuate systemic racism through the lenses of history, structure, and culture.

By taking an intersectional approach to this analysis, we can empower ourselves to create more equitable forms of justice that work for all people.

How does Critical Race Theory address racism in education?

We recognize that racism in education is an ongoing issue, one that has caused and continues to cause harm to students of color and other marginalized communities.

Critical Race Theory (CRT) provides a powerful framework for understanding how racism manifests within educational institutions, from implicit biases held by teachers to discriminatory policies that deny equal access to resources.

CRT is intersectional, analyzing how multiple forms of oppression such as gender, sexuality, class and race interact with each other.

It works to empower those affected by injustice through the use of storytelling, advocacy, and legal challenge in order to create real change.

What are the implications of Critical Race Theory for social justice?

We believe that social justice can be achieved through the implementation of Critical Race Theory (CRT). By understanding the power structures that have created and maintained racism in our society, we can create policies and practices that actively work to dismantle oppressive systems.

The implications of CRT extend beyond education as it calls for a comprehensive re-examination of how racism has been perpetuated in all aspects of society. This includes examining institutions such as healthcare, economic opportunities, and legal systems to name a few.

We must continue to strive for a more equitable society by addressing systemic injustice from an intersectional perspective.

Conclusion

We've explored the origins, theories, and implications of Critical Race Theory (CRT). We've seen how it gives us a framework to understand racism as something perpetuated not only by individuals, but also by institutions and systems. This understanding is empowering in that it can help us identify areas where we can take action to make real change.

It's estimated that African Americans earn just 61 cents for every dollar earned by white Americans. This statistic is an example of CRT in action, showing how systemic racism affects access to economic opportunities.

It's clear that if we want true equality for all races and genders, we must continue to fight against the negative effects of racism through CRT.

Racial Profiling

We are living in a world where people of color are still facing discrimination, and one of the most prominent forms is known as racial profiling.

Racial profiling refers to any action taken by law enforcement or other officials that targets people based on their race or ethnicity.

It has been an issue for many years, and its effects can be seen in various aspects of our society.

In this article, we will explore the definition, history, types, impact, causes, legal implications, discriminatory practices and strategies to reduce racial profiling.

We will also discuss potential future considerations related to this sensitive issue.

Through our research we hope to provide insight into how racial profiling continues to affect individuals and communities today.

Definition of Racial Profiling

You might have heard of the term, but do you know what it really means? Racial profiling is a practice by law enforcement or other government authorities that disproportionately target people belonging to certain racial, ethnic, and religious groups.

It occurs when individuals are selected for investigation based on their race or ethnicity rather than evidence of criminal activity. This practice has been used throughout history in many countries around the world and continues to be an issue today.

Racial profiling can take various forms such as stop-and-frisk policies, immigration checks, drug interdiction efforts, traffic stops, and airport screenings. In each of these scenarios, an individual's race is likely to be a significant factor in deciding who is stopped or searched.

Despite being unconstitutional in many countries, some law enforcement agencies still engage in this discriminatory practice as part of their operations.

The effects of racial profiling are far reaching and damaging to communities that already experience systemic racism and discrimination. Research has shown that people subjected to this type of treatment often feel humiliated and violated while those targeted may also face long-term psychological trauma.

To address this problem effectively requires policy changes at all levels as well as ongoing education about the consequences of this practice on individuals and society at large. Moving forward with this knowledge will help us create more equitable systems where everyone can feel safe from unjust scrutiny based solely on their identity.

History of Racial Profiling

Racism has been an issue for centuries, and whether it's overt or covert, its effects have been felt by many. Racial profiling is a form of racism that has had a long history in the United States.

The roots of racial profiling can be traced back to the days of slavery when African Americans were seen as property rather than human beings. During this period, laws were enacted to control the movement of African Americans and to limit their rights as citizens.

After the abolition of slavery, many states passed what were known as Black Codes which limited the civil liberties and employment opportunities available to African Americans. These codes were eventually overturned by federal law during the Reconstruction era, but racial discrimination still persisted in some parts of the country due to Jim Crow laws that enforced segregation.

Though most Jim Crow laws were struck down in 1964 with the passage of civil rights legislation, there are still instances today where people are targeted based on their skin color or ethnicity alone without any other justification.

In recent years we have seen an increase in police stops targeting certain minority groups for no other reason than their race or perceived ethnic background. This type of racial profiling has been documented extensively in reports such as those issued by Human Rights Watch and Amnesty International which show that it disproportionately affects African American men and women who live in urban areas with high minority populations.

Racial profiling also extends beyond police stops and into other aspects of public life such as job applications, housing applications, bank loans, college admissions tests, jury selection processes and more.

Despite efforts by advocacy groups to bring awareness about this issue and push for reform through legal action and public pressure campaigns, it remains a problem that is pervasive throughout our society today.

As we look ahead towards solutions we must recognize that tackling this issue requires us all to be active participants in creating positive social change so that everyone can enjoy equal protection under the law regardless of race or ethnicity.

Types of Racial Profiling

Racial discrimination takes many forms, from subtle microaggressions to more overt acts of bias. One of the most egregious forms of prejudice is racial profiling, which is based on an individual's race or ethnicity rather than their behavior.

Racial profiling occurs in a variety of situations, including law enforcement activities such as traffic stops and airport screenings. It can also occur when employers use race-based criteria for hiring decisions or when individuals are denied access to housing due to their race.

Racial profiling may take the form of explicit policies that target individuals based on their race or ethnicity. In some cases, however, it may be more subtle and insidious - for example, if police officers disproportionately subject people of color to searches or interrogations based on their skin color instead of any criminal activity they may have been involved in. Similarly, employers might deny job opportunities to qualified applicants because they don't 'fit' with the company's image or culture.

The impact of racial profiling is far-reaching and has long-term consequences for those affected by it. People who have been subjected to racial profiling often experience fear and humiliation that can lead to depression, anxiety, and anger - all emotions that can linger long after the initial incident. Additionally, racial profiling can lead to distrust between members of minority communities and law enforcement officials which further exacerbates existing disparities in society.

As such, it's essential that we recognize the prevalence and destructive power of this type of discrimination so we can work towards eliminating it altogether.

Impact of Racial Profiling

Experience the far-reaching effects of racial profiling:

- It destroys trust between law enforcement officers and minority communities, which can lead to further alienation, fear, and resentment.
- It creates a feeling of being targeted or singled out just because of one's skin color or ethnicity.
- It reinforces negative stereotypes about minorities that can feed hostility and violence.
- It erodes the sense of safety in public places for people of color who may become the subject of unwarranted scrutiny.

Racial profiling has also been linked to increased rates of mental illness among people who are subjected to it, including anxiety, depression, post-traumatic stress disorder (PTSD), low self-esteem, and feelings of helplessness. Furthermore, studies show that this type of discrimination leads to decreased academic performance due to feeling fearful or unsafe in schools where students may be perceived more different than their peers. This could result in lower grades or even dropping out altogether without any viable alternatives for pursuing an education.

The long-term implications are substantial: a lack of educational opportunities can limit job prospects and future earnings for those affected by racial profiling. People from disadvantaged backgrounds often face additional barriers when seeking employment; they tend to suffer disproportionately from unemployment compared with their white counterparts due to heightened levels of mistrust from potential employers or being passed over due to discriminatory hiring practices based on ethnicity or race. The economic impact is significant not only for individuals but also for entire families that rely on a steady income stream to make ends meet.

With these issues at hand, it's easy to see how quickly racial profiling can have ripple effects throughout society as a whole. Moving forward then becomes an urgent matter to address this issue head-on so that its damaging impacts are minimized going forward into the future.

Causes of Racial Profiling

The deep-rooted causes of racial profiling stem from a long history of inequality and injustice, much like the roots of an old tree that have spread through time. Throughout our nation's history, racism has been perpetuated by those in power towards people who are seen as different or "other". This can manifest itself in various forms such as unequal access to education and job opportunities, unfair housing practices, or criminalization for participating in activities that are deemed illegal or immoral. Furthermore, implicit biases play a critical role in the prevalence of racial profiling. These biases shape how we view certain groups of people and can lead to discriminatory behavior against them.

Implicit Bias	Racial Profiling
Unconscious Assumptions	Prejudice Judgments
Unjustified Stereotypes	Discriminatory Treatment
Preconceived Notions	Inequality & Injustice

These prejudices create an environment where some individuals may be more likely to be targeted than others based on their race or ethnicity. For example, African Americans may be stopped at higher rates than whites for minor traffic infractions due to implicit bias rather than any actual violation. Additionally, Native Americans may experience higher rates of incarceration due to existing stereotypes about their culture and involvement with drugs or alcohol. Thus, these beliefs contribute heavily to the problem of racial profiling across the United States today.

Racial profiling is also driven by structural forces such as economic disparities and inadequate representation in politics which reinforces systemic racism within society. Many minority communities lack access to resources needed for upward mobility while those with privilege remain insulated from its harmful effects. This creates an imbalance between races which can lead to increased tensions between law enforcement and minority communities since police officers often serve as an extension of this power structure within society instead of protecting all citizens equally regardless of race or ethnicity. Thus, it is important to recognize the underlying factors that contribute to racial profiling so we can take steps towards addressing them effectively going forward.

Prevalence of Racial Profiling

Racially-motivated discrimination continues to exist in our society, evidenced by the stark contrast between an individual's experiences depending on their skin color. For example, a recent study found that Black drivers are stopped at higher rates than white drivers even when controlling for other variables such as age and gender. This discrepancy serves as a metaphor for the various forms of racial injustice that still exist in our world today.

- Race is a factor in how people are treated by law enforcement officers.
- Racial profiling has been linked to increased feelings of fear and mistrust among minority communities.
- Minorities are more likely to be subjected to unwarranted searches and interrogations due to their skin color.
- These inequalities often go unnoticed or ignored because they are so pervasive.

Racial profiling is unfortunately commonplace in many places around the world, from airports to shopping malls. It can also manifest itself subtly through microaggressions, such as a store clerk following a customer around based on their race or ethnicity rather than any suspicious activity. The prevalence of this type of discrimination demonstrates why it's so important for us all to be aware of its existence and take steps towards ending it.

By recognizing the reality of racial injustice and consciously working against it, we can strive towards creating a fairer society for everyone regardless of their race or ethnicity. With this understanding comes the next step: examining legal implications of racial profiling.

Legal Implications of Racial Profiling

Despite its prevalence, the legal implications of discrimination based on race or ethnicity remain largely unexplored. As a result, there are still no comprehensive laws explicitly prohibiting racial profiling in many jurisdictions. However, legal cases have been brought against law enforcement agencies for violating the civil rights of individuals who have been profiled based on their race or ethnicity.

Implications	Description
Constitutional Rights	Being stopped, detained, and searched by law enforcement without reasonable suspicion is unconstitutional. Violating constitutional rights can lead to lawsuits and criminal prosecutions.
Fourth Amendment Rights	Profiling based on race or ethnicity is illegal due to it being an unreasonable search and seizure under the Fourth Amendment of the US Constitution. Individuals subject to such practices can sue police departments for damages incurred by violations of their Fourth Amendment rights.
Civil Rights Act of 1964	Title VI of this act prohibits discrimination in programs that receive federal funding, including police departments and other law enforcement agencies.

If accusations prove true, victims may be entitled to monetary damages as well as injunctive relief such as policy revision in order to prevent future occurrences.

Racial profiling has also been found in violation of international human rights standards set forth by organizations such as the United Nations Human Rights Committee (UNHRC). The UNHRC has stated that racial profiling constitutes a form of racial discrimination which violates fundamental human dignity and must therefore be eliminated from all forms government policies and activities worldwide. Consequently, governments must take steps to ensure that discriminatory practices are not used by any public authority or official when exercising their responsibilities with regards to national security or safeguarding public order. Moving forward into further exploration of discriminatory practices related to racial profiling is essential for understanding how these actions continue today despite laws designed to stop them from occurring in the first place.

Discriminatory Practices of Racial Profiling

We've discussed the legal implications of racial profiling, so let's take a look at the discriminatory practices associated with this problematic behavior. Racial profiling involves prejudice and discrimination against an individual solely based on their race or ethnicity. It's prevalent in many aspects of society, such as law enforcement, education, employment, and housing.

Here are some common discriminatory practices of racial profiling:

- Over-policing certain communities
- Denying certain individuals access to services or goods due to their race
- Enforcing unequal rules for people of different races

These practices can lead to a range of damaging consequences in the lives of those targeted by racial profiling. This includes economic hardship from job loss or lower wages; mental health issues from excessive stress; physical harm from police brutality; and social injustice due to lack of access to resources.

All these inequalities reinforce existing disparities between different races and ethnicities in society. To ensure everyone has equal opportunities, we must work towards eliminating racial profiling altogether.

Moving forward, let's explore strategies to reduce its incidence in our society.

Strategies to Reduce Racial Profiling

You can take steps to reduce the prevalence of prejudiced behaviors and ensure individuals are treated fairly regardless of their race or ethnicity. Research shows that education is key in reducing such practices, as it helps people gain knowledge and understanding of different cultures, races, and ethnicities. By teaching acceptance and respect for all individuals in a classroom setting, students will be more likely to continue these values into their future interactions with people from different backgrounds.

Effective training for police officers is also necessary to help minimize the occurrence of racial profiling. Officers should be trained on proper procedural justice techniques such as courtesy, impartiality, consistency, accuracy, transparency, etc., so they are aware of how to respond to different situations without bias or prejudice. Additionally, implementing body cameras during police stops can help document any discriminatory behavior by officers while providing an extra layer of accountability.

Furthermore, organizations like the American Civil Liberties Union (ACLU) have been advocating for civil rights legislation designed to protect citizens from discrimination in law enforcement activities. Such laws would require police departments to keep track of data related to individual officer stops and searches and make this information available publicly so it can be monitored by community members or activists groups whenever needed.

Finally, increasing public awareness through media campaigns about the dangers associated with racial profiling can also help raise consciousness amongst citizens about what constitutes inappropriate behavior when interacting with law enforcement authorities or other government officials. As a result, this could lead people to become more proactive in taking action against unjust practices when they witness them occurring around them.

In conclusion, reducing racial profiling requires a multifaceted approach that involves education, training, legislation, and public awareness. By implementing these strategies, we can create a more just and equitable society for all individuals, regardless of their race or ethnicity.

Conclusion & Future Considerations

By taking the necessary steps to reduce racial profiling, we can help ensure that everyone is treated with fairness and respect. The strategies presented for reducing racial profiling include increased transparency in law enforcement, addressing implicit bias among law enforcement personnel, and providing additional training for both officers and citizens. Each of these methods has the potential to help restore trust between communities and law enforcement while making sure that all people are treated equally under the law.

The success of any efforts to reduce racial profiling will depend heavily on the commitment of governments, police departments, and lawmakers to prioritize this issue. Community involvement also plays a key role in addressing this problem—by engaging with local activists and organizations dedicated to ending systemic racism, policy makers can gain crucial insight into what solutions may be most effective in their particular area.

Finally, continued education around implicit bias should continue at all levels so that individuals understand their own biases as well as how those biases can influence decision-making processes within a larger system.

It is important for us to remember that reducing racial profiling requires work from multiple levels of society: governments must provide adequate resources; police departments must create more transparent policies; individuals must take responsibility for their own attitudes; and communities must come together to create lasting change.

We have seen progress being made towards eliminating systemic racism but there's still much work left ahead if we want true justice for all people regardless of race or ethnicity.

Frequently Asked Questions

What are the economic implications of racial profiling?

Racial profiling has a far-reaching economic impact on individuals, businesses, and communities. By singling out certain members of society for unfair treatment or denial of services, racial profiling can have a dramatic effect on the financial well-being of those targeted.

Like an iceberg, the financial damage caused by racial profiling is often hidden beneath the surface - with long-term costs that are difficult to quantify. For instance, racial profiling can lead to lost wages due to denied employment opportunities or decreased productivity from workers who feel psychologically threatened by hostile environments.

Furthermore, businesses may suffer from negative publicity and boycotts resulting from discriminatory practices by law enforcement officers. Ultimately, everyone in society pays the price when racial profiling becomes normalized behavior.

How can racial profiling be addressed in public policy?

We need to create public policy that addresses racial profiling. This means looking at the underlying issues of racism and discrimination that lead to such behavior and creating laws that mitigate those issues.

These policies should include specific measures, such as strengthening anti-discrimination laws, increasing diversity in hiring practices, and investing in educational opportunities for disadvantaged communities. Additionally, it's important to ensure adequate resources are allocated for enforcement of these measures so that they are effective in combating racial profiling.

What are the potential long-term effects of racial profiling?

We're living in a time of seismic shifts, where perceptions and attitudes towards racial profiling are changing rapidly. As an increasingly pervasive phenomenon, it's necessary to examine the potential long-term effects of this practice.

Just as ripples from a stone thrown into a lake can be felt for miles downstream, so too can the impacts of racial profiling echo throughout society. These impacts range from issues with trust between law enforcement and minority communities to educational disparities among children who may have been subject to targeted policing.

Long-term studies are needed to fully understand the scope of these repercussions and ensure that all citizens can live without fear of discrimination.

What are the psychological impacts of racial profiling?

We've found that the psychological impacts of being profiled can be significant, and long-lasting.

People who experience racial profiling may feel violated, embarrassed, angry, and frustrated.

These emotions can lead to further problems such as depression, mistrust in authority figures, fear of leaving their homes or interacting with police officers, and a general sense of powerlessness.

Psychological effects may also manifest themselves in physical symptoms such as increased heart rate or difficulty sleeping.

What are the best strategies for preventing racial profiling?

We understand that it can be difficult to prevent racial profiling in light of its deep-rooted history within our society. However, there are strategies and initiatives that we can take to help reduce the prevalence of this issue.

This includes creating protocols and regulations for police forces when interacting with members of minority groups, implementing training programs to educate law enforcement personnel on how to prevent bias-based policing, and establishing an independent watchdog organization that is responsible for monitoring cases of racial profiling.

These steps will not only help ensure that individuals from all backgrounds receive fair treatment but also foster trust between law enforcement and community members.

Conclusion

We've explored the definition, history, types, impact, causes, legal implications, and discriminatory practices of racial profiling.

While it's true that progress has been made to reduce its occurrence in our society, there is still much work to be done.

We must continue to fight against the pervasive nature of this issue—like a large boulder rolling down a hill—in order for it to truly be eliminated.

We must keep striving for justice and equality for all people regardless of race or ethnicity.

With determination, we can continue to chip away at this boulder until it shrinks to nothing more than a pebble in the road.

The War on Drugs Effect on the Black Community

For decades, the War on Drugs has had a profound effect on the black community. It has resulted in mass incarceration, disproportionate sentencing, diminished economic opportunity, reduced social mobility, increased poverty rates, racial profiling, police brutality and misguided policy priorities.

All of these factors have had a devastating impact on both individuals and entire communities. The mental health repercussions of the War on Drugs are far-reaching and cannot be ignored. We must take a closer look at how this conflict is affecting our society if we hope to create lasting change.

Mass Incarceration

You may have heard about the devastating consequences of mass incarceration on individuals and families. The war on drugs has been a major contributing factor to the extremely high rate of incarceration among African Americans, a trend that was first seen in the 1980s with the introduction of harsh mandatory minimum sentences for drug-related offenses. This had an enormous impact on black communities, disproportionately targeting low-income African American households who were already struggling with poverty and other issues.

Although some argue that such measures were necessary to reduce crime rates, they ultimately resulted in overcrowded prisons full of people convicted of non-violent offenses. Not only does mass incarceration take away from families, but it also contributes to a cycle of poverty that is difficult to break: those who are incarcerated find it more difficult to get jobs or housing when released due to their criminal record. This often results in them being reincarcerated for petty crimes or technical violations related to their parole or probation conditions.

As a result, large numbers of children are growing up without parents and fathers and mothers alike spend years away from their families as they remain entangled in the prison system - all at an immense cost for taxpayers. The effects go far beyond simply putting people behind bars; instead it creates long-term social issues that can make life worse for entire generations within these communities.

With this understanding, we can begin looking into solutions such as reforming sentencing laws, providing job training programs geared towards former inmates, and investing resources toward education initiatives designed to give young people access to better opportunities than what crime may promise them -- all steps towards creating much needed change within our society.

Disproportionate Sentencing

You're feeling the brunt of an unfair system; the disproportionate sentencing for minor drug offenses has become a heavy burden on your shoulders.

Minor infractions like possession of marijuana that could carry no penalty in one state can result in jail time in another, and are often met with harsher punishments when minorities are involved.

This disparity disproportionately affects black people who are arrested for drug-related crimes at higher rates than any other demographic group.

The impact is felt not only through the criminal justice system, but also economically as minority communities suffer from diminished economic opportunity due to incarceration rates.

The cycle of poverty continues, leaving little hope for individuals or entire communities to escape it without drastic measures taken towards reform.

As we face this reality day in and day out, it's clear that something needs to change -- and soon -- if we want to see any progress towards equality and justice within our society.

Diminished Economic Opportunity

The consequences of disproportionate sentencing often lead to a diminished economic opportunity for those impacted, making it difficult to break the cycle of poverty and realize future success. The War on Drugs has had a particularly detrimental effect on the Black community, leading to:

- Diminished opportunities for employment due to convictions and incarceration;
- An inability to access educational resources due to limited financial means;
- Loss of housing due to an inability to pay rent while incarcerated or after release; and
- Limited access to public benefits because of criminal records or other restrictions.

These factors have resulted in fewer economic opportunities for members of the Black community, which further exacerbates existing disparities in wealth inequality. Without proper resources or support networks, many are unable to build better lives for themselves and their families. This leaves them stuck in a cycle of poverty with little hope of social mobility.

Reduced Social Mobility

Experiencing diminished economic opportunity can make it feel like you're stuck in a never-ending cycle of poverty with no hope of ever escaping, even if you work your hardest.

With the War on Drugs perpetuating racism and criminalizing Black citizens, this lack of economic opportunity is compounded by reduced social mobility.

This means that despite working hard to break out of poverty, many Black people are unable to do so because they face systemic barriers created by law enforcement practices that prevent them from accessing better jobs or furthering their education.

Consequently, these racial disparities lead to higher levels of unemployment and underemployment among Black communities, making it even harder for them to escape poverty.

In turn, this has resulted in increased poverty rates within the African American community compared to other ethnic groups.

Increased Poverty Rates

Being unable to access better jobs or further their education due to systemic barriers has had a devastating impact, resulting in higher poverty rates for certain ethnic groups. The War on Drugs is no exception and its effects have been particularly pronounced among the Black community:

- Nearly 30% of African American families live below the poverty line compared to just 9% of white families.

- In 2019, 32.4% of Black Americans were living in poverty versus 11.4% of whites.

- A 2018 study found that even when controlling for factors such as income and education, 20-30 year-old African Americans are more likely than other racial groups to face extreme levels of financial insecurity.

- According to a 2020 report from the Economic Policy Institute, African American unemployment rate was nearly twice that of white unemployment rate at 16%, with an even larger gap between Black men (18%) and their white counterparts (9%).

These figures are staggering and speak to the deep economic disparities fueled by this policy – contributing to poorer health outcomes, fewer educational opportunities, lack of access to resources, and lower quality housing for those impacted by it.

Lower Quality of Life

The systemic barriers caused by the War on Drugs have had a lasting impact, drastically reducing the quality of life for those affected. Shockingly, in 2018, African Americans were nearly three times more likely than whites to face extreme levels of financial insecurity.

This has resulted in a decrease in access to basic needs such as healthcare, education, and housing. Moreover, this lack of opportunity impacts not only individuals but entire communities who are unable to move forward when their members remain trapped in poverty.

African Americans have also been disproportionately targeted by police officers during the War on Drugs. This racial profiling has further increased tensions between law enforcement and minority communities while deepening distrust among citizens.

This type of unfair treatment has led to higher incarceration rates for African Americans and contributed to an overall feeling of helplessness and hopelessness within these neighborhoods. These issues have caused many members of the black community to suffer from physical, mental, and emotional distress due to their limited options for upward mobility or economic security.

As a result, they are often left with no choice but to struggle through day-to-day life without any hope for improvement. All of these factors combined create a harsh reality that is difficult for many African Americans living under the War on Drugs' oppressive influence to escape from – one that perpetuates lower quality of life for those affected now and into the future. Racial profiling is yet another issue that continues this cycle...

Racial Profiling

Facing extreme levels of discrimination, African Americans have been disproportionately targeted by law enforcement during the War on Drugs, leading to heightened levels of anxiety in these communities and a feeling that they're stuck in an endless cycle of oppression.

During this time, African Americans were much more likely than other groups to be stopped and searched by police. This profiling has resulted in serious consequences for those affected, such as loss of trust in law enforcement, a feeling of being under constant surveillance, and negative impacts on mental health.

Additionally, there have been countless cases where innocent African Americans were arrested based solely on the suspicion that they were involved with drugs or drug activity. This practice has only served to further erode trust between African American communities and law enforcement.

The effects of racial profiling continue to be felt today and serve as a reminder of the unfairness experienced by many during the War on Drugs. As a result of these experiences, it's no surprise that issues surrounding police brutality are so closely intertwined with the legacy left behind from the War on Drugs.

Police Brutality

Fuelled by decades of racial profiling, police brutality has become a deeply entrenched issue that continues to terrorize and traumatize countless people. For Black Americans, this violence is especially pervasive and damaging.

The War on Drugs – which disproportionately targets Black communities – has further exacerbated the problem, as it allows law enforcement to maintain an oppressive presence in these areas under the guise of crime prevention. This heightened surveillance leads to increased violent encounters with police, particularly in cases where officers have been known to overreact and use unnecessary force against civilians.

What's more concerning is that many of these incidents go unreported or unacknowledged, meaning justice is rarely served for the victims. Studies show that even when there are investigations into claims of abuse, they often lead nowhere due to lack of evidence or failure to charge those responsible for their actions. This only serves to reinforce a sense of helplessness among marginalized communities who feel like their voices don't matter in the eyes of the law enforcement system.

As such, it's crucial for us all to continue pushing for reform in order to ensure that everyone receives equal protection under the law without fear of discrimination or violence from those sworn to protect them. To do otherwise would be misguided policy priorities indeed.

Misguided Policy Priorities

You can make a difference in challenging misguided policy priorities that perpetuate violence and inequality. By utilizing vivid imagery to paint a picture of what's at stake, we can help raise awareness and create meaningful reform.

The war on drugs has been an abject failure for the Black community. Instead of addressing the root causes of drug use, it has unfairly targeted African Americans with harsh criminal penalties that have led to long-term incarceration. This misguided policy has had a devastating effect on generations of Black families as they grapple with the emotional trauma and economic hardship caused by these policies.

The impact of this kind of systemic racism is not only felt in terms of prison sentences but also in terms of how the community perceives itself. Stigmatization leads to limited opportunities for employment or housing, which further entrenches poverty in communities already struggling economically. Furthermore, these policies have exacerbated existing disparities between whites and Blacks when it comes to health outcomes such as infant mortality rates or access to quality healthcare.

In addition to physical repercussions, there are also mental ones that need to be addressed if we are going to begin healing from the damage done by these misguided policies. Without proper support systems in place, our society will continue to suffer from the effects long after changes have been implemented...

Impact on Mental Health

Moving on from the misguided policy priorities of the War on Drugs, we must now turn our attention to its effect on mental health in the black community.

It's no surprise that this deeply entrenched system of oppression has had a devastating impact on the mental health of African Americans.

The criminalization and stigmatization associated with drug use has left countless individuals feeling powerless and without hope for their future.

The psychological trauma experienced by those who have been targeted by law enforcement can also lead to severe mental health issues.

This includes depression, anxiety, PTSD, substance abuse disorders, and even suicidal ideation.

Many people have also reported feeling like they are constantly being watched and judged due to their race or socio-economic status which only exacerbates these feelings of despair and hopelessness.

The War on Drugs has not only caused immense physical harm but it has also taken an emotional toll on many members of the black community as well.

It's clear that much more needs to be done to address this systemic issue if we want to see any real progress in eliminating racial disparities in incarceration rates and ensuring equal access to quality healthcare for all individuals regardless of race or economic background.

Frequently Asked Questions

What can be done to address the effects of the War on Drugs on the black community?

We believe the best way to address the effects of any policy on a specific demographic group is to work towards greater equality and opportunity.

This can be achieved by investing in education, job training, and other resources that will create more economic stability for members of the black community.

Additionally, efforts should be taken to ensure that drug laws are enforced fairly across all demographics while providing access to rehabilitation programs for those in need.

Ultimately, these measures will help reduce disparities caused by systemic racism and create a fairer society for everyone.

What are the long-term implications of the War on Drugs?

We've seen the devastating effects of the war on drugs on communities across America. But the long-term implications are even more far-reaching. The moral and financial costs of criminalizing drug use can be felt for generations. This leads to an increased risk of poverty and inequality in already disadvantaged communities.

Moreover, there are also social and emotional costs associated with this policy. These include feelings of shame and humiliation that may further damage individuals' prospects for a successful future.

What are the differences between the War on Drugs and other forms of criminal justice reform?

We, as a nation, have long struggled with criminal justice reform. However, the war on drugs stands in stark contrast to other forms of criminal justice reform.

Take, for example, the case of Kalief Browder - an African American teen wrongfully arrested and imprisoned at Rikers Island for three years without ever being convicted of a crime. He was then released after prosecutors dropped all charges against him.

Kalief's story is just one powerful example that demonstrates how the war on drugs disproportionately affects the black community and lacks any meaningful reform initiatives compared to other forms of criminal justice reform.

How have the effects of the War on Drugs been felt in other communities?

We understand that the War on Drugs had a huge effect on the black community, but it's important to note how its effects have been felt in other communities.

For example, people of color and those who are economically disadvantaged often face harsher penalties for drug-related crimes than white individuals, leading to an increase in incarceration rates and disparities in sentencing.

Additionally, laws that were created during the War on Drugs era have led to increased police presence in certain neighborhoods and more aggressive tactics being used by law enforcement against people of color.

As a result, many communities have experienced economic hardship due to the disruption caused by these policies.

What solutions have been proposed to mitigate the effects of the War on Drugs?

We, as a society, have long been aware of the devastating effects of the war on drugs. But what solutions have been proposed to mitigate these impacts?

One interesting statistic is that in 2020, almost 80% of people incarcerated for drug-related offenses were black or brown. This startling fact has led many organizations to propose initiatives and policies aimed at reforming the criminal justice system so that it no longer disproportionately affects communities of color.

Such initiatives include providing treatment and rehabilitation services to those affected by the war on drugs, decriminalizing certain low-level drug offenses, and creating more equitable sentencing guidelines.

Conclusion

We've seen the devastating effects the war on drugs has had on our black community. Mass incarceration, disproportionate sentencing, diminished economic opportunity, reduced social mobility, increased poverty rates, racial profiling, and police brutality are just some of the consequences we face.

The misguided policy priorities that led to this crisis have taken an immense toll on our collective mental health. To make matters worse, these issues seem to be spiraling out of control - it's like a snowball rolling downhill.

We must come together to help break this cycle and create meaningful change for future generations. It's going to take time and effort, but if we stick together, we can turn things around - one step at a time.

Discriminatory Restrictive Covenants

We've all heard of restrictive covenants, but what about discriminatory restrictive covenants? Have you ever stopped to consider the impact these agreements have on minorities and marginalized groups?

Discriminatory restrictive covenants are a form of contract that has been used for centuries to limit the rights of individuals. These contracts can be found in many areas, including real estate, employment, and business.

In this article, we'll take a look at the history of discriminatory restrictive covenants, their impact today, and strategies for challenging them. We'll also explore how US Supreme Court decisions and local regulations are affecting the use of such agreements going forward.

So let's dive in and find out more about discriminatory restrictive covenants!

Definition and History

You may not be familiar with it, but restrictive covenants have been around for a while - they've just been hiding in plain sight.

A restrictive covenant is an agreement between two parties that prohibits one of the parties from using or possessing particular property or engaging in certain activities.

Historically, these types of agreements were used to block African Americans from living in certain neighborhoods and working at specific jobs as part of discriminatory practices. This led to a large amount of economic disparity among racial groups that has lasted for generations.

But now, understanding the implications of these covenants is more important than ever before. As we move forward and strive towards a society free from discrimination, it's essential that we recognize the impact restrictive covenants can have on people's lives and work together to ensure everyone has access to equal opportunities.

With that being said, let's take a closer look at the different types of restrictive covenants out there today.

Types of Covenants

These covenants can come in many forms, but one thing's for sure: if it ain't broke, don't fix it!

Typically, restrictive covenants are used to prevent the sale or lease of land or property to particular individuals. Examples of this include racial and religious discrimination, age restrictions, and other exclusionary practices.

Restrictive covenants also often involve tenant screening criteria such as credit scores, criminal background checks and income qualifications that have a disproportionately negative effect on certain groups. These discriminatory practices can be damaging to communities by perpetuating segregation and inequality.

Fortunately, there are laws in place to protect against these kinds of discriminatory restrictive covenants. But even so, they remain problematic because they often require people who want to purchase a home or rent an apartment to meet certain standards that may not apply equally across different demographics.

This sort of discrimination needs to be addressed in order for everyone to have equal opportunities when it comes to housing rights - without having to worry about being excluded based on their race or religion.

With that said, let's take a look at some examples of discriminatory restrictive covenants.

Examples of Discriminatory Covenants

Discriminatory covenants can take many forms, including those that exclude certain individuals from renting or purchasing land or property based on their race, religion, age, and other criteria.

For example, historically in the United States prior to 1948 some covenants prohibited people of color from purchasing real estate in certain neighborhoods or states. Some covenants excluded Jews or members of other religious groups from owning homes in certain communities.

This type of discrimination has had a long-lasting impact on minorities and marginalized groups who were denied access to housing and employment opportunities due to unfair practices like these.

Consequently, it's essential for legislators to pass laws that protect citizens from discriminatory restrictive covenants.

Impact on Minorities and Marginalized Groups

The effects of discriminatory covenants have had a devastating impact on minorities and marginalized groups, denying them access to housing and other opportunities. This has further entrenched systemic racism, as these communities are unable to achieve the same level of economic mobility that non-minorities enjoy.

Here's an overview of the major impacts this has had:

- It has limited job opportunities for minority workers due to prejudicial hiring practices based on where a person lives instead of their qualifications.
- It has increased poverty in minority neighborhoods, as resources are concentrated away from those areas and into whiter ones.
- It has led to a lack of representation in government positions and decision-making processes, resulting in policies which do not adequately address the needs of minority communities.

These unjust conditions can lead to feelings of hopelessness among minorities and marginalized groups and further entrench systemic racism.

The challenges for businesses and employers in combatting discrimination through restrictive covenants will be discussed next.

Challenges for Businesses and Employers

Businesses and employers face a challenging task in tackling the discrimination that restrictive covenants perpetuate, and you can help make a difference.

It's important for business owners to realize their potential role in making a positive change. This includes creating an environment of understanding with clear rules about how such discriminatory practices won't be tolerated or accepted.

Employers must also take steps to ensure that any existing restrictive covenants are monitored and updated to eliminate any language that would lead to unequal treatment of employees or customers.

In addition, businesses should provide training and resources to ensure all staff have the knowledge necessary to identify potentially discriminatory practices during recruitment and hiring processes.

Taking action now can help prevent future problems as well as offer support for those affected by existing restrictions. By taking these proactive measures, businesses can make sure they're upholding their commitment to fairness, equality, and inclusion - setting an example for others to follow.

As we move forward into this new era of increasing awareness about restrictive covenants, it's essential for businesses and employers alike to remain vigilant so that everyone has an equal chance at success no matter their background or identity - legal implications and restrictions notwithstanding.

Legal Implications and Restrictions

As employers and businesses, we need to be aware of the legal implications that come with discriminatory restrictive covenants. Though these clauses aren't always enforceable, it's important to know what restrictions they impose on our employees.

Here are three key things to keep in mind:

- Restrictive Covenants must be reasonable in terms of geography, duration, and scope.
- The clause shouldn't be overly broad or contain language that could lead to discrimination against a protected class of employees.
- It's important to have a good understanding of the applicable state laws before including a restrictive covenant in an employment contract or offer letter.

It's vital for us to stay up-to-date on potential liabilities when it comes to discriminatory restrictive covenants so our organization can remain compliant and protect its interests going forward. With this in mind, let's consider how Supreme Court decisions have impacted these types of clauses over time.

US Supreme Court Decisions

You may have noticed that US Supreme Court decisions have had a lasting effect on these types of clauses, so it's important to stay informed on their rulings.

Over the years, the US Supreme Court has dealt with several cases involving discriminatory restrictive covenants, determining whether they are legal in certain instances or not.

The court has also determined that when it comes to restrictive covenants which involve race or ethnicity, they are never legally binding because they violate the Equal Protection Clause of the Fourteenth Amendment.

Other types of discriminatory restrictions may be permissible if they don't violate public policy and serve a legitimate business purpose.

The Supreme Court continues to review cases related to discriminatory restrictive covenants and their legality, so staying up-to-date is essential to ensure compliance with applicable laws.

With this in mind, it's important to understand how local and state regulations may affect these types of clauses as well.

Local and State Regulations

In addition to the US Supreme Court decisions on discriminatory restrictive covenants, local and state regulations are also in place to help protect against discrimination. We're all familiar with the basics of anti-discrimination laws: no one should be discriminated against on the basis of race, gender, religion, or other factors.

But many states and localities have gone beyond these basic protections to consider restrictions that might be placed on property owners when they sell their homes or businesses. Here are three ways in which local and state laws address restrictive covenants:

- Preemptive Legislation: Many states have passed laws that make it illegal for developers or property owners to include certain types of discriminatory language in their contracts.

- Local Ordinances: Some cities and towns have passed ordinances that restrict certain types of biased terms from being included in deeds or other contracts related to real estate transactions.

- Anti-Discrimination Laws: A number of states have enacted legislation that prohibits landlords from refusing to rent a house or apartment because of an individual's race, ethnicity, gender identity, sexual orientation, etc.

These various forms of regulation help ensure that individuals' rights are protected when it comes to buying and selling property in their communities. They also provide a framework for challenging any potentially discriminatory restrictions if they arise during a real estate transaction.

By providing protection at both the federal level through Supreme Court decisions and at the local level through legislation and ordinances, we can work together towards a more equitable society free from restrictive covenants based on prejudice or bias. Now let's examine strategies for challenging these kinds of restrictions when they arise so everyone can feel secure when engaging in real estate transactions.

Strategies for Challenging Restrictive Covenants

It's important to understand the strategies for challenging any potentially biased terms that may arise during a real estate transaction, so you can ensure your rights are protected.

One of the most effective strategies is to work with an experienced real estate attorney who understands local and state regulations concerning discriminatory covenants.

This legal professional can help you identify any potential discrimination in the contract and take steps to challenge it if needed. They can also provide advice on how best to proceed should you be presented with a restrictive covenant that is not legally binding.

With their help, you can protect yourself and your interests by ensuring that all parties involved understand their respective responsibilities in the transaction.

Having a clear understanding of how to challenge potentially discriminatory language in a real estate agreement gives buyers peace of mind when entering into such transactions.

It's vital to stay informed about changing laws and regulations as they relate to restrictive covenants, and having a qualified lawyer on your side will make sure that any issues regarding them are addressed quickly and appropriately.

Looking ahead, it's essential to continue staying educated on these topics so we can remain vigilant against unfair practices in the future.

Looking Ahead: The Future of Discriminatory Covenants

As we strive for a more equitable future, it's essential to ensure that any language in real estate agreements is just and fair - not only for ourselves, but also for generations to come. Discriminatory restrictive covenants are a major factor in continued inequality and unfairness in the real estate industry.

Restrictive covenants have been used to keep certain populations from buying or residing on certain properties and these clauses can be difficult to challenge. As such, it's important that we take steps now to avoid creating new discriminatory covenants as well as challenging existing ones.

A key part of this effort is educating people about discriminatory covenants so they better understand their implications. We need to make sure that everyone involved in real estate transactions understands the legal ramifications of restrictive covenants and how they can be challenged if necessary.

Additionally, governments should consider enacting laws that ban discriminatory language from being used in real estate agreements altogether. This would help create a more equitable system for all parties involved and help ensure fairness within the industry for years to come.

Frequently Asked Questions

What is the difference between discriminatory restrictive covenants and other types of covenants?

We all have a subconscious desire for safety, so it's important to understand the difference between types of covenants.

Put simply, restrictive covenants are agreements between two parties that limit what one party can or cannot do. They often prevent someone from competing with another person's business.

Discriminatory restrictive covenants go a step further and involve an element of discrimination. These may include provisions against certain demographics owning property in a certain area.

Ultimately, discriminatory restrictive covenants are more extreme than other types of covenants. They not only restrict behaviors, but also discriminate against specific groups of people.

How do discriminatory restrictive covenants affect individuals and businesses?

We all know the importance of safety in our lives and businesses, but what about covenants?

Covenants are agreements that regulate how individuals and businesses interact with each other, and discriminatory restrictive covenants are a particular type of covenant that can have a big impact.

These covenants can restrict an individual or business from taking certain actions based on characteristics such as race, gender, religion, and more. This means that individuals and businesses may be prevented from doing things like buying property or entering into contracts due to these restrictions - something that could potentially have a huge effect on their livelihoods.

What laws protect individuals from discriminatory restrictive covenants?

We all want to feel safe and secure in our homes, neighborhoods, and workplaces. Unfortunately, discriminatory restrictive covenants can be used to deny people access to these places based on their race, religion, or gender.

Thankfully, there are laws that protect individuals from such discrimination. The Fair Housing Act of 1968 prohibits any sort of discrimination in regards to housing and real estate transactions, while Title VII of the Civil Rights Act protects employees against discriminatory practices by employers.

Additionally, state laws may provide additional protections for those affected by discriminatory restrictive covenants.

Are there any strategies to prevent discriminatory restrictive covenants?

We know that our safety is of the utmost importance, so we want to be sure that discriminatory restrictive covenants are avoided at all costs.

To do this, there are a few strategies we can use to prevent their emergence and implementation. One way is to create clear policies on non-discrimination for businesses, ensuring that all employees receive the same opportunity regardless of their identity or background.

Additionally, making sure that any contracts signed in regard to hiring practices include language explicitly forbidding any type of discrimination.

Finally, companies should also provide ongoing training and education on anti-discrimination laws and regulations which apply to their business model. These measures will help ensure that no one is subject to unfair restrictions based on discriminatory reasoning.

Are there any local or state regulations that apply to discriminatory restrictive covenants?

We're always looking for ways to ensure safety in our communities. Local and state regulations can be a great way to do this. These regulations cover a range of topics. They prevent discrimination based on race or religion. They also ensure that homeowners don't take advantage of their neighbors by creating unreasonable restrictions on the use of their land.

By taking a proactive stance against discriminatory covenants, we can protect our communities. We can create an environment that is safe and equitable for everyone.

Conclusion

We've investigated the truth of the theory that restrictive covenants are discriminatory and have a negative impact on minorities and marginalized groups. From US Supreme Court decisions to local regulations, we've seen how these covenants can cause harm.

We've also explored strategies for challenging them, as well as what businesses and employers must do to work against these restrictions. It's clear that discriminatory covenants are still an issue in our society, but if we continue to take action and challenge them, we can make progress towards a more equitable future.

Let's keep fighting together!

Gentrification

We've all heard of gentrification, but what is it exactly? According to recent data from the U.S. Census Bureau, gentrification is happening in over 13% of neighborhoods across the country.

Gentrification is a process of reinvestment in low-income urban areas that can have both positive and negative effects on local residents, businesses, and communities at large. In this article we will explore what gentrification is, its causes, economic and social impacts, strategies for addressing it with equity in mind, and whether gentrification can be beneficial.

We will also look at how race intersects with the issue of gentrification. Join us as we delve into this complex topic!

Definition of Gentrification

It's a process of change, when wealthier people move into an area and cause the cost of living to rise. This influx of wealth and resources can have profound effects on a neighborhood, both positive and negative.

Gentrification often brings with it improvements like new infrastructure and businesses, as well as increased property values, but these positives come at a cost. Longtime residents may find they are unable to keep up with rising rent prices or pushed out entirely in favor of newcomers.

As such, gentrification has become a controversial topic, particularly among those who are already vulnerable from poverty or racism.

Transitioning now to the causes of gentrification...

Causes of Gentrification

The tide of change has swept through, slowly transforming the once familiar neighborhood into an unrecognizable land, where the old and new exist side-by-side in a state of uneasy coexistence.

There are many factors that can contribute to gentrification:

- An influx of capital from external sources such as investors and businesses;
- A rise in property values due to increased demand for residential housing;
- The displacement of poorer residents as wealthier people move in; and
- Increased pressure on infrastructure due to population growth.

Together, these influences can create a ripple effect that alters the socio-economic composition of a community.

It's important to recognize that gentrification doesn't happen overnight or without consequence. The process is often long, drawn out, and controversial, with both positive and negative impacts for those affected by it.

As we transition into discussing the economic impacts of gentrification, let's consider how this phenomenon affects communities at large.

Economic Impacts of Gentrification

You may have seen the effects of gentrification in your own community, as it affects both individuals and the wider population. At its core, gentrification is an economic process that shifts the balance of housing and other services within a particular area.

In general, this shift is associated with higher property values and increased demand for goods and services in the neighborhood. This can lead to improved infrastructure, such as new roads or public transport links, better access to amenities like shops and restaurants, and rising rents. However, these increases can also mean that lower-income residents are unable to keep up with rising living costs — leading to displacement of existing communities who cannot afford to remain in their homes.

This can have a devastating effect on those affected by it, making them vulnerable to poverty and homelessness due to their inability to pay rent or buy property in gentrified areas. With this in mind, it's important for governments and local authorities to take measures which protect people from being displaced by gentrification while still allowing investment into deprived areas.

The economic impacts of gentrification go beyond just housing prices however — they extend into employment opportunities as well. Gentrifying neighborhoods often attract more businesses looking for cheaper land or labor costs compared to other areas — meaning that locals may find themselves replaced by workers from outside the area who are willing to work for less money.

This can lead to job insecurity among existing residents who now struggle against competition from outside forces in order to maintain secure employment within their local economy. It's vital that initiatives are put forward that ensure current residents benefit from any investment made into their neighborhood so they don't get left behind amid rapid changes taking place around them.

Next, we'll look at how gentrification affects social life within a community — something which has become increasingly contested in recent years as debates about urban development rage on across cities worldwide.

Social Impacts of Gentrification

Gentrification often has a drastic effect on the social fabric of a community, irrevocably altering the lives of those inhabiting it. This can manifest in various ways such as a decrease in affordable housing, an increase in rent prices, and a displacement of longtime residents from their beloved neighborhoods. All this disruption can lead to increased feelings of alienation for these individuals when their sense of belonging is taken away from them.

Even if the new amenities that come with gentrification benefit some community members, they can also lead to more social stratification and segregation. As existing residents are forced out, so too are community ties severed and replaced by unfamiliar faces who may lack empathy for what was once there before them. Ultimately, this process can leave communities feeling divided and fractured - something we all want to avoid.

To prevent this unfortunate consequence of gentrification requires support for existing residents through access to resources like job opportunities or affordable housing solutions. With everyone's collective effort towards creating greater equity and inclusion within our cities, we can ensure that no one is left behind as our cities continue to evolve and change over time.

With that in mind, let's take a look at the cultural impacts of gentrification next.

Cultural Impacts of Gentrification

Discovering how gentrification can affect the culture of a community is an important part of understanding its impacts. The influx of wealthier individuals in a historically low-income area often leads to changes in cultural norms and values.

Here are some of the ways gentrification can affect culture:

- It may lead to increased diversity, as more affluent people move into the area.
- It can also result in reduced access to traditional cultural activities, such as festivals or dances.
- Some local businesses may be forced out due to rising rent prices, leading to a loss of unique cultural offerings.
- Gentrification has been known to alter the social dynamics within a community as well.

These changes are not always positive and have led to a sense of displacement among long-time residents who no longer feel at home in their neighborhoods. This highlights the need for further examination into the effects that gentrification has on communities so that solutions can be found that recognize both new and existing members' needs and desires.

Transitioning into this conversation brings us closer towards understanding how gentrification is related with displacement.

Gentrification and Displacement

Displacement is often an unfortunate consequence of gentrification, and as the old adage goes, 'home is where the heart is'.

For many individuals and families, the gentrification of a neighborhood can lead to displacement from both their homes and communities. People have a natural desire for stability and continuity in their lives, but this can be upended when they're forced out of their homes due to increasing housing costs or changes in zoning laws.

As gentrification increases throughout cities, it becomes increasingly important to find strategies that can help mitigate displacement while still allowing for economic growth.

Strategies to Address Gentrification

Now that we've discussed the displacement caused by gentrification, let's look at how cities can address the issue. There are several strategies that communities can take to mitigate the effects of gentrification:

- Establishing rent control and tenant protection laws.
- Developing more affordable housing options and programs such as inclusionary zoning.
- Funding community programs such as job training and access to financial services for low-income residents in gentrifying areas.
- Strengthening and diversifying small businesses in local neighborhoods through grants and other incentives.

These strategies acknowledge that displacement is part of a much larger problem with existing racial inequalities, inadequate affordable housing options, rising costs of living, stagnating wages, underfunded education systems, etc. They aim to address these problems through proactive measures instead of reactive ones after the damage has been done.

By taking steps towards creating equitable opportunities for all members of a community regardless of socio-economic status or race, cities can ensure they are not displacing vulnerable populations while still allowing progress and development within their boundaries - something necessary for growth but which must be done responsibly if it is to benefit everyone involved.

Gentrification and Equity

Gentrification can have devastating consequences, especially for marginalized communities, so it's important to ensure that any development is done equitably. The scale of gentrification and its impact on communities is often linked to the race and income of the people who are displaced.

In many cases, city policies have enabled or accelerated gentrification without offering equitable solutions for those most affected by displacement. This has the potential to create a lack of affordable housing options and can contribute to increased poverty in these neighborhoods. As a result, it's essential that local governments take proactive steps to promote equity as part of their redevelopment or revitalization plans.

To do this effectively, they must consider how race and class intersect with gentrification in order to create meaningful solutions that protect vulnerable populations from displacement. Moving forward, careful consideration must be given not only to ensuring equitable access but also providing resources and opportunities for those most impacted by gentrification.

With thoughtful planning, cities can work towards creating more inclusive neighborhoods while preserving existing cultural identities.

Gentrification and Race

You may be wondering how gentrification affects different races and communities. As the process of gentrification takes place, it can lead to displacement of people already living in the area, particularly those from low-income backgrounds who often identify with a racial minority group.

This displacement can lead to an increase in economic inequality and tension between different communities as resources become increasingly scarce. Furthermore, this type of displacement has been linked to physical and mental health issues such as stress, depression, and anxiety in affected individuals.

By creating an environment where certain groups are privileged over others based on race or class status, gentrification can have serious negative impacts on overall wellbeing. As a result, it's important that all parties involved carefully consider the consequences of gentrification before proceeding with any changes.

With this in mind, let's now turn our attention to the question: can gentrification be beneficial?

Can Gentrification Be Beneficial?

You may be wondering if there are any potential benefits to gentrification; let's explore this idea further.

While it's important to recognize the challenges gentrification can bring, there are also positive aspects that should not be overlooked:

- Improved access to services and amenities like better schools, healthcare facilities, and improved public transportation can benefit local communities.

- An increase in property values often leads to more tax revenue, which could provide resources for programs and infrastructure improvements.

- An influx of new businesses brings with it a variety of job opportunities for local people.

- Gentrification can help revitalize areas that have been neglected or become unsafe over time.

Ultimately, gentrification is a complex process and its effects vary depending on the context. However, as long as it's done responsibly with an emphasis on protecting existing residents from displacement, it can offer substantial benefits by improving living conditions in neighborhoods where they were previously lacking.

Frequently Asked Questions

What are the long-term effects of gentrification?

We're experiencing the long-term effects of displacement and economic inequality in our communities. As neighborhoods become more desirable, property values increase and lower-income families can no longer afford to stay.

This has resulted in a loss of housing options for those who need it most, as well as an overall decrease in diversity within the community. Gentrification has caused long-term issues with affordability, access to resources, and social cohesion.

It's important that we take steps to ensure that all members of our community are able to benefit from any development projects while still preserving the unique character of each neighborhood.

What is the relationship between gentrification and housing affordability?

We all know the struggle of finding affordable housing in cities. But what if a change came to our neighborhoods that made them more desirable and drove up prices?

Gentrification is the process of renovating and developing an area with new buildings and businesses, often displacing low-income families who can't afford higher rents. It has a ripple effect on surrounding areas, raising property values in the entire neighborhood - but at what cost?

Gentrification can lead to displacement, creating an atmosphere of instability where people feel they don't belong anymore. This can have serious implications for social cohesion, economic opportunity, and even public health.

The relationship between gentrification and housing affordability is complex - it may bring some benefits but also some risks that must be carefully weighed before implementing any changes.

How does gentrification affect local businesses?

When it comes to local businesses, many people are concerned about the impact of gentrification.

When neighborhoods undergo this process of change, it can have a significant effect on small businesses.

In some cases, rents may increase, making it difficult for existing business owners to remain in their locations.

This can lead to an influx of new businesses that cater more towards higher-income residents and don't offer as much support to the local community.

Additionally, gentrification can also cause displacement of existing businesses which could disrupt the culture and character of a neighborhood.

How can gentrification be prevented?

We've all heard stories about how gentrification can drastically change a neighborhood, but what can be done to prevent it?

The truth is that there are several steps cities and communities can take to help mitigate the effects of gentrification. Local governments can implement policies such as rent control, tax incentives for existing businesses, or public housing programs.

They can also create zoning regulations that protect small businesses and prohibit large-scale development projects.

Community members themselves can also organize and advocate for their rights to keep their neighborhoods intact. These strategies are key to preserving the unique character of the community while still allowing room for progress and growth.

What are some of the key differences between gentrification and urban renewal?

We often talk about urban renewal, which can make a city more inviting and vibrant. But what's the difference between it and gentrification?

Gentrification is when wealthier people move into a neighborhood, leading to an increase in housing prices that makes it difficult for existing residents to remain in the area.

On the other hand, urban renewal focuses on improving infrastructure, creating better public services and transportation options, and generally making the city more accessible and livable for all residents.

Thus, while both involve improvements to a city's landscape, they ultimately serve different purposes: one boosts property values at the expense of current residents, whereas the other seeks to benefit everyone equally.

Conclusion

We've explored what gentrification is and its impacts, both positive and negative.

It's clear that gentrification can bring economic prosperity to a neighbourhood, but it can also cause displacement of current residents.

When done with an eye on equity and justice, gentrification can be beneficial for everyone involved.

At the same time, it's important to ensure that no one group is unfairly targeted or excluded from these opportunities.

Gerrymandering

We've all heard of gerrymandering, but what does it actually mean?

In its simplest form, gerrymandering is when politicians use redistricting to gain an advantage for their party.

Politicians do this by manipulating the boundaries of electoral districts in order to ensure that a certain population is represented.

It's been around for centuries and has had a huge impact on modern politics.

In this article we'll be taking a closer look at gerrymandering and how it affects our political system today.

What is Gerrymandering?

Have you ever heard of gerrymandering but weren't sure what it was? Let's dive in and find out!

Gerrymandering is a process used to manipulate the boundaries of electoral districts, so as to give an advantage to a particular political party or group. It is typically conducted by those in power, who can use their control over the boundaries of these districts in order to limit opposition or minority groups from gaining representation. This means that certain communities are not represented fairly in elections, resulting in an uneven playing field when it comes to politics.

To understand why this practice has become so widespread, we need to look at its history - which brings us to our next subtopic.

History of Gerrymandering

The practice of manipulating electoral district boundaries for political gain has a long and storied past, stretching back to the days when its namesake first left his symbolic mark.

In 1788, Elbridge Gerry of Massachusetts signed a bill that created a voting district in the shape of a salamander, hence giving rise to the term 'Gerrymandering'.

In 1812, the United States Supreme Court upheld an Ohio Congressional map that had been drawn by state legislators in order to benefit their own party.

In 1964, there was a landmark Supreme Court case which established legal standards on how election districts could be drawn.

By 2000, computers were being used to create more precise gerrymandered districts than ever before.

The history of gerrymandering is still unfolding today with states like North Carolina facing lawsuits over recent redistricting efforts.

This long-standing practice has been an integral part of politics since its inception and continues to remain relevant in modern times as both parties strive for advantage in elections.

As we continue our exploration of gerrymandering, let's now turn our attention to discussing the different types of gerrymandering currently employed around the world.

Types of Gerrymandering

Gerrymandering has taken many shapes over the years, ranging from blatant partisan manipulation to subtle boundary-shifting tactics. Whether it's done to create an advantage for a particular party or just to protect the incumbents of a certain district, gerrymandering can have far-reaching implications.

This issue is especially concerning when it comes to state legislative and congressional races, where manipulating districts can determine who wins and losses in elections. From packing districts with one party's voters to cracking them up into multiple districts – ensuring that no single district will have enough voting power – gerrymandering can have a profound effect on our electoral system.

As we look ahead to the impact of these tactics, we must understand how they are used in order to ensure fair representation for all citizens.

Impact of Gerrymandering

Gerrymandering effects can be likened to a game of chess, where one side is given an unfair advantage and the other is left at a disadvantage, unable to compete in what should be an even match. This practice results in politicians having more control over their own re-election than the voters, creating a system that works against fair representation and undermines democracy.

Gerrymandering also has ripple effects on the political climate as it leads to increased polarization and division among the voting populace. This makes it harder for people from different parties or ideologies to come together and find common ground, making it difficult for meaningful progress to happen. As such, gerrymandering has wide-reaching implications for our society and further reinforces existing power structures that prevent true democracy from being realized.

The consequences of gerrymandering are clear; however, its prevalence remains high due to its usefulness as a tool for political gain. The result? Politicians across all levels of government have used gerrymandering as a way of gaining electoral advantages while leaving voters feeling powerless and disenfranchised.

Moving forward then, we must address this issue head-on in order to ensure that our elections are free and fair so that every voice can be heard. To do this effectively requires both understanding how gerrymandering works within the context of political parties as well as enacting measures that will safeguard against future abuses of this process.

Political Parties and Gerrymandering

You have the power to help ensure fair representation and prevent further abuses of gerrymandering by understanding how it works within the context of political parties.

Gerrymandering is a practice that has been used to give one political party an advantage over another, particularly in legislative elections. When done correctly, this can be achieved by cleverly drawing district lines or other election boundaries so as to benefit one party's voters. It can also be used to reduce competition between candidates from different parties, which often results in a decrease in voter turnout.

To combat these practices, citizens need to understand how their representatives are being elected and make sure they are held accountable for any unfair advantages they take. By doing so, we can create fairer elections and ensure more balanced representation for all.

Gerrymandering has long been a problem in American politics but recent advancements in technology have made it easier for those with nefarious intentions to manipulate the system even further. Understanding how political parties use gerrymandering is key to preventing further abuses of power and ensuring fair representation for all citizens.

With this knowledge, we can better equip ourselves with the tools needed to hold our elected officials accountable and protect our democracy from any future abuses of power. Moving forward, we must remain vigilant against any attempts at manipulating elections through gerrymandering and work together towards creating a more equitable system of representation.

Technology and Gerrymandering

We've seen how political parties have used gerrymandering to gain an advantage in elections, but technology is also playing a role.

In recent years, computer software and data-driven analysis has enabled more sophisticated partisan redistricting plans than ever before.

By utilizing voter profiles, past election results and population trends, mapmakers can draw district lines with incredible precision that create a highly favorable outcome for one party or the other.

This technology has opened the door to even more extreme forms of gerrymandering than we've seen in the past.

At the same time, these advances in technology are being used by those fighting against gerrymandering as well.

Activists are using algorithmic tools to identify unconstitutional redistricting plans and challenge them in court.

This is helping to bring balance back into our electoral system and give people their voices back at the ballot box -- something that's desperately needed amid today's increasingly polarized climate.

With this new battle over gerrymandering now playing out in courtrooms across America, it's time to take a look at some of its most important cases yet.

Court Cases on Gerrymandering

As the battle over gerrymandering rages on, courtrooms have become the new battleground as citizens fight to reclaim their right to be heard at the ballot box. From federal district courts to state supreme courts, citizens are challenging gerrymandered districts in an attempt to restore fairness and balance in their states' electoral systems.

In many cases, these challenges have been met with success as judges rule that current redistricting plans violate the Constitution or voting rights laws. These rulings often lead to new redistricting plans being drawn up by either state legislatures or independent commissions in order to ensure that all citizens are treated fairly when it comes time for them to vote.

This shift toward judicial oversight of gerrymandering is a welcome one for those who desire fair districting maps and fair elections. With legal challenges continuing around the country, it's likely that more decisions will be made soon which could further strengthen efforts against partisan gerrymandering.

Transitioning into what can be done next to combat gerrymandering, it's clear that much work must still be done if we're going to see lasting change and reform in our electoral system.

What Can be done to Combat Gerrymandering?

Now that we've explored the court cases surrounding gerrymandering, let's take a look at what can be done to combat it.

In order to effectively combat gerrymandering, here are four steps we must take:

- Investigate voting patterns to identify areas where gerrymandering may be occurring.
- Monitor changes in district boundaries over time.
- Utilize directional or independent commissions when drawing up electoral maps.
- Advocate for legislation that promotes fair and equal representation.

Taking these steps will help us ensure that no one party has an unfair advantage over another when it comes to elections.

We must also remember that fighting gerrymandering requires teamwork and cooperation between different political parties and organizations. By working together, we can create fairer systems of representation for everyone.

Now let's turn our attention towards exploring how other countries are dealing with this issue of gerrymandering.

Gerrymandering in Other Countries

Discover how other nations are addressing the issue of unequal representation in their electoral systems. Gerrymandering is not just a problem faced by the United States, but by many countries around the world.

In Germany, for example, the constitution requires that each party receive proportional representation according to its vote share. This ensures that if a party wins 30% of votes, it receives 30% of seats.

Similarly, Japan has implemented an electoral system in which parties and candidates compete in multi-member districts with voters casting ballots for individual candidates rather than parties. These systems ensure fairer representation while still allowing parties to differentiate themselves from one another on policy issues.

The solution to gerrymandering does not have to be limited solely to these two models; there are many alternatives that can be explored as well. From ranked voting systems like instant runoff voting (IRV) and cumulative voting to single transferable vote (STV), there are plenty of options available for countries looking for better methods for electing representatives.

Next up, we'll take a look at some of these alternatives and discuss why they might be a better choice than gerrymandering.

Alternatives to Gerrymandering

Experience the power of fair representation for yourself by exploring some of the alternatives to gerrymandering.

One alternative is a system known as 'multi-member districts.' This system divides a state into several large districts, each of which elects multiple members from different parties through proportional voting. This can result in an electoral outcome that reflects the diversity of public opinion without sacrificing representational accuracy.

Another approach is ranked choice voting, which allows voters to rank their preferences among candidates instead of choosing just one candidate. This encourages more nuanced political engagement and reduces negative campaigning, ultimately leading to greater satisfaction with elected officials and the electoral process as a whole.

Finally, there are independent redistricting commissions, which remove the redistricting process from politicians' hands and put it in those of citizens who may be more likely to consider voter welfare when drawing district boundaries.

All these alternatives offer democratic solutions that can help reduce gerrymandering and ensure fair representation for all.

Frequently Asked Questions

How does gerrymandering influence voter turnout?

We've all heard about the power of voting, but few understand how gerrymandering can influence voter turnout.

Gerrymandering is the practice of redrawing district lines to give an advantage to a certain group or party. This practice has been around since the early 1800s and it continues to shape our electoral process today.

By manipulating district boundaries, politicians often have an edge in winning elections and this can significantly decrease voter turnout in affected areas. This issue is especially worrisome because when fewer people participate in elections, it becomes easier for those in power to make decisions without considering public opinion.

It's time we take a stand against gerrymandering and ensure that everyone has an equal chance to have their voice heard at the polls.

What are the legal limits to gerrymandering?

We all want to make sure our voices are heard in the voting booth. But what if someone was manipulating the system so that your vote wasn't counted? That's where legal limits come in.

Gerrymandering is a form of redistricting that can change the shape of electoral districts and how people vote - but it should always be done within certain boundaries set by law. In general, these limits require that district lines must not be drawn for any discriminatory purpose or in order to diminish an individual's right to vote.

To ensure fair elections, governments must constantly monitor their gerrymandering practices and uphold laws that protect citizens' rights to representation.

What are the most effective strategies to reduce gerrymandering?

We know that the way our voting districts are drawn can have a huge impact on our democracy. But, did you know that gerrymandering is an issue in almost every state in the United States?

This controversial practice has been used by politicians to gain an unfair advantage over their competition and manipulate election results. So, what can we do to reduce gerrymandering?

One of the most effective strategies is to adopt independent redistricting commissions. These independent committees would be made up of citizens rather than political appointees, ensuring impartiality and fairness when drawing district lines.

Additionally, greater transparency around the process could help prevent partisan manipulation and ensure that all voices are represented in the democratic process.

Does gerrymandering disproportionately affect certain demographics?

We've all seen it: areas with oddly shaped voting districts that seemingly have no rhyme or reason for their borders. Unfortunately, this means certain demographics are being disproportionately affected by the way districts are drawn.

This can lead to minority groups being underrepresented in the political process and their voices not heard in important decisions. Gerrymandering is a real issue, and steps must be taken to ensure everyone's vote is accounted for regardless of race, gender, or any other factor.

What is the relationship between gerrymandering and media coverage?

We've seen a massive surge in media coverage of political boundary manipulation over the past few years. It seems to be on everyone's minds. Conversations are swirling like a tornado around every corner. This topic is an absolute juggernaut. Its implications are vast and far-reaching - almost to the point of being too immense for us to fully comprehend.

The reality is that gerrymandering has become so prevalent that it can no longer be ignored. Its effects on our lives cannot be overstated.

Conclusion

We've come to the end of our exploration of gerrymandering. We've discussed its history, various types and effects, political parties involved, court cases that have been brought up against it, and potential solutions.

Gerrymandering is a complex issue with far-reaching consequences and it must be faced head-on in order to create fair and equitable electoral maps. We need to find alternative methods for drawing district boundaries that give everyone an equal voice in our democracy.

To do so, we must work together as citizens to demand accountability from our elected officials and put an end to this form of manipulation once and for all.

The Electoral College

We, as a nation, have relied on the Electoral College since the 18th century to choose our president.

It's a complex system that has been both praised and criticized over its long history.

In this article, we'll cover what exactly the Electoral College is, how it works, its role in deciding presidential elections and some of the arguments for and against it.

Overview of the Electoral College

You're likely familiar with the process of selecting a president through the electoral system; however, this overview will provide a more in-depth look at how it works.

The Electoral College is made up of 538 electors who cast votes to determine the President and Vice President of the United States. Each state receives one elector for each member of Congress they have, plus an additional two electors representing their two US senators.

For example, California has 55 members in its Congressional delegation and thus receives 55 electoral votes. On Election Day, citizens vote for their preferred presidential candidate and those ballots are tallied together to determine who won the majority of the popular vote in that state.

Then on a separate day known as 'the meeting of electors', those appointed by each party meet together and cast their votes for president based off which candidate won the popular vote within that state.

In order for a candidate to win the presidency, they must receive 270 or more out of 538 total electoral votes.

This concludes our overview - next we'll take a look at how this system came into being: the history of the Electoral College.

History of the Electoral College

Ever wondered how the process of choosing a president came to be? Take a look back at the history of the Electoral College to find out!

The Founding Fathers established the Electoral College in 1787 as part of the U.S. Constitution as a compromise between election of the President by Congress and election by popular vote. They determined that each state would appoint electors in such manner as its legislature may direct, equal in number to its senators and representatives combined.

Initially, states had total control over how their electors voted, but this changed when Andrew Jackson was elected President in 1828 after winning more popular votes than John Quincy Adams but losing in electoral votes. This led to some states passing laws requiring electors to pledge support for presidential candidates based on how their state's citizens voted.

Today, electors are chosen through a variety of methods depending on which state they are from and must cast an individual vote for President and Vice-President on separate ballots during their meeting following Election Day - though not all do so faithfully!

As we can see from this brief overview, the history of our country's electoral system has been full of change and evolution throughout time - so let's take a look at how it works today.

How the Electoral College Works

You may be familiar with how the voting process works, but understanding the Electoral College can be a bit more complex. The Electoral College is made up of 538 electors from all 50 US states and Washington D.C., who cast votes for the President and Vice President during an election.

When American citizens vote in a presidential election, they are actually voting for these electors to represent them in their state's electoral college. These electors then cast their votes based on the candidate that won the popular vote in their respective state.

In most cases, whichever candidate wins the majority of Electoral College votes (270 or more) will become president of the United States. To further complicate matters, each U.S state has a different number of Electoral College votes depending on its population size; this means some states carry more weight than others when it comes to deciding who wins an election.

With this in mind, it's easy to see why understanding how the Electoral College works is so important when it comes to electing our leaders! Moving forward, let's take a look at how states receive and allocate electoral votes.

States and Electoral Votes

Every state is allotted a certain number of electoral votes according to its population, making some states more influential than others when it comes to deciding the outcome of an election. The number of electoral votes allocated to each state depends on the size of their congressional delegations. In most cases, that means a state is allocated one vote for every member in both their Senate and House delegation.

This means larger states with higher populations will typically get more electoral votes than smaller states. For example, California has 55 electors for its two senators and 53 representatives in Congress, while Wyoming has only 3 electors for its two senators and one representative. Washington D.C., which does not have voting representatives in Congress, is still given three electors due to the 23rd Amendment.

Additionally, six additional electors are also given to American Samoa, Guam, Puerto Rico, the U.S. Virgin Islands, Northern Mariana Islands and Washington D.C. This allocation system gives citizens from bigger states greater influence over Presidential elections than citizens from smaller ones as they can cast multiple ballots at once rather than just one ballot per person like other voters do across the country.

Consequently, this system allows candidates to focus their efforts on key areas where they can gain maximum electoral votes instead of trying to reach out equally everywhere.

Allocation of Electoral Votes

You've got the numbers now, so let's look at how electoral votes are allocated. The number of electoral votes for each state is equal to the sum of its representatives and senators in Congress. Allocations of electors are based on population size, with larger states receiving more electors than smaller ones. This means that California has the most electoral votes with 55 while seven states have three or fewer.

State	Representatives	Senators	Electoral Votes
CA	53	2	55
TX	36	2	38
FL	27	2	29
NY	27	2	29
PA	18	2	20
OH	16	2	18
IL	18	2	20
GA	14	2	16

It's important to remember that these allocations of electoral votes aren't set in stone and can change due to reapportionment after a census. Now that you understand how electoral votes are allocated, it's time to examine the role political party's play in this process.

Role of Political Parties

Political parties play an important role in determining the number of electoral votes each state receives, so it's essential to understand how they work.

Generally, each state is allocated a number of electors based on its population size, and the political party that controls the legislature decides how these electors are chosen and cast their vote.

Political parties also dictate who will be nominated as potential presidential candidates for election. It's therefore critical for political parties to have strong support from voters across different states to gain sufficient electoral votes.

This connection between political parties and the Electoral College allots more power to those affiliated with major parties compared to those who are not. As such, faithless electors may differ from what the majority of a particular state has voted for, depending on which party they belong to.

Faithless Electors

Have you ever heard of a faithless elector? Here's your chance to find out what they are and why their vote matters!

A faithless elector is an individual who, when they cast their Electoral College ballot, does not do so in the way that the state has instructed them. They may make this decision for any number of reasons - perhaps due to corruption by political parties or simply due to personal opinion.

This means that a candidate might not win the majority vote in the Electoral College, even when they have won the popular vote. Faithless electors have been around since 1808, although only 157 instances of them have occurred throughout U.S history.

Their votes can be decisive in close elections and it's important for citizens to understand how this works as part of our election process. With this knowledge, we can move forward with an understanding of how our government works and how our votes count in determining presidential elections.

Understanding faithless electors allows us to better comprehend the role played by the Supreme Court in election disputes.

Role of the Supreme Court

The Supreme Court plays an important role in deciding election disputes, and its decisions can have a profound impact on the outcome of Presidential elections.

In Bush v. Gore, for example, the court's decision to stop recounting votes in Florida awarded George W. Bush the 2000 presidential election by a margin of just 537 votes.

The court's ruling underlined the importance of every vote, regardless of which candidate it is cast for. As such, it stands as a reminder that Supreme Court rulings hold great power when it comes to determining who will become president in any given election year.

This emphasizes the need for careful consideration when justices are appointed to serve on the bench.

With this in mind, we turn our attention to criticisms of the Electoral College system that continues to be used today.

Criticisms of the Electoral College

You may have heard about the controversy surrounding Presidential elections - but do you understand how the system works? The Electoral College is an antiquated and complicated process that has been criticized for not accurately reflecting the popular vote. Here are a few of the main issues with the system:

- It does not consider population size when allotting electoral votes, allowing smaller states to be more influential than larger ones.

- Certain states are "winner-take-all" where all of its electors will go to one candidate no matter what percentage of people voted for them.

- Third-party candidates may influence which major party candidate wins by taking away votes from them, despite having no chance of winning themselves.

- It is possible for a candidate to win the popular vote but lose in electoral college and therefore fail to become President.

These factors make it difficult for citizens to know their voices are being heard, leaving many feeling disenfranchised by their own government. Moving on from this point, we can explore some potential alternatives to the Electoral College system...

Possible Alternatives to the Electoral College

Gaining an understanding of potential alternatives to the Electoral College system can be like unlocking a puzzle - let's explore some possible solutions!

One possible alternative is the popular vote system, which would involve the direct election of the President by citizens across all states. This system eliminates the need for electors and would ensure that every vote is counted equally.

Another alternative is a National Bonus Plan, which would award bonus electoral votes to whichever candidate wins in each state. This could help prevent a winner-takes-all effect for individual states, and could result in more balanced representation throughout the nation as a whole.

Ultimately, while there are many different approaches that could be taken to replace or supplement our current Electoral College system, it's clear that there are both pros and cons associated with any reform efforts.

Frequently Asked Questions

How does the Electoral College decide the winner of the election?

We all want to know how the winner of an election is decided. The Electoral College plays a major role in this process.

When citizens vote for a presidential candidate, they are actually voting for "electors" who have pledged to support a particular party's nominee. These electors then cast their votes in the Electoral College.

The number of electors each state has corresponds to its population size, so states with larger populations have more influence than those with smaller populations. The candidate who wins the majority of elector votes wins the election and becomes President of the United States.

What percentage of the popular vote does a candidate need to win the Electoral College?

We often hear about the popular vote, but what percentage of it does a candidate need to win the Electoral College?

It's an elusive prize - one that requires strategic maneuvering and an attentive eye on the ballots.

To secure victory, a candidate needs to have 270 of the 538 Electoral College votes, which equates to more than 50% of all votes cast.

In practice, this means that a candidate usually needs at least 51% of the total popular vote in order to clinch a presidential election.

How often have faithless electors changed the outcome of an election?

Faithless electors are members of the Electoral College who don't vote for the candidate they pledged to support.

While this is rare, it has occasionally changed the outcome of an election.

For example, in 2016 seven faithless electors voted against their pledge, three for Hillary Clinton and four for Donald Trump.

Ultimately, these faithless votes didn't alter the outcome of the election, but they still serve as a reminder of how powerful each individual vote can be.

What are the advantages of the Electoral College system?

We believe the Electoral College system is advantageous in that it encourages presidential candidates to campaign on a more national level, rather than focusing solely on certain populous states.

The Electoral College system ensures that all regions and populations are represented in the election process, making sure every person's vote counts, regardless of where they live.

It also prevents any one region or party from dominating an election and allows for third-party candidates to have a voice without completely disrupting an election outcome.

Finally, it gives smaller states more representation than they would have if only the popular vote was counted.

Could the Electoral College be abolished without a constitutional amendment?

We're often faced with a difficult question: could the Electoral College be abolished without a constitutional amendment?

At first glance, it may seem impossible. After all, any change to the way we elect our leaders would require a thorough examination of the current system and its implications.

But on closer inspection, we find that there is precedent for such changes being made without amending the constitution. In fact, many states have done away with their own electoral college systems while still adhering to federal election law requirements.

By looking at these examples and examining how they were implemented without an amendment process, we can gain insight into whether or not abolishing the Electoral College is possible in today's political climate.

Conclusion

We've looked at the history, workings, and criticisms of the Electoral College. After examining all of this information, it's clear that there is still a lot to learn about this system.

It's uncertain what changes may come in the future or if any will be made at all. But one thing is certain: we must continue to investigate and explore the truth behind this complex system in order to make sure that everyone's voice is heard in our democracy.

Only then can we ensure that every vote counts!

Voter Suppression

We all want to believe that our voices are heard and respected in the voting process, but what if they weren't? Voter suppression is a real issue that affects millions of people every election cycle.

It's an insidious force, often hidden behind complex legal structures and policies, preventing citizens from exercising their right to vote.

In this article, we'll explore the history of voter suppression, examine current laws in place, and discuss how these practices impact elections and democracy.

Join us as we take a closer look at voter suppression in America today.

History of Voter Suppression

Over the years, countless people have been denied their right to have a say in democracy--all for the sake of preserving power. Voter suppression has been used throughout history to disproportionately deny certain groups of people their right to vote.

From poll taxes and grandfather clauses, this effectively barred African Americans from voting in some states during Reconstruction era, to literacy tests that targeted Black and Latino voters, numerous tactics have been used by those with power in order to maintain it.

Today, voter ID laws are being used in many states as another way of suppressing the vote. Despite claims that these laws are necessary for preventing fraud at the polls, research shows that there is little evidence of widespread voter fraud and instead suggest that such policies serve more as a tool for keeping certain communities -- mostly minority and low-income — from having a voice at the ballot box.

This leaves them unable to participate equally in our democracy.

Voter ID Laws

You may not be aware, but certain laws in the US require citizens to present a form of ID before casting their vote - a practice that can have far-reaching implications.

Voter ID laws, which are enacted by states, vary widely and can make it difficult for certain individuals or groups to meet the requirements.

For example, some voter ID laws accept only a limited number of types of government-issued photo IDs or have additional requirements like providing a birth certificate or proof of residency. This makes it hard for people who do not have easy access to these documents — such as low-income voters — to obtain valid identification.

Moreover, many forms of identification are not free and can be cost prohibitive for those already struggling financially. As such, voter ID laws disproportionately affect minorities and marginalized populations, inhibiting them from exercising their right to vote.

These issues compounded with the fact that some states target minority voters through purges of voting rolls create an atmosphere where our democracy is threatened by intentional barriers preventing eligible citizens from having their voices heard at the polls.

Voter Purges

It's a disgrace that eligible citizens are being blocked from having their voices heard at the polls due to voter purges. Voter purges are processes used by states to remove names from registration lists, and they have become an increasingly popular tool for suppressing votes in recent years.

Unfortunately, these practices can be discriminatory, as they disproportionately target minority groups such as African Americans, Hispanics and Native Americans. Voter purging can be done through inaccurate methods like cross-checking registration lists with other databases to identify people who may have moved or died; using flawed assessment criteria for determining potential non-citizens or felons; or applying overly strict standards for verifying voters' information. It can also be done through intentional partisan manipulation of the list process, such as implementing burdensome rules like requiring voters to re-register before each election.

The consequences of these practices are clear—millions of legitimate voters are being stripped of their right to vote and shut out of our democracy.

This segues seamlessly into the next section on 'felony disenfranchisement' without needing a step transition.

Felony Disenfranchisement

Disenfranchisement of those with felonies is like a wall blocking citizens from having their voices heard, preventing them from engaging in the democratic process. This kind of voter suppression has an especially large impact on communities of color and low-income areas, as well as women, who are more likely to be incarcerated for minor offenses.

Denying the right to vote to people who have served their sentence forces them into a cycle of exclusion and marginalization that can only be broken if they're allowed to exercise their basic right to participate in democracy. As such, we must push for policies that restore voting rights for those convicted of felonies once they've completed their sentences.

With this in mind, it's necessary to understand how gerrymandering affects our political power and influences our elections. Gerrymandering allows politicians to unfairly draw district lines so they can remain in power despite not having the popular vote—a practice that undermines democracy itself.

Gerrymandering

Gerrymandering is a practice that undermines the democratic process by enabling politicians to craft district lines in order to maintain their hold on power, regardless of the will of the people.

This tactic allows those in power to sway election results before they even begin by manipulating which groups are included or excluded from voting districts. Gerrymandering creates an unlevel playing field and prevents fair representation of all parties and beliefs.

It's an insidious form of voter suppression that can have long-term effects on elections and democracy as a whole. However, it's not just politicians who benefit from gerrymandering; special interest groups and lobbyists also use this technique to influence legislation and policy outcomes.

By redrawing lines, these groups can ensure their favored candidates win seats in Congress and state legislatures, thus giving them more control over future laws and regulations. As such, gerrymandering is a powerful tool for those hoping to gain an advantage in politics—and it's one that should be guarded against at all costs if we want true democracy to prevail.

Looking ahead, then, we must consider how poll taxes further impact the ability for citizens to exercise their right to vote.

Poll Taxes

Poll taxes have historically been used to prevent marginalized citizens from exercising their right to vote, effectively disenfranchising them. This odious tactic has been used for centuries, and it is still employed in some states today.

Here are four key points about poll taxes:

- Poll taxes were declared unconstitutional by the 24th Amendment of the US Constitution in 1964.
- The poll tax was a fee that had to be paid in order to vote, and could only be paid with money or property.
- Poll taxes disproportionately affected African Americans, as many of these individuals did not own land or have excess cash available for such an expense.
- Some states attempted to bypass the 24th Amendment by creating literacy tests or other restrictive measures.

These tactics kept many people of color from voting and curtailed their rights as citizens; they remain yet another example of voter suppression efforts that continue into modern times.

With this troubling history in mind, we now turn our attention to restrictions on voter registration which can also deter individuals from taking part in elections.

Restrictive Voter Registration

Restricting voter registration is another way of keeping people from exercising their right to vote, and it's a real slap in the face for those affected.

This practice can be done through purging voter rolls, instituting overly burdensome ID requirements, and eliminating same-day registration.

Sadly, these measures disproportionately affect marginalized communities who are already struggling for basic rights like healthcare and education.

It's an inexcusable attempt to limit access to the polls and keep certain voices unheard.

And it's time we put a stop to this form of voter suppression so everyone can have an equal opportunity to make their voice heard at the ballot box.

Moving on from restrictive voter registration, another tactic used by those opposed to democracy is voter intimidation.

Voter Intimidation

Intimidating voters is a nefarious way of manipulating the outcome of an election, undermining the will of the people and silencing marginalized voices. Tactics such as threatening language, surveillance, physical intimidation by law enforcement or political operatives on polling sites, and misinformation campaigns can all be used to prevent people from voting.

These actions are deliberately designed to spread fear and anxiety amongst communities that don't support certain candidates or parties in order to discourage them from exercising their right to vote. Such tactics have been used historically to target racial minorities and other marginalized groups. That's why it's important for us today to recognize how insidious voter intimidation can be and take action against it.

The consequences of voter intimidation can be severe. It undermines democracy itself as well as trust in our government institutions. By limiting access to information about where and when people should vote, fewer potential voters may actually show up at polling places. This can lead to limited polling locations being established in areas with large minority populations as well as a decrease in poll workers who are often drawn from those same communities. Both lead to even further disenfranchisement of vulnerable populations.

Limited Polling Locations

By creating limited polling locations, particularly in areas with large minority populations, voter turnout can be significantly reduced and the voices of these communities silenced.

For example, in the 2016 presidential election, 16% of African Americans who tried to vote were unable to due to issues such as difficulty finding their assigned polling place or long lines.

This kind of voter suppression has a direct impact on democracy and elections because it denies certain groups of people the ability to exercise their right to vote. As a result, those individuals are unable to have their voices heard and make an impact on how the country is run.

This type of intentional disenfranchisement leaves citizens feeling powerless and creates an environment that is hostile towards political participation.

Impact on Elections and Democracy

We understand the direct and drastic impact limited polling locations have on democracy and elections. Limiting access to the polls has a far-reaching effect, with marginalized communities particularly vulnerable to this form of disenfranchisement.

It's vital that we recognize the consequences of voter suppression. It undermines our democracy by reducing citizens' voices in government. It limits fair representation by making it harder for certain groups to exercise their voting rights. It curbs civic engagement by discouraging people from participating in elections. And it destroys trust in the electoral system, leading to decreased faith in public institutions.

We must take action now if we're to preserve our democracy and ensure everyone can participate freely and fairly in our democracy's cornerstone - elections!

Frequently Asked Questions

How can I find out if I am eligible to vote?

We've all been there - standing in front of the ballot box, ready to cast our vote but not sure if we're actually eligible. It's a daunting feeling - you want to make sure that your voice is heard and your vote counts, but how can you be sure?

Well, don't worry - finding out if you're eligible to vote is easier than ever! With just a few clicks of the mouse, you'll know exactly what requirements need to be met so that your voice can be heard loud and clear.

No more stressing or worrying about whether or not you can cast your ballot; now it's as simple as pie! So don't wait another minute - find out if you're eligible today and get ready to make history!

How can I register to vote?

We're all eligible to make our voices heard and have a say in who makes decisions that affect us! Registering to vote is easier than ever.

All you need to do is find your state or territorial elections office online and fill out the required forms. You can also visit your local library, post office, or department of motor vehicles for more information about registering.

Make sure you have the necessary documents such as your driver's license or state ID card ready before starting! Once everything is submitted, you'll be able to cast your ballot during election time.

What are the different types of voter suppression?

We all have a voice, and with that come the power to make change. But what happens when that voice is suppressed?

There are several different types of voter suppression, including voter ID laws, gerrymandering, purging of voter rolls, and limiting access to polling places. These tactics are intended to discourage or prevent citizens from exercising their right to vote - a right that should be accessible for everyone.

What can I do to protect my right to vote?

We, as citizens of a democracy, can take steps to ensure that our right to vote is protected. It starts with staying informed about the voting rules and regulations in our state or locality.

We should be aware of any changes that might affect our ability to cast a ballot. Additionally, it's important for us to register early and make sure we have all the necessary documents ready when it comes time to head to the polls.

Finally, if we have any issues while voting, such as being asked for documentation that shouldn't be required by law or having our name removed from voter rolls, then we should immediately contact election officials or an attorney experienced in voting rights law.

By taking these proactive steps, we can help protect our right to participate in this sacred democratic process.

What are the consequences of voter suppression?

We all have the right to vote, but unfortunately, that right isn't always respected or protected.

Voter suppression prevents people from expressing their voices and having an impact on important decisions. The consequences of voter suppression can be far-reaching and devastating.

These consequences include a decrease in civic engagement, a lack of representation for certain groups in government, increased frustration with democracy, lower voter turnout rates during elections, and a decrease in trust for elected officials.

It's essential that we take steps to protect our democratic values by fighting this unjust practice.

Conclusion

We've seen how voter suppression has been used throughout history to keep certain groups of people from exercising their right to vote. It takes many forms, such as voter ID laws, purges, felony disenfranchisement, gerrymandering, restrictive voter registration, intimidation and limited polling locations.

All in all, it's a clear attempt to control the outcome of elections and derail democracy. The fight for voting rights is far from over; we have our work cut out for us if we want to make sure everyone can participate in our political system.

We must speak out against these tactics and do everything in our power to "level the playing field" so that everyone has an equal chance at making their voice heard.

Redlining

We all know the feeling of being discriminated against, but did you know that there is a practice called redlining that has been used to discriminate against individuals and families for decades?

Redlining is the systematic denial of resources, services, and opportunities based on race or geography. It has had a detrimental impact on people's lives - from housing to health care to economic opportunities.

In this article we will take a look at the history of redlining, how it continues to be enforced today, and what can be done to combat it. By understanding how redlining works and its consequences, we can come together as a society to create real solutions for those affected by it.

History of Redlining

It's been around for a while, but what exactly is it? Redlining is a practice of denying or limiting services to certain neighborhoods and communities based on race.

It was first used in the 1930s when banks created "redlines" that marked entire neighborhoods as risky, or off-limits for loans and other financial services. This discriminatory practice has had long-term effects on communities of color by widening the racial wealth gap and creating economic inequality.

Today, redlining takes new forms with different policies and practices that limit access to credit, housing assistance, insurance products, capital investment, healthcare services and more. While these modern versions of redlining may not be explicitly based on race, they still have negative impacts on vulnerable communities—limiting opportunity and perpetuating existing disparities.

As we look ahead at how this history of discrimination continues to affect our society today, understanding how redlining has been enforced gives us insight into the current landscape of inequality.

How Redlining is Enforced

Denying people access to loans and other financial services based on their location is an egregious violation of basic rights. Redlining, the practice of denying or providing fewer services to residents in certain areas based on racial, ethnic, or other characteristics, has a long history in the United States and continues today.

Here are some ways it is enforced:

- Property owners can be denied loans or insurance if they live in neighborhoods deemed as high-risk by lenders.
- Government entities can refuse to approve construction projects that would benefit redlined areas.

- Communities can be denied retail outlets and business investment because they are seen as unsavory investments due to redlining practices.

The effects of this discrimination have been far-reaching and damaging for many communities, causing a disparate impact that cannot be ignored any longer.

The Disparate Impact of Redlining

Redlining has had a devastating impact on communities, creating disparities that have been difficult to ignore. By denying certain neighborhoods access to resources and investments, redlining has caused vast economic inequality between races.

This has resulted in low-income areas with high crime rates and limited educational opportunities for the people living there. The effects of this policy are still felt today, as communities struggle to overcome the legacy of discrimination and lack of investment that redlining perpetuated.

As we'll explore further, these same policies have created a racial wealth gap that'll take generations to close.

Redlining and the Racial Wealth Gap

You've likely heard of the term 'redlining', but you may not be aware of the extent to which it has contributed to the racial wealth gap in America today.

Redlining is a term used to describe how banks, mortgage lenders, and insurance companies denied services to communities of color, resulting in unequal access to financial resources. This practice has had serious repercussions on both housing opportunities and economic stability for generations.

Housing Opportunities:

- People of color were disallowed from buying homes in certain areas that often had better schools and job opportunities than their current neighborhoods.
- As a result, these people were stuck without access to job markets or educational institutions that would have enabled them to get ahead economically.

Economic Stability:

- Due to redlining practices, many people of color are unable to secure loans or build credit necessary for starting businesses or purchasing larger assets such as cars and houses.
- This lack of access has resulted in less intergenerational wealth accumulation among people of color compared with their white counterparts.

This stark difference explains why there is such an extreme disparity between white households and households headed by people of color when it comes to median net worth today - an issue that must be addressed if we're ever going achieve true economic equality.

The next section will explore the impact of redlining on housing further.

The Impact of Redlining on Housing

You may be familiar with the effects of redlining on economic stability, but did you know it also had a huge impact on housing opportunities for people of color?

Redlining was a practice used by banks and other institutions to deny mortgages or home improvement loans in certain neighborhoods based on race. This meant that some communities were denied access to mortgages, which prevented them from buying homes or improving their existing ones.

This led to inadequate housing conditions and further segregation as people of color were unable to live in certain areas due to restrictions like these. The practice also created wealth disparities between white homeowners and those who were excluded from purchasing homes.

As a result, generations of black families have been affected by this legacy of racism which continues today. It's clear that redlining had a significant impact on housing opportunities for people of color, causing long-term damage that still exists today.

With this in mind, it's easy to see why access to education is so important for minorities who are still impacted by the consequences of redlining policies.

Redlining and Access to Education

When it comes to access to education, redlining has had an undeniable impact on minority communities that continues to this day.

From inadequate funding of schools in lower-income neighborhoods to the lack of educational resources available, these issues have resulted in a number of problems for students in these areas:

- Lower quality learning environments due to lack of resources and overcrowding;
- Less qualified teachers assigned to disadvantaged areas;
- Higher rates of student dropout and lower college enrollment rates.

These factors contribute not only to a poorer education experience but also create a cycle which perpetuates poverty and inequality among minority populations.

As such, it's clear that redlining has had long-term implications for access to education—ones that must be addressed if we're ever going to achieve true equity in education for all people.

With this knowledge, we can now move forward towards addressing the effects redlining has had on access to health care.

Redlining and Access to Health Care

As we've discussed, redlining has had a significant impact on access to education. Now, we'll explore the implications of this policy on access to health care.

Redlining set up an unequal system in terms of where people could live and what kind of services were available in those areas. As a result, many areas with residents of color were denied basic infrastructure such as hospitals and clinics that provide much-needed health care.

This disparity has become even more apparent during times of crisis like the current COVID-19 pandemic. Communities of color have been hit hardest by this virus due to the lack of access to quality medical care. This is directly correlated with the fact that these communities are often redlined and underserved.

This systemic racism has had far-reaching effects beyond just access to healthcare—it impacts economic opportunities too.

The Impact of Redlining on Economic Opportunities

The lack of access to healthcare and other resources caused by redlining has had a devastating effect on economic opportunities in many communities of color. Without access to capital, credit, or wealth-building resources, many people have been unable to purchase homes or afford quality education for their children.

This has created an intergenerational cycle of poverty that further perpetuates inequalities between different races and ethnicities. To make matters worse, those who have been denied these economic opportunities have also faced a pay gap compared to their white counterparts: African Americans make only 72 cents for every dollar earned by white workers; Latinx workers earn just 61 cents; and Asian American women earn only 82 cents per dollar earned by white men.

These disparities are difficult to overcome without access to financial services, investment opportunities, and other forms of assistance. By understanding the long-term implications of redlining on economic opportunity, we can begin to address the systemic racism that has caused so much suffering throughout our nation's history.

Existing Laws to Combat Redlining

To combat the devastating effects of redlining, a variety of laws have been put in place to ensure equal access to economic opportunities and resources.

The Home Mortgage Disclosure Act (HMDA) requires lenders to provide information about their mortgages and loan applications, which helps identify discriminatory lending practices.

The Fair Housing Act prohibits discrimination when selling or renting housing on the basis of race, gender, religion, national origin, disability, and family status.

Additionally, the Equal Credit Opportunity Act (ECOA) prohibits creditors from discriminating against applicants based on race or other prohibited characteristics.

By having these laws in place, it creates a level playing field for potential borrowers regardless of their background.

With these protective measures in place, we can begin to explore potential solutions for redlining that could help create equitable economic opportunities for everyone.

Potential Solutions for Redlining

By providing equal access to economic opportunities, we can start to turn the tide of redlining and ensure a brighter future for all. To do this, we must think about how to create solutions that are equitable, effective, and promote sustainable growth in our communities. Here are some potential ways of doing so:

- Providing more access to financial services like credit unions and microloans in underserved neighborhoods.
- Offering fair housing laws that protect renters from discrimination and encourage home ownership in communities of color.
- Creating incentives for businesses to invest in marginalized areas, such as tax credits or grant funding for local entrepreneurs.

These solutions could help foster greater economic inclusion and stability for those who have been excluded from traditional models of wealth building due to systemic racism and prejudice.

We must work together with policy makers and stakeholders to make sure these steps are taken towards creating an economically just society that values everyone's contributions equally.

Frequently Asked Questions

What are the consequences of redlining for communities of color?

We all know the impact of discrimination on communities of color – unequal access to resources, economic inequality, and social marginalization.

When it comes to redlining, these issues are magnified even further. Redlining is a practice that involves denying services and resources to people based on their race or ethnicity, leading to long-term consequences for communities of color.

These consequences include housing inequality, higher rates of poverty, and less access to decent education and healthcare services. All of these factors can have a profound effect on the well-being and prosperity of those affected by redlining.

What actions can be taken to reduce the racial wealth gap caused by redlining?

We're all aware of the racial wealth gap in our society, with communities of color facing immense economic inequality.

To reduce this disparity, we must take action to create more opportunities and resources for these marginalized groups. This includes investing in diverse businesses by providing access to capital and resources, offering job training and education programs, advocating for fair housing policies that prohibit discrimination based on race or ethnicity, and increasing financial literacy among underprivileged communities.

By doing so, we can ensure that everyone has an equal chance at success and prosperity regardless of their background.

Are there any local programs available to address the effects of redlining?

We've all heard the stories of people being denied access to housing and financial services due to their race. But what many people don't know is that there are actually several local programs available in cities across the country that aim to reduce the effects of this discriminatory practice, known as redlining.

From government initiatives providing first-time homebuyers with down payment assistance to city funding for small businesses in minority neighborhoods, there are countless programs out there designed to help those who have been disproportionately affected by redlining.

With a little research, anyone can find these resources and take advantage of them!

Is redlining still legal in certain areas?

We've all heard of the injustice that comes with living in certain communities, but what you may not know is that this is a form of discrimination called redlining.

Redlining is still legal in some areas, where banks and other lenders deny or limit services to certain neighborhoods based on race or ethnicity. This outdated practice isn't just unfair--it's also illegal.

Thankfully, there are steps being taken to address the effects of redlining and ensure everyone has access to essential services and resources.

How can people of color be empowered to fight against redlining?

We, people of color, have the power to fight against redlining. Redlining is not just an act of discrimination, but also a form of systemic racism that has been used for generations to keep us from having access to the same opportunities as our white counterparts.

While it may seem like an insurmountable challenge, there are concrete steps we can take to empower ourselves and work towards changing this injustice. By joining forces with organizations dedicated to fighting redlining, advocating for policy change at the local and national level, and educating our peers on what redlining is and how it affects us all, we can make progress in dismantling these unjust practices.

Conclusion

We've seen how redlining has had a devastating impact on communities of color. From the racial wealth gap to limited access to healthcare and economic opportunities, it's clear that something needs to be done.

As the old adage goes, an ounce of prevention is worth a pound of cure - so we must continue to work together to create more equitable laws and regulations that prevent redlining in its tracks.

It's only through unified action that we can truly make lasting change for our neighborhoods, our cities, and our country.

Hate Groups

We live in an increasingly divided world and hate groups are growing more and more powerful. According to a recent report, the number of hate groups operating in the US has grown by 30% over the last five years. This is a shocking statistic that serves to illustrate how quickly these organizations are spreading their hateful message.

We need to take action now if we want to ensure that our communities remain safe and free from hatred. In this article, we'll look at what hate groups are, the tactics they use for recruitment, the impact they have on society, anti-hate strategies and best practices for countering them.

What are Hate Groups?

Hate groups are a real problem, and it's important to understand what they are.

A hate group is defined as an organized group or movement that advocates and practices hatred, hostility, or violence towards members of a race, ethnicity, nation, religion, gender identity, sexual orientation or any other designated sector of society.

These organizations often use extremist rhetoric to spread their message of intolerance and bigotry.

It's important to be aware of the insidious presence of these hateful entities in our society so we can take steps to fight them.

At the same time, it's also important to recognize that there are different types of hate groups with distinct ideologies and tactics.

Understanding these differences allows us to better assess how to address them appropriately and effectively.

Types of Hate Groups

You may be surprised to learn that, as of 2019, there are over 1000 active hate-related organizations in the United States alone, according to the Southern Poverty Law Center. These groups can broadly be categorized into three distinct types: religious or racial based, anti-immigrant, and LGBTQ related.

Each type has its own unique characteristics, but all share a common goal – to spread hatred and fear. Some of these hate groups have been around for decades, while others are relatively new. They range from small neighborhood gangs to large international organizations with millions of members and supporters worldwide.

All types employ recruitment tactics, such as spreading false information through social media, hosting rallies and events, and creating websites that promote their hateful message. It's important to recognize these tactics so we can work together to stop them from spreading further.

Recruitment and Tactics Used by Hate Groups

You may not realize it, but hate groups employ a variety of tactics to further their agenda and recruit new members. Many times they use subtle and covert approaches such as social media campaigns or engaging with people on college campuses. They also use more extreme measures like rallies, marches and intimidation. In some cases, they even have ties to organized crime which can be used for money laundering and other illicit activities.

All of these tactics are used to spread their message of hatred in order to increase their following. No matter the tactic being employed by hate groups, the overall goal is always the same: to spread fear and violence among people who are different from them. This type of behavior only serves to divide us further, creating an unsafe environment for everyone.

The impact of hate groups should not be understated—it can cause serious harm both emotionally and physically if we don't stop them from gaining traction in our society.

The Impact of Hate Groups

The impact of these organizations can be far-reaching, leaving lasting damage to individuals and communities alike.

Hate groups have the potential to drive wedges between people from different races, religions, cultures, and backgrounds. Their message of intolerance can lead to physical violence as well as emotional trauma for those who become the target of their hatred.

The most vulnerable members of society—children, minorities, immigrants—are often at risk for becoming targets of hate group activity. Moreover, entire communities can suffer from a rise in hate group activity with an increase in crime rates and decreased feelings of safety.

It's essential that we examine the ways in which hate groups can devastate our communities so that we may find ways to prevent such occurrences in the future.

Anti-Hate Groups

Fighting hate takes a collective effort, and that's where anti-hate groups come in. These organizations are devoted to stamping out intolerance and prejudice by advocating for social justice, human rights, and equality.

Here are 4 ways they work to combat hate:

- Educating people about the consequences of bias in society
- Organizing events such as rallies and vigils to bring attention to issues of hatred
- Connecting individuals who have been affected by hate with support services
- Mobilizing communities through legislation, peaceful protests, and other forms of activism

The goal of these groups is simple: creating an inclusive world free from bigotry and discrimination. It's a difficult yet noble aim that requires dedication from all sides if it's ever going to be achieved--and anti-hate groups are playing an essential role in leading the charge.

With their tireless efforts towards promoting understanding and respect between people of different backgrounds, they're providing us with hope that a more tolerant future is within reach--one step at a time.

Laws and Regulations Aimed at Combatting Hate Groups

With laws and regulations in place, you can help make a difference in the fight against prejudice and intolerance. Governments have long had anti-hate laws to protect people from discrimination based on race, religion, gender identity, or sexual orientation.

These laws are designed to ensure that everyone is treated equally under the law, regardless of any differences they may possess. They also seek to punish those who intentionally spread messages of hate or incite violence against certain groups. By creating an environment where diversity is embraced and encouraged, we can combat hate groups more effectively.

The role of technology in countering hate groups has become increasingly important as well. Social media platforms, such as Twitter and Facebook, have implemented policies that restrict users from spreading hatred online by banning accounts that promote it. Additionally, governments have begun using digital surveillance tools to monitor for potential threats posed by radicalized individuals or organizations with extremist ideologies.

With these measures in place, society can better protect itself from the influence of hateful ideas—and thus make a real impact on reducing their prevalence in our world today.

Role of Technology in Countering Hate Groups

The need for laws and regulations to combat hate groups is great, but so too is the role of technology in countering these groups. We must utilize the latest advancements in technology to help identify hate group activities and prevent them from spreading further.

Social media platforms have become a key tool for identifying and counteracting extremist beliefs and activities, with algorithms able to detect hateful language or imagery before it even reaches users. Additionally, artificial intelligence has enabled us to better track user activity, allowing us to identify suspicious patterns that could potentially indicate radicalization or recruitment attempts by hate groups.

By using these technologies effectively, we are better equipped than ever before to monitor online activity associated with hate speech and take action against those who incite hatred or commit acts of violence against certain minority groups.

Our goal must be to create an environment where no one feels threatened or discriminated against due to their identity – this is only possible if we work together as a society to counter hate in all its forms. With the power of modern technology at our fingertips, we can make sure that online spaces remain safe and free from bigotry.

As such, it's essential that we continue pushing for technological solutions when it comes to combating hate groups online.

Countering Hate Groups Online

You can help counter online hate by utilizing the latest technology, so you don't have to worry about your safety or that of others. It's an effective way to ensure everyone can feel comfortable in the digital space.

Taking preventative measures such as reporting and blocking any suspicious accounts, monitoring your social media platforms for inappropriate content, and seeking out reliable sources for facts about hate groups are all great steps to take towards countering their malicious messages.

Additionally, creating a safe space within online communities by promoting tolerance and acceptance is another way to fight against hate groups. With these tactics in place, we can work together as a society to create a more tolerant digital world.

Strategies for Dealing with Hate Groups

Dealing with hate groups can be tough, but there are strategies that can help us combat them effectively:

- Learn about the group: Research their history and ideology. Read accounts from people who have escaped or left the group.

- Intervene in situations where hate speech is being used: Speak up to interrupt hateful rhetoric. Report any online activity that promotes violence or illegal behavior.

These two basic steps can help inform our understanding of how hate groups operate and give us a way to intervene when we observe hateful acts within our communities. Taking these proactive steps is essential for creating an environment where all individuals feel safe and respected. With this knowledge, we can move forward in exploring best practices for countering hate groups.

Best Practices for Countering Hate Groups

Combating hate requires us to take action and implement best practices for countering them. We should learn about their history and intervene in situations where hateful rhetoric is used. Understanding the root cause of a hate group's formation can help us come up with strategies that are effective in counteracting them.

We must also be aware of the language used by these groups and intervene when people use it to spread hatred or incite violence. It's important to recognize when a hate group has infiltrated an organization or online forum, so we can take steps to remove them from our spaces.

Finally, educating ourselves on how to respond appropriately in emotionally charged situations can help ensure that no one gets hurt while we're striving for peace. We must remain vigilant against hate groups as they often try to hide behind seemingly innocuous words or phrases that mask their true intentions.

By actively listening and engaging with those who may have been exposed to hateful rhetoric, we are better equipped to identify potential threats from these groups before they become reality. Taking proactive steps like creating safe spaces for open dialogue, speaking out against discrimination and bigotry, and encouraging others to do the same will go a long way towards diminishing the presence of hate in our communities.

Frequently Asked Questions

What is the definition of a hate group?

We all have something we strongly believe in, and it can be hard to accept when someone disagrees with us.

A hate group is a type of organization that goes beyond simply disagreeing; they are dedicated to spreading messages of prejudice and intolerance towards certain individuals or communities. They use symbols, such as flags and symbols of hatred, to represent their beliefs and ideologies.

These symbols can be very powerful - they evoke strong emotions from those who see them and can even be used to incite violence against the targeted groups.

It's important for us to recognize these symbols for what they are so we can stand up against the message of hate that these organizations spread.

What are the consequences of joining a hate group?

We all have our own beliefs and opinions, but joining a hate group can have serious consequences. When you join a hate group, you're associating yourself with an organization that promotes intolerance, violence, and discrimination.

This puts you at risk of being ostracized by your community, friends, and family. Additionally, participating in a hate group can also lead to legal troubles such as fines or even jail time if you engage in illegal activities.

It's important to remember that everyone has the right to their own opinion and personal beliefs, but it's not okay to act on those beliefs in ways that hurt others or violate the law.

What are the legal implications of hate groups?

We all have a subconscious desire for safety, but what are the legal implications of participating in hate groups?

It's important to understand that forming or joining a group with the intent to discriminate against others based on race, religion, disability, gender identity or expression, sexual orientation or other legally protected characteristics is strictly prohibited.

Alliteration aside, it's essential to note that such activities can lead to serious repercussions including criminal penalties and civil liability.

As such, it's important to be aware of any laws concerning hate groups before getting involved in one.

What strategies can be used to counter hate groups?

We all have a desire to feel safe and secure in our communities. To counter groups that spread hatred and intolerance, it's important to recognize the power of unified action.

We can work together towards creating an inclusive environment by engaging in conversations that celebrate diversity, supporting organizations that promote tolerance, and standing up against hate speech when we encounter it.

By taking these steps, we can create an atmosphere of acceptance and understanding within our community.

How can people protect themselves from hate groups?

We all want to feel safe and protected from harm. That's why it's important to know how to protect ourselves from potential threats, such as hate groups.

It starts by knowing the signs of a hate group and being vigilant about our surroundings. This can include watching for unusual behavior or people who seem out of place in an area, researching any unfamiliar groups that form around you, and keeping up with news related to hate crimes in your area.

Additionally, it's important to trust your instincts if something doesn't feel right; don't be afraid to walk away or contact authorities if necessary. Taking these steps will help ensure that you are well-protected from the threat of hate groups.

Conclusion

We've come to the end of our journey exploring hate groups.

We've discussed their types, recruitment and tactics, impacts, anti-hate groups, and the role of technology in countering them.

We've also looked at strategies for dealing with them and best practices for countering them online.

Hate groups are a complex issue that requires an ongoing effort to combat.

Just like trying to stop the waves from crashing on a beach - it's an uphill battle - but it's not impossible with dedication and collaboration.

By raising awareness, educating people on these issues, and empowering communities to stand up against hate, we can work together to create a more inclusive society free from violence and discrimination.

The Great Replacement Theory

We've all heard of the Great Replacement Theory, but what do we really know about it? Is it an accurate way to explain the changing demographics of some countries or is it a tool used to spread fear and hatred?

In this article, we'll take a look at the various criticisms that have been leveled against the theory. We'll explore why many experts argue that it lacks empirical evidence, ignores historical context, over-simplifies complex issues, overemphasizes immigration, presupposes malicious intent and overlooks domestic population changes.

We'll also discuss why some believe there are no viable alternatives to the theory. By understanding these flaws in the theory and its implications for society, we can make informed decisions about how best to promote diversity and inclusion in our societies today.

Lack of Empirical Evidence

You may find that there's a lack of empirical evidence supporting this concept. The Great Replacement Theory has been criticized for relying on anecdotal evidence and speculation rather than hard data. This theory suggests that non-white immigrants are replacing the white population in Europe and North America, but there's no concrete proof to back up this claim.

Furthermore, many experts have argued that the demographic changes seen in these countries are due to other factors such as increased birth rates among minority populations or decreased death rates due to improved healthcare. Without any reliable data to support it, the Great Replacement Theory remains largely unsubstantiated.

Another criticism of the Great Replacement Theory is that it ignores historical context. Immigration has always been a part of life in Europe and North America, with waves of people coming from different parts of the world throughout history.

In addition, many countries have experienced periods of population decline due to wars or economic downturns which could account for some of the demographic shifts seen today. By failing to take into account these important factors, proponents of the Great Replacement Theory overlook key elements which could explain why certain populations are growing or shrinking over time.

Ignoring Historical Context

Ignoring historical context is a huge mistake when it comes to discussing this issue. We can't just look at the present without understanding how things got here. Looking at the roots of the great replacement theory, it's easy to see how complex and far-reaching this issue truly is.

Yet too many people take a simplistic view of the situation and make broad generalizations that don't account for all its nuances. This over-simplification of complex issues often leads to dangerous mischaracterizations and misunderstandings, making it more difficult to have an honest discussion about solutions and possible outcomes.

It's essential that we consider both current events and their historical contexts if we want to move forward in any meaningful way.

Over-Simplification of Complex Issues

Over-simplifying complex issues can be catastrophic, creating an environment of misinformed opinions and dangerous misunderstandings that can spiral out of control in the blink of an eye.

This is one of the major criticisms leveled against proponents of the Great Replacement Theory, which suggests that mass migration from certain countries into Europe will result in a complete cultural transformation. However, this oversimplifies the complexities involved with immigration, as it ignores social and economic factors like job opportunities or access to public services that often play a much larger role in determining where immigrants choose to settle down.

Furthermore, it fails to account for demographic trends such as declining birth rates among native Europeans which are already contributing to population shifts within European countries. Rather than taking these nuances into consideration, supporters of Great Replacement Theory paint a one-dimensional picture that doesn't reflect reality.

As such, this over-simplification can lead to fearmongering and open up avenues for bigotry and hatred rather than allowing for meaningful dialogue about how best to handle immigration in Europe going forward. To avoid such pitfalls, it's important to recognize all sides of an issue rather than relying too heavily on any single narrative.

Ignoring Social and Economic Factors

Failing to recognize the social and economic forces that shape immigration can lead to an incomplete picture of the issue, preventing meaningful dialogue and potentially stirring up unnecessary fear and hatred. Excluding these factors leads to a one-dimensional view of the issue, which could result in a misunderstanding of what is really driving immigration trends.

Without understanding the underlying causes beyond simple movements of people, it can be difficult to understand how best to approach this complex issue. Additionally, focusing on immigration alone ignores other important factors such as global poverty or changes in climate that may affect migration patterns.

It's essential for any discussion about immigration to take into account all relevant aspects so that solutions are implemented effectively and fairly. In order for meaningful dialogue around immigration issues to occur, it's important that all sides consider both the social and economic elements involved.

Understanding why people are moving from one place to another is key in finding successful policy solutions that benefit everyone involved as well as society at large. To move forward constructively, we must move away from oversimplified views of immigration by examining social and economic conditions with empathy and compassion instead of fear or hatred.

Overemphasis on Immigration

You may be tempted to make immigration the sole focus of your conversations about current events, but it's important to remember that immigration is only one piece of a much larger puzzle.

The Great Replacement Theory (GRT) has been criticized for its overemphasis on immigration as the main cause of population change. According to proponents of GRT, immigrants pose an existential threat to Western civilization and culture. However, this ignores the fact that there are numerous social and economic factors at play which contribute to population shifts across countries and regions.

The idea that migrants are solely responsible for societal changes fails to consider other essential components of migration such as poverty, lack of job opportunities, political instability or war-torn countries. Moreover, this theory does not take into account internal migrations within countries or cross-border economic shifts that can also have an impact on population dynamics.

Consequently, it is essential to recognize migration in its complexity rather than oversimplifying it by attributing all changes exclusively to immigration. To understand these issues better, we must look beyond just immigration and explore the broader implications of population movements around the world.

Unintended consequences resulting from migration must be taken into consideration when discussing current events that involve geopolitical dynamics.

Unintended Consequences of Migration

We've seen how overemphasis on immigration has been used to support the Great Replacement Theory, but let's look now at the unintended consequences of migration.

As people move from one region to another, they bring with them their unique cultures and customs that can often lead to tension or misunderstanding when they're not adequately addressed. This is especially true in rapidly changing societies where traditional values and beliefs are challenged by newcomers.

In this sense, migration can create a ripple effect of unintended effects as different groups encounter each other and attempt to coexist without adequate preparation or understanding. It's therefore important for governments and communities to be mindful of the cultural implications of migration prior to its implementation so that any potential issues can be properly addressed.

As we consider the potential consequences of migration, it's equally important to remember that such actions shouldn't be presupposed as having malicious intent. Instead, it's essential for all parties involved in a given situation - both those affected by migration and those who facilitate it - to understand their roles in creating an inclusive society that strives for mutual understanding and respect.

Presupposing Malicious Intent

It's important to remember that migration should not be assumed as having malicious intent, but instead with an eye towards fostering mutual understanding and respect. This is particularly true of the Great Replacement Theory, which claims that large-scale immigration will lead to the displacement of native populations. However, this presupposes a malicious intent on the part of immigrants, something which cannot be conclusively proven. Furthermore, it ignores other factors such as economic instability or violence in countries of origin that could explain why people choose to migrate in the first place.

Ignoring these factors and assuming malignant intentions on the part of migrants is dangerous and misguided. Furthermore, it leads to an oversimplification of a complex issue and can result in policies that are too harsh or even discriminatory against certain people or groups. It also ignores the voluntary nature of migration—that individuals make their own decisions based on what they deem best for themselves and their families—and instead paints them all with one brush stroke as if they were all part of some sinister plan by political elites. Such assumptions are unfounded and only serve to vilify those who seek better lives for themselves elsewhere.

Moving forward, we must ensure our policies reflect our values and that immigrants are welcomed with open arms instead of suspicion and distrust.

Ignoring Voluntary Migration

By disregarding the fact that most migrants choose to move voluntarily, we are denying their right to pursue a better life for themselves and their families. This is an immoral act, as every individual has the right to choose where they live.

Ignoring this reality makes it easy to paint all immigration as something negative or malicious in nature, which feeds into the idea of the Great Replacement Theory. However, this theory fails to consider the positive impacts immigration can have on a country's economy and culture. It also overlooks the fact that many immigrants may be fleeing violence or persecution at home and simply trying to find safety in another country.

Therefore, by ignoring voluntary migration, we are failing to recognize its potential benefits while simultaneously demonizing those who seek refuge abroad.

Furthermore, overlooking domestic population changes also undermines any claims made by proponents of the Great Replacement Theory. Migration patterns often fluctuate over time due to changing economic conditions or other factors such as war or natural disasters.

As a result, populations in certain countries can fluctuate drastically without outside influence from other nations or cultures. Therefore, it's important that we recognize these changes before making assumptions about why certain demographic shifts occur within our society.

Doing so will help us better understand how populations change over time and will ultimately lead us towards more informed policy decisions when dealing with issues of immigration and cultural diversity.

Overlooking Domestic Population Changes

You may be overlooking domestic population changes when discussing immigration and cultural diversity, but they can have significant impacts on the makeup of a society. It's true that voluntary migration can shift demographics, but it doesn't always tell the full story.

Birth rates and death rates within a population are also important indicators in understanding how a culture is shaped over time. Low birthrates or high mortality rates due to medical advances or an aging population can significantly affect the composition of a nation's citizens without any outside influences. Therefore, these internal shifts should also be taken into consideration when examining the great replacement theory as they may be playing an even bigger role than previously thought.

In addition to this, there's another issue with the great replacement theory that needs to be addressed: lack of alternatives.

Lack of Alternatives to the Theory

Critics of the great replacement theory often point to a lack of alternatives, seeing it as a one-sided view of population dynamics. Taking a closer look, however, reveals that there may be more to the story than meets the eye - like the proverbial tip of the iceberg.

When examining population dynamics closely, we can begin to uncover other possible explanations for changes in population composition. Immigration and refugee policies, changing economic opportunities within countries, and even cultural shifts may all play roles in population movements. Without exploring these alternatives, we're likely missing out on important factors that could impact how policymakers respond to global migrations and displacement.

For example, an understanding of how local economies influence migration flows could help inform strategies to reduce conflict between locals and migrants in host countries. Similarly, investigating why people migrate could lead to better ways to support those who choose not to leave their country as well as provide aid for those who do emigrate.

In this way, delving into alternative theories can bring forth new ideas about how best to address issues related to population changes globally.

Frequently Asked Questions

Who are the proponents of the Great Replacement Theory?

We've all heard of the Great Replacement Theory, but who are the people behind it?

The main proponent of this theory is French author and political activist Renaud Camus.

He first articulated his ideas in a 2000 book titled Le Grand Remplacement (The Great Replacement).

Other prominent figures associated with the idea include white nationalist Richard Spencer as well as conservative authors such as Andrew McCarthy and Peter Brimelow.

While these theories have been met with some controversy, what's important to remember is that everyone has the right to express their opinion - no matter how unpopular it may be.

What are the implications of the Great Replacement Theory?

We often hear about the Great Replacement Theory and its implications, but what exactly does it mean?

This theory suggests that the demographic makeup of a certain population is changing rapidly due to immigration or other factors. It implies that one population is being replaced by another, which has sparked debates and raised questions about cultural identity and social cohesion.

The implications of this theory are complex: on the one hand, some believe it could lead to increased cultural diversity; while on the other, others worry that it could cause existing populations to become marginalized or even disappear.

Ultimately, whether we support or oppose this theory will depend on our own beliefs and values.

How does the Great Replacement Theory compare to other theories?

We often compare the Great Replacement Theory with other theories, such as those of racial supremacy and population control. However, when we look at the facts more closely, it's clear that these theories don't quite match up.

The idea behind the Great Replacement Theory is that one particular group of people is being replaced by another due to a variety of factors, which could include economic or political considerations. This theory does not promote any type of racial superiority nor does it suggest population control; instead, it simply highlights a shift in demographics that has been happening for centuries and discussing its potential implications.

What is the historical origin of the Great Replacement Theory?

We've all heard of the Great Replacement Theory, but do you know where it originated from?

This highly controversial idea was first proposed by French philosopher Renaud Camus in his book Le Grand Remplacement (The Great Replacement) published in 2012.

It suggests that native populations of European countries are being replaced and 'outbred' by immigrants from other cultures around the world. Camus argued that this is an intentional process which is deliberately encouraged by governments and leaders, often with negative consequences for the original population.

In recent years, this theory has been widely criticized as a form of racism or xenophobia, but its historical origins remain a subject of debate.

Does the Great Replacement Theory have any real-world applications?

We've all heard of the Great Replacement Theory, but does it have any real-world applications?

The answer is yes and no.

On one hand, this theory has been used to explain some of the population shifts we've seen in certain parts of the world over recent years.

On the other hand, it doesn't account for many other factors that can also play a role in these changes.

While there are certainly criticisms of the Great Replacement Theory, it's important to remember that its implications could still be relevant today.

Conclusion

We've seen that the Great Replacement Theory has come under fire from many angles. From lack of empirical evidence to ignoring social and economic factors, it's clear that this theory is far too simplistic to be taken seriously.

Despite its sweeping popularity, it fails to offer any tangible solutions or address any real-world issues. All it does is breed fear and suspicion, painting a picture of sinister forces 'replacing' us with immigrants for nefarious purposes. We can only shake our heads in disbelief at such a ludicrous notion!

Let's all take a step back and look at the facts; immigration isn't something we should be afraid of: it's an opportunity to embrace new cultures, new ideas, and fresh perspectives on life.

White Supremacy

We, as a society, cannot ignore the issue of white supremacy any longer. It's been ingrained in our history since the very beginning and it still affects us today. We must understand how this ideology has impacted people from all walks of life and how it continues to affect numerous aspects of modern life.

Through education, awareness, and action we can work together to combat white supremacy, but first we need to understand what it is and how it works. In this article we will explore the historical origins of white supremacy, its ideology, systemic racism, economic inequality, educational inequality, political power dynamics, media representation and stereotypes as well as intersectional impacts of white supremacy.

Finally we'll discuss strategies for combating white supremacy. Now let's dive in!

Historical Origins of White Supremacy

You might not realize it, but white supremacy has been a part of our history for centuries. It began as early as the 1600s when Europeans colonized and enslaved African people to work on their plantations in the Americas. This was done through the ideology of white superiority, which argued that people with lighter skin were superior to those with darker skin.

Since then, this idea has been used to justify systemic racism and oppression against minorities around the world. It is important to understand how this ideology shaped our society in order to dismantle it today.

To truly understand white supremacy, we must also look at its underlying beliefs and values. White supremacists view themselves as superior because of their race and believe that other races are inferior or deserving of subjugation. They advocate for laws, policies, and social practices that promote racial segregation and inequality between different groups of people.

This dangerous ideology has resulted in violence against minority communities across the globe over many years. Understanding the roots of white supremacy helps us recognize how pervasive it is today so we can better fight back against it.

The Ideology of White Supremacy

You're likely familiar with the belief that one race is superior to all others, but do you understand why this ideology exists?

White supremacy is an idea that has been around for centuries, and it often relies on the notion of racial superiority to justify its existence. The reasons behind this are varied and can range from a need to feel powerful or more important than other races, to a desire to preserve one's culture and heritage.

This ideology also tends to rely on stereotypes and false claims about certain groups in order to maintain its status. Even though some may claim that white supremacy is rooted in history or tradition, it's an outdated and dangerous idea that should not be tolerated.

White supremacy isn't just a set of beliefs; it's also an oppressive system which has been used by those in power as a tool for subjugating minority groups. Systemic racism occurs when institutional policies and practices create advantages for some while disadvantaging others due to their race or ethnicity.

Thus, understanding the ideological roots of white supremacy is essential if we're going to truly tackle systemic racism within our society.

Systemic Racism

Being a part of a minority group can often mean facing systemic racism that disadvantages you and keeps you from the same opportunities as others.

Systemic racism is based on a set of laws, policies, practices, and customs that create and maintain unequal power relations between different racial groups.

This form of racism is deeply embedded in our social institutions, such as education, healthcare, employment, housing, criminal justice system, politics etc.

It works to keep certain groups at an economic disadvantage by limiting their access to resources and opportunities.

It also reinforces stereotypes about certain races or ethnicities which further limits individuals' ability to succeed or gain recognition in society.

The effects of systemic racism are long-lasting and far-reaching; it affects generations of people who may never have experienced direct discrimination themselves but still feel its impact in their lives.

As such, addressing this form of prejudice requires more than just individual action – it requires collective effort and commitment to prevent discrimination from becoming entrenched in our culture.

With this in mind, it's important to understand how economic inequality is connected to systemic racism.

Economic Inequality

Economic inequality is often connected to systemic racism, and it can be seen in the disparities that exist between different racial groups when it comes to access to resources and opportunities.

This gap in economic opportunity has been exacerbated by historic policies that were designed to create and maintain white supremacy, such as redlining and discriminatory lending practices.

Furthermore, this economic inequality has had a lasting impact on communities of color, making it even more difficult for them to gain access to the same educational and other life opportunities available to white people.

All of these factors contribute to a cycle of poverty that perpetuates racial inequality, ultimately contributing significantly to the prevalence of white supremacy today.

With this in mind, we must also consider how educational inequality plays an important role in reinforcing these dynamics.

Educational Inequality

It's ironic that educational opportunities, which are meant to level the playing field, can instead increase existing disparities between racial groups. White supremacy has long been an issue in the realm of education, and its effects are still felt today.

Despite progress that has been made in recent years, inequalities in educational attainment remain an obstacle for many people of color:

- Access:

- Low-income communities lack access to quality schools and resources.

- Minority students may face discrimination when applying to college.

- Expectations:

- Black and Latino students are often stereotyped as not being "college material".

- Minorities may be expected to take lower level courses or discouraged from taking Advanced Placement classes.

- Representation:

- The majority of teachers do not reflect the racial makeup of their student population.

- There is a disproportionate representation of minorities among school suspensions and expulsions.

These issues serve as a reminder that white supremacy has far-reaching implications on educational opportunities for people of color—and it's evident that there's much work left to be done if we want to create equitable systems for everyone.

It's only through understanding the role that race plays in educational disparities that we can begin to address social exclusion and move towards more inclusive solutions.

Social Exclusion

The prevalence of social exclusion can be seen in the disparities between those with access to educational opportunities and those who are denied them due to systemic biases. These disparities are further perpetuated by white supremacy, which enables certain groups to have more political power than others.

This power often translates into unequal access to resources like education, employment opportunities, and other basic necessities that enable individuals to succeed in life. As a result, some people are relegated to the margins of society and excluded from mainstream institutions such as schools and universities.

Social exclusion has far-reaching consequences for individuals, families, communities, and societies at large. It creates an environment where inequality continues to thrive while preventing people from achieving their full potential.

This unfairness is further entrenched through the political power dynamics that shape our world today. White supremacists have long been able to use their influence to create policies designed solely for their benefit at the expense of marginalized populations—policies that limit these populations' rights and freedoms while also limiting their access to resources like education.

Such policies contribute significantly to social exclusion by making it harder for minority groups to achieve success or find meaningful employment opportunities. Consequently, this creates a cycle wherein minorities remain underprivileged and unable or unwilling to escape poverty or seek better lives for themselves and their families.

With all this in mind, it's clear that addressing the issue of social exclusion requires tackling its root cause: white supremacy.

Political Power Dynamics

You have the power to shape the political landscape, and when you do, be sure not to overlook those who have been pushed to the fringes of society—those who have been denied access to resources like education due to systemic bias. Let's give them a voice and help break the cycle of exclusion with our actions.

We must recognize that white supremacy is still used today as a tool for maintaining power dynamics within politics. This means that we need to actively challenge these oppressive systems in order to create an equitable society where all people are valued and respected.

With this in mind, it's important that we understand how media representation and stereotypes can further perpetuate white supremacy in our political system.

Media Representation and Stereotypes

We've discussed the political power dynamics of white supremacy and how it has continued to shape our society, but there's another aspect that needs to be addressed: media representation and stereotypes.

The way people of color are portrayed in film, television, music, and other forms of media shapes the public's perception. Unfortunately, these representations are often limited or flat out wrong with characters being used as props for comedy or violence. This perpetuates a false narrative about people of color which leads to a greater acceptance of racism and discrimination.

This type of misrepresentation can have an insidious impact on the self-worth and confidence levels of those affected by it, leading to feelings of shame or guilt instead of pride. It also affects how we interact with each other since our opinions about certain groups are based on what we see in the media rather than personal experience.

For example, we might view certain cultures as dangerous because they're depicted that way in films when in reality this may not be true at all. To truly understand the impacts of white supremacy, we need to recognize how its influence is felt through media representation and stereotypes - something that has far-reaching implications beyond just politics.

Intersectional Impacts of White Supremacy

Understanding the intersectional impacts of white supremacy is key to recognizing how it affects our lives and the lives of those around us. White supremacy has a far-reaching impact on communities in terms of access to resources, such as healthcare, education, and job opportunities that aren't equally available for all people regardless of their race or gender identity.

The ability to have one's voice heard in conversations about policy-making and decision-making processes that affect those same communities is also impacted by white supremacy. The psychological effects of being exposed to stereotypes and systemic racism can lead to feelings of powerlessness and lack of self-worth.

Additionally, white supremacy has economic impacts as some groups are pushed into poverty due to discrimination while others are given advantages because they fit certain standards set by white supremacy culture.

It's essential that we acknowledge these issues before moving forward with strategies for combating white supremacy so we can make sure everyone is included in the solution.

Strategies for Combating White Supremacy

Taking action against racism and discrimination is vital for creating a more equitable society, so let's explore some strategies for fighting back.

One effective way to combat white supremacy is through education. We should be educating ourselves and others on the history of oppression and injustice faced by people of color, as well as promoting an environment that encourages open dialogue about these issues.

We can also help create change by supporting organizations and initiatives that focus on dismantling systemic racism, such as donating money or volunteering our time.

Additionally, we must work to actively support Black-owned businesses in our communities, while challenging any instances of racial profiling or prejudice we encounter in everyday life.

Finally, it's important to remember that conversations about race are uncomfortable but necessary; if we don't speak up when we witness injustice, then nothing will ever change.

Frequently Asked Questions

What is an example of a white supremacist group?

We often think of the world as a safe place, but there are many dark corners that can quickly turn dangerous. The term 'white supremacist group' is one such corner, a metaphor for an organization that promotes the idea of racial superiority based on skin color.

Such groups have been around for centuries, and today some of their most prominent examples include neo-Nazi organizations like The National Alliance and racist hate groups like The Ku Klux Klan. These organizations rely on fear and hatred to spread their message, which has no place in our society.

How does white supremacy manifest itself in everyday life?

We often see subtle forms of white supremacy manifesting in everyday life. From microaggressions to discriminatory practices, it's clear that white supremacist ideals are still prevalent and accepted by many people.

The most common examples include the normalizing of racial stereotypes, the privileging of certain cultures over others, and unequal access to resources based on race or ethnicity. These systemic issues can have a profound effect on those who don't fit into the societal norms of whiteness.

It's essential that we acknowledge these issues and strive to create an equitable society for all.

What is the impact of white supremacy on marginalized communities?

We all know the feeling of being excluded and oppressed. Unfortunately, marginalized communities experience this on a daily basis due to white supremacy.

Systemic racism is still prevalent in our society, creating an unbalanced power dynamic that disproportionately affects these communities. This has resulted in various forms of discrimination such as unequal access to resources like education, employment opportunities, healthcare, and housing; as well as physical violence and verbal abuse.

The impact of white supremacy on marginalized communities is undeniable and can have devastating consequences if not addressed.

How can we teach young people about white supremacy?

We all want to empower young people to become informed citizens and to make a positive impact in the world. Teaching them about white supremacy is an important part of this process, as it helps them understand how systems of privilege operate in our society.

We can best teach young people about white supremacy by introducing them to its history, exploring current examples of it in action, and discussing strategies for dismantling oppressive structures. Through these conversations, we can help foster greater awareness and empathy among our youth so that they may become agents of change.

How can we create meaningful dialogue about white supremacy?

We all have a desire for safety and security, but how can we create meaningful dialogue about the things that make us uncomfortable?

To start, let's take a step back in time to a simpler era before white supremacy was even an issue. Let's look at this as if it's any other topic that we must openly discuss; understanding that by doing so, we can foster meaningful conversations.

With open minds and empathy in our hearts, together we can create an atmosphere of understanding and progress.

Conclusion

We must come together and challenge white supremacy. We have to confront the systemic racism, economic inequality, educational disparities, and political power dynamics in our society.

Our collective efforts can make a difference if we stand up for what's right and just. How much longer will we allow these oppressive systems to exist? It's time to take action and create a better future for all of us.

Let's commit ourselves to dismantling white supremacy by supporting initiatives that promote diversity, equity, and inclusion at all levels of our society. Together, we can end this oppressive system once and for all.

Ku Klux Klan

We have all heard of the infamous Ku Klux Klan - a secret society that has been around since the Reconstruction Era in America. It seems strange to think that such an organization could exist for so long and even stranger to think of its lasting legacy.

Even though it was formed with the intention of white supremacy, we must look back on its history and ask ourselves what it truly stands for today. How did this group become so powerful? What were their rituals and practices? And how has it evolved over time?

These questions will be answered as we explore the history of the KKK.

Origins of the Ku Klux Klan

Since the late 19th century, the Ku Klux Klan has been a dark presence in American history, shrouded in secrecy and provoking fear among those it sought to intimidate. The organization was founded in 1865 by Confederate veterans in Pulaski, Tennessee who wanted to resist Reconstruction policies and restore white supremacy.

In its first incarnation, KKK members used fear tactics such as physical violence, assassination threats and economic intimidation to deter African-Americans from voting or engaging in other political activities. As time progressed, new incarnations of the KKK emerged with different goals ranging from anti-Catholicism to labor union suppression.

While the initial Klan dissolved into obscurity during the 1870s, it reemerged at several points throughout US history as a powerful hate group focused on bigotry against racial minorities and religious groups. Throughout the 20th century, violent acts committed by members of this organization have resulted in numerous deaths and injuries nationwide.

Today's version is much diminished but still active in some parts of the country. It continues to spread its message of hatred through rallies, parades, and other public events despite numerous attempts by law enforcement agencies to shut down their activities.

As we move forward into an era where more Americans are embracing diversity than ever before, it's important that we remember how far our nation has come since those dark days when racial tension ran rampant across our land.

The Reconstruction Era

After the Civil War, a new era of hope and challenge emerged - the Reconstruction Era - that would shape the future of America. With Union victory in 1865 and the emancipation of slaves, came a period of readjustment for both North and South.

In an effort to bring Southern states back into the Union, Congress passed two important pieces of legislation: The Thirteenth Amendment abolished slavery, while the Fourteenth Amendment granted citizenship to all persons born or naturalized in the United States.

The Reconstruction Era also brought about a transition from an agricultural to an industrial economy as well as changes in voting rights for African Americans. Although these changes were met with resistance from many Southerners, they ultimately increased political representation for African Americans throughout the region.

Despite these advances, however, racism remained strong throughout much of America's South during this time. This led to outbreaks of violence against African Americans within certain parts of society—the rise of groups like the Ku Klux Klan being one example.

As such, it's clear that while some progress was made during this period in terms of civil rights for African Americans, there was still much work left to be done. Transitioning into this work is what will drive us into looking at 'the rise of the first klan' next.

The Rise of the First Klan

The Reconstruction Era saw the emergence of a dangerous and violent force that threatened African Americans' civil rights: the first Ku Klux Klan. This organization was founded in Pulaski, Tennessee in 1865 by six former Confederate soldiers as an effort to restore white supremacy. The KKK's goals included opposing social change, preventing African Americans from exercising their right to vote, restricting their access to public spaces such as schools and churches, forcing them out of positions of political power, terrorizing them through intimidation tactics, violence, lynchings, and murder, and demonizing their culture through false rumors and propaganda.

As a result of the actions taken by the KKK during this period, many states passed anti-Klan legislation which enabled authorities to prosecute members for their crimes. Unfortunately, these laws were rarely enforced due to widespread racism within law enforcement agencies at the time.

As a result, the Klan was able to remain active throughout much of Reconstruction and beyond until it disbanded in 1869. With this backdrop set, we can now examine how ideas associated with the first Klan resurfaced decades later and formed the basis for its second incarnation.

Second Klan's Ideology and Intent

Roaring like a wildfire, the Second Klan's ideology of white supremacy and oppression spread across the nation, engulfing all in its path. The Second Klan sought to restore white supremacy through intimidation and violence against African Americans and other people of color.

In addition to their core beliefs, they also wanted to protect Protestant values and promote traditional gender roles. Fearful of the changing demographics in America during the Reconstruction period, they adopted a hard-line stance against civil rights reforms that would have provided greater economic opportunities for African Americans.

Through their influence on politics, they were able to create laws that restricted voting rights and made it harder for people of color to find decent jobs or own property in certain areas. The members of the Second Klan believed that their mission was ordained by God himself.

They used rituals such as cross burnings and public rallies to instill fear into those who opposed them. Through these activities, they aimed to establish an atmosphere where anyone who didn't subscribe to their views could be punished or even killed without consequence.

Despite some efforts from local law enforcement officers to prevent such injustice, many people suffered at the hands of this terror group throughout its existence. Their presences had a profound effect on society at large — forcing individuals across racial lines into positions of compliance with their extreme views or suffer dire consequences.

With no end in sight for this oppressive reign over American culture, it's now time to explore how this group conducted themselves through rituals and practices.

Rituals and Practices

You'll explore how the Second Klan conducted themselves through their rituals and practices, a reign of oppression that has had profound effects on American culture.

The Second Klan was founded in 1915 in Pulaski, Tennessee by William Joseph Simmons as an organization dedicated to white supremacy and violence against African Americans, Catholics, Jews, immigrants, and other minorities. The group's mission was to restore America to its former glory when it was dominated by Protestants of Northern European descent.

To this end, they employed intimidation tactics such as night riding, lynching, and cross-burning - all meant to signal their anger towards those who opposed them or threatened their power base.

The rituals and practices of the Second Klan were also used to provide justification for racial segregation laws known as Jim Crow laws which legalized discrimination against African Americans in many parts of the country until the mid-20th century. The Klan advocated for these laws which barred certain people from voting or even attending school together with whites. They argued that segregation would help preserve "white purity" and prevent interracial relationships which would weaken the nation's moral fabric.

The legacy of the Second Klan still lingers today with some groups using similar symbols such as hanging nooses or burning crosses, though thankfully much more rarely than during its heyday. Despite attempts at civil rights legislation over time, there is still bias towards minority groups evident in our society - something we must continue to fight if we are ever going to make progress toward true equality for all citizens regardless of race or religion.

With this understanding, we now turn our attention to looking at how the KKK and Jim Crow Laws intersected with one another...

KKK and the Jim Crow Laws

Experience the powerful symbolism behind the Jim Crow laws and how they were used to oppress minority groups for decades. The Ku Klux Klan (KKK) was a white supremacist group that infiltrated American society in order to further enforce these oppressive laws. This organization had an incredible impact on civil rights issues throughout history.

They campaigned against interracial marriage and employment of African-Americans in certain jobs. They intimidated African-Americans by burning crosses and holding rallies. They used violence to keep people from voting or attending school. They spread propaganda in order to justify their beliefs about racial superiority. They targeted those who supported civil rights movements, including members of Congress and Presidents like Abraham Lincoln and John F Kennedy.

The KKK's activities have been largely condemned by the public today, but it's important to remember their role in creating an atmosphere of fear during a crucial time for civil rights in America. Unfortunately, this type of discrimination still exists today as we continue to strive towards racial equality. However, looking back at our history allows us to reflect on the progress we have made since then and gives us hope for the future.

With that being said, let's now explore how these Jim Crow laws related directly with the Civil Rights Movement...

The Civil Rights Movement

You can see how the Civil Rights Movement directly responded to the Jim Crow laws in an effort to achieve racial equality. The movement was a series of protests and acts of civil disobedience that aimed to challenge segregation, discrimination, and other forms of racism in America. Protests included boycotts, sit-ins, marches, and more peaceful forms of protest.

Action Taken	Goal
Boycotting	Protest Segregation
Sit-Ins	Desegregate Lunch Counters
Marches	Call for Racial Equality

 The most famous example is Martin Luther King Jr's March on Washington for Jobs and Freedom which took place in 1963 with over 200,000 people attending. This march highlighted the importance of achieving economic justice as well as political freedom and helped pass legislation like the 1964 Civil Rights Act. Through this legislation it became illegal to discriminate based on race or color when hiring employees or providing services. This marked a huge victory for civil rights activists across America who had worked hard to combat institutionalized racism through peaceful means. As a result of these efforts African Americans were finally given the same legal protection from discriminatory practices that white Americans had enjoyed since the founding of the nation. With this newfound protection they were able to pursue their dreams without fear or intimidation from those seeking to keep them down because of their skin color - enabling them to become fully equal members of society. Moving forward into a new era where all individuals are respected regardless of race or ethnicity would not have been possible if not for the courage shown by so many during this time period who stood up against injustice despite all odds being against them.

The Third Klan

Shrouded in mystery and cloaked in fear, the Third Klan's resurgence in the 1920s saw them terrorizing minority communities with their hateful rhetoric and violent tactics. The Third Klan had a different purpose than its predecessor, seeking to promote white supremacy through strict immigration policies and anti-Catholic sentiment. The group also wanted to keep African Americans from voting, achieving economic freedom, or even having any rights or representation at all.

Here are four defining characteristics of this era of the KKK:

- An emphasis on white Protestantism and nativism
- Adherence to traditional gender roles
- A focus on criminalizing non-white immigrants
- Intimidation tactics used against minorities

The Third Klan was highly effective at creating an environment of fear among minority groups by publicly displaying their symbols, burning crosses in yards, and organizing rallies aimed at spreading their message. This was further exacerbated due to the lack of legal protection for those targeted by this organization as well as local law enforcement turning a blind eye to their activities.

Even though it has largely been forgotten today, the impact of this period in history is still felt through current social issues such as police brutality against people of color and systemic racism. Its legacy continues to shape our society today; understanding what happened then is essential if we're ever going to move forward into a more equitable future.

Without meaningful change, we'll be doomed to repeat past mistakes, perpetuating injustice and inequality for generations to come. Moving forward requires looking back so that we can understand how far society has come while recognizing how much further there is left to go before true equality is achieved for all people without prejudice or discrimination.

The Klan Today

Today, the Klan has reemerged in a new form, though its ideologies remain largely unchanged. They've adopted more modern methods of recruitment and communication, utilizing internet forums and private messaging to build their membership base. Though they lack the same level of influence as before, they still carry out hate-filled propaganda campaigns targeting various minority groups like immigrants, Jews and African Americans. The group has also been linked to several acts of violence in recent years such as arson attacks on churches and homes.

In spite of these efforts by the KKK to spread their message of hate, counter-protests from other civil rights organizations have made it difficult for them to gain much traction. Though their attempts at creating new chapters across America have been largely unsuccessful due to public opposition, there are still areas where the organization is active and can be found gathering members or attending rallies.

This includes states like Georgia where an influx of anti-immigration sentiment has allowed them to increase their presence among certain demographics that share their views. The KKK also continues to be active in politics with candidates running for office on platforms supporting white supremacy ideals or attempting to introduce racist legislation into state laws.

The Klan's attempt at modernizing itself may not have brought them back into mainstream society but it has enabled them to reach more people than ever before with their messages of hate and intolerance. Moving forward, it's important that we continue our commitment towards fighting against racism by standing up for what's right regardless of how many people may oppose us.

With this goal in mind, let's explore further into the legacy of the KKK and what can be done about it today.

The Legacy of the KKK

You've heard of the Ku Klux Klan, but have you considered their long-lasting impact? The KKK has been an active group in America for over 150 years.

Despite its decline in activity and membership in recent decades, the legacy of the KKK still lingers today:

- Racism is still embedded in our society and laws.
- Racial discrimination is rampant throughout many occupations and industries.
- Hate crimes are a common occurrence across the United States.
- White supremacy groups continue to exist and propagate their message of intolerance.
- Schools continue to teach a skewed version of history that focuses on white perspectives while leaving out different voices or experiences from minority populations.

The effects of racism can be seen from all angles – social, economic, political, etc. Policies that were created by the KKK are still being used today such as voter suppression tactics or anti-immigration policies designed to target certain racial groups.

It's clear that these remnants remain long after the organization itself has been disbanded. We must take steps to create an inclusive society where everyone can live together without fear or judgment based on race or ethnicity.

Only then will we fully move past this dark period in American history and begin to heal from its impacts on our culture today.

Conclusion

We've seen how the Ku Klux Klan has changed and evolved over time.

From its inception during the Reconstruction Era to its decline after the Civil Rights Movement, it has left behind a legacy of racism and hatred.

Even with its diminished presence today, we must remain vigilant in our fight against hate and bigotry.

How can we ensure that this cycle doesn't repeat itself?

With more education and understanding, perhaps we can make sure that history doesn't repeat itself.

Neo Nazism

We shudder at the thought of it.

Neo-Nazism is a nightmarish ideology that has tormented our world for decades and continues to be a threat to global peace and security.

It's a vile virus, slowly spreading its infectious hatred through radicalized individuals, groups, and organizations with dark ambitions.

This article will explore the history, symbolism, ideology, activism, violence and countermeasures associated with neo-Nazism on a global scale.

Join us as we take an in-depth look into this unsettling phenomenon.

Definition of Neo-Nazism

Fueled by hate and bigotry, this movement has become a terrifying force in our world today. Neo-Nazism is an ideology that combines elements of white supremacy, nationalism, and anti-Semitism - all of which are rooted in Nazi Germany's totalitarian regime.

This extremist movement attempts to revive the lost glory of the Third Reich and Adolf Hitler's doctrines. It seeks to promote white power through discrimination against immigrants, Jews, Muslims, people of color, LGBTQIA+ individuals, disabled people and other minority groups.

Neo-Nazis also adhere to ideas like Holocaust denial or revisionism that aims to rewrite history so as to deny any blame for Nazi atrocities. Consequently, neo-Nazism is considered a form of extreme right-wing nationalism and racism by scholars across the globe.

In light of this background information on neo-Nazism, it's important to understand its history and development over time.

History of Neo-Nazism

Motivated by hatred and prejudice, a radical right-wing ideology emerged in the early 20th century, aiming to revive Nazi Germany's vision of racial superiority. The roots of neo-Nazism can be traced back to 1919 when the German Workers' Party (DAP) was founded. The DAP would later become the National Socialist German Worker's Party, commonly known as the Nazi party.

After World War 1 ended, Germany was left economically weakened and politically unstable. This allowed Adolf Hitler to gain control of Germany through his political party. In 1933, Hitler became Chancellor of Germany and began implementing his extreme views on race and ethnicity. His rhetoric against Jewish people and other minority groups led to the Holocaust - an event that resulted in millions of deaths.

The legacy of Nazism has remained with us for generations since then. Neo-Nazis have adopted many aspects from their predecessors such as white supremacy beliefs or anti-Semitism. From its inception, this ideology has been based upon fearmongering tactics and seen numerous upsurges across Europe throughout the last century.

By understanding this history, we can better understand why neo-Nazis exist today—and how we can confront them effectively.

Neo-Nazi Ideology

Driven by hatred and bigotry, a radical right-wing ideology has taken root in modern society, embodying an extreme form of nationalism and racism. Known as neo-Nazism, this movement seeks to revive the beliefs of Nazi Germany and Adolf Hitler.

Neo-Nazis are united by their belief in racial superiority, anti-semitism, xenophobia, and homophobia. Their rhetoric is often characterized by xenophobic language that suggests some races or religions are superior to others. Neo-Nazis also deny the Holocaust ever happened and promote white nationalist ideals.

This extremist ideology has been linked to domestic terrorism in both Europe and the United States as well as hate crimes targeting minority groups. To many people's dismay, neo-Nazi rhetoric continues to spread across social media platforms unchecked. As a result of this hateful propaganda, it's essential that we understand how neo-Nazis express their beliefs through symbolism in order to better combat its spread.

Neo-Nazi Symbolism

You hear it in their words and you see it in their symbols; neo-Nazi hatred has no place in our society.

From the swastika to the Celtic cross, neo-Nazis have adopted many symbols throughout history to signify their allegiance to white supremacy. The most common of these is the swastika, which originates from ancient Hindu culture and was later adopted by Nazi Germany. Other symbols commonly used by neo-Nazis include variations on the Iron Cross, Thor's Hammer, and runes like Odal or Tyr.

Neo-Nazi symbolism also includes flags such as the Confederate battle flag and various combinations of black, white, red, and blue colors that are meant to evoke feelings of racial superiority. It is clear why this type of symbolism has been so pervasive among neo-Nazis: they use it as a way to intimidate those who disagree with their views while at the same time rallying around an easily recognizable banner for their cause.

As long as these hateful messages remain present in our society, we must continually stand against them in order to protect those who are targets of neo-Nazi hate speech. With that said, let's now examine how these same symbols are being used by neo-Nazi groups today.

Neo-Nazi Groups

Today, neo-Nazi groups continue to use these symbols to spread their message of hatred and intolerance.

Neo-Nazi groups remain active in many parts of the world, ranging from small local hate cells to larger organizations that span multiple countries. No matter the size or scope of the group, they all share a common thread: their commitment to using violence and intimidation as tools to further their extremist views.

This often includes carrying out physical attacks on people or property associated with those who oppose them, such as immigrant communities or minority religious groups. Additionally, neo-Nazis have been known to employ propaganda tactics like distributing leaflets and making public speeches in an effort to draw attention and support for their beliefs.

These materials are often filled with racially charged language or false information designed to stir up fear and hatred in order to further their cause. As a result, it's important for us all to stay vigilant against any attempt by neo-Nazis – both large and small – at spreading this kind of hateful rhetoric in our communities.

To do this effectively requires recognizing not only some of the symbols used by neo-Nazis but also understanding how they use these symbols as part of a larger strategy intended to incite hatred among populations around the globe.

Moving forward, we must recognize that this fight extends beyond simply identifying symbols; it involves actively countering neo-Nazi propaganda wherever it appears.

Neo-Nazi Propaganda

You've certainly heard about the symbols associated with neo-Nazi groups, but have you ever stopped to consider how they use propaganda to spread their message of hate and intolerance?

Neo-Nazis often rely on posters, flyers, websites, and even graffiti to indoctrinate the public. These messages are often heavily focused on anti-Semitic themes or white supremacist messages. They also attempt to promote a sense of superiority over other racial groups by emphasizing the supposed greatness of an Aryan race. Often times these same tactics are used to recruit new members into their cause as well.

The hateful messages that neo-Nazis present through their propaganda can be deeply damaging for those who come in contact with it. It can lead people to believe false notions about different races or ethnicities and foster feelings of hatred and exclusion against those who don't share their beliefs.

As such, it is important for us as a society to recognize the danger posed by this type of rhetoric and take steps towards stamping out its spread wherever we find it. Moving forward, let's explore how neo-Nazis manifest themselves in activism.

Neo-Nazi Activism

Though they may attempt to hide behind their hateful rhetoric, neo-Nazis still engage in activism to further their agenda of intolerance and bigotry. They often target young people, using online platforms such as social media and forums to spread their messages of hate.

Here are a few examples of neo-Nazi activism:

- Holding rallies and marches in public areas
- Engaging in political campaigns by running candidates for local office
- Posting flyers with white supremacist slogans or symbols

The goal of these activities is to make the neo-Nazi message appear normal and acceptable, no matter how extreme it might be. Unfortunately, this type of activism can lead directly to violence.

Neo-Nazi Violence

It's a sad reality that neo-Nazis often resort to violence in order to spread their message of hate and intolerance, leaving innocent people hurt or killed.

Neo-Nazi groups have been responsible for countless attacks on minorities, immigrants, and members of the LGBTQ+ community, religious minorities, and other vulnerable populations.

These violent acts have included physical assaults, vandalism targeted at places of worship and cultural centers, as well as arson attacks against businesses owned by ethnic minorities.

Such acts of violence are not only morally wrong but also illegal; yet unfortunately these groups continue to operate with impunity in many parts of the world.

We must take action to stand up for those affected by neo-Nazi violence and ensure that justice is served.

To do this, we must recognize the threat posed by these hate groups and work together to counter it.

Countering Neo-Nazism

It's clear that neo-Nazism has caused violence, and it's our responsibility to take action.

We must look beyond violence and consider the bigger picture of how to counter neo-Nazism in our communities.

To do this, we need to:

- Educate ourselves and others on the history and dangers of neo-Nazism.

- Demonstrate solidarity with those affected by neo-Nazism through peaceful protests or social media campaigns.
- Support organizations providing aid to those targeted by neo-Nazis around the world.

These are just a few of the ways we can take a stand against intolerance, hatred, and discrimination within our society.

Whether it's through education or support for organizations fighting injustice globally - together, we can make a difference in countering neo-Nazism in our communities and beyond.

Now let's turn our attention towards combating neo-Nazism globally...

Combating Neo-Nazism Globally

Taking a stand against neo-Nazism doesn't have to be limited to our own backyard - we can fight it on a global scale as well.

We need to build bridges between countries and cultures, creating an environment of understanding, acceptance and mutual respect. This can be achieved by organizing international events that celebrate diversity and provide support for those affected by hate crimes.

We should also increase awareness about the dangers of neo-Nazism through education initiatives in schools and universities.

In addition, governments should create legal frameworks that protect vulnerable populations from discrimination and bigotry.

Finally, we must use our voices to speak out in solidarity with those who are standing up against neo-Nazism around the world so they know they're not alone.

By joining forces together at a global level, we can make sure that everybody's respected regardless of their backgrounds or beliefs.

Frequently Asked Questions

Are neo-Nazis considered a terrorist organization?

The question of whether neo-Nazis are considered a terrorist organization is one that has been asked for decades. While it may be tempting to think of them as nothing more than dangerous radicals, the truth is that their activities can constitute terrorism in some cases.

In order to be labeled as terrorists, neo-Nazi groups must meet certain criteria such as using violence or threats of violence to intimidate or coerce people into doing something they wouldn't otherwise do. Governments around the world have taken steps to combat these groups, including criminalizing certain activities and increasing surveillance on suspected members.

Ultimately, while it might not always be easy to label neo-Nazis as terrorists, there is no denying that their actions can have serious repercussions and should be taken seriously.

How do neo-Nazis view other races and religions?

We, as humans, are often taught to respect those who are different from us. However, neo-Nazis take a vastly different approach. From their point of view, any race or religion that is not their own is viewed with contempt and hatred. They see themselves as superior to all other races and religions, believing they have the right to subjugate anyone who does not share their beliefs.

This twisted ideology has led to countless acts of violence and terror in the past. It is clear that neo-Nazism is an extreme threat to public safety.

What is the origin of neo-Nazi symbols?

The neo-Nazi movement has a long history, and its symbols are an important part of that legacy. Neo-Nazis have appropriated symbols from Nazi Germany, such as the swastika, double lightning bolt symbol, and Black Sun.

Other symbols include variations on traditional Germanic runes and Aryan imagery. Many of these images evoke feelings of white supremacy or experiences of violence associated with the Nazis' regime.

The use of these symbols is meant to inspire fear in those who oppose their beliefs, while at the same time unifying members within the neo-Nazi movement.

What methods do neo-Nazis use to spread their message?

We were recently surprised to discover just how many methods neo-Nazis use to spread their message.

From organizing rallies and protests, to using social media – especially apps like Telegram – to distribute hateful literature, neo-Nazis are a dangerous force online and offline.

They even take advantage of technology by creating highly sophisticated websites that run on cryptocurrencies or anonymous networks.

It's no wonder they've been able to spread their hate so far and wide. The scary part is that it looks like they're not going away anytime soon.

Are there any laws in place to prevent neo-Nazi activity?

Yes, there are laws in place to prevent neo-Nazi activity. Governments around the world have implemented a range of measures designed to protect citizens from these dangerous extremist groups.

These measures include restrictions on propaganda and incitement of hatred, as well as criminal penalties for those who engage in violence or discrimination against certain groups.

Many countries have also enacted hate speech laws that criminalize public expressions of racism or bigotry.

These laws can help to ensure that people feel safe and secure in their communities, free from the fear of neo-Nazism.

Conclusion

We've seen the horrific effects of neo-Nazism, but there's much we can do to combat it worldwide.

We must take a firm stance against bigotry and hatred, and work together to create a society that rejects this kind of extremism.

We need to teach our children the importance of acceptance and respect for all people.

And we should strive to create an environment where everyone is free from discrimination or hate speech.

But most importantly, we must ask ourselves: how can we ensure that neo-Nazism doesn't continue to spread its vile ideology?

Together, by taking action in our own communities, we can make sure that neo-Nazism never again takes root in the world.

Non-State Armed Groups

We've all heard about non-state armed groups (NSAGs), but what exactly are they?

Generally speaking, NSAGs are organizations that challenge the authority of a legitimate state and use violence to achieve their goals.

These groups can have political or criminal agendas, and often cause serious human rights abuses wherever they operate.

In this article, we'll explore NSAGs in greater detail, looking at their impact on international security, arms trafficking activities and recruitment practices.

We'll also examine the regional impacts of such groups and discuss ways in which the threat posed by them can be countered.

Definition of Non-State Armed Groups

You don't have to be part of a government to wield power – just look at the influence of non-state actors.

Non-state armed groups (NSAGs) are organized entities that use force or the threat thereof independently from any state, and they occupy a wide range of roles in international relations. NSAGs can include irregular military forces such as guerrillas, militias, gangs, or other paramilitary organizations with an array of political objectives ranging from separatist movements to nationalist insurgencies, criminal enterprises and revolutionary groups.

They often operate in weakly governed states with limited capacity for providing security. The presence of NSAGs has varied implications for international security depending on their size and level of organization; larger and more organized groups tend to present greater threats to regional stability due to their potential ability to gain control over certain areas and resources.

They also pose direct risk to civilians because they may not adhere to established norms around warfare such as the Geneva Conventions or prohibitions against targeting civilians or using weapons of mass destruction like chemical weapons. Furthermore, they may fund activities through illegal means such as drug trafficking or human smuggling, which exacerbates already existing problems related poverty and social inequalities within fragile societies.

Despite these challenges, NSAGs are highly adaptive actors: some have managed to coexist with states during times when governments lack authority while others provide protection services where the state is unable or unwilling do so itself. As a result, understanding how these groups form and function is essential for developing effective strategies that address their potential threats while taking advantage of any opportunities they might offer for positive change in conflict-prone contexts.

Political Agenda NSAGs

Political agendas of NSAGs are often fiercely contested, with struggles for power raging like a wildfire. Many non-state armed groups have political goals that focus on overthrowing the current government and establishing a new one that reflects their ideology. These groups may also seek to create an independent state or region within the existing nation-state, which involves both violent and nonviolent tactics such as civil disobedience and boycotts. They may also be fighting for greater autonomy within a nation-state's existing framework or even just to gain recognition as an autonomous entity by other governments.

Additionally, some non-state armed groups form around causes related to social justice, such as the struggle against racial inequality or land rights violations. Others may pursue religious or ethnic based grievances such as separatism or secession movements in areas where minority populations feel disenfranchised. The motivations behind each group's agenda vary greatly depending on its particular context, but they all share a common goal: to achieve power through various means of resistance and challenges towards the status quo.

These political objectives can lead these groups into direct conflict with governments and international organizations alike who oppose their proposals or actions. Such clashes can take place in both conventional warfare settings as well as asymmetric conflicts in which non-state actors use unconventional methods of attack in order to achieve their goals without escalating into full scale war.

In this way, non-state armed groups are able to wield considerable influence on global politics while operating outside of formal channels of governance and diplomacy. With this in mind, it's clear that understanding the political agendas of these organizations should be at the forefront when attempting to assess their significance for international security.

Moving forward, it's important to consider how criminal activities factor into these complex dynamics between NSAGs and other stakeholders in any given conflict situation.

Criminal Agenda NSAGs

From gaining power to achieving financial gain, non-state armed groups often have criminal agendas that drive their actions and conflict with governments and international organizations. In many cases, these groups will use illegal activities such as extortion, kidnapping, human trafficking, drug smuggling, arms dealing, and piracy to achieve their goals. Such activities are often used by NSAGs as a way to generate revenue in order to fund their operations or purchase weapons.

Additionally, these crimes can be used by NSAGs as a form of leverage over government forces or other local actors in an attempt to gain control of territory or resources. The impact of NSAG criminal activities is far-reaching; they can cause significant harm to both individuals and communities in the areas where they operate. These groups can exploit vulnerable populations for financial gain which can create mistrust between them and the local population who may view them as exploiting the community for personal benefit rather than working towards shared objectives.

Furthermore, these criminal activities are often highly disruptive within societies as they undermine state authority and disrupt economic activity through violence or intimidation tactics such as corruption or bribery. The prevalence of criminal activities conducted by NSAGs has led to increased scrutiny from both governments and international organizations alike. Efforts are being made to combat such actions through increased monitoring of illicit networks and improved law enforcement actions in affected regions.

Additionally, efforts have been made to engage with non-state armed actors in order to deescalate tensions between them and governmental forces while incorporating them into established political processes when possible. It's clear that the issue of criminal activity conducted by non-state armed groups must be addressed in order for peacebuilding efforts around the world to be successful moving forward - especially when it comes to addressing human rights abuses committed by NSAGs on vulnerable populations throughout conflict zones worldwide.

Human Rights Abuses by NSAGs

You'll be surprised to hear the outrageous stories of human rights abuses these criminal organizations can get away with; it's almost like they've got their own set of laws! Non-state armed groups (NSAGs) have been increasingly responsible for gross violations of human rights, including crimes against humanity, war crimes and other serious violations.

From kidnappings and extortion to torture and extrajudicial killings, these acts often go unpunished as NSAGs are not bound by international laws or agreements. Even more concerning is that some governments provide support or safe havens to non-state armed groups who commit egregious acts without being held accountable for their actions.

The scale and scope of human rights violations committed by NSAGs vary widely across different regions and contexts. In many cases, civilians are targeted through indiscriminate violence or deliberate attacks on schools, hospitals, markets and places of worship. Women in particular have become victims of various forms of gender-based violence such as rape, forced marriage and abduction while children are exposed to recruitment into armed forces or sexual exploitation.

Moreover, the destruction caused by these violent activities often results in displacement which further exacerbates poverty levels within affected communities.

Despite efforts from civil society organizations to promote accountability for perpetrators, there still remains a lack of deterrence mechanisms due to limited resources available for monitoring or investigating abuses perpetrated by NSAGs. This has implications not only at the local level but also at the international level as failure to address such atrocities can lead to instability that threatens global security.

In light of this situation, it's imperative that countries take swift action towards strengthening existing legal frameworks in order to guarantee accountability for perpetrators and create an environment where human rights are protected moving forward – without this step we risk returning back into a state of chaos again soon enough.

Impacts of NSAGs on International Security

Non-state criminal organizations are wreaking havoc on international security, leaving devastation in their wake. The presence of these groups can lead to destabilization, greater regional tensions, the spread of violence and terrorism, and an increase in human rights abuses.

NSAGs often have a global reach, with access to powerful weapons and financial resources that enable them to act outside the bounds of legitimate governments. As a result, they can cause political unrest through coups or assassination attempts against government officials. Additionally, their activities are not bound by international law and treaties; therefore they can easily violate the sovereignty of nations by taking control of territory or committing acts of terror without consequence.

The proliferation of NSAGs has resulted in increased military spending around the world as states attempt to protect themselves from these groups' activities. This shift in resources away from social development projects has caused economic harm in many countries as well as further insecurity due to weakened state capacities.

Furthermore, NSAGs are often involved in illicit activities such as drug trafficking and arms smuggling which undermines efforts at global security governance as it is difficult for states to effectively address these issues when actors exist outside their jurisdiction.

The negative consequences created by NSAGs cannot be understated; however there is still hope for finding ways to better manage this threat through improved intelligence gathering capabilities and international cooperation between states affected by NSAG activity. In order to do so though, a clear understanding must be developed regarding how these organizations operate and how they finance their operations...

Financing of NSAGs

As the impacts of non-state armed groups (NSAGs) on international security have become more apparent, it's important to investigate their sources of financing. Financing for NSAGs can come from a variety of sources, both legal and illegal, some more well-established than others.

The main source of funding often comes from donations or taxation collected by NSAGs from local populations in exchange for providing services or protection. Some may receive donations from Diaspora communities abroad.

Drug trafficking, extortion, and kidnapping are other common sources of income for many organizations that have been classified as non-state armed groups. Furthermore, arms trafficking have provided a lucrative form of financing for certain NSAGs. Buying weapons at low prices and then reselling them at higher market prices can generate significant financial profits to sustain operations over long periods of time.

This type of activity has increased the complexity concerning the regulation of arms transfers around the world, making it difficult to limit their access to resources necessary to maintain or increase their power base. As we move forward into exploring arms trafficking and NSAGs further, it's essential that we continue understanding how these powerful organizations acquire their means in order to act accordingly going forward.

Arms Trafficking and NSAGs

Investigating the link between arms trafficking and non-state armed groups can help us better understand how these powerful organizations sustain their power and activity. Armed groups have been found to obtain weapons through illicit means, which include illegal importation of weapons from other countries as well as domestic production. These activities are largely funded by criminal activities such as drug smuggling, human trafficking, or kidnapping for ransom. These sources of funding enable armed groups to acquire materials that would otherwise be difficult to obtain and may even provide them with access to certain technologies.

In some cases, political connections also play a role in allowing access to more advanced weaponry. Arms trafficking have enabled many non-state armed groups to increase their military capabilities beyond what they could acquire through legal channels alone. This is especially true in conflict zones where government control over security forces is weak or nonexistent; in this context, arms traffickers can often operate with relative impunity due to limited law enforcement oversight and corruption among local governments or security forces.

By providing access to sophisticated weaponry without requiring payment up front, arms traffickers also allow these organizations to allocate funds for other purposes such as recruitment campaigns and infrastructure development. In addition, arms traffickers often act as intermediaries between non-state actors seeking weapons and foreign suppliers willing to sell them on the black market at discounted prices; this provides a significant financial benefit for both sides since it reduces costs associated with transportation or legal fees that would normally be incurred when obtaining weapons directly from manufacturers or dealers abroad.

As a result of this relationship, arms trafficking networks are increasingly becoming integral components of international security dynamics - allowing non-state actors greater autonomy in acquiring the resources needed for continued operations while simultaneously enabling foreign governments or private entities looking for profit opportunities in unstable regions of the world. With this in mind, understanding how these networks operate is key if we hope to combat the proliferation of violent extremist organizations around the globe and promote stability throughout fragile states and conflict zones.

Recruitment by NSAGs

Having discussed the issue of arms trafficking and its relationship to non-state armed groups (NSAGs), we now turn our attention to another important factor in understanding these organizations: recruitment.

Recruitment is a major challenge for NSAGs, as they rely on recruiting members in order to stay active and maintain their presence. They have several methods through which they can recruit fighters, ranging from voluntary enlistment to forcibly conscripting people.

Voluntary enlistment is the most common form of recruitment for NSAGs, as it allows them to draw upon local populations who may sympathize with their cause or who are simply seeking employment or adventure. These recruits often come from socio-economically disadvantaged backgrounds, and are often motivated by economic insecurity or the promise of higher social standing within an organization. However, this type of recruitment has been declining due to increased government monitoring and suppression of potential recruits.

Forced conscription is another method that some NSAGs use in order to bolster their ranks. This involves kidnapping people from villages or towns and forcing them into service against their will. This tactic has been used extensively by some groups, such as Boko Haram in Nigeria, who have used forced conscription as a way to spread fear among local populations while simultaneously increasing the size of their forces.

The methods used by NSAGs for recruitment vary greatly depending on the particular group and region in question; however, one thing remains constant: recruitment is a key factor in understanding how these organizations operate and survive over time. To further explore this topic; let us now turn our attention away from individual NSAG's recruiting strategies towards examining how regional dynamics can influence the activities of such groups.

Regional Impacts of NSAGs

Understanding the impacts of non-state actors (NSAGs) on a regional level is essential to comprehending how they operate and remain active. NSAGs have a variety of effects that can be seen in both immediate and long-term contexts:

- Immediate Impacts:

- Displacement of civilians due to physical violence, destruction of property, and other human rights violations.

- Reduction in economic productivity due to disruptions in trade, commerce, infrastructure, etc.

- Political instability resulting from the breakdown of government control over certain areas or resources.

- Long Term Impacts:

- Increase in poverty levels as a result of prolonged conflict and lack of investment in development projects.

- Social tension between different groups due to heightened mistrust and divisions caused by the presence of NSAGs.

- Security threats posed by terrorist activity and illicit trafficking activities conducted by NSAGs, which can spread across borders or regions.

The impacts discussed above illustrate why it's important for governments to take a proactive approach when countering the threat posed by NSAGs. Without appropriate action, their influence can continue even after they're no longer actively operating in a given region. To effectively address the problem, it's necessary to develop comprehensive strategies that seek not only to contain these groups but also work towards preventing them from taking root again in the future.

Countering the Threat of NSAGs

You can take steps to counter the threat of these powerful forces by developing strategies that both contain and prevent them from regaining a foothold in the region. One approach is to increase collaboration between local governments and regional stakeholders to share intelligence on NSAGs, their activities, and potential threats. This would allow for more effective operations against these groups, as well as better implementation of policies aimed at mitigating their influence.

Proactive Measures	Reactive Measures
Strengthen security forces	Surveillance & monitoring
Promote economic development	Targeted airstrikes/military operations
Increase regional collaboration	Diplomatic interventions & sanctions
Build public support systems for peacebuilding initiatives	Negotiations with leaders of NSAGs (if possible)

Another way to reduce NSAG's influence is through long-term socio-economic investments geared towards improving infrastructure, education opportunities, and access to resources. More inclusive government policies and greater access to employment could also help create an environment in which people are less likely to join or support NSAGs. Finally, it is important to invest in building strong civil society networks that will be able to monitor local trends and provide early warning indicators before any new conflicts arise. Such measures can create sustainable strategies for countering future NSAG threats while promoting stability in the region.

Frequently Asked Questions

What is the most prevalent form of recruitment used by non-state armed groups?

Recruitment for any organized group is crucial for their success, and non-state armed groups are no exception. The most prevalent form of recruitment used by these organizations tends to be coercion or persuasion.

Coercion is often done through physical force or threats, while persuasion consists of methods such as offering money or other benefits in exchange for joining the organization. By combining both tactics, non-state armed groups can attract more members and expand their power base.

How has the financial support of non-state armed groups changed over time?

We've seen a remarkable evolution in the financial support of non-state armed groups over time. From humble beginnings, where these groups often relied heavily on donations from sympathetic publics, to now having access to multi-billion dollar investments from private entities and governments alike.

These funds have allowed these groups to take action on a much larger scale than ever before. They can purchase weapons, gain access to more sophisticated technology, and increase their recruitment capabilities.

What measures are being taken to counter the threat of non-state armed groups?

We're taking multiple steps to counter the threat of armed groups. We're increasing surveillance and intelligence gathering, implementing sanctions, strengthening regional security forces, and developing counterterrorism strategies. Governments around the world are making concerted efforts to reduce the operational capabilities of such organizations. In addition, diplomatic channels are being used to engage in dialogue with leaders of these groups to de-escalate tensions and negotiate peace agreements.

Are there any organizations that provide support to non-state armed groups?

We're asking a provocative question: are there organizations that provide support to non-state armed groups?

To answer this, we need to take a step back and consider the context. Non-state armed groups exist in conflict zones around the world and generally don't have access to resources or external assistance, making them vulnerable to exploitation and manipulation by outside forces.

While there's no definitive answer as to whether any organizations actively provide support, there are reports of indirect assistance such as foreign governments providing weapons or other forms of aid through proxies or third parties.

Ultimately, it remains unclear if any organization explicitly provides direct support for non-state armed groups.

What are the long-term impacts of non-state armed groups on local and regional communities?

We've seen that non-state armed groups can have a significant impact on local and regional communities. These impacts can be both positive and negative, depending on the context of the situation.

In the short term, these groups may bring increased stability to an area or provide essential services for those in need. However, over the long-term, there are often unintended consequences that can cause more harm than good.

This could include economic instability due to militarization or environmental degradation caused by conflict. It's important to consider all possible outcomes before engaging with any non-state armed group to ensure that their actions won't lead to long-term detrimental effects for local and regional communities.

Conclusion

We've seen that non-state armed groups (NSAGs) pose a significant threat to international security. Their political and criminal agendas, human rights abuses, arms trafficking, recruitment techniques, and regional impacts all contribute to their dangerous impact on the world.

In conclusion, we must recognize NSAGs as a symbol of violence and destruction. They are a stark reminder of the risks associated with global instability. We must come together to counter this threat in order to safeguard our collective future.

By promoting peace building initiatives, investing in development projects, and strengthening international cooperation against these groups, we can work together to create a safer world for us all.

The Aryan Brotherhood Prison Gang

We've all heard of the Aryan Brotherhood, and it's safe to say that they have a notorious reputation. But what exactly is the Aryan Brotherhood?

The Aryan Brotherhood is an organized prison gang formed in 1964 by white inmates in California prisons. The AB was originally created for protection against other gangs, but has since become a powerful and dangerous criminal organization involved in drug trafficking, extortion, money laundering, and murder.

In this article we'll take a look at the history of the Aryan Brotherhood, their structure, membership requirements and goals as well as their various criminal activities and law enforcement response.

History of the Aryan Brotherhood

The past of this organization is riddled with a darker side that speaks to its power and influence. The Aryan Brotherhood, also known as the AB or Brand, is an American white prison gang formed in 1964 by two Irish-American brothers at San Quentin State Prison. It was initially formed as a support network for white inmates who were facing racial discrimination from African American gangs.

Over the years it has grown to become one of the most powerful prison gangs in the United States, with members operating both inside and outside of prisons. The group's activities include drug trafficking, extortion, arms dealing and murder both in and out of prisons. They often target rival gangs as well as African Americans and other ethnic minorities within prisons, using violence to maintain their status within the prison system. In addition to these crimes, they are also known for being involved in organized crime on the outside such as money laundering and illegal gambling operations.

The Aryan Brotherhood is highly structured with each member having a distinct role within the gang's hierarchy. Although membership fluctuates due to incarceration cycles, it is estimated that there are currently between 15000-20000 members worldwide. This structure allows them to operate relatively safely on both sides of prison walls despite facing numerous law enforcement efforts against them over the years.

With their strong presence across US prisons and criminal activities beyond bars, it appears likely that they will remain a major force in organized crime for some time yet. To understand more about how they operate, we now need to turn our attention to their structure and activities within prisons.

Structure of the Aryan Brotherhood

You'll learn about the structure of this powerful organization, how its members interact and how it operates. The Aryan Brotherhood is a prison gang with a hierarchical structure, led by an allegedly all-powerful 'Commission'. This Commission is said to be comprised of five leaders who make all major decisions for the gang. It's rumored that 'generals' are appointed by the Commission to lead their own divisions in different regions and states.

The group also has local chapters or sets, which meet regularly to discuss business and plan activities inside and outside prison walls. These meetings are held at various locations within prisons or on visitor days between family members visiting inmates associated with the gang.

While there is no formal membership process, potential members must prove themselves through violent acts or drug deals before being accepted into one of these local sets.

Members operate under an unwritten code called "The Book" which is passed down from generation to generation of Aryan Brotherhood members. This code dictates rules about loyalty, respect, punishment for breaking the rules, initiation rituals and more. By following "The Book" each member shows his commitment to furthering the goals of the Aryan Brotherhood while ensuring their own safety within it.

With such a strict system in place, it comes as no surprise that this infamous prison gang continues to remain one of the most feared criminal organizations today - ready to transition into our next topic concerning membership of the Aryan Brotherhood.

Membership of the Aryan Brotherhood

Gaining entry into this powerful organization requires dedication and commitment, with potential members having to prove themselves through often violent acts or drug deals before being accepted. To be considered for membership in the Aryan Brotherhood, candidates must meet certain criteria:

- They must demonstrate a commitment to the white race and a willingness to protect fellow members of the gang at all costs;
- They must be willing to commit criminal activities on behalf of the gang; and
- They must adhere strictly to the code of conduct established by the gang's leadership.

Those who are deemed suitable for membership are allowed access to an exclusive network that provides them with protection and support from within prison walls as well as on the outside.

Once accepted, they become part of a larger family that shares common beliefs, values and goals - providing its members with not only physical protection but also emotional security.

From here, it's possible to move up in rank within this organization based upon one's loyalty and contributions to its cause.

Moving forward without saying "in conclusion" or "finally," let's explore the goals of this notorious prison gang next.

Goals of the Aryan Brotherhood

You'll quickly notice that the organization's purpose goes far beyond physical protection and security; they have a much bigger goal in mind. Symbolically, this gang is like a ship sailing through turbulent waters- its mission to assure the safe passage of its members to their ultimate destination. The Aryan Brotherhood is an organized crime group with racist ideologies at its core. It seeks to maintain white supremacy by engaging in criminal activities such as drug trafficking, extortion, murder-for-hire services, and more.

Although it may seem counterintuitive for a prison gang to seek power outside of prison walls, there are still tangible benefits from maintaining control both inside and out. Primarily, the Aryan Brotherhood seeks financial gain so that they can continue their operations without external interference or limitation. Additionally, having access to resources outside of prison provides them with leverage over other inmates within the facility who do not have connections outside the walls.

The Aryan Brotherhood also has an ideological agenda: establishing a homeland for whites where they will be free from racial persecution and oppression; creating their own set of laws based on social Darwinism; and promoting violence against non-whites as well as Jews and homosexuals. They view themselves as modern day crusaders for white supremacy - willing to use any means necessary to ensure their vision becomes reality. By utilizing fear tactics both inside prisons and on the streets, they are able to spread their influence throughout society while maintaining power amongst fellow prisoners who share similar beliefs or interests in organized crime activity.

To further strengthen their hold on society, the Aryan Brotherhood also engages in acts of intimidation which serves two purposes: keeping rival gangs at bay while simultaneously strengthening loyalty amongst its own members by providing proof that violence can reap rewards--key components needed for effective leadership within a criminal enterprise such as this one. With strong ties between existing chapters across multiple states along with support from outside sources (i.e., wealthy donors), it's clear that the goals of the Aryan Brotherhood are much larger than simply gaining power within prisons - they have set out on a mission which transcends boundaries both real and imagined.. As we move into discussing criminal activities of this notorious prison gang, we must keep these ambitions in mind when evaluating their actions further down line.

Criminal Activities of the Aryan Brotherhood

The Aryan Brotherhood's criminal activities are an attempt to achieve their larger ambitions, using a combination of fear and loyalty to gain control over society.

The Aryan Brotherhood has been linked to numerous criminal activities ranging from drug dealing and money laundering to extortion and murder. In addition, they've also been known to target law enforcement officials in order to deter potential investigations into their operations. This is often done through intimidation or threats of violence against those who don't cooperate with the gang's wishes.

By instilling fear in both members of the public and law enforcement alike, the Aryan Brotherhood is able to maintain a reign of power that allows them to further expand their operations without interference. The gang's use of extreme violence has also enabled them to take control over certain areas within prisons, making it easier for them to recruit new members as well as carry out their other nefarious activities.

By controlling these spaces within prisons, they can provide protection for new recruits while also intimidating those who challenge them or cross them in any way. This creates an atmosphere where the Aryan Brotherhood can thrive by utilizing its resources more efficiently than if operating outside prison walls. The harsh methods employed by the Aryan Brotherhood make it clear that they'll go above and beyond what's necessary in order to protect themselves and increase their power base - all while attempting to stay one step ahead of law enforcement agencies.

With this kind of ruthless approach, it's no wonder why recruitment tactics are so important for gaining new adherents and ensuring total domination over their rivals.

Recruitment Tactics of the Aryan Brotherhood

Discover how the Aryan Brotherhood recruits people and why their tactics are so effective by reading on. The gang typically looks for inmates who are already serving hard time, as they consider them to be more trustworthy and dependable. They also look for those with a history of violence, which helps to build up their reputation within the prison system. Additionally, they often rely on word-of-mouth referrals from current members looking to strengthen their connections in the gang.

Here's a quick summary of some of the recruitment tactics used by the Aryan Brotherhood:

- Utilizing existing relationships among inmates
- Relying on word-of-mouth referrals from current members
- Looking for prisoners serving long sentences or hard time
- Preferring those with a history of violence

The Aryan Brotherhood is notorious throughout correctional facilities because of its ruthless recruitment tactics and loyalty to its members. It uses intimidation and fear as primary tools in order to gain respect among other gangs and inmate populations. Their power has been known to extend outside the prison walls, where they can influence criminal activities that take place in communities across America.

With this understanding, it's clear that the impact of this powerful gang goes far beyond just recruiting new members inside prisons; it reaches into our streets too. Understanding the methods used by this gang for recruitment gives us insight into how they maintain control over those both within and outside prison walls.

Next, we will explore further into how this affects prisons today.

Impact of the Aryan Brotherhood on Prisons

Gain a better understanding of the influence the Aryan Brotherhood has on prisons today and how it affects you, with just a few clicks. As one of the most notorious prison gangs in America, the Aryan Brotherhood operates within many US state and federal prison systems. They are known for their extreme violence against both rival gangs and even individual members who do not follow their rules. The gang's presence in these facilities can be seen through their recruitment tactics, drug trafficking, extortion schemes, and intimidation of other inmates.

Influence	Example
Recruitment Tactics	Targeting vulnerable inmates for protection or access to resources
Drug Trafficking	Using smugglers to bring drugs into prisons
Extortion Schemes	Threatening other inmates or guards to gain power or money inside prisons
Intimidation Tactics	Physical force used to maintain control over certain areas in prison systems

The impact of the Aryan Brotherhood on prisons is far-reaching. Their presence creates an atmosphere of fear that affects those living within these walls. It also leads to increased tension between rival gangs as well as decreased safety for correctional officers tasked with keeping order. In addition, their illicit activities often lead to overcrowding and resource scarcity due to limited supplies available from outside sources. All these problems have led law enforcement agencies around the country to take a tougher stance on gang activity in correctional facilities—which we'll discuss further below....

Law Enforcement Response to the Aryan Brotherhood

We've discussed the impact of the Aryan Brotherhood on prisons, but what about law enforcement? The response by law enforcement to the presence of this prison gang has been complex and multifaceted. Here are four ways in which they have responded:

- Increased Monitoring: Law enforcement have increased their monitoring efforts within prisons where the Aryan Brotherhood is present. This includes more frequent checks on inmates and their cells, as well as greater surveillance of inmate interactions.

- Disruption Tactics: Law enforcement agencies have also implemented disruption tactics to interrupt the communication channels used by members of the group. This can include intercepting phone calls or disrupting meetings between members.

- Segregation Policies: Law enforcement has enforced segregation policies that separate known Aryan Brotherhood members from other inmates in an attempt to reduce gang-related violence and activity within prisons.

- Targeted Arrests: Law enforcement have also targeted arrests at suspected Aryan Brotherhood members, including those involved in criminal activities related to drug trafficking or weapons smuggling.

Overall, law enforcement's response has sought to reduce the influence of this prison gang and protect both inmates and staff from harm caused by its violent activities. As a result, we can now explore what risks individuals face when joining the Aryan Brotherhood organization without worrying about further endangering those around them.

Risks of Joining the Aryan Brotherhood

Joining this organization may seem enticing, but it comes with serious risks that could cost you more than you bargained for. The Aryan Brotherhood is a prison gang and its members often use extreme violence to take care of business, both inside and outside of the prison walls.

Being caught in possession of any drugs or weapons can lead to serious charges, especially if they're found on an AB member. Additionally, anyone associated with the gang can come under scrutiny from law enforcement agents even if they haven't committed a crime.

Moreover, those who join this organization face potential retaliation from rival gangs as well as government authorities. This type of organized crime group is targeted by law enforcement agencies due to their notoriety and connections with other criminal activities such as drug trafficking and money laundering.

As a result, joining the Aryan Brotherhood carries the risk of being arrested or facing lengthy sentences for their involvement in illegal activities. The consequences are costly - not only financially but also personally - and should be considered carefully before making the decision to join this organization.

Joining can result in loss of freedom, physical harm, property damage, or even death; thus taking steps to avoid joining the brotherhood is essential for protecting one's safety and wellbeing.

Steps to Take to Avoid Joining the Aryan Brotherhood

As someone looking to avoid joining the Aryan Brotherhood prison gang, the most important thing to remember is that prevention is key. Once you've joined a prison gang, it can be very difficult to leave.

To prevent yourself from becoming part of this dangerous organization, there are several steps that you should take.

First and foremost, if you're not already affiliated with the Aryan Brotherhood, don't make contact with any members or associates of the group. It's important to stay away from people who may be involved in criminal activities or who may know someone involved in the Aryan Brotherhood. This includes avoiding places where members of the gang might hang out and being careful about what information you share about your whereabouts and activities on social media sites.

Secondly, if you feel threatened by anyone associated with the Aryan Brotherhood or other gangs, reach out for help right away – don't wait until it's too late! Talk to trusted friends or family members or contact local law enforcement.

It's also a good idea to familiarize yourself with laws in your area related to gangs and potential punishments for engaging in gang activity so that you can better protect yourself from involvement in criminal activity related to gangs like the Aryan Brotherhood.

Taking these steps will help ensure that you stay safe and remain free from ties with this potentially deadly gang.

Conclusion

We've seen that the Aryan Brotherhood is an intimidating prison gang, with a history of violence and organized crime. Joining them can lead to serious repercussions, both in terms of legal action and personal safety. It's like walking into a minefield- one wrong step could be catastrophic.

The best way to stay safe from the Aryan Brotherhood is to avoid joining them altogether. If you see any signs of their presence in your prison, report it immediately and take the necessary precautions to keep yourself out of harm's way.

Remember: knowledge is power in these situations, so arm yourself with information and stay vigilant.

American Hypocrisy

We live in a world full of hypocrisy.

The United States is no exception.

From racism and gender inequality to foreign policy contradictions, there are many examples of American hypocrisy that have been exposed over the years.

Despite the fact that the nation prides itself on its core values, it often fails to hold itself accountable for injustices both domestically and around the globe.

In this article, we will explore some of these hypocrisies and how they continue to shape US society today.

Definition of Hypocrisy

Can't we all relate to the idea of being a hypocrite at one time or another? Hypocrisy is defined as the practice of claiming to have moral standards or beliefs but acting in ways which are contradictory. It's an affront to justice, equality, and truth.

When hypocrisy becomes pervasive in society, it can lead to an atmosphere of public discontent and cynicism.

The American political sphere has become increasingly rife with hypocrisy in recent times. Politicians frequently express their condemnation for issues such as racism while simultaneously engaging in policies that perpetuate systemic racism. This cognitive dissonance between words and actions creates feelings of distrust among citizens who feel betrayed by elected officials who fail to live up to their own standards.

At its worst, hypocrisy can be used as a tool by those in power for personal gain; however, it also serves as a reminder that no one is free from making mistakes or having lapses in judgment. Each person should strive for greater self-awareness and make an effort towards holding themselves accountable when they make hypocritical statements or decisions.

With this understanding, we move forward into the next section on racism in the US with renewed commitment towards creating lasting change through collective action.

Racism in the US

It's ironic that the same nation that claims to stand for justice and equality is rife with racism.

Even though slavery was abolished in the US more than 150 years ago, its legacy still lingers on in many forms today.

The facts speak for themselves: African Americans are disproportionately represented in prisons and suffer from poverty at much higher rates than other ethnicities.

On top of this, they often face discrimination when it comes to employment opportunities, housing, and education.

The current system has led to a wide knowledge gap between different racial groups in terms of access to resources and wealth.

This has resulted in disparities that can be seen across all aspects of life – from healthcare and economic opportunity to education and political power.

Unfortunately, these issues have been around since the beginning of America's history and little progress has been made over time despite attempts by advocates for change such as civil rights activists or organizations like Black Lives Matter.

This reality exposes a fundamental problem with American society: we talk a lot about equality but our actions don't quite reflect that sentiment.

It's clear that if we want real progress on social justice issues, we need more than just words – we need concrete policy changes that will make an impact on people's lives moving forward into the future.

Foreign Policy Contradictions

America claims to promote democracy and human rights abroad, yet its own foreign policy decisions often contradict these values. For example, the US has been a vocal advocate for freedom of expression in other countries while simultaneously silencing journalists domestically. It has also provided military aid to autocrats around the world who have committed human rights abuses against their own citizens.

This behavior does not match with America's self-proclaimed commitment to international justice and egalitarianism but rather reveals an extreme hypocrisy that undermines its moral authority among other nations.

Another area where American foreign policy is hypocritical is when it comes to trade practices. The US regularly criticizes foreign countries for protectionist policies that hurt small businesses, yet it routinely enacts its own import tariffs on goods from certain trading partners. As a result, American companies are able to gain an unfair competitive advantage over their counterparts operating in different markets.

By doing so, the US continues to demonstrate a clear double standard when it comes to economic matters on the global stage. These examples illustrate how the United States frequently falls short of upholding its ideals when engaging with other countries through diplomacy and commerce. Such discrepancies between rhetoric and reality damage America's international reputation even further as they expose the inherent contradictions within its foreign policy agenda.

With this in mind, there's still much work that needs to be done if America hopes to live up to its lofty promises about providing support and stability abroad—starting with addressing gender equality issues at home and abroad.

Gender Equality Issues

You can think of gender inequality as a two-way street—one paved with good intentions and the other with broken promises. Despite its commitment to promoting human rights around the world, the US has failed to provide equal opportunities for women in its own society, let alone abroad.

The gender gap is evident in areas such as education, healthcare, labor force participation, and wages. Women are often relegated to lower paying jobs and are subject to discrimination when seeking higher positions of power in both public and private sectors.

Moreover, there is a stark contrast between what the US preaches about equality and what it practices at home - this double standard has only perpetuated gender inequality. For example, even though the US has made strides towards empowering women through legislation such as Title IX that seeks to close educational gaps between sexes, female students continue to face discrimination on college campuses across the country.

The fact that American hypocrisy continues to hinder progress when it comes to achieving real gender equality speaks volumes. This reality suggests that despite all the rhetoric about promoting human rights around the world, there remains a lot of work left undone within our own borders if we hope to make meaningful change for women everywhere.

To move forward, we must take actionable steps towards eliminating existing disparities and create an environment where everyone can thrive regardless of their gender identity or expression.

Environmental Double Standards

Despite its commitment to protecting the environment, the US has often failed to live up to its own standards. Perhaps nowhere is this more evident than in its environmental double standards.

In the US, it's generally accepted that certain practices such as dumping hazardous waste are unacceptable and illegal. However, when it comes to international trade, the same regulations do not apply. For example, a company can ship products overseas with hazardous chemicals that would be illegal for them to use domestically.

This discrepancy between domestic and international law creates an environment of hypocrisy where companies can exploit weaker countries that may not have the resources or political will to enforce their own regulations. The lack of enforcement of international environmental laws allows companies from developed nations like the US to continue polluting at levels higher than what would be permitted domestically or even internationally without consequence.

This double standard has resulted in a global increase in pollution and degradation of natural resources beyond what could've been achieved if all countries had adhered to similar standards. It also serves as a sad reminder that economic interests still trump environmental protection when it comes down to decision-making on a global scale.

This imbalance means that poorer countries end up bearing more of the burden for environmental damage caused by multinational corporations while richer nations get away with little accountability or responsibility for any impacts they might have on other parts of the world. As long as these hypocrisies exist, true sustainability will remain out of reach and issues like climate change will continue unabated until meaningful action is taken by all involved parties—including those primarily responsible—to address them head on.

Moving forward, it's essential that governments prioritize meaningful collaboration over short-term economic gains if we're ever going to make progress in protecting our environment from further harm caused by irresponsible industry practices abroad.

Discrepancy between Domestic and International Law

We've already discussed the environmental double standards that exist in the United States, but there's another source of American hypocrisy. The discrepancy between domestic and international law reveals a troubling lack of consistency when it comes to policy-making.

There are several areas where this discrepancy exists:

- **Economic Policy**: The U.S. has taken a much more protectionist stance when dealing with its own economy compared to other countries, such as China and India, which have been allowed to take advantage of free trade agreements while the U.S. imposes tariffs on goods from both countries.

- **Immigration Laws**: While the U.S. insists on strict immigration laws for those entering its borders, it fails to adequately enforce them for those leaving its borders illegally or overstaying their visas. This creates an enormous strain on resources both domestically and abroad and leads to a large number of undocumented immigrants living in fear within the country's borders without any legal recourse or protection against exploitation by employers or law enforcement officials.

- **Military Intervention**: The U.S., despite its claims of being a beacon of democracy, often engages in military interventions at home and abroad that violate international standards. This includes drone strikes that kill innocent civilians as well as support for oppressive regimes such as Saudi Arabia's monarchy, which has engaged in human rights abuses against its citizens with impunity while receiving billions of dollars in arms sales from the U.S.

These inconsistencies between domestic and international policies create an atmosphere where it's difficult for citizens to trust their government or believe that justice will be served fairly no matter what side of the border they're on. Whether they're American citizens within their own country or foreign nationals outside it who are subject to different sets of laws than those enjoyed by Americans themselves. This raises serious questions about how seriously America takes its commitment to upholding international standards and protecting global human rights when so many violations occur unchecked within its own borders without consequence - something which calls into question how committed America truly is towards justice and equality worldwide rather than just domestically.

Without making progress towards closing these discrepancies between domestic and international law, America will continue facing criticism from both foreign governments as well as its own citizens who demand better accountability from their leaders - especially when it comes to issues like immigration policies which have become increasingly contentious due not only to ideological differences but also due to rampant discrimination based upon nationality or race/ethnicity among other things.

Immigration Policies

Immigration policies have long been a source of contention, creating a patchwork quilt of confusion that leaves many feeling like they're walking through a minefield.

As the US has become increasingly divided along partisan lines, immigration policy has become an ever more contentious debate in political discourse. The double standard for citizens and non-citizens is especially glaring when one considers the fact that while some are welcomed with open arms, others are demonized as dangerous criminals. This hypocrisy between domestic and international law serves to further highlight the unequal treatment of immigrants in this country.

The consequences of such policies are far reaching, not only impacting those detained at the border but also their families who remain behind. Those attempting to enter the US face lengthy waits for visas or asylum hearings; children separated from their parents; and even outright rejection of individuals seeking refuge from violence or poverty.

It's clear that our current system is broken and fails to recognize both human rights and American ideals of freedom and justice for all.

In spite of calls for reform, politicians remain entrenched in their positions on either side of the issue with little willingness to compromise or negotiate a reasonable solution. It remains to be seen if any meaningful progress will be made, yet it seems unlikely until Americans can come together in agreement on how best to address this complex problem—one that affects us all regardless of race or nationality.

With corporate greed driving much of the debate around immigration policy, it may be time for true change rather than empty rhetoric.

Corporate Greed

We've now come to the issue of corporate greed.

Our current system is designed to reward those at the top, while leaving many behind in poverty and without a chance for upward mobility.

To make matters worse, these companies are often able to dodge taxes through loopholes or offshore accounts, further widening the gap between the rich and everyone else.

Here are some examples of how corporations have taken advantage for their own gain:

- The 2017 Tax Cuts and Jobs Act significantly lowered corporate tax rates in an effort to incentivize businesses to keep jobs in America, but it didn't include any provisions that would ensure wages would be raised.

- Corporate lobbying has allowed them to influence policy decisions that benefit only them instead of working people as a whole.

- Big banks were bailed out after 2008's financial crisis with taxpayer money, yet never faced criminal charges or had anyone held accountable for their actions leading up to it.

It's clear that there's an inherent imbalance in our current economic system which disproportionately favors big business over everyday citizens.

This leads us directly into our next topic: wealth inequality.

Wealth inequality is a major issue facing American society today and understanding its roots can help us create meaningful solutions for all Americans moving forward.

Wealth Inequality

The issue of wealth inequality has become increasingly apparent, with the gap between the haves and have-nots widening at an alarming rate. It's a situation caused by decades of government policies favoring the privileged, leaving others behind. This has resulted in a system where the wealthiest individuals and corporations control a disproportionate amount of resources, while large segments of society are denied opportunities to climb out of poverty.

Moreover, it has enabled some to hide their ill-gotten gains through tax avoidance schemes or by taking advantage of loopholes designed to help them evade taxation. This stark reality highlights the hypocrisy of American society, where rhetoric about equality and opportunity fails to match what's happening on the ground.

The idea that everyone should have access to equal opportunities, regardless of social standing, is often touted but rarely put into practice, leaving many without any real chance for upward mobility. At the same time, those who already hold vast amounts of money and power can take advantage of loopholes or lax regulations to maintain their status quo.

This creates an environment where wealth inequality continues to grow unchecked with no end in sight. The injustice inherent in this situation serves only to further highlight how broken America's economic system truly is, with too much power concentrated among too few people leading to rising levels of discontent and frustration within society.

Without meaningful reforms that address these imbalances head-on, it seems unlikely that anyone will be able to bridge this ever-widening chasm between class divisions - making political corruption all but inevitable in this new landscape.

Political Corruption

We've seen how wealth inequality is a major issue in America, and related to this is the issue of political corruption. To understand why this happens, we need to look at both the short-term and long-term causes behind it.

In the short term, there are many issues that can lead to political corruption:

- Political campaigns that rely heavily on private donations from wealthy individuals and corporations
- Lobbyists who use their money and influence to push for laws that benefit them personally
- Politicians willing to trade favors in exchange for financial or other benefits
- A lack of oversight or accountability when it comes to campaign finances.

The long-term effects of these issues can be just as damaging as the short-term ones. Corruption erodes public trust in government, which can lead to decreased voter turnout and apathy towards democracy. It also perpetuates a cycle of wealth inequality, where those with money have more power than those without it.

This creates an unbalanced playing field which further limits opportunities for those without financial resources. This not only affects our society today but will shape our future generations as well.

It's clear that American hypocrisy isn't an isolated problem; rather, it's part of a larger system that has been in place for centuries. From special interests groups influencing policy decisions, to politicians trading favors for personal gain, it's time we acknowledge these issues and make changes if we want any real progress towards creating a more equitable society for everyone involved.

Frequently Asked Questions

What have been the long-term consequences of American hypocrisy?

We often talk about the consequences of American hypocrisy, but what have been the long-term implications?

Like an insidious cancer, it has spread far and wide, permeating every corner of our society. It has become a part of the cultural fabric, making it difficult to unravel its effects on generations to come.

We can see how it has led to a loss in trust within our communities and institutions as well as a decrease in international respect for America's values and ideals. Its legacy is one that will take generations to overcome if we're ever able to do so.

What role has the media played in perpetuating American hypocrisy?

We've seen the media play a significant role in perpetuating American hypocrisy. From news outlets to social media, they've been instrumental in amplifying and normalizing certain perspectives and beliefs while simultaneously ignoring or marginalizing others.

This has resulted in certain ideologies becoming entrenched in our society, while opposing viewpoints are continually ignored or silenced. It's become clear that the media is often complicit in maintaining an unequal power structure within our country.

How do social and economic disparities in the US contribute to American hypocrisy?

We often hear of the disparities between social classes in America, and how they contribute to an unequal playing field.

However, it's important to consider how these disparities are perpetuated by American hypocrisy.

Wealthy individuals and corporations often take advantage of loopholes that enable them to pay lower taxes or receive preferential treatment from the government, while those with fewer economic resources are unable to access similar opportunities.

This creates a situation where people from different backgrounds experience vastly different levels of success, which serves to further entrench the existing power structures in society and exacerbate existing social and economic divides.

How can American hypocrisy be addressed on an individual level?

We all have a responsibility to ourselves and our society to address American hypocrisy on an individual level. To do this, it is important to understand how social and economic disparities can contribute to it.

According to the U.S. Census Bureau, nearly one in five Americans lives in poverty, which is only the tip of the iceberg when it comes to understanding these systemic issues. We must recognize that our privilege allows us access to resources that are not available for everyone, and use our power in a way that works towards making a more equitable future for all.

By utilizing our personal networks, donating money or time towards meaningful causes, and engaging with our elected officials about their policies on these issues we can make a difference in combating hypocrisy at the grassroots level.

What are the global implications of American hypocrisy?

We live in a globalized world, and the actions of one nation often have far-reaching implications for the rest of the world. This is particularly true when it comes to hypocrisy. When a powerful nation acts inconsistently with its own values or fails to keep promises to other nations, it can lead to mistrust and resentment, as well as disruption of diplomatic relations.

American hypocrisy has the potential to disrupt trade agreements, destabilize international markets, and undermine alliances that are essential for maintaining peace. To ensure that America upholds its responsibilities on an international level, we must work towards holding ourselves accountable and ensuring that our behavior matches our rhetoric.

Conclusion

We've seen that American hypocrisy is rampant in many areas of life. Racism, foreign policy, gender inequality, environmental double standards, immigration policies, corporate greed, wealth inequality, and political corruption - the list goes on and on.

We must remember the old adage: "actions speak louder than words". If we continue on this path of hypocrisy, our words will be meaningless. Our actions will be judged harshly by ourselves and by future generations.

We must recognize these injustices for what they are and take steps to address them. Only then can we become a truly just society.

White Christian Nationalism

We've seen it before: a wave of white Christian nationalism that washes over our nation. It's a dangerous movement, driven by an ideology of domination and hatred. Too often, this toxic form of extremism has been allowed to fester in the shadows, unchecked and unchallenged.

But now more than ever, we must recognize the power and reach of white Christian nationalism--and act to counter its influence. In this article, we'll explore the historical origins and modern manifestations of this dark force in American society; examine how religion is used to promote its ideals; investigate the connection between white Christian nationalism and white supremacy; discuss critiques of its beliefs; provide strategies for countering it; explore educational efforts aimed at prevention; consider alternatives to this ideology; and ultimately offer hope for a brighter future.

Historical Origins of White Christian Nationalism

Tracing its roots to the post-WWII era, white Christian nationalism has become a powerful force in recent decades. This form of ultra-nationalism emerged as a response to the rapid shifts in American culture, politics, and demographics that marked the late 20th century. It was rooted in an attempt to preserve what were seen as traditional values and beliefs by attempting to maintain an idealized version of American Christianity that focused on white racial supremacy and exclusionary policies.

This ideology was particularly attractive to many white Americans who felt threatened by changing norms and rising diversity. White Christian nationalism is often expressed through political action and policy making, including restrictive immigration laws, opposition to civil rights legislation, support for religious education requirements in public schools, attempts to limit access to abortion services or contraception access, efforts towards banning same-sex marriage or transgender rights recognition, among others.

These actions are typically framed as moral issues rather than racially motivated ones. In terms of rhetoric, it often involves appeals based on patriotism and moral authority rather than explicit racism or bigotry. As this ideology spreads throughout communities across America, it has become increasingly mainstreamed within the Republican Party as well as certain religious denominations that have embraced these principles either overtly or tacitly.

This has implications not just for how people view their own identity but also for how they interact with those who do not share their views; creating deep divides between those who subscribe to white Christian nationalism and those who do not. Its modern manifestations have had serious repercussions both domestically and abroad with increasing levels of intolerance becoming commonplace within our society today. To better understand where we are heading, it is important to understand the history behind white Christian nationalism, which provides insight into its current resurgence and prevalence.

Modern Manifestations of White Christian Nationalism

Paint a vivid picture of modern manifestations of this ideology, from its extreme factions to its more subtle influences.

White Christian Nationalism is an ideology that has found renewed vigor in the 21st century. It is a belief system that promotes white supremacy and often uses Christianity as a tool for oppression.

Extreme forms of white Christian nationalism can be seen in events like the 2017 Unite the Right rally where self-proclaimed white supremacists marched with tiki torches chanting "Jews will not replace us". This event was widely denounced by religious leaders, yet it reflects the presence of some extremist elements within this movement.

At the same time, there are more subtle aspects to this ideology which can be seen in statements such as "America was founded on Christian principles" or calls for laws based on Judeo-Christian values. These statements may seem innocuous but they serve to reinforce traditional notions of whiteness and Christianity as superior and exclude other religions or ideologies from public discourse.

White Christian Nationalism also manifests itself through attempts to promote prayer in public schools or pass legislation that would restrict certain civil rights protections to members of particular religious groups.

White Christian Nationalism is thus an evolving force with both extreme and more subtle expressions, each requiring careful attention if we are to understand its true nature and implications for our society today.

We must now turn our focus towards exploring the role religion plays in this ideology and how it shapes its development over time.

The Role of Religion in White Christian Nationalism

You may be surprised to learn that a staggering 77% of white supremacists identify as Christian, highlighting the deep entanglement between religion and this ideology. Religion can play an important role in the formation and perpetuation of white Christian nationalism. Specifically, it provides a sense of unity through shared beliefs and values, an identity for those who feel marginalized by society, and a moral justification for discriminatory practices based on racial or religious superiority.

White Christian nationalists often cite scripture to support their views on race and immigration. They take passages out of context from the Bible and other religious texts to promote a narrative that justifies exclusionary policies toward minorities. Furthermore, they use their faith as a platform to legitimize oppressive ideals such as white supremacy without having to consider any counterarguments from a moral standpoint.

Consequently, religion has become an integral part of the ideological basis for white Christian nationalism. This intertwinement between religion and white nationalist ideologies is something that needs to be examined more closely if we're ever going to address these issues effectively. To do so, we must understand how religion is used to further the agenda of those who subscribe to this ideology in order to combat its influence over our society.

With this in mind, let's turn our attention now towards exploring the ideology behind white Christian nationalism itself.

The Ideology of White Christian Nationalism

Discovering the underlying ideology of exclusionary and oppressive beliefs can help you understand why some people are drawn to white Christian nationalism. At its core, this belief system revolves around maintaining a predominantly white, Christian nation, with traditional values and conservative ideals.

It is rooted in the idea that non-white races and non-Christian religions should be excluded from participating or having authority in government. This ideology also focuses on preserving traditional gender roles, while rejecting progressive social movements like same-sex marriage and abortion rights. Furthermore, it is based on a fear of immigrants coming to "steal" jobs from native citizens and diluting the culture of the country through religious or cultural practices associated with their home countries.

White Christian nationalists believe that they must take action to keep these outsiders out so that their superior belief system will remain unchallenged in society. To this end, they use tactics such as limiting immigration policies, promoting English only laws for communication between government officials and citizens, attempting to control what students learn about other cultures in school curriculums; all measures which have been used historically to oppress minorities.

White Christian nationalists also often display an intense hostility towards Muslims due to their religion being seen as incompatible with Christianity itself.

White Christian nationalism is closely linked to white supremacy since both ideologies share common goals: maintaining power structures which prioritize whiteness over other races and religions, while simultaneously oppressing them by denying equal access to resources like education or employment opportunities. Therefore, understanding how this exclusionary philosophy works can provide insight into why some people actively seek out these dangerous beliefs systems as a way of protecting their own sense of identity from perceived threats posed by outsiders.

With this knowledge, we can move forward towards more inclusive solutions that embrace diversity instead of rejecting it outright.

The Connection between White Christian Nationalism and White Supremacy

Understanding the link between exclusionary beliefs and oppressive power structures is essential to recognizing why some individuals are drawn to this dangerous ideology. White Christian Nationalism has been a long-standing source of racism, xenophobia, and white supremacy in the United States. It is rooted in the idea that America belongs only to white Christians who validate their claims of racial superiority through a combination of religious scripture and historical interpretation.

This ideology relies heavily on systems of oppression such as slavery, colonialism, Jim Crow laws, segregation, and discrimination to maintain its power structure. As a result of these beliefs, many people of color have faced significant socio-economic disadvantages throughout history.

White Christian Nationalism also promotes an us-versus-them mentality which encourages exclusivity and marginalization based on race or religion. The rhetoric used by supporters of this movement serves to further divide society into two distinct camps – those deemed worthy and those seen as inferior. These messages can be found everywhere from political discourse to religious services where 'true Americans' are praised while anyone seen as foreign or non-Christian is demonized.

Ultimately, this ideology reinforces existing prejudices by fostering a sense that 'others' are undeserving or unfit for full acceptance within American culture. The implications of White Christian Nationalism's embrace of white supremacy go beyond hurtful speech; it actively seeks out policies that would disadvantage minority groups in areas such as education, employment opportunities, voting rights protection—the list goes on. The effects are far reaching with regard to how it shapes our society today; from denying medical care due to religious convictions to influencing public policy decisions like immigration reform or affirmative action initiatives—all while reinforcing the notion that 'white' should be at the top of every hierarchy in America.

To truly understand its impact requires looking at its consequences through an intersectional lens which acknowledges both oppressive power structures and individual experiences alike.

Transitioning now into examining the impact these ideologies have had on society...

The Impact of White Christian Nationalism on Society

Gaining an insight into the ramifications of this divisive ideology can help us appreciate how it has shaped our society and communities. White Christian Nationalism has had a major impact on our social, political, and religious structures in a variety of ways:

- It has exacerbated existing divisions between people of different religions, ethnicities, and races.

- Its rhetoric is often used to justify bigotry and discrimination against those who don't share its beliefs.

- It reinforces certain traditional gender roles that limit the potential for many individuals to fully express themselves or explore their fullest potentials.

The effects of this movement have been far-reaching. It has impacted individual lives and influenced entire countries' laws and policies. This movement has also served as a rallying point for those who feel threatened by cultural shifts such as immigration or increased diversity in traditionally homogenous societies.

As we strive to create more inclusive spaces for all people, it's important that we understand the implications white Christian nationalism has had on our societies. This will help us effectively recognize and combat its influence moving forward without sacrificing progress towards greater equality and justice.

Moving on from this section, let's turn our attention to examining some of the criticism leveled at white Christian nationalism specifically.

Criticism of White Christian Nationalism

Criticizing this divisive ideology is essential for appreciating the extent of its reach and impact in our society, and can help us combat its influence going forward.

White Christian Nationalism has been criticized as a form of racism that perpetuates white supremacy by oppressing people from minority backgrounds. This form of racism, which is deeply entrenched in American culture, has been used to justify policies such as discriminatory immigration laws and the reification of racial segregation. Additionally, some have argued that while these policies are often framed as being based on religious beliefs, they actually serve to bolster power structures that maintain privilege for those who already hold it.

White Christian Nationalism has also been criticized for threatening long-standing social progress by creating an atmosphere of fear and distrust amongst those who do not share the same beliefs or values. This type of nationalism can lead to exclusionary practices that impede the ability of individuals from different backgrounds to participate fully in society. It can also foster xenophobia and intolerance towards people from other countries or cultures, making it more difficult for them to integrate into their new communities.

Critiquing White Christian Nationalism is part of understanding how this ideology works within existing power structures and how it shapes public discourse on issues related to race and religion. Understanding its effects can help us move forward with strategies aimed at countering its influence so that all members of society feel safe, respected, and included regardless of their background or beliefs.

To do this effectively we must work together to challenge existing systems of oppression while building bridges between diverse communities based on mutual respect and understanding.

Strategies for Countering White Christian Nationalism

You're not alone in wanting to counter the oppressive force of this ideology; together, we can work towards creating a more inclusive society.

There are many strategies to be implemented when countering white Christian nationalism, such as dismantling power structures that perpetuate racism and inequality, creating safe spaces for marginalized communities to have their voices heard, and educating people on the history and impacts of white Christian Nationalism.

It's important to understand that countering white Christian nationalism requires more than just talking about it. Action must be taken. This means engaging in conversations that challenge oppressive systems, recognizing privilege, amplifying the voices of those affected by racism and oppression, and holding people accountable for their words and actions. Only then can real progress be made towards achieving true equity and justice.

The role of education in combating white Christian nationalism cannot be overstated. It's vital for individuals to educate themselves on the issue to gain a better understanding of how it affects different populations. Education can also provide an opportunity for people to learn about alternative ideologies that promote acceptance and respect for all members of society regardless of race or religion - something which is essential if we're ever going to move away from this divisive ideology.

To put it simply: knowledge is power, so use it!

The Role of Education in Countering White Christian Nationalism

As we discussed previously, there are a variety of strategies available to counter white Christian nationalism. Another approach is through educational programming. By recognizing the origins of white Christian nationalist ideology and understanding the potential danger it poses to our society, we can help people become aware and combat this belief system.

To further illustrate this point, let's look at how education can be used to counter white Christian nationalism:

Tool	Usage	Benefits
Textbooks & Curricula Updates	Encourage students to learn about the history of racism in America and the development of white supremacist movements over time. Educators should also focus on stories from people from different backgrounds who have worked for social justice.	This will foster critical thinking skills in students as they analyze their own biases and assumptions while developing empathy for those with lived experiences that differ from their own. Additionally, teachers will become more aware of their own role in perpetuating systemic racism.
Mentorship Programs & Guest Speakers	Invite guest speakers from various backgrounds to come into classrooms or host mentorship programs where students can ask questions and engage in dialogue about topics related to race and identity formation without fear of judgement or backlash.	This allows students to explore issues related to race beyond what is provided in textbooks, deepening their knowledge base on the issue while allowing them to interact with a range of perspectives outside of those presented by educators alone. It also creates an opportunity for dialogue among classmates which may challenge any preconceived notions they have about race or other identities.
Community-Based Learning Projects	Engage students in projects that involve interacting with diverse communities, addressing real-world issues related to race, and applying classroom learning to practical situations.	This hands-on approach helps students understand the impact of systemic racism in real-life scenarios. It promotes active participation, collaboration, and empathy as students work towards solutions. It also connects classroom learning to the broader community, fostering a sense of responsibility and a deeper understanding of the complexities of racial issues.

Utilizing community-based learning projects helps build relationships between schools, local businesses, organizations, government agencies, etc., allowing students opportunities for hands-on learning activities related to social justice issues such as racism or white supremacy that may not be covered in traditional curriculums alone. The benefits here include fostering civic engagement by connecting classroom instruction with real world applications while providing meaningful experiences that lead towards greater understanding across diverse groups within our communities – ultimately leading towards a more inclusive society free from ideologies like white Christian nationalism.

In order to truly create lasting change against white Christian nationalist beliefs within our communities it is essential that we use education as part of our strategy; only then will we be able to actively work towards creating more equitable societies for everyone involved in them. With this understanding firmly rooted within us, it's time now to turn our attention towards exploring alternative models that can serve as alternatives instead—models which do not rely upon tenets espoused by white Christian nationalists but instead work against them..

Alternative Models to White Christian Nationalism

Discover alternative models to white Christian nationalism, and explore how they promote a more equitable society for everyone.

One example of an alternative model is the Black Church Movement, which emerged after the Civil War as a tool to help African Americans gain access to education and resources in a racist society. This movement encouraged communal worship, service-oriented work, and civil rights activism, which all work together to challenge white supremacy. The Black Church Movement has been instrumental in empowering African American communities by giving them power within institutions that were once oppressive.

The queer liberation movement is another example of an alternative model that challenges white Christian nationalism. This movement seeks to overcome heteronormative oppression through LGBTQIA+ advocacy, education, and support services. It works towards creating safe spaces for members of the LGBTQIA+ community by challenging traditional gender roles and binary structures that have been put in place by white nationalist ideologies. Additionally, this movement promotes visibility for queer identities so that those who do not fit into traditional gender boxes can be seen and heard without fear of judgment or discrimination.

These two examples demonstrate how alternative models can fight against white Christian nationalism by creating inclusive environments that celebrate diverse identities while also working towards justice and equity for all people. By promoting understanding among different groups within our society, we can create a more equitable future where everyone is welcome regardless of their beliefs or identities.

Frequently Asked Questions

What are the key differences between White Christian Nationalism and other forms of nationalism?

We often think of nationalism as a unifying force, but there are different forms that draw on various cultural and religious influences. White Christian nationalism is just one example, and it differs from other forms in several ways.

Whereas many traditional forms of nationalism focus on a shared language or culture, white Christian nationalists tend to emphasize their faith as the primary source of national identity. This has led to an emphasis on exclusionary policies such as immigration restrictions and preferential treatment for certain religious groups.

Additionally, white Christian nationalists often view themselves as superior to others, creating an atmosphere of intolerance and racism.

Is White Christian Nationalism still prevalent in today's society?

We've seen a rise in nationalism across the world, and it can take many forms. One form that's particularly relevant today is white Christian nationalism - a belief system that promotes the idea of a superior white Christian culture and identity.

Is it still prevalent in today's society? The answer to that question depends on who you ask, but there are those who argue that its influence continues to be felt in some areas, from politics to religion and beyond.

What are the potential legal implications of White Christian Nationalism?

We've all heard the saying 'actions speak louder than words', and when it comes to the potential legal implications of any kind of nationalist movement, this maxim is particularly relevant.

From increasing scrutiny on hate speech laws to potential challenges on immigration policies, there are numerous ways in which any nationalistic ideology could be challenged in a court of law.

It's for this reason that those who support such movements must tread carefully and ensure their actions aren't in violation of existing laws and regulations.

How does White Christian Nationalism intersect with other forms of racism?

We've seen how racism has evolved over centuries, leading to forms of bias and discrimination against marginalized groups.

White Christian nationalism intersects with these other forms of racism in subtle ways, such as through the use of religious rhetoric to justify racial inequality or by creating a false narrative that Christianity is only for white people.

This type of racism can be both intentional and unintentional, making it difficult to identify and address.

It's important to recognize the connections between white Christian nationalism and other forms of racism in order to create meaningful dialogue about race and religion.

How can individuals and communities effectively respond to White Christian Nationalism?

We believe that the most effective way to respond to any form of racism is through education and understanding. This includes learning about how different cultures, religions, and systems impact each other, as well as having conversations with people who've experienced racism firsthand.

It's also important to recognize the power of our own words and actions. Even if we don't intend it, language or behavior that privileges one group over another can perpetuate racism. We must all strive to be aware of our own biases and challenge them when they arise.

Finally, it's essential for us to spread awareness by standing up against injustice whenever we encounter it, whether directly or indirectly.

Conclusion

We've seen the origins, manifestations, ideology, and criticism of white Christian nationalism. It's clear that this movement is rooted in racism and white supremacy.

We must take action to counter these ideologies before they become further entrenched within our society. For example, a small town in the South had a long history of racial segregation until one brave student-led organization decided to confront it head on by organizing peaceful protests against discriminatory policies.

This inspiring story shows us that we all have a role to play in combating white Christian nationalism and its toxic ideas. Let's use this example as motivation to create positive change in our own communities.

Police Street Gangs

We have all heard of street gangs, but what about police street gangs? Police street gangs are a relatively new phenomenon that is becoming increasingly more common in many parts of the world. They are organized groups of law enforcement officers who operate outside the scope of their professional duties and use their power to engage in criminal activity.

In this article, we will explore how police street gangs are formed, who their members are, what they aim to accomplish through their activities, what tactics they employ to achieve these objectives and the risks associated with them. We'll also examine how police street gangs can be controlled and discuss the impact that they have on communities.

Finally, we'll look at the future of police street gangs and see where this phenomenon is heading.

What is a Police Street Gang?

A police street gang is an organized group of individuals that often use violence and intimidation to gain control of a particular area. These gangs are highly organized and have complex hierarchies, with members ranging from enforcers to lieutenants who answer directly to the leader. Police street gangs tend to be more heavily armed than their civilian-based counterparts, as they may not only carry weapons illegally but also have access to police-issued equipment. As such, they pose a greater threat to public safety due to their level of power and influence.

Police street gangs are typically formed in response to various social conditions in the community or region they inhabit. These may include inequality, poverty, unemployment, discrimination, and other forms of marginalization which can lead some individuals into crime as a form of survival or economic opportunity. The presence of police street gangs can also be an indicator of higher levels of criminal activity within the area due to their territorial nature and propensity for violence.

In order for police street gangs to survive and thrive in their environment, they must create connections with other criminal organizations both locally and internationally in order to maintain resources necessary for continued operations. This means engaging in activities like drug trafficking or human smuggling while relying on networks that allow them access money laundering services or covert arms deals, amongst others. Understanding how these groups operate is essential if we're going to effectively combat them moving forward.

How are Police Street Gangs Formed?

You may be wondering how these groups of people come together, so let's explore how they form.

Police street gangs are created whenever a group of like-minded individuals bond over shared interests, goals, and values. Often times, this comes in the form of a shared feeling of disillusionment with law enforcement or government institutions. This can include feelings surrounding racial inequality or unfairness in the justice system. It may also be caused by a deep sense of mistrust towards the police and other authorities.

There is often an element of secrecy to their meetings as well; many members aren't aware that their peers have joined such a group until later on into their involvement. Members typically have to meet certain criteria before being accepted into the gang as well - a sense of loyalty and trustworthiness is expected from all participants. They must also demonstrate commitment to upholding any laws or codes set forth by the group's leaders, as well as actively participating in activities that align with their mission statements and ideologies.

These gangs also tend to share common symbols or identifiers that serve as unifying markers among members, helping to create a stronger sense of camaraderie between them.

By providing an outlet for those who feel disenfranchised from society, police street gangs become formed through trust and solidarity within its membership base. With this knowledge, we can now move on to understanding who the members of police street gangs are.

Who are the Members of Police Street Gangs?

Feel disenfranchised from society and looking for an outlet? People of all backgrounds join police street gangs, hoping to find solidarity and support within a tight-knit community.

Although membership is often exclusive to those with some form of law enforcement experience, many members come from the streets or have prior criminal convictions. Many even have active gang affiliations outside the organization.

The diversity of its members creates unique dynamics within police street gangs that challenge traditional notions of social order and hierarchy. Members are held to a high standard of loyalty and commitment as they strive towards collective goals in an effort to provide for their families and protect their neighborhoods.

A sense of camaraderie develops between members as they share common struggles in navigating difficult life circumstances.

Police street gangs may be seen as an alternative way for individuals to make connections, seek protection, or express themselves without having to conform to societal expectations or norms. As such, the interactions among members require respect, understanding, and communication in order to create a safe space where everyone can thrive.

This level of trust allows the gang's objectives—whether legal or illegal—to carry out more smoothly than if each member acted individually or on their own accord. With this type of structure in place, it's no surprise that police street gangs remain popular today despite facing frequent scrutiny from both authorities and civilians alike.

Moving forward, it's important for us to understand what these groups' goals are so we can better understand their impact on our communities.

What are the Goals of Police Street Gangs?

The goals of police street gangs may vary, but ultimately they strive to create a sense of connection and security in an otherwise hostile environment. For many members, the main aim is to provide an outlet for individuals who share similar life experiences or come from the same background. These groups can also act as a support system, providing protection and support for vulnerable members of their communities.

Additionally, some gangs seek to wield power over rival gangs through violent tactics such as intimidation and threats. Furthermore, they often use illegal activities such as drug dealing, theft, and extortion in order to gain money and resources for their members. In some cases, gang members are also involved in organized crime operations that involve large amounts of cash or illicit goods. By taking part in these activities, police street gangs can increase their wealth and influence within a given area.

Although there are many positive aspects associated with being part of a police street gang—such as camaraderie amongst its members—there are also serious risks involved due to the criminal nature of these organizations. As such, it's important for individuals considering joining one of these gangs to be aware of what they're getting themselves into before making any commitments.

With that said, understanding what drives people to join police street gangs can help us better address this issue on a wider scale moving forward. So, what tactics do police street gangs use?

What Tactics Do Police Street Gangs Use?

We often think of street gangs as criminal organizations operating outside the law. However, there are also police street gangs that operate within the law enforcement community. These gangs use a variety of tactics to gain power and influence, such as intimidation, extortion, and illicit activities like drug dealing and theft.

Here are four key strategies police street gangs employ:

- Unite members through shared experiences in order to create a sense of loyalty and camaraderie.
- Discourage cooperation with internal affairs investigations by threatening members or their families with violence or job loss if they cooperate with investigators.
- Use surveillance techniques to monitor the activities of other officers in order to ensure compliance with gang rules.
- Create an atmosphere of fear among civilians by intimidating them into not reporting incidents involving gang members or cooperating with local authorities when applicable.

These tactics enable police street gangs to maintain control over their turf while simultaneously avoiding detection from higher-ups in the department who might seek to bring them down if they knew what was going on beneath the surface level operations of their departments.

As a result, these tactics have allowed police street gangs to remain largely undisturbed by external forces for decades despite efforts from both inside and outside the law enforcement community to curb their influence and power within urban areas across America. With this understanding, we can now move on to explore what benefits these powerful groups may provide in our next section about what are the benefits of police street gangs?

What Are the Benefits of Police Street Gangs?

You'd think police street gangs would only bring trouble, but surprisingly they can actually offer some benefits too!

When it comes to crime prevention, police street gangs can be a valuable asset. By having their presence in certain neighborhoods and actively engaging with the public, they can help deter criminal activity by showing that there's law enforcement nearby. They can also act as a sort of mediator between the police and community members who may be wary of law enforcement. This helps build trust between both groups and create an environment where people feel safe to report any criminal activity without fear of retribution.

Police street gangs are also beneficial in terms of surveillance and intelligence gathering. By being part of a gang, officers have access to information about criminal activities that might not otherwise be known or reported by civilians. This allows them to stay one step ahead and proactively prevent crimes from occurring in their jurisdictions.

In addition, these gangs provide extra manpower for special operations such as raids or undercover operations which could prove useful when investigating more serious cases like drug trafficking or organized crime rings.

Lastly, police street gangs can also serve as a source of support for officers who are dealing with difficult situations on the job. These gangs often develop close bonds with each other which provide moral support during stressful times while on duty or after traumatic events occur within the department. With this kind of camaraderie and solidarity among members, officers are better equipped to handle dangerous situations that arise during their service without feeling isolated or overwhelmed by the circumstances at hand.

Without question, police street gangs offer some unique advantages that should not be overlooked when considering ways to reduce crime in communities across America. That being said, it's important to consider what risks come along with this type of policing before making any decisions about utilizing them for crime prevention efforts—especially since they've been linked to corruption and abuse in certain areas in the past.

What Are the Risks of Police Street Gangs?

Being part of a gang can come with risks, particularly when it comes to law enforcement. Police street gangs are no exception to this rule, and they pose several potential dangers that must be considered. Some of these risks include:

- Legal Risks: The members of police street gangs often engage in criminal activities that could lead to prosecution or disciplinary action by the police department. There's also the potential risk of civil litigation if the gang's actions violate someone's rights or cause injury or damage.

- Physical Risks: Gang members may be exposed to physical violence from other gangs, as well as from rival officers within their own department. The high-stress environment associated with being part of a gang can also lead to physical and psychological health problems for its members.

Furthermore, police street gangs have been known to use their position and influence within law enforcement agencies to further their own interests at the expense of others. This has resulted in misuse of resources, corruption, and abuse of power that can have serious consequences for both those involved in the gangs as well as innocent bystanders who may become victims due to such activities.

It's essential that steps are taken to ensure these risks are minimized in order to protect everyone involved and prevent any further damage from occurring. Without proper oversight and control, police street gangs can do more harm than good and cause serious harm both physically and legally if left unchecked.

How Can Police Street Gangs be controlled?

Knowing the risks associated with police street gangs is only the first step; taking action to control them is essential for protecting those involved and preventing further damage.

One way to address this problem is by increasing public education on police street gangs, as well as providing resources to those affected. This would help raise awareness of the dangers that they present and allow people to recognize signs of gang activity in their own communities.

Additionally, more resources should be allocated towards law enforcement efforts targeting these groups. This could include increased surveillance and improved intelligence gathering capabilities, allowing authorities to identify potential members and disrupt criminal activities before they spread.

Finally, creating better relationships between police officers and citizens can also be beneficial in controlling police street gangs. Community policing initiatives can encourage communication between parties, building trust and providing a platform for addressing concerns about gang activity without fear of retribution.

These steps are necessary for reducing the prevalence of police street gangs and ensuring safer communities overall.

What is the Impact of Police Street Gangs on Communities?

Police street gangs have a devastating impact on communities, leaving lingering effects of fear and violence that can last for years. In many cases, these gangs become entrenched in neighborhoods, taking advantage of vulnerable populations and creating an atmosphere of intimidation and mistrust. This is especially true in areas where economic insecurity or a lack of access to quality education is already present.

From this environment emerges a cycle of crime and poverty that becomes difficult to break. The presence of police street gangs also affects the relationship between law enforcement officers and communities they serve. It's not uncommon for members of gangs to be employed by local government agencies such as the police force or other organizations that provide public services.

As such, it's easy to understand why citizens might feel less than trusting toward those in uniform; it creates a divisive atmosphere which undermines community trust in authority figures. The long-term implications are profound: without trust between citizens and public officials, it becomes harder to create meaningful change within the community through legitimate means such as education reform or job training initiatives.

Without trust, even well-intentioned efforts often fail due to lack of participation from residents who feel their voices will not be heard anyway. Moving forward, addressing the issue of police street gangs must involve finding ways for everyone—citizens and authorities alike—to work together towards solutions that benefit all members of society equally.

What is the Future of Police Street Gangs?

You can shape the future of your community and break the cycle of fear, violence, and poverty caused by police street gangs.

Police street gangs have become an increasingly serious problem in many communities, with devastating consequences for public safety. The rise of these gangs has created a culture of crime that further perpetuates itself through illegal activities such as drug trafficking, extortion, and bribery.

In order to counteract these negative effects, it's essential to develop strategies that focus on prevention and intervention. Here are three ways to make a positive change:

- Strengthen local law enforcement by increasing resources dedicated to combating police street gangs
- Support local anti-gang initiatives that provide education and resources for at-risk youth
- Facilitate more meaningful cooperation between law enforcement agencies and community members

These efforts can help build stronger relationships between residents and police while helping to reduce gang activity in the long run.

It's also important for cities to invest in programs that help those who have been involved with gangs find employment or training opportunities so they can transition away from criminal behavior.

By working together, we can create safer neighborhoods where everyone feels secure and respected without having to worry about the presence of police street gangs.

Frequently Asked Questions

How do Police Street Gangs Recruit New Members?

We often hear stories of gangs recruiting new members, but how do police street gangs go about it? With the rise of law enforcement-affiliated gangs, recruitment methods have had to evolve.

Coincidentally, most of these groups focus on peer-to-peer outreach and word of mouth as their primary strategies. Tactics such as offering safety in numbers, a sense of belonging and camaraderie are used to entice members and draw them into the fold.

Additionally, some police street gangs also use personal connections with current officers or former gang members to influence potential recruits. Understanding this approach gives us an insight into how these groups operate and why they're so successful at bringing in new members.

How Does the Legal System Treat Police Street Gangs?

The legal system treats gangs generally harshly, and police street gangs are no exception. Law enforcement is particularly hostile towards such organizations, as they involve police officers in criminal activities.

Police street gangs often face stiffer penalties than other gangs due to the public's fear of law enforcement corruption and abuse of power. Furthermore, these groups are quickly targeted by prosecutors in an attempt to make examples out of them and deter similar behavior in the future.

This results in harsher sentences handed down by courts, with some gang members even receiving life sentences for non-violent offenses.

What Role Does Technology Play in Police Street Gangs?

Technology has become an integral part of many aspects of modern life, and police street gangs are no exception. Gangs use technology to facilitate communication between members, organize criminal activities, and even recruit new members by using social media platforms.

They also use encrypted messaging apps to keep their operations hidden from law enforcement agencies, while tracking their rivals' movements though GPS systems. Technology can also be used for surveillance purposes such as monitoring phone calls or text messages of rival gang members.

In conclusion, technology plays a major role in the operations of police street gangs.

How Can the Public Get Involved in Preventing Police Street Gangs?

We, as a public, are all familiar with the concept of street gangs and their negative impacts on our communities.

To prevent police street gangs from forming and growing, we must take an active stance and get involved in prevention strategies at the local level.

From attending town hall meetings to engaging in community dialogue with members of law enforcement, it's vital that citizens take part in any initiatives aimed at reducing gang activity.

By taking action as a collective unit, we can create an environment where police street gangs have no place to exist.

How Can Communities Respond to Police Street Gangs?

We understand the need for communities to respond to the presence of street gangs. It's important for citizens to come together and build strong relationships with police officers, civic organizations, and local government to ensure safety and security in their neighborhoods.

This could include working with police departments to create neighborhood watch programs, attending community meetings about gang violence, or developing strategies to reduce gang activity in public areas.

These efforts will help create an environment that is safe from gang activity and that encourages positive development within the community.

Conclusion

We've seen how police street gangs form, what their goals are, and the tactics they use to achieve them. We also know the risks of these gangs, and how they can be controlled.

But one question remains: what is the ultimate impact of police street gangs on communities? Unfortunately, this isn't an easy answer; police street gangs often have lasting effects on neighborhoods for generations to come.

It's up to us as a society to recognize the dangers posed by these groups and work together to prevent them from taking root in our communities.

Black Historical Moments

We have been witness to some truly remarkable black historical moments throughout history. From the abolition of slavery, to the elections of Barack Obama and Kamala Harris, these events have made a lasting impact on our society that will never be forgotten.

Our minds are filled with awe and admiration as we look back at these powerful figures and movements who fought against injustice and racism in order to create a better future for us all. With each event comes a feeling of hope, pride, and strength that radiates through our veins like a warm embrace from the ancestors who came before us; it's almost too overwhelming for words!

We can only imagine what could come next in this ongoing saga of Black excellence.

The Abolition of Slavery

You've heard the stories of freedom and liberation - now learn how it all began with the Abolition of Slavery. It was a key moment in history that marked the end of an era where hundreds of thousands of people were enslaved without choice or recognition.

The Abolitionists, such as William Lloyd Garrison and Harriet Tubman, fought for freedom long before it was granted. Their resistance helped pave the way for future generations to gain access to rights, liberties, and justice.

As we look back on this period in our nation's history, we remember its significance and honor those who courageously stood up against oppression.

With these new-found freedoms came opportunities for progress. African Americans started to mobilize politically, educationally, and economically; leading the charge was Rosa Parks with her refusal to move from her seat on a segregated bus in Montgomery – sparking what later became known as 'The Montgomery Bus Boycott'.

This bold act set off a chain reaction which revolutionized race relations in America during the Civil Rights Movement.

The Montgomery Bus Boycott

You're likely aware of the famous boycott, but did you know it took over a year to achieve its desired results? The Montgomery Bus Boycott was one of the most significant actions taken in support of civil rights during the 1950s and 1960s.

It began on December 1st, 1955 after Rosa Parks refused to give up her seat on a public bus in Montgomery, Alabama. This event sparked a protest movement that spread across the nation and spurred on the civil rights movement.

The boycott lasted 381 days and resulted in a Supreme Court decision declaring segregation on buses unconstitutional. Throughout this time period, African Americans organized carpools and walked long distances to get around town as an act of non-violent defiance against racial injustice.

The boycotters' courage inspired many people around the world to recognize that they had power when working together for change. Despite facing discrimination and violence, they persevered until their goal was achieved, showing us all what is possible when we stand up for something we believe in.

Their strength paved the way for future generations hoping to create a more equitable society – leading us into our next topic about 'the civil rights movement'.

The Civil Rights Movement

The civil rights movement was an incredibly powerful time when people of all backgrounds came together to fight for justice and equality. It started as a peaceful protest against the unfair treatment of African Americans in the United States.

This spanned from protests, sit-ins, marches, rallies, and other forms of civil disobedience to challenge oppressive laws that discriminated against Black Americans. The movement brought attention to issues such as education reform, voting rights, police brutality, and economic inequality, which were all deeply rooted in racism and segregation.

The bravery and courage of those who fought for change during this challenging time eventually led to the passing of the Voting Rights Act of 1965, which made it illegal for states to use discriminatory practices to keep minorities from voting.

The Voting Rights Act of 1965

You can make a real difference in your community by exercising your right to vote, so don't let anything stop you from making your voice heard!

The Voting Rights Act of 1965 was a monumental moment for civil rights in the United States. It prohibited racial discrimination in voting and ended literacy tests as a requirement for voting eligibility. As such, it granted African Americans the right to vote and gave them access to the ballot box after decades of oppression.

This act had an immense impact on the black community, as it allowed them to have their voices heard and participate in democracy like never before. Transitioning into the era of Black Power, this newfound access to political power enabled African Americans to push for further equality and justice within our nation.

The Black Power Movement

Fueled by the momentum of the Voting Rights Act, African Americans began to organize and advocate for full equality during the Black Power Movement. This movement sought to change the status quo in regards to civil rights and economic power.

It was a period marked by increased militancy and protest against injustices done to black people, with calls for self-determination, pride in African heritage, and empowerment through education and political organization.

Organizations such as the Student Nonviolent Coordinating Committee (SNCC), The Black Panther Party (BPP), and The National Black Political Assembly were founded during this time. These organizations sought to create a better life for African Americans through grassroots activism, community service programs, voter registration drives, educational initiatives, employment schemes, and legal support services.

From advancing civil rights legislation to challenging police brutality on behalf of minority communities, these groups worked tirelessly towards achieving their goals of racial justice and equality. With their determined effort they set an example of solidarity that would continue long after their work was done.

As such, they remain an integral part of black history today—and will forever be remembered as vital figures that helped shape a brighter future for all African Americans.

The Black Panther Party

The Black Panther Party fought fiercely for African American rights, famously organizing a 'Free Breakfast Program' that fed thousands of underprivileged children in need. This dedication to helping the community was emblematic of their commitment to justice and equality - an inspiring example of what can be achieved when people stand together.

Through peaceful protest, they demanded economic equality, a living wage, and access to quality education. They also called for an end to police brutality. Through self-defense, they protected themselves from violence and established armed members to patrol neighborhoods and provide security at political events. Additionally, they protected activists on marches and rallies.

Their unwavering courage in the face of adversity set a powerful example for all people fighting for social justice. With this legacy in mind, it's no wonder that the Million Man March was such a prominent event.

The Million Man March

You'll never forget the stirring sight of hundreds of thousands of people coming together in one unified movement, a moment that will remain etched in your memory forever.

The Million Man March was a powerful gathering for African Americans to put their collective foot down and let their voices be heard. It was an uplifting experience to see so many people from all walks of life come together peacefully to stand up for what they believed in.

The march highlighted the importance of solidarity amongst African Americans and sent a message loud and clear: We're here, we matter, and we won't be silenced. Despite the challenges our nation has faced since then, this event will always remain an inspiring example of what can happen when we stand up together as one.

And just as it did then, it continues to give us hope now that things can get better if we work towards it with passion and purpose.

The spirit of unity that was seen during the Million Man March carried on into the historic election of Barack Obama as President in 2008 - another remarkable milestone for black history which ignited a sense of pride across America like never before.

This moment showed how far this nation had come since its troubled past, proving that anything is possible if you set your mind to it despite any obstacles that may arise along the way.

With Obama's election came newfound optimism for generations both present and future - optimism about what could be achieved if we continue working towards progress with courage and resilience.

The Election of Barack Obama

The Million Man March was a significant moment in history that demonstrated the power of solidarity and unity among African Americans. It showed the world that when we come together, we can make a difference.

Now, building on this momentum, we had the opportunity to witness an even more historic event: The election of Barack Obama as President of the United States. His election not only marked a new era for African Americans but also for people all around the world who felt inspired by his message of hope and progress. With his victory, he became our nation's first black president - a monumental achievement that will be remembered in history books forever.

His presidency was an inspiring example of what is possible when people come together to work towards common goals. As we look back on this remarkable time in our nation's history, it serves as a reminder that anything is achievable with hard work and determination.

Our next step is to reflect on how this period has informed our current understanding of civil rights -- namely, the Black Lives Matter movement.

The Black Lives Matter Movement

You're likely familiar with the Black Lives Matter movement, a powerful civil rights movement that has been gaining traction in recent years. From peaceful protests to slogan t-shirts and hats, BLM is everywhere and it's here to stay.

This movement seeks justice for all Black people who have been systematically oppressed by police brutality and racism throughout history. One example is the 2014 shooting of Michael Brown in Ferguson, Missouri. Another is the 2018 killing of Botham Jean in his own apartment by an off-duty police officer. And yet another is the death of George Floyd in 2020 due to excessive force used by Minneapolis officers while he was handcuffed face down on the ground. These are only a few examples of countless cases where innocent Black people were not given fair treatment by those sworn to protect them - showcasing why this movement matters so much today and why we must continue fighting for racial equality going forward.

The fight for justice doesn't end here though - it extends beyond this momentous civil rights struggle into other areas such as voting rights and representation in government, setting up a path towards Kamala Harris' historic election as Vice President of the United States, thus continuing our journey towards achieving true equity across all races...

The Election of Kamala Harris

We all watched with excitement as Kamala Harris, the first woman of color to become Vice President-elect in the United States, was elected.

This momentous event marked a significant milestone in black history and was a powerful reminder of how far we've come since the Black Lives Matter Movement began.

The election of Kamala Harris is an inspiring example of what can be achieved when people work together towards change.

The breakthrough achievements have meant that now more than ever, not only are African Americans being heard but also given positions of power and influence in society.

This is proof that progress and equality can be achieved through hard work and determination.

Frequently Asked Questions

What impact did the Abolition of Slavery have on the economy?

The abolition of slavery had a profound impact on the economy. By removing free labor from the equation, industries and businesses had to adjust their costs and production models.

This resulted in significant increases in wages for laborers and an overall shift in how business was done across multiple sectors. This economic transformation was difficult but necessary, creating new opportunities for those who were formerly enslaved and setting the stage for a brighter future.

What other civil rights issues were addressed during the Montgomery Bus Boycott?

We've all heard about the Montgomery bus boycott, but what other civil rights issues were addressed during this historic event? To understand the full scope of its impact, we must investigate the truth of this theory.

During the boycott, African Americans in Alabama were actively protesting against segregation laws that limited their access to public transportation and employment opportunities. They also fought for their right to vote and for equal pay for equal work.

The Montgomery bus boycott was a catalyst for change in civil rights legislation throughout America and was instrumental in paving the way towards greater racial equality.

How did the Civil Rights Movement influence the Black Power Movement?

The Civil Rights Movement of the 1950s and 1960s laid the foundation for the Black Power Movement that followed. This movement was a response to ongoing racial inequality and discrimination, which had been going on in the US since its founding.

It sought to empower African Americans by encouraging them to take charge of their own destinies through activism, education, and economic independence. The Black Power Movement aimed to create systemic change within society, advocating for civil rights as well as black pride and dignity.

The struggle created by this movement resulted in new legal protections for African Americans and gave rise to a new wave of activism that is still seen today.

How did the Voting Rights Act of 1965 affect voter turnout?

We can't help but feel a sense of accomplishment and pride when we look back at the Voting Rights Act of 1965. This critical moment in history played an important role in ensuring that people of all colors had their voices heard at the ballot box, leading to increased voter turnout across the United States.

Allusion is often used to add richness and depth to stories, and this act is no exception – it stands as a beacon for our nation's commitment to equality and justice. In an era where many were still denied basic freedoms, this monumental act was crucial in bringing us towards a more equitable society.

What are the main objectives of the Black Lives Matter Movement?

We strive for equality and justice in the Black Lives Matter movement. The main objectives are to create a world where Black lives are no longer systematically targeted for demise, and to achieve a sense of safety through the recognition of our human rights.

We focus on ending police brutality, challenging unjust laws and institutions, and recognizing global impacts of white supremacy. We advocate for self-determination, work towards liberation from all forms of oppression, and build healthy communities with sustainable resources.

We also seek to honor those who have been lost due to racial injustice. Together, we fight for freedom and justice until every Black life is valued equally in this society.

Conclusion

We've come a long way since the abolition of slavery.

From the Montgomery Bus Boycott to the Black Lives Matter Movement, we've seen countless moments in history that have pushed us forward.

These moments represent our struggles and our resilience, our pain and our triumphs.

We remember them as an allegory of sorts – a reminder that together, we can overcome anything.

Our journey is not over yet, but with each step taken towards progress, we gain strength and courage to continue on this path of liberation and justice.

Now more than ever, it's time for us to unite and create real change.

Let us all keep marching until freedom rings true for everyone!

The Contributions of Black People in America

We have all heard of the many contributions made by black people in America.

From music and art, to literature, education, activism, business and science – these are just some of the areas where African Americans have achieved great progress.

But what we often don't acknowledge is the sheer force of determination that has been behind each success story.

Despite centuries of oppression and discrimination, black people around the country have worked tirelessly to make a positive difference in society – and continue doing so today.

Music

You can hear the influence of African-American culture in all kinds of music today! From gospel to hip-hop, blues to jazz and R&B, black musicians have helped shape the music we listen to.

Many artists have used their music as a means of expressing themselves and advocating for social change. African-American musicians have also been incredibly successful in breaking down barriers and paving the way for greater inclusion in the industry. From Dizzy Gillespie to Aretha Franklin, Ella Fitzgerald to Beyonce, black American musical talent has left an indelible mark on our culture and society.

The contributions of African-Americans extend far beyond music though. Art is another powerful way that black people have expressed themselves throughout history. For centuries, their art has served as an important vehicle for cultural expression and political resistance.

Artists such as Jean-Michel Basquiat, Kara Walker, Jacob Lawrence, Faith Ringgold and many others have made tremendous contributions to our understanding of Black life through their works.

Art

Discover how African-American artists have painted a stunning tapestry of culture and creativity, weaving together unique perspectives that are sure to move you.

From jazz legends like Miles Davis and John Coltrane to visual artists like Romare Bearden and Jacob Lawrence, African American art has left an indelible mark on our culture:

- Music:

- Jazz greats like Louis Armstrong, Duke Ellington, and Ella Fitzgerald continue to influence modern musicians.

- Blues singers such as Bessie Smith and Robert Johnson laid the foundation for popular music today.

- Visual Arts:

- Portraits by renowned painters such as Henry Ossawa Tanner capture the strength of African Americans throughout history.

- Sculptors like Richmond Barthe created powerful works that celebrate black identity in art form.

These artistic contributions show us how far we've come in recognizing the vast cultural impact of Black Americans across all fields of art—and how much further we still need to go in celebrating their accomplishments.

With this understanding of past achievements, let's explore how African American literature has shaped our world view.

Literature

African-American literature has captivated generations with its vibrant stories of struggle, resilience, and joy. Authors such as Maya Angelou, Toni Morrison, and James Baldwin have crafted works that explore the African-American experience in a powerful way. Their words are filled with emotion and insight into the multifaceted nature of being black in America.

From historic figures like Harriet Tubman to modern day icons like Ta-Nehisi Coates, African-American authors have created a canon that is essential for understanding the culture of the United States. By weaving together elements of history, philosophy, and personal narrative, these authors provide an invaluable contribution to American literature.

As we move forward into new literary eras, it's important to remember this legacy and ensure that it continues to be celebrated for many years to come.

Moving from literature to education, we find yet another area where African Americans have made significant contributions throughout history.

Education

Education is an invaluable resource for all communities, and African Americans have made groundbreaking strides in the fight for quality education throughout history. Even when faced with systemic racism and inequality, they continue to push forward for greater access to educational opportunities that can help build a brighter future.

Black scholars and educators have long advocated for improved resources, increased funding, and more equitable access to higher education institutions. They have fought to make sure that African American students receive the same level of academic support as their peers from other backgrounds. The labor of these individuals has helped create better educational environments for all students in both K-12 schools and universities across America.

As a result, African Americans are now able to pursue educational opportunities on par with those of other races or ethnicities. This progress helps ensure that everyone has equal chances at success regardless of race or background.

With this hard work paving the way for better futures, activism is the next step towards achieving true equity in education.

Activism

Activism has been a crucial part of African Americans' efforts to ensure educational opportunities for all, helping to create a more equitable learning environment for everyone regardless of race or background.

From the civil rights movement to protests against police brutality, black activists have been at the forefront of numerous struggles that sought to bring about widespread change and greater social justice.

African American leaders such as Martin Luther King Jr., Malcolm X, Fannie Lou Hamer, and Ella Baker were instrumental in leading marches and sit-ins that brought attention to discrimination and inequality.

Their advocacy helped shape public opinion on issues like voting rights, education reform, and desegregation.

These movements were successful in achieving significant victories for African Americans but also played an important role in advancing the cause of equality for all people.

With this momentum, black activism can continue to drive positive changes that benefit everyone.

This spirit of activism is equally applicable when it comes to sports—another area where African Americans have made tremendous contributions over the years.

Sports

As activists, African Americans have been an integral part of the movement to improve civil rights in the U.S. But they've also made a huge impact on sports, both in America and around the world.

From Jackie Robinson breaking barriers in Major League Baseball, to Venus and Serena Williams dominating tennis courts throughout their career, African Americans have used sports as a platform to show that black people can achieve anything they put their minds towards.

African American athletes have been an inspiration for generations of young people to pursue their dreams no matter what obstacles may be standing in their way. Lebron James has even become a vocal leader on social justice issues with his "More Than An Athlete" initiative.

It shows that while having success on the field or court is important, there's also great power in using your platform for something greater than yourself. This spirit of activism and resilience carries over into other areas like business as well – where African Americans are making strides every day.

Business

African Americans have made an immense impact in the business world, proving that with hard work and determination anything is possible.

From major corporate success stories such as Ursula Burns, who became the first African American woman to become CEO of a Fortune 500 company when she led Xerox from 2009-2016, to Robert Smith becoming one of the wealthiest African American men in America after founding Vista Equity Partners, many inspiring stories demonstrate that anyone can achieve success in the business world regardless of their race or gender.

The contributions of African Americans are not limited just to corporations; they've also been integral innovators when it comes to small businesses.

Over 2 million black-owned businesses contribute over $150 billion annually to the US economy - a number which has grown substantially since 2007 due to the increasing number of entrepreneurial opportunities available for people of color.

These businesses provide jobs and economic security for countless families across America, demonstrating how powerful and resilient African Americans can be when given the opportunity.

Moving forward into invention...

Invention

You too can make strides in invention, just like many African Americans have done. It is clear that innovation knows no bounds when given the chance. Black Americans have made significant contributions to the world of invention and technology.

From inventors such as Lonnie Johnson who developed the Super Soaker water gun to Lewis Latimer who helped perfect the light bulb, it's evident that creativity and ingenuity are not limited by race.

Here are just a few examples of black inventors and their groundbreaking creations:

- Granville Woods created a telephone-telegraph system known as "Induction Telegraphy"
- Dr. Patricia Bath invented a laserphaco probe for cataract surgery
- Dr. Mark Dean co-invented a personal computer with an integrated motherboard

Although obstacles may stand in our way, we should never forget that it is possible to overcome them and reach great heights in any field of endeavor, especially invention!

Science

African Americans have made remarkable advances in the field of science, pushing boundaries and expanding horizons with their innovative ideas and groundbreaking discoveries.

From George Washington Carver's pioneering work in agricultural sciences to Mae Jemison becoming the first African American woman to go into space, countless Black scientists have left an indelible mark on history.

Their contributions to medicine, physics, chemistry, astronomy, engineering, microbiology, and more have helped shape modern society and opened up new possibilities for generations of future inventors.

As we look ahead with hope for a brighter future, we can be sure that African Americans will continue to make invaluable contributions in the field of science.

With this knowledge comes an empowered sense of responsibility; a commitment to taking action and building upon our collective successes for the benefit of all people.

This is why it's so important that we recognize these incredible individuals who have come before us and strive to create even greater opportunities for those who will follow after us.

With this spirit of progress driving us forward, let us now turn our attention towards politics.

Politics

Political progress has been made by African Americans, opening up new doors for generations to come and allowing them to make their mark on the world.

From the first black congressman, Joseph Rainey in 1870 to the election of Barack Obama as President of The United States in 2008, black people have broken through centuries-old barriers that held them back from achieving political power. This achievement is especially significant considering that until around a century ago they were denied basic rights and freedoms due to Jim Crow Laws.

Today, African Americans are able to run for office at all levels of government and many have had success in doing so. They are also represented well among civil servants including judges, diplomats, cabinet members, mayors and more.

This increased visibility helps ensure that issues important to the African American community are not ignored or forgotten about but instead given proper consideration when decisions are being made.

Overall, political progress has been made by African Americans which helps create a more equitable society where everyone's voice can be heard and respected.

Frequently Asked Questions

What are some of the barriers that have historically prevented black people from achieving success in these fields?

Have you ever wondered what's prevented black people from succeeding in their respective fields? Despite the contributions of Black Americans to our country, there are still many barriers that have historically hindered them from achieving success.

These barriers range from a lack of access and resources to educational discrimination and systemic racism. In addition, there's a lack of representation in leadership roles, which creates an environment where it can be difficult for Black professionals to advance their careers.

By understanding these challenges, we can work together to break down these barriers and create more equitable opportunities for all members of our society.

How have black people been able to overcome these obstacles?

We've seen how black people have had to battle against insurmountable odds throughout history, but there are many inspiring stories of achievement and success in spite of them.

From the courage of those who risked their lives for civil rights, to the hard work and dedication that's been put into entrepreneurship, education, politics, arts, and sciences - black people have shown immense resilience and determination in overcoming these obstacles.

This is a testament to their strength as individuals and as a community.

How have the contributions of black people been acknowledged and honored in America?

We've all seen the incredible contributions of black people to America. From the arts and sciences, to civil rights and more, their impact has been undeniable. We can't help but marvel at how they've been able to overcome such insurmountable obstacles with grace and strength – like a flower blooming through concrete.

Their achievements have deservedly been acknowledged and honored in many ways across our nation. We can see this through statues erected of important figures, streets named after them, and awards given out in recognition of their hard work; to name just a few examples.

How have the contributions of black people shaped American culture?

From the music we listen to, to the sports we watch, to the art that adorns our walls and fills our homes, Black people have shaped American culture in countless ways.

From jazz and blues, to hip hop and rap, Black artists have pushed the boundaries of creativity in music.

Black athletes have broken records on the court and on the field while inspiring generations of kids with their athleticism.

Painters and sculptors such as Romare Bearden, Elizabeth Catlett, and Augusta Savage have used their art to express themes of resilience, perseverance, beauty, identity, and so much more.

The influence of Black people on American culture is undeniable.

What are some of the ways that black people have been able to achieve success in spite of systemic racism?

We've seen countless examples of black people succeeding in spite of systemic racism. One such example is Barack Obama. He grew up in a single-parent home and eventually became the 44th President of the United States. Against all odds, he was able to work hard, acquire an education, and climb the ladder to success.

This proves that despite racial discrimination and disparities in resources, it's possible for black people to achieve their dreams and reach their goals. Through dedicated effort and determination, even those without much opportunity can overcome daunting obstacles and create a better life for themselves.

Conclusion

We've seen the incredible contributions black people have made in America, and it's truly awe-inspiring.

From music to art, literature to education, activism to business, invention to science, and politics - there's no denying that without the tireless efforts of black Americans, our nation would not be where it is today.

We can't express enough how much they've changed and shaped our way of life. Their legacy will live on forever!

Contributions of Black Soldiers in American History

We, as Americans, owe a great debt of gratitude to the many African American soldiers who have served in our armed forces throughout history.

Take for example James Robinson, an African American soldier in the Revolutionary War. He fought bravely at the Battle of Bunker Hill and was honored with a Purple Heart for his courage.

While stories like his are well known, there are countless others that may not be so familiar. The contributions of Black soldiers to our nation's history are far reaching and innumerable, from their service during wartime to their impact on civil rights movements and culture.

In this article we will explore the major contributions made by African American servicemen throughout American History.

African American Contributions during the Revolutionary War

From fighting in the Continental Army to providing essential supplies, African Americans had a vital role in securing America's independence during the Revolutionary War.

Among these contributions was James Armistead Lafayette, a former slave who served as a spy for General Lafayette. His intelligence-gathering allowed the rebel forces to gain insight into British movements and plans.

Additionally, local militias recruited free blacks to bolster their ranks and prevent desertion from among their white troops. These black soldiers fought alongside whites at major battles such as Saratoga and Cowpens where they earned recognition for their bravery and skill.

African American contributions did not end with military service alone; many also provided resources like food and clothing that were desperately needed by the army. Groups of freedmen living near Philadelphia even formed associations tasked with collecting funds to purchase goods for Washington's troops.

In some cases, slaves themselves managed to escape bondage by enlisting in patriot armies or taking up arms on behalf of the republicans themselves. These self-liberated men went on to become valuable assets both inside and outside of battle lines.

The legacy of African American contributions during the Revolutionary War is still felt today within communities across America; it serves as an example of how individuals can make a difference when faced with adversity no matter what color or creed they are.

With this courage in mind, we can now turn our attention to examining African American involvement during the War of 1812 when once again they rose up against oppression despite overwhelming odds stacked against them.

African American Contributions during the War of 1812

During the War of 1812, African Americans fought bravely to defend their country and their freedom - often with little recognition.

Hundreds of free black men joined the Patriot forces during this war. For example, in 1814, Colonel Thomas Ludlow Ogden of New Jersey raised a regiment of African American soldiers who were recruited from Philadelphia and its surrounding area. The all-black unit was known as the 'Bucks of America' and they helped repel a British invasion at Bladensburg, Maryland.

In addition, some enslaved people were also able to join the fight by taking advantage of offers for freedom made by various states. For instance, Massachusetts promised freedom to any slave who enlisted in her militia forces; up to three thousand slaves gained their freedom through this offer alone.

The contributions that African American soldiers made during the War of 1812 are significant. Not only did these soldiers demonstrate extraordinary courage and loyalty on the battlefield, but they also played an important role in helping secure victory against Britain for America's future independence. Despite facing discrimination within military ranks due to racism and segregationist policies, African American soldiers continued to serve valiantly throughout the war effort.

And while there has been much discussion about how white soldiers contributed to winning this conflict, it is equally important that we recognize how black soldiers fought just as bravely and made invaluable contributions towards American success at this time too.

Though largely forgotten today, African Americans' service during the War of 1812 should not be overlooked or minimized; these courageous individuals deserve recognition for their bravery in defending our nation against one its fiercest enemies – Britain – when so much was at stake for both our present and future generations alike.

Moving forward into the Mexican-American War era next, we can see yet another example where African Americans demonstrated tremendous resolve in protecting our country's interests despite being denied equal rights back home.

African American Contributions during the Mexican-American War

Bravely battling against bias, African Americans fought fervently for freedom during the Mexican-American War. Many black soldiers found themselves involved in the war, which lasted from April 1846 to February 1848. They used their skills and knowledge to fight bravely on both sides of the conflict with some serving in the U.S. Army and others joining Mexican forces in defense of their homeland. Despite facing racial discrimination from many officers, African American soldiers served with distinction and courage throughout the war, displaying a loyalty and dedication that transcended racism.

In addition to fighting on battlefields, African Americans also contributed to the war effort by providing essential supplies such as food rations, ammunition, clothing, medical attention, and transportation services for troops stationed around Mexico City. This support was key in helping both armies survive until victory could be declared.

Additionally, several freed slaves joined up with General Stephen Kearny's expeditionary force as they moved across New Mexico toward California during the summer of 1846. In doing so, these individuals helped lay claim to vast amounts of land that would one day become part of a larger United States—a nation made possible by courageous soldiers like them who were willing to risk everything for freedom's cause.

By taking part in this tumultuous era, African Americans demonstrated their commitment to defending democracy regardless of race or ethnicity. Their contributions not only played an important role in achieving victory but also provided a lasting legacy that continues to inspire generations today—a reminder that no matter how difficult it may seem at times, we're all capable of uniting together for a brighter future when our freedoms are threatened.

With this same spirit, African Americans soon marched into battle again during the Civil War where they faced even greater challenges yet never wavered from their determination to defend liberty at all costs.

African American Contributions during the Civil War

You can't talk about American history without mentioning the remarkable efforts of African Americans during the Civil War. This conflict was a turning point for African Americans in the struggle for civil rights and their important contributions to the Union's victory cannot be overstated.

Over 180,000 black men served in the Union Army as free men and former slaves, making up 10% of its forces at its peak. They fought with courage and bravery in some of the most iconic battles of this war including Bull Run, Shiloh, Vicksburg, Antietam, Gettysburg and Appomattox Court House.

African American soldiers were also integral members of the United States Colored Troops (USCT) which was formed in 1863 by a presidential order from Abraham Lincoln. In addition to combat roles they filled positions such as cooks, servants and laborers and their service not only bolstered Union forces but also helped to break down racial barriers within society.

The USCT proved to be an effective fighting force that would go on to fight until 1866 when it was disbanded after all Confederate forces had surrendered.

Despite facing great challenges such as discrimination from white officers and unequal pay compared to white soldiers, African American men played an essential role in securing victory for the Union side during this conflict. Their brave contributions enabled them to gain greater respect and recognition among their fellow citizens while paving a path towards greater equality for generations to come.

Going forward these hard-fought freedoms would continue to shape America's future as they prepared for another major war just two decades later - The Spanish-American War.

African American Contributions during the Spanish-American War

African Americans courageously rose to the occasion during the Spanish-American War, making significant strides towards greater equality and recognition.

The Buffalo Soldiers of the 9th and 10th Cavalry regiments played a crucial role in subduing Filipino resistance against American forces. Similarly, the 24th Infantry regiment helped to secure Puerto Rico from Spain. African American soldiers were also among the first American service members sent into combat in Cuba as part of Theodore Roosevelt's Rough Riders Regiment. Black sailors served on naval vessels such as USS Texas and USS Maine, while others performed dangerous missions behind enemy lines as part of an elite force known as McKinley's Guerillas.

Their courageous actions laid a foundation for future generations of African Americans to serve their country with distinction in times of war and peace alike.

Despite facing significant discrimination both at home and abroad, African American veterans returned home with newfound respect from many fellow citizens. This shift was further solidified after Congress passed anti-discrimination laws that allowed them to serve alongside their white counterparts without fear or prejudice.

As a result, they were finally able to receive equal pay for equal work regardless of race or ethnicity which was a major victory not only for African Americans but all minorities across America.

This marked an important milestone in our nation's history that has since become a source of pride and inspiration for millions around the world.

As we move forward into World War I, it's clear that this wouldn't have been possible without the brave contributions made by black soldiers during the Spanish-American War.

African American Contributions during World War I

During World War I, you stepped up to the plate and risked your lives for a greater cause, painting a lasting portrait of heroism that will be remembered in our collective memory. African-American soldiers offered their services and put themselves on the line for America, showing tremendous courage and bravery.

More than 350,000 Black soldiers enlisted in the military. The 15th New York National Guard made up of African Americans was sent to France as part of the 93rd Division. In total, more than 1 million African Americans served during WWI including about 40,000 women. Hundreds were awarded medals for their service in battle due to their acts of valor. They helped secure victory for the Allied Forces while fighting against prejudice and segregation from other military personnel.

Despite all these efforts, they still faced racism upon returning home. Although they had proven their worthiness through selfless actions on behalf of their country, Jim Crow laws continued to spread throughout many states. Despite this injustice, these brave men and women had left an indelible mark on history as they proudly marched off into war with courage and hope.

With this legacy of strength behind them, African American soldiers moved onward towards a brighter future; one that included contributions during World War II.

African American Contributions during World War II

Despite the racism and discrimination they faced, African-Americans courageously stepped up to serve their country once again during WWII. Approximately 1.2 million African Americans served in the military during this time. They served in every branch of the military, from the Army to the Navy to the Marines and Coast Guard.

Contributions	Branches	Total Number Served
Combat	Army	881,000
Aviation	Navy	19,000
Other Roles	Marine/Coast Guard	200,000

African-Americans served with distinction and bravery throughout World War II. They were involved in major battles such as Iwo Jima and Okinawa while others flew missions for the Air Force or Navy over Europe and Japan. Despite being denied opportunities that other soldiers received due to segregation laws at home, they still managed to make significant contributions towards achieving victory abroad. From these brave men we learn that courage and strength can be found even under difficult circumstances. With this knowledge in mind, it is important to recognize their sacrifices as we move forward into learning about African American contributions during the Korean War.

African American Contributions during the Korean War

You won't believe the impact African Americans made on the Korean War - it's a story that needs to be told!

During this conflict, almost all of the Army's divisions were integrated and African Americans made up a significant portion of the fighting force. They served in every branch of service, from infantry to engineering, and their bravery was recognized by many awards such as Distinguished Service Crosses and Silver Stars. Despite facing discrimination from both enemy forces and their own countrymen, they sacrificed much for their nation.

African American contributions went beyond just battlefield engagements; they played an important role in providing support roles such as medical technicians, supply specialists, military police officers, transportation personnel, and signal corps members. These individuals helped keep morale high among troops in combat with respect for one another regardless of race or ethnicity.

Furthermore, many black soldiers provided invaluable intelligence gathering services which aided US strategy in Korea significantly.

These brave men and women should be remembered for their dedication to protecting freedom around the world during the Korean War. Their courage is an inspiration to us all - it exemplifies what it means to serve one's nation selflessly without thought of reward or recognition.

Continuing our exploration into these stories of heroism leads us towards understanding African American contributions during the Vietnam War.

African American Contributions during the Vietnam War

We've discussed the contributions of African American soldiers during the Korean War, but now let's look at their brave efforts during the Vietnam War.

African American soldiers had a major role in fighting in this war, and they made significant contributions to its success. They served with distinction on all fronts and proved themselves as capable leaders.

Here are some key points about their service:

- Over 700,000 African Americans served in the Vietnam War, making up roughly 12 percent of all U.S. forces involved in the conflict.

- They received more medals for bravery than any other ethnic group, including two Medals of Honor awarded posthumously to Sgt Henry Johnson and Pfc Milton Olive III for heroic actions in battlefield combat operations, saving others from death or serious injury.

- African Americans suffered disproportionately high casualties when compared to white troops. However, this was due largely to their being assigned more hazardous duties than whites serving alongside them were given.

- Despite these hardships, African American soldiers willingly faced danger and fought valiantly for freedom and justice against an enemy determined to take it away from them.

The courage and commitment of these men should be remembered as we move forward into future wars, such as The Persian Gulf War, which will surely have its own unique set of challenges for our brave soldiers to face.

African American Contributions during the Persian Gulf War

You can picture the African American heroes of the Persian Gulf War, risking their lives for justice and freedom in a foreign land. From all branches of the United States Armed Forces, African Americans made significant contributions.

Type of Contribution	Number of African American Participants
Ground Combat	78,000+
Naval Combatants/Support Personnel	24,000+
Air Force Combatants/Support Personnel	7,500+

African American servicemen and women stepped up to serve in positions that were often dangerous or difficult. They provided support to troops in Kuwait and Iraq by delivering supplies as truck drivers or serving in medical roles such as nurses and medics. In addition to their service on the ground, they also took part in missions aboard naval vessels and flew combat missions with Air Force fighter jets. Together these brave individuals made tremendous sacrifices for their country. Their courage will never be forgotten. The legacy of African American military personnel continues today with their involvement in conflicts around the world such as Afghanistan.

African American Contributions during the War in Afghanistan

Despite the dangers of war, African Americans have bravely and selflessly volunteered to serve in Afghanistan, making an invaluable impact on our nation's efforts abroad. The contributions of black soldiers during this conflict were vast and varied. They provided critical logistical support to coalition forces by manning supply lines, preparing food, and maintaining military equipment. They served on frontlines as infantrymen, medics, and special operations personnel in some of the most dangerous areas of the country. Additionally, they provided valuable cultural insight into Afghan customs, which was instrumental in navigating conflicts between coalition forces and local populations.

The bravery displayed by African American servicemen and women resulted in many awards for their service; thirteen Medals of Honor were bestowed upon them for their courage under fire, including former Army Specialist Monica Brown, who became the first woman to receive this award since the Vietnam War for her heroic actions rescuing injured soldiers from a live grenade explosion. Furthermore, there are countless stories of heroism that remain untold due to their classified nature, such as those serving as members of Delta Force or Navy SEAL units.

African American contributions during the War in Afghanistan have been essential for success overseas and pave the way for future generations to take up arms in defense of freedom around the world - setting an example for all service members regardless of race or gender. As we look ahead to consider similar involvement during other conflicts, such as Iraq, it's important to remember these courageous individuals who made great sacrifices while providing necessary aid on foreign soil.

African American Contributions during the War in Iraq

You have the opportunity to be part of a legacy, to honor those who bravely and selflessly risked their lives for freedom abroad. African Americans in particular made significant contributions during the War in Iraq, as they did in many other wars before it.

Many African American soldiers served in combat roles on the front lines, while others provided vital support services from further behind. African American soldiers were among some of the first troops to enter Iraq after the initial invasion and were integral in helping to secure major cities like Baghdad.

The courage and resilience of African Americans was particularly inspiring as they faced extreme dangers amid heavy fighting with enemy forces. The bravery and fortitude demonstrated by these brave men and women helped lead to eventual victory over Saddam Hussein's regime.

African American soldiers also gave back to local communities by providing humanitarian aid such as medical assistance, food, water, shelter, supplies, education programs and more.

Their efforts were not just limited to military service - they also played an important role in rebuilding Iraq after hostilities ceased. Through their tireless dedication towards peacekeeping operations, these brave individuals continue to help bring stability and prosperity back into the country even today.

As we look ahead towards a better future for all affected by this conflict, let's never forget the immense contribution that African American veterans made during this era of war and peacekeeping missions.

African American Contributions during Peacekeeping Missions

As war and conflict continues to plague the world, African American individuals have continued to be an integral part of peacekeeping missions, bringing their courage, resilience, and dedication in order to help bring stability back to affected regions.

Throughout history, African Americans have served admirably in these positions—from helping to keep the peace in Iraq during Operation Iraqi Freedom all the way back to Reconstruction after the Civil War. Whether it was putting out fires between warring factions or providing much needed humanitarian aid and relief services, African American soldiers have been a critical part of these efforts.

African American servicemen and women have also played key roles in helping restore democracy within countries whose governments had destabilized due to civil unrest or war. During such operations as Restore Hope in Somalia and Uphold Democracy in Haiti, African Americans provided essential support for local elections by providing security at polling locations and maintaining order throughout the country. They also helped train citizens on how to vote properly while ensuring that their votes were counted correctly.

Beyond just keeping the peace abroad, African Americans have also made significant contributions towards civil rights movements here at home. From marching alongside Dr Martin Luther King Jr., participating in sit-ins across America's segregated South during the 1960s, and pushing for more equitable representation of minorities within law enforcement agencies today—African Americans continue to fight for justice both abroad and at home.

As we move forward into a new era of global peacemaking initiatives, we can only hope that African Americans will remain an essential component of our efforts towards achieving lasting peace worldwide.

African American Contributions to Civil Rights Movements

You won't believe the impact African Americans have had on civil rights movements - it's absolutely incredible! From marching with Dr. Martin Luther King Jr. to fighting for equitable representation in law enforcement agencies today, these individuals have left an indelible mark on our country and our history.

African Americans were a driving force behind the Civil Rights Movement of the 1960s, participating in boycotts, marches, sit-ins, and other non-violent forms of protest to demand equal rights and opportunities for all citizens regardless of race or ethnicity. They also played a major role in shaping public opinion by speaking out against racism through speeches, writings, and other media outlets.

Their courage and commitment to make sure everyone is treated fairly has helped create a more equitable society for generations to come.

African American contributions to the civil rights movement continue today as activists work hard to ensure that people of color are adequately represented in government institutions such as police departments, school boards, and legislatures. For example, African American leaders are advocating for policy changes that would eliminate racial disparities in criminal justice practices such as police brutality and harsh sentencing laws. Additionally, they are pushing for more funding for historically black colleges and universities (HBCUs), which provide valuable educational opportunities to many students across the nation who otherwise wouldn't be able to access them due to financial constraints or lack of resources available in their communities.

The progress made by African Americans towards achieving equality is inspiring but there is still much work yet to be done before all citizens can truly experience justice without prejudice or discrimination. As the fight continues for full civil rights protections across America, let us remember those brave individuals who fought tirelessly so we can enjoy the freedoms we do now – their legacy will live on forever!

To further honor this legacy of activism and service, let's now turn our attention towards understanding African American contributions to arts and culture...

African American Contributions to the Arts and Culture

Discover how African Americans have used their creativity to shape the cultural landscape of our nation, from creating beautiful works of art to inspiring iconic musical genres.

Throughout centuries of oppression and marginalization, African American artists have made lasting contributions that continue to influence and inspire today.

Visual arts have been a powerful expression of culture in America as far back as the 18th century. When slavery was still prevalent in the United States, many enslaved people found solace in expressing themselves through painting, drawing, and sculpting.

In more recent history, visual artists such as Jacob Lawrence and Romare Bearden created vivid works that depicted both the struggles and triumphs of African American life.

Music is another art form where African American individuals have left an indelible mark on society. Jazz music originated in New Orleans during the late 19th century with roots stemming from traditional West African music combined with European influences.

Other influential genres include hip-hop which emerged in the 1970s and has since become one of the most popular forms of music worldwide; blues which developed out of work songs sung by enslaved people after emancipation; reggae which gained international fame through Bob Marley's success; and gospel whose sound has heavily influenced other genres like soul over time.

African American contributions to the arts are vast and varied - from visual arts to musical styles - but all demonstrate a creative resilience meant for celebrating culture while addressing challenging issues faced by black communities throughout history.

These contributions offer insight into an often overlooked part of our country's past as well as ongoing efforts towards equality among all races today.

Frequently Asked Questions

How did African Americans contribute to the development of the US economy?

We, the great people of the United States of America, have always been proud to point out how much African Americans have contributed to our economy. But what we often fail to recognize is that their contributions span far beyond just monetary value.

They shook up traditional economic systems and created new industries that benefit us all today. From clothing lines to technology companies, they've been instrumental in creating jobs and helping propel our country into a better financial future.

We can thank them for pushing us forward economically and making sure we remain competitive in an ever-changing global market!

What were the long-term impacts of African American contributions to US history?

African Americans have had a lasting impact on the history of the United States, contributing to it in many meaningful ways. They fought for their rights in the Civil Rights Movement and made great contributions to music and literature. African Americans left a legacy that will never be forgotten.

Perhaps their most significant contribution was their service during times of war. During World War I and II, African American soldiers fought bravely for their country despite facing discrimination and unequal treatment. These acts of courage not only helped secure victories for America but also laid the groundwork for greater civil rights.

The bravery of these soldiers paved the way for future generations of African Americans to pursue equality and become an integral part of American culture.

How did African Americans contribute to the development of the US military?

African Americans have made immense contributions to the development of the US military since its inception.

During the Revolutionary War, they fought alongside white soldiers in battles such as Bunker Hill and Saratoga.

During the Civil War, nearly 200,000 black soldiers enlisted in the Union Army.

In World Wars I and II, African Americans served with distinction in segregated units and were awarded numerous medals for their bravery.

They also played an important role in desegregating the military after World War II and continue to serve today in all branches of service.

What were the most significant contributions made by African Americans to US culture?

We, African Americans, have made a huge impact on American culture. Our contributions are significant and varied. We have developed new music genres and influenced fashion trends.

But perhaps the most noteworthy are those we've made in the fields of science, education, and civil rights. We have paved the way for future generations of African American students to pursue higher education. We have also fought for equal rights under the law.

Through our efforts, we have helped shape this great nation into what it is today.

How did African Americans contribute to the US civil rights movement?

African Americans have played a significant role in the US civil rights movement. They risked their lives to challenge injustice and paved the way for future generations of civil rights activists. From the early 1900s, African American activists like W.E.B Dubois and Ida B Wells protested against lynching and segregation. In the 1960s, Martin Luther King Jr., Rosa Parks, and others led the march for desegregation and voting rights. African Americans have been at the forefront of this historic struggle.

Conclusion

We, African Americans, have made countless contributions to our nation's history.

From the Revolutionary War to the Civil Rights Movement, we've been at the forefront of progress and justice.

We fought for freedom on foreign battlefields and defended our rights in the streets.

We've enriched our culture with art, music, and literature.

Our legacy is one of courage, strength, and resilience.

As a people, we're unstoppable - no matter what obstacles stand in our way, we'll continue to strive for greatness with pride in our hearts.

Let's not forget those who came before us; their sacrifices shall forever be remembered as an inspiration for generations to come!

NAACP

We, the National Association for the Advancement of Colored People (NAACP), have been fighting for civil rights since 1909. Our mission is to ensure the political, educational, social and economic equality of all people and eliminate race-based discrimination.

Throughout our history, we have advocated for African Americans' civil rights by pursuing legal action, educating communities on their rights, and promoting diversity and inclusion. We strive to create a more just society where everyone has access to opportunities regardless of race or ethnicity.

We are dedicated to advancing racial equity through social justice initiatives both nationally and locally through our many chapters across the United States.

History of the NAACP

You can almost hear the echoes of civil rights pioneers as you learn about the long and powerful history of the NAACP. Originally founded in 1909, the National Association for the Advancement of Colored People (NAACP) is a leading civil rights advocacy organization that has been on the frontlines in defending people of color against racism and discrimination.

At its founding, it was only comprised of nine members but quickly grew to include thousands across all 50 states. With groundbreaking legal battles such as Brown v Board of Education, Freedom Riders, and desegregation efforts in Little Rock, Arkansas, they have been instrumental in changing American laws to promote equality and justice for all citizens.

The NAACP has also served as a beacon for change by providing opportunities for people from marginalized communities through education initiatives like voter registration drives throughout many Southern cities during Jim Crow era. It also worked closely with organizations like CORE and SCLC during The Civil Rights Movement to ensure that African Americans would have access to equal voting rights.

Additionally, their lobbying efforts were instrumental in passing several pieces of legislation such as The Voting Rights Act of 1965 which granted Black Americans full access to polling places throughout America without discriminatory practices or intimidation tactics used by local governments.

Throughout its existence, the NAACP has played an integral role in promoting civil liberties and protecting human rights regardless of race or ethnicity. They continue to be an important voice in advocating for social justice while empowering communities across America with invaluable resources needed to combat bigotry today.

As we look ahead into our future together, let us remember this vital organization's immense contributions towards achieving greater racial equity—a task that remains unfinished until true justice is realized everywhere. Moving forward into a more equitable tomorrow requires dedication from all who believe that everyone deserves fair treatment without prejudice or discrimination no matter their background; this is where mission and goals come into play...

Mission and Goals

The Mission and Goals of the NAACP demonstrate its commitment to fighting for civil rights and social justice. The organization strives to ensure the political, educational, social, and economic equality of rights of all persons.

They aim to achieve equality of rights and eliminate race prejudice among the citizens of the United States. Their goal is also to remove all barriers of racial discrimination through democratic processes and to seek enactment and enforcement of federal, state, and local laws securing civil rights.

The NAACP works to empower individuals who are legally denied their basic human rights as well as advocating for policies that will end racism in our nation's institutions such as education, health care, housing, and employment opportunities. They also fight for voting access for those traditionally disenfranchised based on disparities in income or race.

In addition to these efforts, they provide leadership training programs that focus on developing skills related to community organizing and civic engagement, which helps equip people with the knowledge necessary to lead their own communities towards progress.

Their work does not stop there, however. They also strive to educate both adults and children alike about issues related to civil liberties by hosting events nationwide such as youth summits or college campus visits that help spread awareness about various topics like voter suppression or gender equity.

This commitment is what makes them an integral part of our society's movement towards true equality for all people regardless of race or background - something we should strive for every day until it is achieved in its fullest form. As we continue this journey towards a brighter future, let us remember that together we can build a better world where everyone has access to opportunity without fear or discrimination holding them back from achieving their dreams.

Civil Rights Advocacy

Nobody ever said achieving civil rights would be a cakewalk, but with the NAACP leading the way, it's sure to be a piece of (equality) pie!

For more than a century, this organization has been at the forefront of advocating for civil rights and working to eliminate racial discrimination in America. From organizing marches and protests to filing lawsuits and lobbying Congress, they have tirelessly pursued justice for all Americans regardless of their race.

This is no small feat given the long history of systemic racism and inequality in our country. The NAACP continues to fight against injustice today by helping people understand their legal rights, providing support to individuals who have experienced discrimination, and pushing for policy changes that will ensure equal treatment under the law.

They also work hard to educate communities about civil rights issues as well as rally public support for causes that advance racial equity. Their grassroots efforts are inspiring people across the country to stand up for what's right – something we should all aspire to do every day.

It's clear that advocacy is essential if we want real progress on civil rights issues in our nation. But it must be paired with education and outreach if we are truly going to create lasting change...

Education and Outreach

Through education and outreach, the NAACP works to empower people with the knowledge they need to understand their civil rights and stand up for them.

This includes educating communities on current issues, such as voting laws, voter suppression, police brutality, and social justice.

The organization also reaches out to youth groups and families in order to engage them in meaningful dialogue about civil rights. They host dialogues between policy makers and communities, participate in grassroots advocacy efforts, teach educational seminars on racial justice topics, and organize events that encourage civic engagement.

The NAACP continues its work by engaging the public through an extensive media presence that amplifies the voices of those who have been silenced or ignored for far too long. Through these strategies, they continue their mission of advocating for equality and justice for all people regardless of race or ethnicity – a goal that is more urgent than ever before in today's political climate.

To further advance this cause, the NAACP takes legal actions against injustice when necessary.

Legal Actions

You're not alone in your fight for justice; the NAACP stands with you and will take legal action when necessary to ensure that civil rights are protected.

The National Association for the Advancement of Colored People (NAACP) is committed to using all available resources to advocate on behalf of African Americans, other people of color, and all disadvantaged communities. This includes utilizing the courts and filing lawsuits against those who violate civil rights laws.

The NAACP has a long history of taking legal action to advance constitutional protections and challenge discriminatory practices in areas such as education, housing, employment, voting rights, healthcare access, economic opportunity and environmental justice. The organization has also worked to secure compensation for victims of police brutality or wrongful convictions.

For more than 100 years, they have been instrumental in leading some of the most important civil rights cases before state supreme courts and even the United States Supreme Court.

The NAACP's commitment to legal action is part of its mission to ensure that everyone has equal access to their civil liberties regardless of race or ethnicity. They continue to work diligently on behalf of individuals who have experienced discrimination based on their race or culture so that everyone can enjoy equal opportunities under the law.

As we move forward into membership and community engagement with the NAACP, we can rest assured knowing that they will always be there standing up for our basic human rights through legal actions when necessary.

Membership and Community Engagement

By joining the NAACP, you can be part of a powerful movement that works to ensure all individuals have equal access to their civil rights and liberties. Through membership in the organization, members become connected with a nationwide network of activists dedicated to achieving social justice for all.

Members are also able to gain access to educational resources and participate in community-based events that promote civic engagement and advocacy initiatives. Membership in the NAACP also provides members with an opportunity to engage with their local communities through volunteerism, such as participating in voter registration drives or helping out at local soup kitchens.

The organization also encourages members to take an active role in addressing issues related to racism, sexism, poverty, education inequality and more. With its long history of activism aimed at improving life for marginalized communities across America, joining the NAACP is one way of taking action towards creating a more equitable society.

The NAACP offers its members support and resources so they can stay informed on important topics related to social justice. Members are provided with information on legal developments related to civil rights cases as well as legislative updates on policy changes that may affect their rights. Additionally, they receive advice from lawyers and other experts on how best they can use their voices for meaningful change within their own communities.

With these resources available, members are equipped with the knowledge needed for them to be effective advocates for equality and justice everywhere. Moving forward into the next section about 'support and resources', let's explore what kind of help is available through this organization.

Support and Resources

You can count on the NAACP to provide you with the support and resources you need to stay informed on important social justice topics. From access to educational programs, advocacy tools, and legal assistance, to a network of local chapters and community activism initiatives, we ensure that our members have the knowledge and skills necessary to lead their communities in positive change.

The organization provides a range of resources for individuals looking to deepen their understanding of civil rights issues or take action against injustice. Our online library includes reports, articles, videos, podcasts, and other materials about current events as well as historic milestones. The NAACP also hosts regular forums open to the public where experts discuss pressing social justice subjects like racism, voter suppression, immigration reform, police brutality, and more. We strive for continuous learning so our members are always equipped with the latest information on how best to advocate for social change.

The NAACP serves as an invaluable source of reliable data and analysis regarding diversity initiatives across various industries including education, healthcare, and business. We understand that true progress requires a multifaceted approach based on inclusionary practices and strong representation from many different backgrounds. To help promote this goal, we offer advice on creating equitable policies within organizations while also highlighting best practices from companies dedicated to increasing diversity amongst their staffs.

Additionally, we provide resources aimed at informing potential allies about how they can support marginalized groups without taking away from their voices or agency. By drawing attention towards these issues through both research-backed publications as well as grassroots activism efforts, we're able to create meaningful conversations about equity in society today while paving the way for a better tomorrow.

From advocating for policy changes at the state level all the way down to empowering people within individual communities with knowledge - it is clear that no matter what form it takes, the NAACP is committed to pushing for equality through continuous learning opportunities, supportive services, and innovative solutions. With our help, your voice will be heard loudest when demanding systemic change - leading us towards a brighter future where everyone has equal rights regardless of gender, race, religion, or sexual orientation. Onward together!

Diversity and Inclusion

The NAACP is dedicated to promoting diversity and inclusion in all areas of life, so you can make a real difference by getting involved with our organization. Our members come from all walks of life, but are united by a commitment to social justice and racial equity.

We have chapters across the country that strives to break down barriers and create an equal playing field for everyone. Our efforts are focused on raising awareness of issues affecting marginalized communities, fighting discrimination in any form, and advocating for policy changes that will benefit those who are most vulnerable.

We believe that education is key to helping people understand the importance of diversity and inclusion. Through our many initiatives such as voter registration drives, youth leadership programs, legal advocacy campaigns, and community outreach events we strive to educate and empower individuals from underrepresented backgrounds.

We also provide support services such as crisis counseling for victims of hate crimes or discrimination and educational resources on topics like affirmative action.

Our ultimate goal is to create an environment where everyone feels safe, respected, accepted, and appreciated - regardless of race or ethnicity - so they can contribute their unique skill sets towards making our society better for us all.

To get involved with the NAACP's mission of creating a more inclusive world through diversity and inclusion efforts, join one of our local chapters today! With your help, we can continue striving towards progress in achieving social justice and racial equity.

Social Justice and Racial Equity

Making the world a more equitable place for all is at the heart of the NAACP's mission to promote social justice and racial equity. Every day, the organization works tirelessly to ensure that everyone is treated fairly regardless of race or ethnicity.

The NAACP focuses on voting rights, economic justice, health care access, education reform, and criminal justice reform to create lasting systemic change in society. Through its advocacy work, it has overturned discriminatory laws and policies across the country.

The NAACP also spearheads initiatives which provide resources and support services for underserved communities through national and local chapters. It organizes forums such as town hall meetings where community members can discuss issues impacting them as well as participate in workshops that teach leadership skills. In addition, its outreach efforts include providing legal assistance to those facing discrimination due to their race or ethnicity.

The NAACP continues to light a path forward towards greater racial equity by inspiring activism in young people through its Youth & College program. By equipping youth with knowledge about civil rights history and how they can be agents of change in their own communities, this program helps cultivate future generations of activists working towards social justice and racial equity around the world.

As a result of these efforts throughout its 113-year history, the NAACP remains an essential voice on matters related to social justice and racial equity today. With this momentum propelling it into tomorrow, there's no doubt that it will continue making strides towards achieving greater equality for all people everywhere.

National and Local Chapters

You're never alone in your fight for social justice and racial equity with the NAACP's National and Local Chapters.

The National Association for the Advancement of Colored People (NAACP) is one of the oldest civil rights organizations in America, founded in 1909 to fight against racial discrimination and injustice. The organization spans 2,200 units located throughout the United States, making it a powerful force for change at both local and national levels.

With its network of branches, chapters, youth councils, and college divisions, the NAACP is committed to providing grassroots support to members who are dedicated to promoting equality through activism. The organization does this by providing resources such as legal assistance from its Legal Defense and Education Fund (LDF), training sessions on racial bias prevention conducted by its Education Department, participation in educational forums hosted by its Youth & College Division, health screenings provided by its Health department, and more.

Additionally, its leadership development program empowers members to become more active advocates in their respective communities. The NAACP also has an impressive list of successful campaigns that have helped win victories for civil rights around the world.

From leading protests against police brutality to filing lawsuits against discriminatory employers or advocating for voting rights legislation - no matter what kind of impact you want to make on social justice issues - you can count on the support of your local or national branch of the NAACP every step of the way.

Through collective action across generations we can ensure that everyone experiences true freedom and equal opportunity regardless of race or ethnicity.

Frequently Asked Questions

What is the NAACP's stance on current civil rights issues?

We believe that civil rights are essential for everyone and should not be denied to anyone on the basis of their race, gender identity, sexuality, or any other factor.

We strive to ensure that everyone has equal access to their rights and can exercise them without fear of discrimination or violence.

We actively work to eliminate racism and oppression in all its forms and advocate for a more equitable society.

We stand with those who have experienced any form of injustice and fight for justice at every turn.

Our mission is to protect the civil rights of all individuals by advocating for social justice, equality, and fairness in our communities.

How can I support the NAACP financially?

We all want to make a difference in the world, and one of the best ways to do that is by supporting the NAACP financially. By donating money, you can help fund their important work on civil rights issues. This ensures that they have the resources they need to continue advocating for justice.

Your contribution will go towards initiatives like voter registration drives, legal defense funds, educational programs, and more. Every dollar counts when it comes to making sure everyone has equal access to their rights. So join us in supporting the NAACP today – your donation could be what makes a real difference!

Who are the current officers of the NAACP?

We're here to provide information on the current officers of the NAACP. The National Association for the Advancement of Colored People (NAACP) is a civil rights organization that's been fighting for racial justice since 1909.

Currently, it's President and CEO is Derrick Johnson, who was elected in 2017. The Chairperson of the Board of Directors is Leon Russell and Vice Chair is Karen Boykin-Towns. Additionally, there are five Regional Directors across the United States as well as a Youth & College Division Director, an Economic Department Director, and several other positions held by various officers dedicated to advancing social justice through education and advocacy.

How can I join a local NAACP chapter?

We've all been inspired by stories of people coming together to make a difference in their communities. Joining a local NAACP chapter is an easy way to help further the cause of equality and justice for African Americans.

By becoming part of this powerful organization, you can join forces with like-minded people to create meaningful change in your area. You'll get access to resources and tools that'll help you take action and become a leader in your community.

Plus, you'll be connected with other members who share your passion for advocacy and social justice. It's an empowering way to make a positive impact on the world around you!

What are the NAACP's plans for the future?

We're committed to continuing our work towards achieving racial justice and equality for all. Our plans for the future include:

- Expanding our advocacy efforts
- Increasing public education on civil rights issues
- Engaging in grassroots organizing to build power within communities of color

We'll continue to fight for:

- Voting rights
- Criminal justice reform
- Economic opportunity
- Health equity
- Educational access

We'll also strive to create a more inclusive society by promoting diversity and inclusion in all aspects of life.

Conclusion

We've come a long way since the NAACP was founded over 100 years ago. The mission and goals of this organization have evolved, but the commitment to civil rights advocacy, education, legal action, and social justice remain unwavering.

Today, the NAACP continues to be a beacon of hope for our communities – fighting for fairness and equality through diversity and inclusion initiatives that promote racial equity. With their support and resources, we can continue to build a more just society for everyone.

Let's take it one step at a time – because in this day and age, every little bit counts!

HBCUs

We have all heard of historically black colleges and universities (HBCUs) but may not know what they are or why they exist.

HBCUs are institutions of higher education in the United States that were established before 1964 with the primary mission to serve the African American community.

These schools have a rich history and culture, having been created as an alternative to traditional predominantly white institutions during a time when many African Americans were denied access to those schools due to racism and segregation.

We'll explore how HBCUs serve their students, alumni, and communities today.

Origins of HBCUs

From slavery to segregation, African Americans had a long history of educational exclusion, so creating HBCUs was essential for providing access to higher education.

Historically, the first HBCU in the U.S. began with Cheyney University of Pennsylvania, founded in 1837 by Quakers who wanted to educate freedmen and their descendants. It wasn't until later that other states followed suit and began founding more HBCUs.

However, these institutions were still limited due to segregation laws and discriminatory policies such as literacy tests used against Black citizens attempting to vote at the polls. As a result of these unequal practices, Black people were unable to receive equal educational opportunities despite having legal access under the 14th Amendment.

Thus, it is no surprise that HBCUs become a vital part of the Black community during this era for those seeking higher education. The establishment of HBCUs provided an invaluable space where students could learn without fear of discrimination or persecution based on race while being surrounded by like-minded peers from similar backgrounds and experiences.

Furthermore, many faculty members at these schools were African American themselves which meant they could relate firsthand to the struggles that their students faced beyond just academics - making it possible for students to find mentors who could offer advice on how best confront racism in society.

Lastly, rather than solely focusing on traditional academic subjects such as math and science like predominantly white institutions (PWIs), most HBCUs also placed emphasis on civil rights related courses while also helping alumni gain entry into political movements after graduation - thus allowing them to make major contributions toward social justice throughout America's history.

HBCUs have been an integral part of African American culture since their inception as they have consistently provided greater educational opportunities for generations of Black people even when faced with systemic oppression from PWIs and government entities alike. Without these special institutions it would not be possible for many individuals today who are making strides within various industries from politics to business ownerships - all thanks largely in part due to the legacy that each one has left behind them over time.

Moving forward then, we must work together ensure future generations continue receiving equitable resources needed in order succeed both inside out outside of academia so that everyone can achieve their dreams regardless of race or background.

The Impact of HBCUs

You must be aware of the influence HBCUs have had, so don't even try to deny it! It is undeniable that these institutions have made a significant impact in providing higher education opportunities for African Americans and other underserved populations. HBCUs are more than just educational institutions; they are social hubs and cultural centers.

They provide an environment where students from diverse backgrounds can come together to form a community of learners who share common experiences. This includes creating supportive spaces for dialogue on issues such as racism, sexism, classism, and homophobia.

They also offer unique courses tailored to their student population that focus on topics such as African American history and culture. Their alumni networks serve an important role in helping graduates find jobs or mentorships within their respective fields. Many prominent politicians, educators, civil rights activists, business leaders, entertainers, etc., have graduated from HBCUs over the years. These alumni often return to their alma mater to give back by offering financial support or mentoring current students.

HBCUs play an integral role in uplifting underrepresented communities. They strive to create equitable pathways for students of all backgrounds to pursue higher education opportunities while cultivating a sense of belonging among its members. In addition to providing quality instruction and resources for its students and faculty members alike, HBCUs also serve as incubators for new ideas that promote progress within marginalized communities.

As we look ahead towards the future of our nation's educational system, let us not forget the invaluable contributions these historical Black colleges and universities have made throughout history—contributions that will continue to shape our society for decades to come without question! Without them, many individuals would lack access or opportunity when it comes to receiving quality higher education. Thus, it is necessary for us to move forward with addressing the financial challenges facing HBCUs today.

Financial Challenges Facing HBCUs

You're likely aware of the financial challenges facing HBCUs, and it's essential that we work together to ensure they remain successful.

Challenge	Effect on Students	Solution?
Decreased state funding	Higher tuition costs for students	Increase donations from alumni & private sources
Reduced federal grants & loans	Less aid to cover expenses like housing, textbooks, etc.	Improve access to additional loan programs & scholarships
Higher enrollment requirements	Fewer opportunities for low-income students to attend college	Increase funding for need-based aid programs & support services

These challenges are not only threatening the future of HBCUs but also have a lasting impact on their student body. Low-income students face an even greater barrier when attempting to attend these universities – with limited resources available to them; they may not be able to afford higher tuition costs or necessary supplies. Additionally, fewer resources means less opportunity for much needed campus improvement projects and building renovations that would better serve the student population. We must recognize the need for increased support from alumni and other private sources so that these vital institutions can remain competitive and continue developing generations of leaders in our community.

It's clear that there is much work yet to be done in order to secure a successful future for HBCUs across America, but this isn't a challenge without hope or solutions. Through collective action and continued commitment from both public and private organizations alike, we can bridge the gap between stability and success by providing increased access to scholarships, grants, and loan programs as well as supporting services that will help more individuals gain entry into these historically significant schools. These efforts will allow current students – including those who come from underprivileged backgrounds – receive a quality education while laying a foundation for generations of future leaders within our community. Ultimately, investing in our HBCUs today is an investment in our communities tomorrow - let's make sure we create an equitable environment where everyone has equal access to higher education opportunities! And with that said let's explore the benefits of attending an HBCU...

The Benefits of Attending an HBCU

Attending an HBCU can be a life-changing experience, offering students the opportunity to learn in a setting that celebrates their culture and heritage. For example, one graduate noted that their experience at an HBCU was like 'planting a seed of pride' that blossomed into a career full of self-confidence and success.

At an HBCU, students are exposed to classes and activities tailored to African American history, literature, art, music, and more, often taught by black professors who are knowledgeable about the cultural backgrounds of their students. This type of environment allows for learning with a unique perspective on topics typically seen through a Eurocentric lens in other higher education institutions.

In addition to fostering understanding within different fields of study, many graduates have reported feeling empowered by the sense of community found at HBCUs; something not easily found elsewhere. Through clubs, organizations, student unions, and more, there is an unwavering support system dedicated to helping each individual reach his or her fullest potential. This support helps create lasting bonds between members of the same class year as well as alumni long after graduation day passes.

HBCUs provide more than just educational opportunities and social networks; they offer hope for brighter futures rooted in confidence and empowerment. With this knowledge, comes an increased chance for success in personal lives as well as careers after college ends – allowing individuals from all walks of life to achieve greatness regardless of where they come from or how much money they make. Thus, transitioning us into discussing some prominent alumni coming out from these historically black colleges...

Prominent HBCU Alumni

Discover how many inspiring and successful individuals have come out of HBCUs, and find out what you can accomplish with a degree from one! From entertainment to politics, the list of distinguished alumni is long and impressive.

Oprah Winfrey attended Tennessee State University, Shonda Rhimes graduated from Dartmouth College but was a student at Howard University for two years, while Chadwick Boseman graduated from Howard University with a Bachelor's in Fine Arts. Other notable graduates include Denzel Washington (Fordham), LeBron James (University of Akron), Thurgood Marshall (Lincoln University) and Toni Morrison (Howard).

The accomplishments of these prominent alumni have not gone unnoticed. Many universities have honored their most successful former students by creating awards such as the Oprah Winfrey Scholarship at Tennessee State or the Chadwick Boseman Leadership Award at Howard. These awards serve as an inspiration for current students to strive for greatness both within and outside the university walls.

It's clear that attending an HBCU can open doors to success on many levels. With access to renowned faculty members, countless opportunities for personal growth, strong networks of support and mentorship, and now having seen some amazing examples of what can be achieved with an HBCU degree - it's no wonder why so many African-Americans choose to attend historically black colleges and universities each year.

And now let's take a closer look at some prominent faculty members who teach there.

Prominent HBCU Faculty

With renowned faculty members like Dr. Michael Lomax, professor of African American Studies at Dillard University, or Dr. Ivory Toldson, professor of Education and Executive Director of the Quality Education for Minorities Network at Howard University, HBCUs are paving the way for success for their students.

From prominent academics to esteemed intellectuals in a range of fields, these distinguished professors help ensure that HBCUs remain competitive in both research and educational offerings. For example, Dr. Lomax is acclaimed for his work on race relations and Black history while Dr. Toldson leverages his expertise in education policy to advocate for diversity on college campuses across the country.

HBCU faculty also focuses on providing an enriching educational experience for students through mentorship opportunities and research collaborations with their peers and colleagues throughout the United States as well as abroad.

Through this level of engagement between faculty and students, students can gain invaluable insights into different disciplines from some of the most experienced practitioners in their fields. Furthermore, these meaningful connections with faculty will often last long after graduation day as alumni continue to rely upon their academic mentors well into adulthood and beyond.

The commitment to excellence demonstrated by HBCU faculty creates a unique atmosphere within each institution that promotes academic achievement among its student body while also providing them with a sense of belonging within their own communities—a bond that helps prepare them to be successful citizens wherever they find themselves later on down life's path.

Moving forward then, we turn our attention towards exploring various academic offerings available at HBCUs...

Academic Offerings at HBCUs

Explore the range of academic offerings available at HBCUs and discover how you can benefit from the unique learning environment they offer.

From diverse majors to cutting-edge research opportunities, HBCUs have something for everyone. Their curriculums are designed to prepare students for successful careers in many industries such as business, healthcare, technology, and engineering.

With experienced faculty members who are passionate about their work and knowledgeable in their field of study, HBCUs provide an ideal educational experience that fosters critical thinking skills while promoting inclusive excellence.

HBCUs offer an array of courses that allow students to explore different areas of interest outside their major. Whether it's a course on African American Literature or one on Environmental Science, these courses give students exposure to new perspectives and topics they may not have otherwise encountered.

Furthermore, many classes use experiential learning techniques such as engaging field trips or hands-on activities to make lectures more engaging and memorable.

Because of this commitment to excellence in education, graduates from HBCUs often go on to become leaders in their respective fields. With the support of dedicated faculty members who mentor them along the way, these alumni serve as examples of what is possible with hard work and dedication — making them assets both within their communities and beyond.

As you embark on your college journey at an HBCU institution, consider all the possibilities that await you — academically and personally — during this time period in your life. With so much potential ahead, nows a great opportunity to start exploring what makes HBCUs so special when it comes to academics – so don't wait any longer!

As we move into discussing 'HBCU student life', let's take some time to consider the impact these institutions have had on countless individuals over generations past - and present!

HBCU Student Life

Experience the rich and vibrant culture of HBCUs, where you can truly immerse yourself in an environment unlike any other - one that's sure to open your eyes to a world of possibilities beyond your wildest dreams!

From student-run organizations like dance troupes and debate teams, to campus-wide activities such as Step Shows and Homecoming celebrations, there is something for everyone at an HBCU. You'll find a wide variety of clubs and organizations that cater to every interest imaginable, from community service initiatives to artistic endeavors. Whether it's academic excellence or social engagement, you'll find plenty of ways to get involved with life on campus.

The spirit and pride that radiates from each HBCU is contagious and will undoubtedly enrich your college experience. You'll make lifelong friends while taking part in the many traditions unique to HBCUs: tailgating at football games, attending concerts featuring renowned artists from all over the country, participating in cultural events like Juneteenth and Kwanzaa celebrations -- even living in residence halls named after esteemed alumni who have paved the way for students today!

In addition to these experiences, there are also countless opportunities outside the boundaries of campus that allow you to explore nearby communities or take advantage of internships offered by some of the most influential companies around.

At an HBCU, you'll gain invaluable knowledge about yourself as well as issues impacting our global society on a daily basis. With its diverse population and dynamic atmosphere, this type of learning environment gives students the opportunity to engage with topics they may not have encountered previously -- helping them become more aware citizens who can make meaningful contributions throughout their lives.

With so much available for exploration both inside and outside the classroom walls, it's no wonder why so many people choose an HBCU as their destination for higher education. As we transition into discussing 'HBCU Athletics', there's no doubt that fans across all campuses have much for which they can cheer!

HBCU Athletics

Cheer on the teams of your favorite HBCU, from football to basketball and more - it's an exciting way to show your school spirit! Historically Black Colleges and Universities (HBCUs) are renowned for their commitment to excellence in athletics. From Division I sports programs to intramural clubs, these institutions offer a wide range of athletic activities that keep students engaged and energized.

Here are some highlights of the HBCU athletic experience:

- Rivalries – Whether it's between two schools or within a single school, rivalries fuel the competitive spirit among students that make attending games thrilling.
- Unique Traditions – Many HBCUs have unique pre- and postgame rituals that bring together students, alumni, staff, and faculty in celebration.
- Supportive Environment – The stands at any given game will be filled with passionate supporters cheering on their team as one unified voice.
- Diverse Sports Programs – From tennis to track & field to volleyball, there's something for everyone when it comes to sports at HBCUs.
- Professional Opportunities – Many student athletes use their time in college as an opportunity to hone skills towards joining professional leagues after graduation.

At HBCUs across the nation, athletics serve as a powerful vehicle for unifying campus communities while providing invaluable learning experiences for student athletes. Whether you choose to attend games or cheer from home, participating in the world of HBCU athletics is sure to bring excitement into your life.

With support from alumni associations and boosters clubs providing financial aid for athletes' tuition costs and equipment needs, these institutions continue making remarkable contributions towards ensuring all participants have equitable access to achieving their goals both on and off the court.

As we take a closer look at how rankings play an important role in fostering success among HBCU sports teams, let's consider how far they've come over the years since they first began competing against one another decades ago.

HBCU Rankings

See how your favorite HBCU teams stack up in the rankings, and cheer them on as they strive to reach their goals. It's no surprise that historically Black colleges and universities (HBCUs) have been working hard to make their mark in the world of college sports. From football to basketball, these schools are competing with some of the most prestigious programs around the country.

Rank	School	Conference
1	Howard University	Mid-Eastern Athletic
2	North Carolina A&T	Mid-Eastern Athletic
3	Alcorn State	Southwestern Athletic
4	Grambling State	Southwestern Athletic
5	Jackson State	Southwestern Athletic

As seen in the table above, Howard University is currently ranked number one among HBCUs with North Carolina A&T at number two followed by Alcorn State, Grambling State, and Jackson State rounding out the top five. These rankings are based on a combination of team performance over time as well as academic success for student athletes. While overall rankings may fluctuate from year to year due to shifting dynamics within different conferences and divisions, it is clear that HBCUs have earned a place among some of the nation's best collegiate athletic programs. We can all be proud of our alma maters for continuing to excel in both academics and athletics!

Frequently Asked Questions

What are the application requirements for HBCUs?

We often hear about the importance of higher education, but not all colleges are created equal. Historically black colleges and universities (HBCUs) offer a unique educational experience that can provide students with skills to thrive in today's competitive job market.

To apply for an HBCU, applicants generally need to have their high school diploma or GED, complete the admissions application, and pay any associated fees. They also need to submit official transcripts from previous educational institutions attended (if applicable) and provide scores from college entrance exams such as the SAT or ACT.

Additionally, many HBCUs may also require letters of recommendation and/or an essay to demonstrate the applicant's commitment to their academic goals.

How much does it cost to attend an HBCU?

Attending college is a huge financial commitment, and for many of us, the cost of tuition can be daunting. Fortunately, there are historically black colleges and universities (HBCUs) that offer an affordable education option.

While tuition costs vary between schools, many HBCUs strive to keep their tuition prices competitively low compared to other universities. For example, at the University of Maryland Eastern Shore – one of the oldest HBCUs in the United States – yearly tuition currently stands at $6,744 for in-state undergraduates and $15,907 for out-of-state students. This is significantly lower than some non-HBCU universities which charge upwards of $30,000 per year or more!

The affordability offered by HBCUs makes them an attractive option for those seeking higher education without breaking their budget.

What types of scholarships are available for HBCU students?

We know that college can be expensive and it's important for students to find ways to finance their education. That's why we're here to discuss scholarships available for college students.

There are many scholarships out there specifically designed for Historically Black Colleges and Universities (HBCU) students, ranging from full tuition awards to small grants. These scholarships come from a variety of sources, including the federal government, private companies, nonprofits, individual donors, and more.

It's important to do research on the different types of scholarship opportunities available in order to maximize your chances of obtaining financial aid for school.

Is there a difference between HBCUs and other universities?

Yes, there is a difference between Historically Black Colleges and Universities (HBCUs) and other universities.

HBCUs were established to provide educational opportunities for African Americans in the United States during a time when they were denied access to many mainstream higher education institutions. These schools have been around for over 150 years, providing students with an opportunity to pursue their dreams regardless of race or ethnicity.

In addition to providing access to higher education, HBCUs are focused on creating culturally conscious environments that celebrate diversity while cultivating a sense of community among its students. This is something that many traditional universities lack as they tend to be less attentive to the needs of minority students.

How do HBCUs compare to other universities in terms of resources and support?

We're often asked how historically black colleges and universities (HBCUs) compare to other universities in terms of resources and support. From our experience, HBCUs provide an unparalleled level of personal attention, guidance, and mentorship that can make a world of difference in a student's college career.

Their dedication to diversity, inclusion, and cultural awareness is evident in the way they approach education - not as a one-size-fits-all model but rather as a tailored journey which recognizes each individual's unique strengths and needs.

Furthermore, their commitment to providing access to resources such as scholarships, financial aid, and career counseling is unparalleled when compared to other institutions.

In short, HBCUs offer students the opportunity to grow academically while having their social wellbeing taken care of - something few other universities can match.

Conclusion

We've seen that HBCUs offer a unique educational experience, with an emphasis on cultural understanding and the advancement of Black people.

There are many benefits to attending an HBCU, including strong support networks, career opportunities, and a greater chance at success after graduation.

Nearly half of African American professionals in the U.S. today are graduates of HBCUs!

Clearly, these institutions have made a lasting impact on our society and should be valued for their contributions to advancing the Black community.

Black Fraternities and Sororities

We've all heard stories about Black fraternities and sororities, with their members representing a diverse array of backgrounds and talents. But what is it that makes these organizations so special?

From academic excellence to community service, leadership development to an unbreakable network of support - the impact of black fraternities and sororities can be felt everywhere. In fact, they are like a force of nature - powerful enough to move mountains!

They have shaped generations, created leaders and been integral in the fight for civil rights. So let's dive into this fascinating topic as we explore the history, purpose, recruitment process and more that make up Black fraternities and sororities.

History of Black Fraternities and Sororities

You've heard of them, but do you know their history? Discover the story behind these iconic organizations.

Black fraternities and sororities have a rich history in the United States, stemming from a need to create an environment that fosters academic excellence, community service, and social awareness among African-Americans. Founded in 1906 by African-American students at Cornell University, Alpha Phi Alpha was the first intercollegiate Greek letter fraternity established for black men.

The National Pan-Hellenic Council (NPHC) was founded soon after in 1930 and is composed of nine historically black international Greek letter sororities and fraternities. These organizations eventually spread throughout college campuses around the country, providing an opportunity for students of color to come together with a shared sense of common identity and purpose while also developing strong relationships with their peers.

Throughout their long histories, these organizations have been dedicated to uplifting people of color through leadership development programs as well as philanthropic projects such as voter registration drives and health initiatives. They've also been essential in providing networking opportunities within professional fields like medicine, law, business, government, and education - all aimed at improving educational access for African Americans who otherwise may not have had it available to them.

As such, members of these groups often take great pride in being able to pay dues that help support the mission of these powerful institutions that strive to make positive changes in our society. These organizations are more than just symbols; they represent a commitment to empowering individuals from all walks of life through education and activism while building a stronger sense of community among its members.

By working together on various projects both inside school walls and out in public spaces across our nation's cities and townships alike - black fraternities & sororities play an invaluable role in unifying communities around social justice issues that affect us all today. From this perspective, we can see how these venerable institutions continue to be instrumental forces for good within American culture - inspiring future generations towards greatness on many levels.

As we move forward into uncharted territory, it's important that we remember the impactful legacy created by those who came before us - setting forth examples for others so they too can achieve success no matter what obstacles stand before them.

Academic Excellence

Education is the key to unlocking a world of endless possibilities, and for generations, these organizations have been helping members open those doors. Black fraternities and sororities have always valued an education as more than just getting good grades but also about developing critical thinking skills that can be used in everyday life.

They promote academic excellence through setting high standards for their members, providing support systems to help them reach those goals, such as study sessions and mentorship programs. As a result, members of these organizations continually strive to meet higher academic expectations while being proud representatives of their communities.

These organizations are not only focused on achieving high GPAs and graduating with honors; they also focus on how to use the knowledge gained in college to make meaningful contributions back to their respective communities. In fact, many require community service hours or other forms of outreach in order for students to remain active members in good standing.

From tutoring local elementary school children or helping out at shelters for the homeless, black fraternities and sororities are committed to creating positive change through service projects both near and far from home.

By stressing the importance of academics while simultaneously pushing for social responsibility among its members, black fraternities and sororities create a balanced environment that allows individuals to find success at any level no matter what path they choose. As leaders both inside and outside the classroom, they provide resources that allow students to become well-rounded individuals who understand how their words can shape history.

With this type of guidance behind them, it's no wonder why so many alumni go on to achieve greatness within their chosen fields. And looking ahead into the future, there is no doubt that these same ideals will continue inspiring greatness for generations yet to come – now that's something worth celebrating!

Moving forward then into our next section about community service...

Community Service

Giving back to the community is a great way to make an impact and gain invaluable life experiences, and these organizations are committed to helping their members do just that. Black fraternities and sororities have long been at the forefront of this effort, providing opportunities for volunteers to give back through service projects in their communities.

These organizations also provide resources and support for members who wish to get involved in service projects on a larger scale. For example, some chapters host annual 'Day of Service' events where members come together to volunteer with local charities or non-profit organizations. The service provided by black fraternities and sororities goes beyond one-off volunteer initiatives such as 'Days of Service'.

Many chapters have established formal partnerships with charity groups or non-profits that are working on larger scale projects; such as building homes for those in need, creating scholarship funds for underprivileged children, or helping out at food banks. There's also often an emphasis placed on mentoring youth from disadvantaged backgrounds - both through volunteering activities as well as providing academic guidance - all with the goal of giving them the best possible chance at success in life.

This commitment to community service has enabled black fraternities and sororities to not only impact their immediate neighborhoods but also society as a whole by inspiring others to take action and contribute positively towards it too. With this focus on civic engagement, there's no doubt that these organizations will continue making meaningful contributions towards improving our communities well into the future - leading us into the subsequent discussion about leadership development within these societies.

Leadership Development

You're about to be blown away by the incredible leadership development taking place in these organizations - it's absolutely awe-inspiring!

Black Fraternities and Sororities play a major role in developing their members into strong, capable leaders. The organizations provide members with invaluable mentorship and support from experienced professionals who can offer guidance and resources to help them reach their goals.

Members are also trained on critical skill sets such as communication, problem solving, decision making, networking, public speaking and more -- all of which give them the confidence they need to take on any challenge. Furthermore, members learn how to effectively manage people and projects while growing in their own personal development.

They gain an understanding of working with different kinds of people while building relationships along the way. This kind of experience is key for learning how to lead others through tough situations or complex tasks. In addition to providing professional growth opportunities, these organizations also build a sense of community among its members.

Through shared experiences such as volunteering together or attending conferences and events, members form an unbreakable bond that will last long after they graduate from college. From sharing ideas and inspiring each other to pushing each other towards success, this network of support helps foster individual growth that will ultimately benefit the larger community as well.

Network of Support

You're part of a tight-knit group that provides each other with unwavering support and encouragement. As a member of one of the many Black fraternities and sororities, you have access to a whole network of people who can help you out in times of need. Here are some of the benefits that come with this extended family:

- **Mentoring** - You get access to individuals who can offer advice and guidance as you navigate through life.

- **Networking** - The fraternity or sorority has connections with people in various fields that can help you professionally.

- **Financial Assistance** - Your brothers or sisters may be able to provide financial assistance if needed for anything from school fees to rent payments.

- **Emotional Support** - In addition to all these tangible benefits, your fraternity/sorority members will also provide emotional support when facing difficult times, lift up your spirits when feeling down, and share achievements together during good times!

This extended family is an invaluable asset on your journey through life, offering both practical resources and moral support throughout your journey – something that money can't buy! Everyone needs a helping hand at some point, especially those trying to make their way in the world, so it's great knowing that such reliable resources are available whenever they're needed most.

This bond between members adds an extra layer of security which makes being part of a fraternity/sorority even more rewarding – it's like having another family looking out for you! Moving forward into the next section about the benefits of joining a fraternity or sorority, we can see just how beneficial membership really is for its members!

Benefits of Joining a Fraternity or Sorority

One of the biggest benefits of joining a fraternity or sorority is the opportunity to form close relationships with people who share similar values. Beyond networking, members can provide each other with emotional and moral support. We've seen how this network of support can be invaluable for those pursuing academic and career goals alike.

Joining a fraternity or sorority also provides access to professional development opportunities and resources that help members grow personally and professionally. From attending workshops on enhancing leadership skills to taking part in exclusive job fairs, there are plenty of ways that fraternities and sororities assist their members in achieving success. Additionally, becoming a member gives you access to scholarships which may not otherwise be available, including those from your own organization as well as outside entities such as corporations and foundations. This helps open doors for furthering education beyond college, opening up even more opportunities for personal growth.

Membership in black fraternities or sororities is also an opportunity to make lasting connections with like-minded individuals who value building strong communities through service and collaboration. These organizations serve an important role in providing mentorship where it's needed most, creating bonds between younger generations while supporting programs that enhance the quality of life within our local neighborhoods, nationally, and even internationally.

With so many advantages for personal growth, it's no wonder why so many people choose to join these groups year after year. As powerful forces for good that bring together individuals from different walks of life, we must take the time to understand what sets fraternities apart from sororities. It's important to look at factors such as mission statements, social activities, and membership qualifications before making any decisions about our future involvement in either one.

Differences between Fraternities and Sororities

Comparing fraternities and sororities is like looking at two sides of a coin; each has its own unique culture, values, and goals that intertwine to form an interconnected whole. At the core of these differences lies the gender divide: while fraternities are traditionally exclusive for men, sororities are typically reserved for women.

Here are some other notable distinctions between them:

- Fraternities and sororities often have different recruitment and intake processes.
- Activities within a fraternity or sorority can differ significantly in terms of their focus (e.g. leadership development vs. philanthropic work).
- Social events hosted by fraternities or sororities usually follow traditional gender roles with regard to expectations about behavior, dress code, etc.

These disparities demonstrate how the two types of organizations vary in many ways beyond just gender-based exclusivity — they also involve distinct rituals, values, codes of conduct, and more. As such, it's important to understand these nuances before making a decision on which organization one should join; this will ensure that members get the most out of their experience as part of either a fraternity or a sorority.

With this knowledge in mind, individuals can make an informed choice about which organization best fits their interests and goals — ultimately leading to fruitful experiences both inside and outside the Greek system. Without further ado, let's now turn our attention to understanding recruitment and intake processes associated with joining black fraternities and sororities.

Recruitment and Intake Processes

Discovering the unique cultures and values of black fraternities and sororities can be an exciting journey, so take the time to explore their recruitment and intake processes.

Each fraternity and sorority has its own specific process for selecting new members, with some allowing potential members to join during any semester or term while others allow membership only at certain times. Generally speaking, there are two types of recruitment/intake processes - formal and informal.

For formal processes, a period of information sessions is organized by the chapter where potential new members can learn about the organization's history and values, as well as ask questions about dues and other associated costs. Informal processes rely on existing members reaching out directly to potential new members through word-of-mouth or social media campaigns.

During both types of recruitment/intake processes, it is important to emphasize that hazing in any form is not tolerated within most organizations.

Once a potential member shows interest in joining a fraternity or sorority they will go through an interview process conducted by current active members known as 'potential new member educators'. This allows them to get more information about the organization before committing or being invited to join a particular chapter.

After this process, if the individual is selected for membership they will have to accept an invitation letter from the organization's leadership board which outlines all terms related to becoming a member such as dues payments, meeting expectations for academic performance, participation in events etc. Once accepted into a chapter, each individual will also need to sign a contract outlining their commitment to uphold organizational policies laid out by national headquarters such as no hazing policy and anti discrimination policies among others.

The recruitment/intake process provides individuals with ample opportunity to learn more about each particular fraternity or sorority prior making decisions regarding membership which generally lasts for life once initiated into said organization. Furthermore, it also helps chapters ensure that their prospective candidates are aware of all commitments associated with being part of these organizations prior signing up so that no one is blindsided by additional requirements after initiation ceremony takes place.

With this knowledge in hand, then transitioning into discussing 'hazing in black fraternities and sororities' should be easier than ever before!

Hazing in Black Fraternities and Sororities

As you embark on your journey to learn about the cultures and values of these organizations, be mindful that hazing is not tolerated within them; sometimes it takes just one wrong step to undo all the progress made.

Hazing is a form of socializing which involves initiates going through physical or psychological abuse in order to gain acceptance into a group.

In the black fraternity and sorority community, there have been allegations of hazing for many years. Although most members are committed to upholding their organization's principles, some individuals engage in activities that can put other members at risk. Reports show that incidents ranging from verbal humiliation to physical harm have occurred during recruitment and initiation ceremonies.

Organizations such as National Pan-Hellenic Council (NPHC) have implemented anti-hazing policies and provided educational programs to raise awareness around the issue of hazing in their chapters. Some NPHC member organizations even require potential new members to take part in training sessions prior to joining their chapter. These sessions cover topics like understanding organizational goals, building leadership skills, respecting diversity, honing communication skills, setting boundaries and expectations for oneself and others – all with the aim of eliminating any potential risks associated with hazing activities.

Hazing has no place in black fraternities and sororities - it violates both public safety laws as well as traditional cultural standards set by African American communities throughout history.

To ensure a safe experience for everyone involved in joining a fraternity or sorority, organizations must continue educating new members about what constitutes acceptable behavior while also holding those who violate policies accountable for their actions.

As we look towards the future of black fraternities and sororities, we must strive for an environment free from any forms of intimidation or abuse so they can continue fostering relationships based on mutual respect and understanding between its members.

The Future of Black Fraternities and Sororities

Now that we've discussed the issue of hazing in Black fraternities and sororities, let's look to the future. As one of the oldest African American organizations in the US, it's important for these groups to continue to exist and grow.

The most important thing for Black fraternities and sororities is to stay true to their mission while adapting with the times. This means continuing their commitment to social justice, academic excellence, service work, and sisterhood/brotherhood. They should also strive to make access easier by providing more scholarships and waiving membership fees when possible.

These organizations need to be aware of opportunities for members outside of campus life too, such as internships or job prospects with alumni networks or mentorship programs that encourage professional growth within members. By doing so, Black fraternities and sororities will remain relevant through networking initiatives that help create meaningful relationships between current students and alumni – something which was not always available in previous years due to racism or lack of resources.

In short, these organizations must embrace change in order to sustain their longevity well into the future.

Frequently Asked Questions

How much does it cost to join a fraternity or sorority?

Joining a fraternity or sorority can be an expensive commitment. Costs vary widely between organizations, but typically include one-time fees for initiation and membership dues that are paid every semester.

The one-time fee usually ranges from $300 to $1,000 while the semesterly dues may cost anywhere from $50 to $500 depending on the organization. Other expenses may include social event tickets or apparel such as t-shirts or pins.

Are Greek organizations open to non-students?

Greek organizations aren't just exclusive clubs for college students; they can be open to non-students as well. Some exist outside of collegiate environments and accept members who aren't currently enrolled in school.

Joining one of these non-student Greek groups requires an application process. Applicants must meet certain requirements such as having a clean criminal record and passing a background check. Additionally, there may be fees associated with joining the organization, though the amount will vary depending on the group.

How do I know which fraternity or sorority is right for me?

Choosing the right fraternity or sorority is a big decision, and it requires some research. The best way to figure out which organization is right for you is to learn more about each group's history and purpose.

Get in touch with members of different fraternities and sororities, either through online forums or in person, and ask questions about their goals and values. Consider what kind of activities they organize, as well as the type of people who join them.

Most importantly, make sure the group aligns with your own beliefs and ideals before committing to membership.

Are there any age restrictions for joining a fraternity or sorority?

When it comes to joining a fraternity or sorority, age restrictions can vary. For example, some organizations have a minimum age of 18 for college freshmen while others may require that members be at least 21 years old.

Generally speaking, most fraternities and sororities require potential new members to be in college and of legal drinking age, which is typically 21 in the United States. Also, many organizations have set upper limits on how old one can be before they are no longer eligible to join.

That said, there are exceptions to these rules as some organizations will allow individuals over the typical upper limit if they demonstrate an exceptional commitment to their organization's values and ideals.

Is there a minimum GPA requirement for joining a fraternity or sorority?

Joining a fraternity or sorority can be an exciting experience, but there are certain requirements that must be met in order to qualify. One of those requirements is typically a minimum GPA requirement.

While the exact numbers vary between individual fraternities and sororities, most require at least a 2.5 GPA for consideration. This number may vary depending on the organization's specific standards, so it's important to research the particular chapter you're interested in before applying.

Conclusion

We've seen the impact that black fraternities and sororities have had on generations of students and alumni. With a long history of academic excellence, community service, leadership development, and a network of support, it is no wonder why so many people choose to be part of these organizations.

While there are differences between fraternities and sororities, they both share common goals that revolve around bettering their communities.

We can't deny the unfortunate presence of hazing in some parts of Greek life, but we believe that with continued support from all members, these organizations will continue to grow in strength and purpose.

As we move forward into the future together, let us continue to stand in solidarity with one another as we strive for success.

The Black Elite

The black elite are a powerful and influential group in society. In the United States, African Americans make up just 13% of the population, but hold 48% of all top-level executive positions in Fortune 500 companies.

We've come a long way since the days when black people had to face discrimination and oppression, but there is still work to be done.

Our article will explore what it means to be part of the black elite, how they have impacted society so far, and what challenges still lie ahead.

Definitions of the Black Elite

The upper crust, the crème de la crème, and an exclusive group - these are all definitions of the cream of society. And for those in the black community, this elite group is known as 'the black elite.'

It could be argued that the journey to reach such a lofty status takes more than just money and power; it requires courage and determination to succeed in a system designed to oppress them. As such, those who have achieved success despite these barriers should be honored and respected as part of this exclusive group.

From well-known celebrities to powerful politicians and business moguls, we'll now explore some famous figures within the black elite.

Famous Black Elite Figures

From business moguls to world-renowned athletes, these collections of renowned figures have made their mark, achieving the highest levels of success. Here are just a few names that come to mind:

- Oprah Winfrey - entrepreneur and philanthropist
- Barack Obama - former U.S. President
- Michael Jordan - basketball legend
- Nelson Mandela - revolutionary leader
- Jay-Z - music mogul

These amazing individuals are inspiring role models for our generation and beyond. They're leaders who've demonstrated resilience, courage, and discipline in their respective fields. It's no wonder they've achieved such incredible heights!

As we look ahead, its clear there's much more work to be done to continue the progress made by these iconic members of the black elite.

Accomplishments of the Black Elite

These iconic figures have accomplished impressive feats, breaking boundaries and pushing the limits of what was believed to be possible. From Oprah Winfrey becoming the first African American Billionaire to Barack Obama becoming the 44th President of the United States, these individuals have made a lasting imprint on society. They demonstrated that success could be achieved through hard work, determination, and dedication - regardless of race or gender. Their accomplishments are evidence that anything is possible with a strong will and perseverance.

This legacy of excellence has not only been set by individuals, but also organizations such as Black Lives Matter, which has become an international movement for social justice. The Black Elite have shown how those with privilege can use their resources to create positive change in their communities and beyond.

As we continue to strive for equality in all aspects of life, these powerful examples should serve as inspiration and motivation for us all. With this in mind, it becomes clear why education is so important for furthering the progress made by the Black Elite today - setting up future generations to follow in their footsteps towards greater success.

Education and the Black Elite

Through their accomplishments, the Black Elite have demonstrated the power of education in achieving success, illustrating that it's a crucial tool for overcoming barriers and creating lasting change.

From notable leaders such as Barack Obama to everyday entrepreneurs and professionals, many African-Americans owe much of their success to having obtained an education. This has translated into improved economic opportunities for black communities across America, from better wages to more job opportunities.

Education has also been instrumental in reducing long-standing disparities between African Americans and other minority groups. By giving them access to resources and knowledge not previously available, higher education has had a positive impact on the lives of many African Americans.

In turn, this has helped create a wealthier and more diverse middle class that's now seen in large parts of the country. As such, it's clear that education has played an essential role in helping members of the Black Elite reach greater heights than ever before.

With these successes come a new set of responsibilities – namely, the responsibility to use their influence to continue amplifying voices which have yet to be heard and empower those who remain marginalized or disadvantaged by society today.

The Role of the Black Elite in Business

Examining the role of African-Americans in business, it's clear that they have made tremendous strides in creating a more diverse and equitable economic landscape.

The black elite have proven to be instrumental in leading this charge, with many entrepreneurs becoming successful business owners and executives. They have shown that success is possible despite facing systemic racism, and have often used their own wealth to create opportunities for others in the community.

Their work has also helped increase diversity within corporate America, as well as providing access to capital for minority-owned businesses. This has led to improved economic mobility for African-Americans across all sectors of society.

As a result, the black elite has become an essential part of the fabric of our economy, setting an example that can inspire future generations. With continued support from both public and private sectors, there's no telling what heights African-American businesses could reach in the coming years.

Moving forward though it's important to ensure that these leaders are given equal opportunity and resources so they can continue making lasting changes within our economy.

The Black Elite and Politics

You may not be aware, but many members of the African-American upper class are also making waves in politics. From local legislators to heads of state and even the current president, the black elite have been making strides in government for decades.

Barack Obama's historic election as President of the United States was a testament to this fact, with his predecessor being a member of the Congressional Black Caucus. The black elite have also made their presence known in other political realms, such as lobbying and advocacy work.

Recent movements such as Black Lives Matter have highlighted how important it is to our society that people from all walks of life can voice their opinions and be heard. As a result, more influential members of the African-American community are beginning to enter politics on both sides of the aisle in order to ensure that their perspectives are taken into consideration when important decisions are made.

This marks an exciting time for those who want to see greater diversity represented in American politics and beyond. With this momentum building, it remains to be seen how much further these efforts will take us towards a truly equitable society — one that values everyone regardless of race or background.

And with that thought in mind, let's turn our attention now to explore 'the black elite in the media'.

The Black Elite in the Media

Discover how members of the African-American upper class are influencing the media and making their voices heard on important issues. We're seeing a new wave of black elite who are utilizing their platforms to speak out on topics such as racial justice, education reform, and economic inequality.

- Ava DuVernay, director of films like 13th and Selma
- Issa Rae, creator of HBO's Insecure
- Taraji P. Henson, star of Fox's Empire
- Beyonce, singer and performer
- Janelle Monae, singer and actress

The black elite have used their influence to draw attention to important causes and start conversations that need to be had about racism in America. Their presence in the media is helping to shape public opinion on these topics - giving people an opportunity to learn more about them while also creating a space for dialogue.

With this newfound power comes responsibility; they must use it wisely in order for it to have a lasting impact on society.

The Impact of the Black Elite on Society

You can see the influence of the African-American upper class on society today – from increased representation in media and entertainment, to pushing for social change. They're making their mark and inspiring a new generation by challenging the status quo and promoting equality.

Their presence has opened up more opportunities for those traditionally excluded, providing Black people with greater visibility and access to resources that create a better future. This wave of progress is just beginning as they continue to break down barriers and stand as role models in their communities.

Still, there are many challenges facing the black elite – from expectations of success that can be difficult to meet, to stereotypes that shape how they're perceived by others. While some members of the community are able to use their wealth or privilege to benefit themselves or others, not all have access to these same resources.

The impact of this reality is felt throughout society as economic inequity remains an issue within minority communities, often leading to disparities in health care, education, employment opportunities, and more. To truly level the playing field will require ongoing effort – both from individuals within the Black elite community and allies outside it – but together we can make lasting positive change.

Challenges Facing the Black Elite

Though many members of the African-American upper class have access to resources that can benefit themselves and others, those without such advantages face a multitude of challenges.

Imagining their struggle, one can see the immense barriers they must overcome to level the playing field for all.

From finding mentors and role models in an unwelcoming environment to dealing with racism and microaggressions even within their own communities, these individuals have to work harder than ever to create a better future for them.

Thus, it's essential that we recognize these challenges facing the black elite today if we're to hope for any progress in the future.

The Future of the Black Elite

Despite the many obstacles they face, members of the African-American upper class remain determined to create a brighter future for themselves and their communities. With concerted efforts, they're working hard to break down systemic barriers and serve as role models in their respective fields.

This passionate drive motivates them to blaze trails, challenge existing paradigms, and pursue excellence in all facets of life. The Black elite are optimistic that progress will be made in areas such as education, employment, housing, and health care.

They believe these improvements will benefit not only their own lives but also those of others in the broader African-American community. The hope is that this progress will help erase persistent racial disparities and create an environment where everyone can thrive regardless of background or skin color.

Frequently Asked Questions

What are the economic benefits of being part of the Black Elite?

We're the privileged few, standing at the pinnacle of success. Like a lighthouse in a storm, we serve as an example for those seeking safety and stability.

Being part of the black elite brings immediate and lifelong economic benefits. Better job prospects and access to high-end investments open doors often closed to others. Not only do they give us greater financial freedom, but they also provide added security in uncertain times.

What strategies have been used to address the challenges facing the Black Elite?

We've been working to address the challenges facing those in power, including the unique needs of the black elite. We're dedicated to finding innovative solutions, from creating more economic opportunities to empowering members of our community through education and mentorship.

We recognize that these issues are complex and require a multifaceted approach from both private and public sectors. Our goal is to ensure equity for all members of our society, regardless of race or social class.

We believe that by coming together, we can make meaningful progress towards achieving this vision.

How has the Black Elite used their influence to create positive change?

We've seen a surge in the number of influential members of society who are using their platforms to create positive change. From celebrities to businesspeople, there's an increasing trend towards action and awareness to bring about meaningful reform.

The Black elite have been no exception. They frequently employ their influence and resources to support causes that seek to improve their communities, uplift marginalized voices, and advocate for justice. Whether it's through philanthropy or advocacy work, they're working hard to make sure that their impact reaches further than ever before.

How has the Black Elite's presence in the media impacted their public image?

As the saying goes, all publicity is good publicity. The presence of the black elite in media has had a huge impact on their public image, and it isn't always positive - but it's certainly attention-grabbing.

From debates over controversial figures to representation of black success stories, their visibility in the media has been both polarizing and eye-opening for viewers around the globe.

It's clear that regardless of opinion or controversy, they've created an impactful presence that can no longer be ignored.

How has the Black Elite's educational background contributed to their success?

We've seen many successful individuals in the public eye, and it's no secret that education plays a major role in their success. For those who are part of the black elite, having an impressive educational background has been a key factor for them to reach higher levels of success.

Not only do they receive a quality education, but they also gain invaluable skills such as problem-solving, critical thinking, and communication which are essential to become leaders within their respective fields.

By combining these characteristics with hard work and dedication, the black elite is able to use their education to achieve great things.

Conclusion

We've seen how influential the black elite has been, and continue to be, on many aspects of society. From the business world to the media, the accomplishments of these individuals are undeniable.

However, they still face many challenges that limit their potential for further success. We must strive to create more equitable opportunities so that everyone can reach their full potential.

By leveraging technology like never before, we can revolutionize what it means to be a part of the black elite and create a future where all people have access to resources and opportunity - no matter their background.

The Black Panther Movement

We were the powerful pioneers of progress, pushing past prejudice to propel our people forward. Proudly proclaiming our principles and purposeful in our pursuit of power, we were the leaders of the Black Panther movement.

Our mission was to bring about lasting change for African Americans in America through a combination of political action and community service. We sought to build a better future by advocating for minority rights, challenging systemic racism and acting as a beacon of hope for those who had been oppressed by white supremacy.

With an unshakeable commitment to justice and equality, we worked tirelessly to make sure that African American voices were heard loud and clear in society's halls of power.

History of the BPP

Founded in 1966, the BPP was a revolutionary organization focused on protecting and empowering African-American communities. Led by Bobby Seale and Huey Newton, the party fought for civil rights against institutionalized racism and economic inequality.

The BPP's main ideology focused on Black self-determination, community control of political power, and full employment opportunities for African Americans. It also sought to improve education and housing options in black neighborhoods. They organized rallies, protests, and even armed patrols to combat police brutality in their communities.

Their efforts were often met with police repression and violence but they continued to push forward. As a result of their actions, they were able to make huge strides towards greater racial justice in the U.S., inspiring other liberation movements around the world along the way.

With this momentum, they achieved many victories such as free breakfast programs for kids or gaining access to legal services for those who could not afford it otherwise. This paved the way for subsequent generations of activists who have continued to work towards dismantling systemic racism today.

In short, the Black Panther Party is remembered as an important catalyst in starting conversations about race relations that are still continuing today.

Ideology and Goals

Uncompromisingly determined to fight for social justice and racial equality, the Black Panther Party sought to achieve its goals through non-violent means.

The party's 10-Point Program consisted of demands that included full employment, decent housing, an end to police brutality, and a call for black self-determination. Its members also sought to create and implement programs such as free breakfast programs for children in impoverished neighborhoods, sickle cell anemia testing centers, and free health clinics.

The ideology of the BPP was based on a combination of socialism and nationalism with Marxist influences. These foundational ideas were outlined in their 'What We Want Now' manifesto which detailed the group's main goals - economic security for all people of color, access to education opportunities, an end to colonial oppression worldwide, and complete liberation from institutionalized racism within the U.S.

They strove to build communities that would be self-sufficient while still engaging in grassroots political organizing in order to bring about long lasting systemic change. With this vision firmly implanted in their mindsets and hearts, they continued fighting for what they believed was right all throughout their existence, moving forward with these principles guiding them along their path towards justice.

Organizational Structure

You can structure your own future and take control of the narrative by joining a movement that's committed to justice, equality, and liberation.

The Black Panther Party organized itself into a hierarchical structure with national leadership at the top and local chapters underneath. Each chapter was led by a Minister of Defense or Field Marshall who reported back to the National Leadership. The party also had a specific set of rules for each member who included upholding the Ten Point Platform and Program, following orders from their superiors, attending meetings regularly, maintaining secrecy about party activities, and keeping up with their dues payments.

In addition to this formal organizational structure, members could also participate in informal actions such as speaking out against injustice or joining protests. By being part of an organization dedicated to social change, members were able to have greater influence on their communities than they would have been able to do on their own.

With solidarity comes strength; together we can create lasting change that'll benefit our society for generations to come. To achieve this goal, it takes action beyond just words – it takes action!

Strategies for Social Change

We must take action to create lasting change, and that requires strong strategies for social change beyond just words. The Black Panther Party was a revolutionary movement that sought to address the systemic racism and injustice in their communities by developing creative tactics to challenge oppressive structures.

They employed the use of public demonstrations, rallies, marches, and petition drives to bring attention to issues such as police brutality, poverty wages, and inadequate housing. Additionally, they produced educational materials that informed people about their rights under the law and how they could exercise them. Through these efforts, the party was able to influence policy changes at both local and state levels.

The Black Panthers also worked on projects such as food pantries and health clinics in order to better meet their community's needs. By providing essential services that were otherwise not available or accessible due to institutionalized racism or poverty, they were able demonstrate concretely the power of collective action towards social transformation.

Moreover, through strategic alliances with other civil rights movements of the time period such as women's liberation groups or student protest organizations they increased their effectiveness by amplifying each other's impact. Ultimately, it is clear that successful strategies for social change require more than just rhetoric but also a commitment to tangible actions. If we are going to transcend beyond mere words into meaningful outcomes, this is what makes the Black Panther Movement so powerful then—and still today: its ability to build bridges across diverse communities in pursuit of justice while engaging society at all levels in an effort create lasting positive change.

To further this cause, community programs and services must be implemented...

Community Programs and Services

In order to bring about lasting change, it's essential that we provide necessary community programs and services to support those in need.

During the Black Panther Movement, members organized a variety of initiatives such as free breakfast programs for school-aged children living in poverty, health clinics and ambulance services.

The goal was to meet the needs of people who were not receiving adequate support from government agencies and other authorities.

Through these various initiatives, they provided tangible help while also making a powerful statement that all members of society should be given equal access to resources, regardless of their race or socioeconomic status.

As a result, many impoverished communities saw massive improvements in quality of life over time.

To take further steps towards social justice and equality, the movement also advocated for armed self-defense.

Armed Self-Defense

As a means of protecting themselves and their communities, many members of the movement advocated for armed self-defense. This was especially true in areas where police did not provide adequate safety or protection for African American people.

The Black Panther Party had various methods of achieving this type of defense:

- They held regular firearms training sessions to provide members with the necessary skills.

- They created programs that provided free breakfast and lunch to local schoolchildren.
- They monitored law enforcement officers' activities in an effort to protect citizens from abuse and intimidation.
- They set up community patrols that could respond quickly when violence occurred in African American neighborhoods.
- And they organized rallies and marches to demonstrate their commitment to justice and freedom for all people regardless of race or class.

The Black Panthers believed that political education was essential if they were going to build a better future for their communities, so they began teaching classes on revolutionary history, politics, economics, legal rights, self-defense tactics, martial arts, nutrition, and health care.

By empowering themselves through political knowledge, the Panthers sought to create lasting change in society.

Political Education

You too can take steps to create lasting change in society, beginning with educating yourself on revolutionary history, politics, and legal rights. The Black Panther Party is an example of a group that took this approach.

They began as a small organization in Oakland, California in 1966 and quickly grew into a nationwide movement advocating for the liberation of African Americans from systemic oppression. Through political education workshops that focused on topics like racism and civil rights legislation, they provided members with the tools to understand their oppressors and fight back against discrimination.

By cultivating an understanding of the power structures at play in society, they empowered individuals to become active participants in shaping their own futures and those of their communities. As part of this strategy, they also developed relationships with other social justice groups whose goals aligned with theirs in order to build larger coalitions for greater impact.

In doing so, they created a legacy that continues to inspire people today who are looking for ways to make meaningful change.

Government Repression

You've seen how powerful political education can be, but unfortunately it has also been met with government repression.

The Black Panther Party was targeted by the FBI and other law enforcement agents to try to disrupt its activities.

Along with surveillance, raids and harassment, members were arrested on trumped-up charges and sentenced to long jail terms or even executed without due process.

This created a hostile environment for the Panthers' work and threatened their safety.

However, despite this fear of retribution, they continued to organize and struggle for their vision of freedom.

The legacy of this movement is one that remains strong in spite of all the attempts by authorities to stifle it.

Legacy of the Movement

Despite the government's attempts to suppress it, the legacy of this powerful struggle for freedom lives on. The Black Panther Movement has left a lasting imprint on our society today. It has become an enduring symbol of strength and resilience in the face of oppressive systems. It stands as a reminder that we can accomplish great things when we come together and fight for what's right.

It serves as a blueprint for grassroots organizing and coalition building. It helps us remember why it's so important to speak out against injustice. The legacy of this powerful struggle continues to inspire people around the world.

As we look ahead towards creating a more equitable future, we must continue to draw inspiration from those who have fought diligently before us. With their example as our guide, let's strive together towards creating a world that's truly free from oppression.

Continuing Influence on Activism

Through their legacy of strength and resilience, the brave few have created an enduring symbol that shows us what can be achieved when we come together to fight for justice.

The Black Panther Movement continues to have a lasting impact on activism today, as it has inspired numerous individuals to take a stand against social injustice. It stands as an example of how collective action can lead to meaningful change in society, and its message is still relevant in our current times.

For many activists, the Black Panthers serve as a source of hope and courage; they show that no matter how daunting the struggle may seem, with enough dedication and unity, success is possible.

In spite of its tumultuous history, the movement remains an integral part of America's civil rights narrative – one which serves to remind us all of what can be accomplished if we're willing to fight for our beliefs.

Frequently Asked Questions

What events led to the rise of the Black Panther movement?

We've seen a rise in activism around civil rights and social justice in recent years. However, the roots of this movement can be traced back to the Black Panther Party of the 1960s. The group began as a response to police brutality and racial inequality in Oakland, California.

Fueled by frustration with discrimination and lack of opportunity for African Americans, the Black Panther Party drew attention to these issues through protests, rallies, and voter registration drives. As their influence spread across the country, they became an important force in inspiring people to fight for equal rights and social change.

How did the Black Panther movement impact the civil rights movement?

We've come a long way since the civil rights movement of the 1960s. The Black Panther movement had a huge impact on pushing progress forward and ensuring that African Americans were given equal rights and opportunities. They used civil disobedience, protest marches, and other forms of activism to guarantee that all people would be treated equally under the law. The Panthers' radical stance on social justice issues helped shape public opinion and eventually led to changes in legislation at both the state and federal levels. Their efforts ultimately gave rise to sweeping reforms for African-Americans across the United States.

How did the Black Panther movement gain popular support?

We, like many Americans in the 1960s, sought to protect our civil rights and challenge systemic racism. The Black Panther Movement provided a powerful platform for this cause, one that quickly gained popular support.

Through organized protests and community outreach initiatives, the movement sparked a nationwide conversation about inequality, civil rights, and social justice that continues to reverberate today.

What did the Black Panther movement do to challenge racism and oppression?

We've long believed that racism and oppression are powerful forces in our society. However, it's only recently that we've seen a movement challenge them head-on. The Black Panther movement was one of the first to confront these issues directly. They used their ideology and activism to demand justice for all.

The Black Panthers organized protests against police brutality. They also held educational seminars to teach about the power of voting. Additionally, they established numerous social programs, such as free breakfasts for children. Through their actions, they inspired others to take up the cause and fight for an end to racial discrimination and oppressive systems.

How did the Black Panther movement influence future movements for social justice?

We're proud to have witnessed the influence of the Black Panther movement on future movements for social justice. Their work in challenging racism and oppression laid a foundation that others could build on. They inspired generations to come with their dedication to fighting injustice and advocating for civil rights.

Through creative tactics like protests, pickets, and petitions, the Black Panthers are remembered as one of the most important catalysts of social change in our nation's history.

Conclusion

We've come to the end of our exploration of the Black Panther Party and its impact on activism.

It's remarkable to think that, at its peak, membership in the BPP was estimated at around 5,000 people.

Despite government repression and powerful opposition, they still managed to have a lasting influence on communities across the nation.

Today, many of their strategies are still used by activists nationwide.

From community service initiatives to political education campaigns, we continue to be inspired by their tireless commitment to bringing about a more just society for all.

As their slogan said: "Power to the People!"

Black Lives Matter

We stand in solidarity with the Black Lives Matter movement.

This powerful collective of activists and advocates has been working tirelessly to bring attention to the systemic racism that exists within our society and to fight for justice for those who have suffered from it.

We must recognize that this is an issue which has been present for a long time, and we can no longer ignore its presence in our lives.

By understanding the history of the movement, examining its impact on various aspects of society, and looking at ways we can move forward together, we can make meaningful progress towards creating a more equitable world.

History of the Movement

The Movement has been around for decades, but it's only recently that its voice has been heard loud and clear. The Black Lives Matter movement began in 2013 after the acquittal of George Zimmerman in the shooting death of Trayvon Martin. Since then, it has grown into a global network of activists fighting against systemic racism and police brutality.

It is an intersectional movement that seeks to address issues such as racial injustice, economic inequality, gender discrimination, and LGBTQ+ rights. The BLM movement is rooted in centuries-old struggles for civil rights and social justice. Its founders have drawn inspiration from the civil rights movements of the 1950s and 1960s as well as more recent efforts like Occupy Wall Street.

The organization works to bring attention to issues such as mass incarceration, police violence, voter suppression, immigration reform, and environmental justice. Through protests, rallies, marches, petitions, boycotts and other forms of direct action they are working to create lasting change in our society. BLM activists have made significant progress over the past few years by raising awareness about systemic racism and inspiring people around the world to take action against injustice.

They have also helped spark conversations about race relations in America that were long overdue. As we move forward with understanding systemic racism, we must continue to listen to those who are most affected by it - black people - so that real change can be achieved.

Understanding Systemic Racism

You can gain a better understanding of systemic racism by looking at examples such as the recent case of Breonna Taylor, an African-American woman who was fatally shot by police in her own home. This case is one example of how Black people are disproportionately affected by systemic racism.

From healthcare to education, Black people are treated differently and are often denied access to basic rights and services. Systemic racism has been embedded into institutions for decades, leading to economic inequality that further impacts communities of color.

For instance, studies have found that even when controlling for race and socioeconomic background, Black students are more likely than white students to be suspended or expelled from school. This speaks volumes about the inequity that exists within our society today.

It's clear that addressing systemic racism is essential in creating a more equitable society where everyone can flourish regardless of their racial identity. Systemic racism must be addressed through policy reform and public education initiatives which focus on educating people on the history of marginalization experienced by Black Americans throughout history and how it continues to impact them today.

Moreover, there needs to be meaningful conversations between all stakeholders in order to create lasting solutions rather than just quick fixes or band-aid solutions.

As we strive towards a more just future, it's important to consider the role media plays in perpetuating negative stereotypes about Black people as well as reinforcing ideas which uphold white supremacy culture. It's only through recognizing these issues and taking active steps towards dismantling them that true change will be achieved.

The Role of the Media

You play a critical role in combating systemic racism by understanding how the media perpetuates negative stereotypes about people of color and white supremacy culture.

The media is an influential tool that has the power to shape public opinion and attitudes toward certain groups, whether it be positive or negative. It can manipulate viewers into believing what it wants them to believe, without considering any underlying truth.

This can manifest itself in the form of damaging representations of people of color, which reinforces harmful stereotypes and reinforces white supremacy culture. Furthermore, news coverage often overlooks issues directly related to racism or frames incidents involving people of color as 'crimes' while ignoring similar actions taken by white individuals.

By recognizing these patterns within the media's coverage, we can better understand how systemic racism works and challenge unjust systems of oppression. Media literacy initiatives are one way to do this - they teach us how to identify bias in our news sources, recognize implicit messages behind stories, and question information presented as fact.

Additionally, supporting independent news outlets that amplify marginalized voices helps counter mainstream narratives and creates more equitable representation for all communities. These efforts have led to some progress in changing the way mainstream media covers issues related to race – however there is still much work left to be done in order for society to truly move towards a more just world where everyone's lives matter equally.

As we continue on this journey towards justice for all peoples regardless of race or ethnicity, understanding the role that media plays in perpetuating systemic racism provides an important foundation from which we can build upon as we strive towards equity and inclusion for all individuals impacted by its effects. With this knowledge base established, we can now turn our attention towards exploring BLM and the fight for justice going forward.

BLM and the Fight for Justice

Embark on a journey with us to explore how the Black community is striving for justice and equity in the face of systemic racism. Join us as we uncover the ways that BLM is challenging oppressive structures and advocating for freedom and liberation.

From protests and rallies to social media campaigns, Black Lives Matter has become a global movement dedicated to addressing racial injustice. In addition to advocacy work, BLM also focuses on policy change such as reforming police departments, increasing public resources in marginalized communities, and creating restorative justice systems.

The primary goal of BLM is to end institutionalized racism by dismantling unjust systems of power, privilege, and oppression. This includes disrupting anti-Blackness in all forms including education, employment opportunities, criminal justice system discrimination, healthcare disparities and more. To do this effectively, BLM seeks to shift cultural norms through education while also elevating awareness about issues facing Black people worldwide.

BLM has been successful in bringing attention to issues that have long existed but gone unchecked or ignored by many people outside of the Black community—including government officials. The momentum garnered from sustained activism has helped propel conversations around these topics into mainstream dialogue while putting pressure on organizations to be held accountable for their role in perpetuating inequality or not addressing it at all.

With this increased visibility comes greater potential for real change as we look ahead towards a more equitable future for all individuals regardless of race or ethnicity. As we move forward into this new era of progress toward true equality and inclusion let's continue our collective fight against injustice together which will ultimately lead us closer to achieving true liberation for everyone.

The Impact of BLM on Education

We've seen an unprecedented call for change in recent years, with the Black Lives Matter movement demanding justice and equality. This fight for justice has had a profound impact on education, both in terms of how students are taught and the curriculum that is offered.

The BLM movement has highlighted how systematic racism is still pervasive within schools, from implicit biases to outright discrimination. As such, there is an urgent need to create an educational system that truly values diversity and inclusion.

To this end, many schools have taken steps to revise their curricula by introducing new courses that focus on black history and culture. In addition, many institutions are also taking steps to tackle discriminatory practices against students of color by introducing initiatives like restorative justice programs or hiring more diverse faculty members.

By making these changes, we hope to build a future where all students can feel safe and respected within their learning environment. We must continue our efforts towards creating a more equitable educational system so that everyone can access the same opportunities regardless of race or socio-economic status.

With ongoing advocacy and commitment from all stakeholders involved in education, we will move closer towards achieving true equity in our society – something which cannot be accomplished overnight but instead requires continued effort over time.

Now let's examine how BLM has impacted the economy as well as other sectors of society.

The Impact of BLM on the Economy

As we've discussed, the Black Lives Matter movement has had a significant impact on education. Its message of justice and equality for all races has sparked conversations in schools about racism and its effects.

Now, let's turn to the economic impacts of this movement.

Numerically speaking, BLM protests have had an impressive effect on the economy:

- A 2020 report from Goldman Sachs estimated that nearly $4 billion was added to the U.S. economy as a result of BLM-related spending during 2020 alone.

- In response to calls for racial justice, many corporations pledged financial support for businesses owned by people of color—over $16 billion in 2020 alone according to Color of Change's "Corporate Accountability Index" report.

- The value of stocks related to diverse hiring or investment in black communities increased by 29%, while companies that did not make pledges saw stock prices drop 3%, according to data from Morningstar analyzed by Bloomberg News.

- Companies like Microsoft and Apple have dedicated millions of dollars towards diversity initiatives such as scholarships and internships for minority students and entrepreneurs within their respective companies and industries overall - this is expected to create hundreds if not thousands of jobs over time with these investments into minority owned businesses or initiatives led by people of color nationwide.

The ripple effect resulting from corporate donations has already begun; job creation, economic development projects, increases in wages, access to capital are just some examples where progress is being made across various sectors due to direct investments into people and organizations advocating for social change through their work at the local level or nationally under the banner of Black Lives Matter (BLM).

The Impact of BLM on Health Care

You've seen the economic impacts of the movement, now take a look at how it's affecting healthcare!

Black Lives Matter has had a significant impact on healthcare in many ways. One way is increased awareness of disparities in healthcare access and quality for minority communities.

The BLM movement has inspired people to speak up against racism within the healthcare system, bringing attention to issues such as unequal access to medical resources, discrimination from healthcare providers, insurance companies, and pharmaceuticals. This awareness has led to discussion about potential solutions including improved representation of minority voices in medical decision-making roles and expanded mental health services for minority communities.

Another way that BLM has impacted healthcare is through increased support for public health initiatives related to social justice issues. For example, many organizations have taken steps towards eliminating racial bias in medical research by making sure studies accurately represent diverse populations and reflecting their unique needs when it comes to treatments and medicines. There has also been an increase in funding for programs that provide better health outcomes for marginalized communities by addressing underlying factors like poverty or housing instability.

These efforts are making a difference but there is still much work left to be done before all individuals can receive equitable access to quality healthcare regardless of race or ethnicity. As we continue this conversation on social justice reform, it's essential that we keep in mind the progress made so far and stay committed to working towards greater equality moving forward—so everyone can enjoy the same standard of care they deserve.

Now let's move onto discussing how Black Lives Matter has shaped police reform efforts across the country.

The Impact of BLM on Police Reform

The BLM movement has sparked some much-needed changes in the way law enforcement treats citizens, and it's high time we all took notice! From demanding more policing accountability to advocating for body cameras on police officers, this movement is making a big difference in how we view law enforcement.

It's also important to recognize that these changes are coming from both grassroots and institutional levels. For example, the U.S. Department of Justice recently issued guidelines for state and local governments to reform their policing policies to ensure they are fair and just. These reforms have been shown to reduce misconduct cases, strengthen trust between police departments and communities, and promote greater transparency when handling citizen complaints against the police.

At the same time, there is still much work to be done. There are a number of areas where further change is needed before true equality can be achieved in our criminal justice system.

This includes reforming qualified immunity laws that protect officers from civil lawsuits; enacting fairer sentencing guidelines; eliminating racial profiling; introducing independent oversight bodies; among many others.

Fortunately, with continued pressure from activists as well as support from government agencies such as the Department of Justice, it appears that progress can continue to be made towards creating a more equitable society for all Americans regardless of race or ethnicity.

These advances made by the BLM movement show us what can happen when people come together to make real change happen - but they also demonstrate how far we still need go if everyone truly wants equal rights under the law for all citizens. Going forward, it will be critical for individuals at all levels of power - both within government institutions and in civil society - to recognize this need for reform and take action accordingly so that no one is left behind or denied basic rights due them simply because of who they are or where they come from.

With sustained effort on everyone's part, perhaps we can finally start down a path towards lasting justice for everyone in America today.

International Support for BLM

Since the emergence of the Black Lives Matter movement, it has garnered a tremendous amount of support from people and organizations around the world.

From major cities to small villages, many have made it clear that they're standing in solidarity with those protesting against police brutality and systemic racism in the United States.

International protests have taken place in countries such as Canada, Australia, New Zealand, France, Germany, India and Nigeria to name just a few.

Online petitions calling for justice have been signed by millions abroad.

Social media campaigns amplifying the message of BLM have reached far beyond US borders.

This international show of support is significant not only because it brings attention to an important issue but also because it serves as an example that this struggle isn't unique to America—racism is alive and well all over the world.

It demonstrates that what happens in America doesn't stay in America; its ripples can be felt around the globe.

This cross-cultural connection has helped fuel momentum within the movement which continues to evolve with each passing day.

It's become increasingly clear that if there's ever going to be real change then everyone needs to work together for a common cause—no matter where they're from or what language they speak.

As we move forward into new strategies for positive social reform, we must do so with this global perspective at heart.

Strategies for Moving Forward

As we look to the future, it's essential that we continue to join together in our efforts to create meaningful and lasting change. To do this, it's important to recognize there are multiple strategies required for moving forward.

These strategies include grassroots organizing, policy reform, education campaigns, and direct action. By coming together with diverse tactics, we can build more powerful coalitions and amplify our collective voice.

Grassroots organizing involves creating networks of people engaged in mutual support and collective action. It includes things like forming local chapters who are dedicated to educating their communities about issues of racism and injustice through workshops and discussions.

This type of networking allows us to pool resources and share knowledge on how best to advocate for change within our own communities as well as on a broader level.

Policy reform is another key strategy for achieving real progress in the struggle against racism. Through targeted lobbying efforts at the local, state, or federal levels, we can ensure that legislation truly reflects the values of justice and equity that we all strive towards.

Additionally, engaging with government officials through letters or public forums creates an opportunity for greater dialogue between those affected by current policies and those tasked with revising them -- leading to more effective outcomes for everyone involved.

Ultimately, it's imperative that we continue working together towards meaningful change both locally and globally as part of our ongoing effort towards creating a more equitable society for all people regardless of race or ethnicity. By uniting under these common goals while also utilizing a range of different tactics such as grassroots organizing or policy reform -- we are able to turn visions into reality so that justice may finally be served for all people across the world.

Frequently Asked Questions

What is the significance of the color black in the BLM movement?

We, as a society, have long associated the color black with strength and resilience. This is no different in the case of the BLM movement.

To many, wearing black symbolizes solidarity and resistance to systemic racism that disproportionately affects people of color in our country. Black has become an iconic representation for justice and freedom from oppression, just as it has been throughout history.

By wearing black, activists stand united against police brutality and racial injustice. The power of this color lies not only in its visual representation but also in its metaphorical implications—it serves as a reminder that there's more work to be done until true equality is achieved.

Are there any non-violent tactics used by the BLM movement?

Yes, there are many non-violent tactics employed by the BLM movement. These tactics include:

- Marches, rallies, and other forms of protest
- Engaging in civil disobedience such as sit-ins or boycotts
- Starting petitions and letter writing campaigns
- Participating in public education campaigns to spread awareness about racial injustice
- Creating support networks to help those affected by racism

All these activities work together to create long-lasting change and progress towards a more just society.

How has BLM impacted the lives of people of color outside of the U.S.?

We're standing at a crossroads, looking out across a global landscape of colors, cultures, and stories. The Black Lives Matter movement has had a profound impact for people of color outside of the United States.

It's been like a beacon of light in the dark night, offering hope that justice is possible and that change is possible. Through organizing and protests, they've created an international platform for their voices to be heard and to demand accountability from those in power.

They've sparked conversations about racism around the world and have opened up opportunities for dialogue about racial injustice on an unprecedented level.

How can allies of the BLM movement support without engaging in activism?

As allies of the movement, we can support without engaging in activism in a variety of ways.

We can stay informed on current events and issues concerning people of color, use our resources to contribute financially or donate supplies to organizations that are actively advocating for change, and speak out against racism and injustice where appropriate.

Additionally, we can share relevant articles, videos, or other media with our social networks to help spread awareness and understanding.

Finally, we can encourage those around us to have open conversations about race and privilege in order to create an environment of acceptance and understanding.

How can BLM help to create long-term solutions to racial inequality?

We, as a society, have the opportunity to create long-term solutions to racial inequality that go beyond just raising awareness.

To do this, we must take a holistic approach that involves not only recognizing and condemning oppressive systems but also actively engaging in conversations about how to dismantle them.

This means looking at racism and other forms of oppression from an intersectional perspective; seeing how different forms of discrimination are interrelated and connected.

It's also important to acknowledge the importance of education, both within traditional educational institutions and through community outreach programs such as BLM initiatives.

By working together, we can create sustainable change on a local and global level.

Conclusion

We've seen the power of solidarity and collective action in the Black Lives Matter movement.

We've come to understand systemic racism, and how it has played out in our educational systems, healthcare, and law enforcement.

While there's still much work to be done, we must also take pause and recognize the progress that's been made.

BLM has become a global phenomenon uniting people around the world in pursuit of justice for all.

By working together, we can continue to push for key reforms that make a meaningful difference in our communities.

Let's stand united with those who fight for an equitable future where everyone's lives are valued equally.

What Is Antifa?

We've all heard the term 'Antifa' but what does it mean? Antifa is a political movement that has gained significant attention in recent years, due to its stance against fascism and white supremacy. It's a controversial subject with strong opinions on both sides of the debate.

In this article we'll be exploring the origins, ideology, tactics and reactions to Antifa. We'll also look at the impact and media coverage of Antifa as well as whether or not it should be considered a terrorist group.

Finally, we'll take a look into the future of Antifa and what that might entail. Let's dive in and get to know this powerful political movement!

Origins of Antifa

The origins of this movement go back quite a ways. It's believed that the first antifascist groups may have formed in response to the rise of fascism in the early 20th century, with some even forming before World War II started.

After the war, groups known as 'antifaschistische Aktion' or 'Antifa' began popping up throughout Germany. Antifa quickly spread around Europe, and eventually made its way to North America in the 1980s.

Today, Antifa stands for anti-fascism and is seen as a form of radical protest against right-wing extremism and white supremacy. Supporters of Antifa are known for their commitment to direct action and confrontation of those they perceive as oppressive or discriminatory towards minority communities.

While their tactics can be controversial at times, they often subscribe to nonviolence principles like those put forward by Gandhi and Martin Luther King Jr. This commitment to challenging oppressive systems through direct action has been taken up by many activists around the globe who see fascism as an ever-present threat.

As such, many antifascist groups today remain vigilant in monitoring far-right activity online, in politics, and on university campuses – always ready to challenge it head on whenever possible. This vigilance allows them to work towards ensuring that everyone has access to safety regardless of socioeconomic status or identity.

With this goal in mind, antifascist activism continues to evolve and grow as we move into a new era of societal change - aiming always for greater equity and justice for all people.

Ideology and Goals of Antifa

Opposing fascism, Antifa's goals are clear; yet they remain shrouded in mystery. Antifa is a decentralized movement that seeks to combat the rise of far-right ideologies and movements.

Their goals are:

- To challenge oppressive systems of power

- To protect vulnerable communities from hate groups
- To promote social justice and equity for all people
- To create an inclusive society free from discrimination and bigotry

The ideology behind Antifa is rooted in anti-authoritarianism, anarchism, socialism, communism, and other left-wing philosophies that prioritize collective action over individualism. They believe that direct action is necessary to confront oppressive forces such as racism, sexism, homophobia, transphobia, xenophobia, ableism, and classism.

Through protests and demonstrations, they aim to disrupt the status quo by challenging those who seek to maintain it through violence or intimidation tactics.

Antifa activists strive to create a world where everyone can live with dignity regardless of race or gender identity. They envision a world where everyone has access to basic human rights like healthcare and education without fear of persecution or oppression. Their ultimate goal is a world free from hatred and injustice – a world where everyone can live peacefully together without prejudice or discrimination.

With this vision in mind, they continue their fight against fascism wherever it may arise, ready to take on whatever challenges come their way in pursuit of a better future for all humanity.

Tactics Used by Antifa

You can witness Antifa's commitment to their cause through the variety of tactics they employ to challenge oppressive forces. One of the most visible strategies is non-violent direct action, which consists of protests, boycotts, and occupations. This type of protest has been used by many civil rights activists in order to draw attention to a particular issue or movement.

Antifa also utilizes digital tools such as social media campaigns and online petitions to spread awareness and amplify their message. In addition, Antifa members are willing to engage in physical confrontations with fascists or those who support them if necessary. They often use protective gear such as helmets and masks when engaging in these activities so that they can remain anonymous while still making their presence known.

Antifa also engages in educational outreach efforts aimed at raising awareness about fascism, racism, xenophobia, homophobia, and other forms of oppression. Through workshops, lectures, film screenings, and other events, they attempt to educate people on why it is important for everyone to stand up against injustice wherever it may be found. By sharing stories from real people who have faced discrimination or violence due to their identity, they strive to create greater empathy among allies and encourage more people to take part in anti-fascist actions.

In addition to these public activities, Antifa also engages in research aimed at uncovering information about fascist groups and individuals who are actively working against progressive values. By doing this research, they hope not only to inform others about the dangers posed by far-right ideologies but also to make it easier for law enforcement agencies to identify a potential threat before any harm is done.

With these various tactics combined, antifascists seek not only to oppose fascism but also to build solidarity amongst those on the left who share their core values of justice and equality for all persons regardless of race or identity. As we move forward into an uncertain future, we must remember that even though some battles may be lost, there is always strength in numbers when standing together against hate.

Reactions to Antifa

Antifa's commitment to their cause has led to mixed reactions, ranging from admiration for their bravery to condemnation of their tactics. Many people applaud the courage they show when taking a stand against social injustice.

Others view them as an extremist group and are critical of the violent methods they employ in pursuit of their goals. Some also believe that Antifa's actions are counterproductive and further polarize different sides of an issue instead of finding common ground.

Despite this criticism, there is no denying that Antifa helps draw attention to issues which would otherwise be neglected by those in power. By making themselves visible at protests and through other channels, they help amplify the voices of those who have been marginalized or silenced for too long.

Through their efforts, many injustices have been brought into the spotlight and have become part of mainstream conversations about important topics such as racism, sexism, homophobia, xenophobia, etc.

Overall, while opinions on Antifa remain divided even among activists fighting for similar causes, it cannot be denied that they provide an often-needed reminder that we still live in a world where justice is not always served equally or fairly. This serves as a galvanizing force for positive change so that all people can enjoy equal rights under the law regardless of skin color or any other factor.

Moving forward into a more equitable future requires us to build bridges across divides rather than erecting walls between groups - something which Antifa strives towards with every action they take.

Criticism of Antifa

Despite their goals of creating a more equitable future, Antifa's tactics have been heavily criticized, leaving many to question the efficacy of their means.

Antifa has been accused of using violent tactics that can result in property damage and injury, recruiting minors into their activities, failing to differentiate between peaceful protests and those advocating for violence, and not providing clear solutions or alternatives to oppressive systems.

Critics argue that these strategies put protestors at risk and do little to advance the cause they are fighting for. It is also argued that they do not engage with those who disagree enough and use confrontational methods rather than constructive dialogue which could be more effective in achieving long term change.

Some fear that by responding too aggressively, it only strengthens the resolve of those against them. This leaves many people feeling uncertain about supporting Antifa's efforts or even attending political demonstrations at all.

This criticism calls into question whether Antifa's approach is beneficial or detrimental for the movement towards social justice. As debate continues, it is important to consider how best we can support meaningful progress while maintaining our safety as individuals and as a society.

Support for Antifa

You may not agree with their methods, but as the old adage goes: "the ends justify the means" when it comes to supporting Antifa.

Supporters of Antifa view them as a necessary counterweight to right-wing extremism and white nationalism.

They believe that in order for society to continue progressing towards a more equitable future, it is essential that these movements be combated firmly.

It is also argued by many supporters of Antifa that they are taking action on behalf of people who cannot do so themselves due to systemic forces such as racism or sexism.

Antifa supporters argue that because fascism has been so effective in turning democracies into dictatorships, preemptive measures must be taken to prevent this from happening again.

To them, this means using any means necessary to prevent the spread of hate speech and violence propagated by far-right groups.

As such, they see themselves as freedom fighters working towards an inclusive society where everyone can live peacefully without fear of oppression or bigotry.

The support for Antifa is strong among those who have faced discrimination at some point in their life - whether it be racial minorities or LGBT+ individuals - and understand how dangerous unchecked extremism can become if left unaddressed for too long.

This collective understanding drives people from all walks of life to stand behind Antifa's mission and push back against oppressive ideologies wherever they may surface — both online and offline — in order to protect our right to live free from fear and hatred.

With this in mind, it's clear why so many people express their support for Antifa's cause despite its controversial tactics; they recognize that sometimes drastic actions are needed in order for true safety and justice to prevail.

Moving forward, attention must now turn towards exploring how antifascist activists interact with the media landscape...

Antifa and the Media

You may not always agree with their tactics, but their presence in the media is a testament to how seriously Antifa takes its mission of combating hate and bigotry.

The success of Antifa's message relies on the attention it receives from news outlets and other media channels. This means that Antifa must actively maintain a positive presence in order to ensure that its messages are heard by wide audiences.

In recent years, there has been an increase in coverage of both positive and negative aspects of Antifa's activities. While some view this as necessary for public safety, others argue that it serves only to inflame tensions between those who oppose hate and those who support it.

No matter which side you take, one thing is certain: Antifa has had a significant impact on the way people perceive issues related to racism, sexism, homophobia and other forms of discrimination. Through their actions in the media—whether through protests or through interviews—Antifa has made sure that these issues remain at the forefront of public discourse.

Whether or not one agrees with all of their strategies, it cannot be denied that they have caused many people to reconsider their attitudes towards prejudice and inequality in society today.

As we move forward into this uncertain future, it is clear that Antifa will continue to play an important role in shaping popular opinion about these topics. Their involvement creates opportunities for dialogue and understanding between different sides, while also providing a platform for marginalized voices to have their say on matters concerning social justice.

With this in mind, the next step for us should be exploring how best we can use our collective power to create real change going forward.

Impact of Antifa

Antifa's work has undeniably had a powerful impact on society, sparking conversations and inspiring action against hatred and prejudice. They have become a beacon of hope for many who face bigotry and persecution in their everyday lives, providing a platform to speak out against oppressive systems.

Their presence at protests has been seen as an act of courage, especially when they stand up to armed police officers or white supremacist groups. With their boldness comes great risk, however; Antifa members are often targets of violence from the very people that they oppose.

Although there is still much debate over the efficacy of Antifa's methods, many acknowledge that their actions have pushed the conversation forward in regards to difficult topics such as racism and fascism. The combination of civil disobedience tactics with direct action has created a unique form of activism that resonates with large numbers of people around the world.

In particular, young people recognize Antifa's willingness to put themselves in harm's way for what they believe in and are more likely to engage in similar acts themselves.

By standing up for those who cannot stand up for themselves, Antifa has forced individuals and governments alike to confront uncomfortable truths about our societies and take steps towards creating more inclusive environments free from oppression. It is clear that whatever your opinion may be on their methods, their presence is here to stay - making it even more important for us all to think critically about how we can create positive change together without resorting to hatred or violence.

With this goal in mind, let's move towards answering the next question: Is Antifa a terrorist group?

Is Antifa a Terrorist Group?

Considering the current debate, it's clear that Antifa stands at a crossroads, with two paths diverging before them like a fork in the road.

One path leads to recognition as a legitimate organization with their political views being taken into account, while the other leads to condemnation as a terrorist outfit and further exclusion from mainstream society.

Proponents of labeling Antifa as a terrorist group point to violent actions they have taken in response to far-right groups such as neo-Nazis and white supremacists.

Detractors argue that this violence has only been used in self-defense or in defense of others who are vulnerable and cannot protect themselves.

The discourse about whether Antifa is a terrorist group or not has become increasingly heated, with both sides unwilling to concede ground.

Those who consider Antifa's methods too extreme are quick to point out unsupervised acts of vandalism by some antifascists while ignoring the peaceful protests that many members take part in.

On the other hand, those defending Antifa often neglect to recognize when its members cross a line into violent behavior without provocation or cause for concern.

Both sides need to take into account the fact that there are multiple faces of antifascism and accept responsibility for understanding what these mean on an individual basis rather than painting all antifascists with one broad brushstroke.

No matter where one lands on this issue, it's important to remember that violence should never be seen as an acceptable response when dealing with any political issue – even if it's done out of frustration or desperation for change.

However, it would be wrong for us to simply ignore the grievances which led individuals down this path in the first place and view them simply as perpetrators instead of people trying desperately (though misguidedly) to make their voices heard within our society.

With this understanding of past events firmly established, we can now look forward towards what lies ahead for antifascism and how its outlook could shape up over time.

The Future of Antifa

As the debate surrounding Antifa continues, it's important to consider what the future will hold for this group of activists. While their methods and tactics may be controversial, there is no denying that Antifa has been successful in achieving some of its goals.

The goal of any activist group is to make change happen, and as long as those goals remain relevant, it's likely that Antifa will continue to exist in some form or another. It's also worth noting that many people view Antifa as a positive force for good in society, helping to bring about much needed social change.

The future of Antifa is uncertain; however, it seems likely that they will continue to fight for what they believe in despite potential backlash from certain powerful individuals or groups. As their numbers grow and more people become aware of their cause, the impact they have on society could become even greater than before. This could lead to more widespread acceptance and understanding of the issues they are fighting for, which could help create lasting positive changes within our society.

No matter how one feels about Antifa, it's clear that this organization has already had an impact on society since its inception. Whether their presence remains strong or wanes over time remains to be seen but it's undeniable that they have made a difference in people's lives by standing up for what they believe in.

Going forward, we can only hope that these activists continue to succeed in creating necessary social change and ultimately a better world for all inhabitants.

Frequently Asked Questions

How does Antifa recruit members?

We've all heard of Antifa, but how do they recruit members?

In an effort to create a safe and secure society, Antifa actively encourages individuals to join their cause. Engagingly, they seek out those who share their passion for justice and equality in both word and deed.

Alliteration emphasizes their ability to attract advocates through accessible avenues; from email list servers to community meetings, there are plenty of opportunities for potential participants to get involved. In addition to online outreach, Antifa is also known for hosting public events which demonstrate solidarity and strength in numbers.

With these open-ended approaches, it's easy to see why so many choose to answer the call for justice by joining the ranks of Antifa.

Is Antifa a global movement?

We've been asking ourselves if Antifa is a global movement. The answer is yes; it has become an international movement that seeks to oppose fascism wherever it may exist.

Antifa's members are spread across the world, from North America to Europe and beyond, where they utilize peaceful protest tactics as well as more direct action against oppressive regimes.

Their message of solidarity and resistance has resonated with people around the globe, making them a powerful force in the fight for human rights.

Is it legal to be a part of Antifa?

We often hear about the Antifa movement, but is it actually legal to be a part of it? It depends on where you're located and what activities are taking place.

In most countries, peaceful protests and non-violent civil disobedience are allowed under local laws. However, if the actions become violent or break other laws then participating in Antifa could be seen as illegal.

That being said, it's important to remember that all people have the right to peacefully protest without fear of retribution from authorities.

Does Antifa receive any financial support?

We've all heard of the mysterious Antifa, but does it receive any financial support?

Reports suggest that Antifa has been able to rely on an underground network of donors and supporters to fund their activities. It seems that those who believe in the cause are willing to part with whatever funds they can spare, whether it is a few dollars or hundreds.

This grassroots approach is allowing Antifa to stay afloat and continue fighting for what they believe in. Though there's no concrete evidence of how much money they have access to, it's clear that Antifa is determined to make its voice heard no matter the cost.

What role does Antifa play in current social and political movements?

We, as citizens of the world, are witnessing a new wave of social and political movements that are shaking up the status quo. Antifa is at the forefront of this movement; its members are actively advocating for change by engaging in protests and demonstrations to raise awareness about issues such as racism, police brutality, and white supremacy.

They also serve to support other progressive causes such as LGBTQ rights, gender equality, and environmental protection. By standing up for these important causes, Antifa serves as an important voice in pushing for positive change in our current society.

Conclusion

We've seen that Antifa has had a major impact on the US and other countries around the world. Their tactics have been met with both support and criticism, but there's no denying their presence in today's society.

For example, when demonstrations against police brutality took place across the country in 2020, Antifa was present at many of them. They served as protectors from potential violence caused by counter-protesters and even law enforcement.

Ultimately, while it remains to be seen what the future holds for Antifa, we can say with certainty that they will continue to challenge oppressive systems wherever they find them. Whether you agree or disagree with their methods is up to you - one thing's for sure: Antifa isn't going away anytime soon.

Call to Action to Save Black History Studies in Our Schools

We've all heard about the importance of Black history studies, but it's never been more crucial than today.

It's no exaggeration to say that without urgent action, black history studies could disappear from our schools forever!

The future of education needs to include a greater focus on the history of African Americans and other people of color.

This article explores why this is so important and offers practical suggestions for how we can ensure that black history remains a major part of school curricula going forward.

Understanding the History of Black People

It's essential to recognize the need for a comprehensive understanding of the rich and varied history of African Americans in order to truly appreciate its significance.

From slavery, to Jim Crow laws, to the civil rights movement, Black history is an important part of American history that must be fully explored.

An appreciation for African American culture can also be gained by studying both traditional and contemporary art forms such as music, literature, dance, and visual arts. Not only do these expressions provide insight into the experiences of Black people in America throughout time, but they also allow us to understand the ingenuity of a people who have been forced to endure oppression and yet find ways to express themselves creatively.

Gaining knowledge about African American history is only one step towards embracing inclusivity within our educational systems. It is equally important that we create curriculums that reflect diverse perspectives and foster environments free from racism and discrimination.

This means creating spaces where all students feel seen, heard, appreciated and respected regardless of race or ethnicity; classrooms where teachers are provided with adequate resources to teach accurate accounts of marginalized groups; and providing extra efforts towards bridging gaps between different communities through collaboration initiatives like mentorship programs or cross-cultural dialogues.

To move away from narrow narratives about Black people's presence in this country requires an intentional effort on behalf of educators everywhere.

Recognizing the need for comprehensive education about Black histories lays a strong foundation for inclusive learning experiences that are necessary for true academic growth among all cultures represented in our schools today.

In turn, this will lead to more equitable access across all disciplines while deepening our collective understanding around what it means to be a part of this nation's complex tapestry made up of individuals with unique backgrounds and stories worth preserving now—and into future generations—for years to come.

Moving forward requires urgency on behalf of educators everywhere who recognize the value in empowering students with diverse perspectives so that together we may build bridges instead walls when it comes time to honor our shared histories as Americans no matter how different they might appear at first glance.

The Need for Inclusive Education

We must fight for an education system that embraces diversity and inclusion, or else this crucial chapter of the past will be lost to future generations like a forgotten meme.

The lack of Black history studies in our schools is a symptom of a larger problem: systemic racism. It's not enough to simply add more Black history studies into the curriculum; we also need to ensure that these courses are being taught in an inclusive environment, free from bias and discrimination.

We must strive towards creating educational spaces where all students feel safe and respected regardless of race or ethnicity; only then can we truly learn from our shared histories. By taking action now, we can ensure that this important part of our history is preserved for generations to come—and more importantly, it'll help us continue the work towards dismantling systemic racism and other forms of inequality.

The impact of systemic racism on education is vast and complex—but by taking steps today, we can make sure that this critical piece of our national identity isn't forgotten in the future.

The Impact of Systemic Racism

You've got the power to make a difference in addressing systemic racism and its far-reaching effects on our education system. Systemic racism is entrenched in all aspects of society, from the criminal justice system to educational institutions. It's been perpetuated for centuries and continues to present day, creating disparities between racial groups within educational systems.

Here are five ways systemic racism impacts our education system:

- Racial segregation still exists in many school districts today, with some schools having student populations that are nearly exclusively one race or another.

- Students of color often face harsher discipline than white students for similar behaviors.

- Schools in low-income areas often lack resources such as qualified teachers, advanced course offerings, and extracurricular activities.

- There is a history of exclusion of people of color from higher education opportunities.

- Educational materials used by teachers may contain biases about people of color.

These disparities create an environment where black students can feel marginalized and less valued than their white peers. This contributes to lower test scores and graduation rates among black students.

The impact of systemic racism on our education system threatens future generations' access to quality educational opportunities. It's up to us to take action now so that we can usher in more equitable learning environments for all children. By making black history studies part of our curriculum, we'll help ensure that the next generation is equipped with knowledge that acknowledges the full history and contributions of African Americans throughout US history.

The Importance of Black History Studies

Nobody can deny the fact that introducing Black History Studies into our educational system is absolutely essential to combat systemic racism, and it's a task that needs to be taken on with lightning speed. In order to fully appreciate the importance of Black History Studies, one must first recognize the contributions African Americans have made throughout history. From inventors like George Washington Carver to musicians like Louis Armstrong, African American individuals have been responsible for some of the most influential moments in history. Furthermore, understanding Africa's complex history is paramount in order to understand its Diaspora and how this has shaped identities all over the world.

Advantages	Disadvantages
Allows for deeper appreciation of black culture	Requires additional resources and time from educators
Encourages conversations about difficult topics such as slavery and oppression	May cause students discomfort or distress when discussing sensitive topics
Connects current events with historical context for better understanding of social inequalities today	Curriculum may be too broad or too narrow depending on school district size/resources available

By giving students an accurate representation of African American culture, we can create more inclusive classrooms where everyone feels safe and respected. Additionally, having an enlightened view of our shared past allows us to move forward together in creating a more equitable society. It is clear that teaching Black History Studies in schools is not only beneficial but also necessary if we want to address systemic racism head-on. With great care and consideration for diverse student backgrounds we can bridge gaps between cultures while simultaneously tackling inequality within our education system.

Addressing Inequalities in Education

Taking bold steps to address inequalities in education is the only way to truly make a difference, and the saying 'knowledge is power' couldn't be more true.

In order for black history studies to be saved in our schools, we must start by recognizing and addressing existing educational inequalities. This means:

- Ensuring that all students have access to high-quality resources
- Providing equal learning opportunities for all regardless of race or socio-economic status
- Offering culturally relevant curricula that celebrates diverse histories and cultures
- Hiring a diverse staff that reflects the student population
- Investing in programs like mentoring and after school activities

It's also important to acknowledge the systemic racism present within many of our current education systems, which often results in fewer opportunities for black students compared to their white peers. We must challenge these systems if we want to create an equitable educational environment where everyone can thrive.

To do this, we must take concrete steps towards creating an inclusive culture of respect and understanding among educators and students alike. These efforts could include providing ongoing professional development trainings on cultural competency as well as implementing policies that actively protect against discrimination or harassment at school.

By taking actionable steps towards creating an equitable learning environment, we can ensure our schools are safe spaces where every student feels respected and supported.

Transitioning into the next section about 'the benefits of inclusive education', it's clear that promoting diversity in classrooms has numerous advantages not just for those identifying with minority backgrounds but also for society as a whole.

The Benefits of Inclusive Education

Inclusive education has the potential to bring about positive changes that benefit everyone, not just those identifying with minority backgrounds. It is an opportunity to address disparities in educational access and outcomes by creating a learning environment that welcomes all students regardless of race, gender or socio-economic background. This form of inclusive education can provide multiple benefits for students, teachers and society alike.

Benefits	Impact
Increased Accessibility	More equitable opportunities for learning among students from different backgrounds
Improved Social Skills	Enhanced collaboration between diverse groups of students through classroom interactions and team activities
Motivation to Learn	Increased performance when students feel included and valued due to an inclusive learning environment
Better Understanding of Diverse Perspectives	Deeper comprehension of different cultures through direct engagement with peers from various cultural backgrounds
Positive Cultural Identity Formation within Students	Cultivated appreciation for one's own culture as well as respect for other cultures amongst youth during their formative years.

Inclusive education promotes understanding among diverse groups which helps create a more cohesive society in the long run. Furthermore, it encourages critical thinking skills in young people by providing them with multiple perspectives on any given topic. Moreover, it also makes classrooms more welcoming and safe spaces where everyone can express themselves without fear of judgment or discrimination. All these advantages demonstrate why there is such a strong case to be made for including black history studies into our school curriculums so all our children can gain knowledge about the rich diversity found in our country's past and present societies. By leveraging resources to increase access to black history studies we will enable today's youth to become better educated global citizens tomorrow.

Leveraging Resources to Increase Access to Black History Studies

You can help create a more equitable future by leveraging resources to increase access to black history studies in our educational system. For example, according to the National Center for Education Statistics, only 8% of educators teaching American History are African-American professionals. This speaks volumes about the lack of representation when it comes to including Black history in our classrooms.

To bridge this gap and ensure that Black students have access to culturally relevant curriculum, we must work together with organizations and institutions that specialize in preserving and promoting African American history and culture. By utilizing these resources, we can create partnerships between schools and community centers that provide meaningful opportunities for Black students to engage with their own heritage while strengthening their understanding of the larger US narrative.

Additionally, through collaboration with museums, libraries, universities, and other institutions dedicated to African American scholarship and artistry, we can bring diverse perspectives into our classrooms - enabling teachers to develop truly inclusive curriculums that celebrate the contributions of all cultures not just those traditionally taught in academic settings.

We must also recognize the need for financial support from both public and private entities as well as individual philanthropic efforts if we are going to make any real progress towards providing accessible black history studies across all levels of education. Only then will our children be able to benefit from a comprehensive view on what it means to be an American citizen – one where they feel empowered by their cultural identity rather than ashamed or excluded from it.

By investing in resources that prioritize inclusionary education initiatives, we can ensure a brighter future for generations yet come.

Developing Effective Curriculum and Teaching Strategies

We're committed to helping teachers bring Black History studies into their classrooms, and we want to share our knowledge about developing effective curriculum and teaching strategies.

Discover how you can develop effective curriculum and teaching strategies to promote the inclusion of diverse perspectives in the classroom. In order to ensure all students are able to benefit from Black History studies, it's important that educators make sure these topics are integrated across multiple disciplines.

For example, a history class should not be the only place where a student learns about the civil rights movement – they should also learn about it in an art or music class as well. Additionally, educators should strive for an inclusive environment where open dialogue and critical thinking around different perspectives is encouraged.

To truly make Black History studies part of a student's education, we must understand what sorts of materials are available for use in the classroom and how best to use them so that all students feel safe and respected while learning.

Educators should focus on finding materials that provide accurate information about both past and current events related to race relations, as well as those which illustrate how people with different racial identities have made significant contributions throughout history. By utilizing these types of resources, teachers can create meaningful learning opportunities for their students while ensuring that their unique experiences are respected at all times.

With these considerations in mind, we now turn our attention towards engaging with the community in order to further increase access to Black History studies in our schools.

Engaging with the Community

Now that we've discussed developing effective curriculum and teaching strategies to make sure black history studies are represented in our schools, it's time to turn our attention to engaging with the community. We need to recognize that learning about the unique contributions of black people throughout history is not just about what happens in the classroom. It's also essential for us to receive support from other members of our community who can help us ensure this important part of history remains front and center.

One way we can engage with the community is by hosting events such as lectures, workshops, or panel discussions on topics related to black history studies. These events give us an opportunity to share information about the importance of understanding this aspect of history with the larger community. Additionally, they allow members of the broader community to be involved in helping us achieve our goal of making sure Black History Studies are taught in our schools.

We must also reach out to local organizations and leaders who may be able to offer their support or assistance in any way possible. This could include connecting us with resources such as books, films, and guest speakers which can deepen students' understanding and appreciation for black history studies. Furthermore, these individuals might even be interested in coming into classrooms during certain periods throughout the year when teachers are covering relevant topics related to African-American heritage so that students have a chance to learn from people directly affected by these issues firsthand.

By taking these steps towards engaging with members of our local communities, we can create a network of supporters who will ultimately help further our mission: ensuring black history studies remain part of educational curricula today and for many years into the future.

With everyone working together toward this common goal, we can take action now so that future generations will benefit from knowing all facets of American History without exclusion or prejudice. As we move forward together toward achieving this shared vision for education equity, let's remember that it starts with each one of us joining forces and taking action right now!

Taking Action to Ensure Black History Studies in Schools

As we strive for educational equity, it's essential to take steps now to ensure Black History Studies remain part of our school curricula for generations to come. We must recognize that Black History Studies is more than a one-time course or lesson; it needs to be embedded into the fabric of the culture and curriculum within our schools.

Starting with faculty, administrators need to create an environment that is supportive of these studies and encourages students' learning in this area. Administrators should also provide resources such as books, articles, films, and other materials about African American history.

The next step is involving parents in their children's education. Parents can help by attending meetings on curriculum updates and advocating for more diverse teaching methods. They can also volunteer as mentors at local schools or assist teachers in creating engaging lessons about African American history. Additionally, they can work with community leaders and organizations on initiatives like book drives or fundraisers that support Black History Studies programs.

We must continue to push for more inclusive education systems so our classrooms accurately reflect the diversity found throughout society today. To do this, we must commit ourselves to taking actionable steps towards ensuring Black History Studies are included in all levels of education — from elementary school all the way through college — so future generations will have access to a fuller understanding of America's past and present history.

It's up to us now to stand up for what's right and make sure these important studies remain part of our schools.

Frequently Asked Questions

What resources are available to help implement black history studies in schools?

We've been on a quest to uncover resources that could help us implement Black History studies in our schools, and the results are exciting!

We've found numerous online tools that make it easy for educators to find resources for their classes. From interactive lesson plans and educational videos to engaging activities and comprehensive curriculum materials, there is no shortage of options available.

And with the right guidance, these resources can be used by teachers to create an engaging and meaningful experience for students as they learn about the significant contributions made by African Americans throughout history.

How can we ensure that black history studies are integrated into the school curriculum?

We must ensure that black history studies are integrated into the school curriculum if we want to adequately represent and recognize the vital contributions of African Americans.

To accomplish this, we need to take action by advocating for curricula that incorporates black history into core classes.

Additionally, we should push for increased funding of supplemental programs and materials that teach about African American culture and history in a meaningful way.

We also need to urge schools to hire more diverse staff who can bring their unique perspectives on race, culture, and history into the classroom.

By taking these steps, we can ensure that black history is honored and respected in our educational institutions.

How can we best support teachers to effectively teach black history?

We can best support teachers to effectively teach black history by providing them with resources, training, and a platform to share their knowledge.

Ensuring that they have access to the latest research, teaching materials, and technology will empower them to bring the subject matter alive in the classroom.

Creating an open dialogue between administrators and teachers about how best to incorporate black history into their curriculums will foster an environment of collaboration that leads to meaningful learning experiences for students.

How can we ensure that the community is engaged in the push for black history studies in schools?

We, as a community, are passionate about preserving and celebrating Black history in our schools. According to recent studies, an astounding 90 percent of Americans believe that Black history should be taught in schools.

That's why it's imperative that we work together to ensure our local schools are actively engaged in teaching this important subject. We can do this by reaching out to school boards and administrators to discuss the importance of including Black history studies into the curriculum.

We can also organize educational events for parents and students within the community to inform them about the value of learning black history. With our collective efforts, we can help create a more equitable future for all students through making sure that black history is never forgotten or overlooked again.

How can we measure the impact of black history studies on student outcomes?

We're interested in understanding how black history studies can affect student outcomes. To measure this impact, we need to establish an evaluation system that tracks both qualitative and quantitative data.

This could include surveys of students to gauge changes in attitudes towards diversity and inclusion, as well as tracking metrics such as grades, attendance rates, and standardized test scores. By gathering this information over time, we can gain a better understanding of the long-term effects of introducing black history into our schools.

Conclusion

We have a duty to ensure that the history of Black people isn't forgotten or overlooked. We must take action now and work together to create an educational system that gives due respect and recognition to Black history studies in our schools.

Symbolically, we can visualize a future where all children are given equal access to education, regardless of their racial background. It's time for us to come together as one voice and make sure this vision becomes a reality.

Let's stand up for what's right, speak out against injustice, and strive towards true equality for all.

Call to Action for Young Black Children to Become Activist for Social Change

We all know the world isn't perfect, and it's time we do something about it!

We hear about social injustices every single day – and now is the time for young black children to step up and make a change.

It's an exciting time to be alive: with so many tools at our fingertips, there are plenty of ways to create awareness and take action.

From joining organizations to writing letters, there's never been a better opportunity for young people to become activists for social change.

So let's get started – it's time for us to get involved and make our voices heard!

Understanding Social Justice Issues

Gaining an understanding of social justice issues is essential for making a meaningful impact in the world. To do this, young black children should be encouraged to explore the history of marginalization and oppression that has been faced by minority groups throughout history. By learning about moments where people have fought against injustice and won, they can gain inspiration for how to make a difference in their own communities.

This includes looking at examples from civil rights movements such as the push for LGBTQIA+ rights or the fight for reproductive health access. When young black children understand these struggles, it will help them develop empathy and understand what it means to stand up for what's right.

In addition, educating kids about microaggressions and privilege will help them recognize how subtle forms of racism and discrimination are still present today. Teaching them how to use language that's inclusive of all genders is also important so that they can create positive conversations around identity and respect differences among one another.

Making sure young black children are aware of implicit bias within institutions like education or employment opportunities will also be beneficial since it shows them how small actions can have large effects on society as a whole.

By having an awareness around systemic inequalities, young black children will be better equipped with knowledge when it comes time to take action towards social change. Understanding these topics first provides a basis for further learning about movements such as Black Lives Matter so they can become informed activists who work towards creating an equitable society where everyone is respected and valued equally.

Learning About the Black Lives Matter Movement

Discovering the Black Lives Matter Movement can be truly inspiring and empowering, encouraging us to stand up for our rights! The BLM movement is a powerful call to action for young black children to recognize the history of oppression and inequality that their communities have faced.

It's an opportunity for them to learn about how they can take action and make a positive difference in their own lives and in the world around them. Young black children can use this knowledge to become activists, advocating for social justice issues such as police brutality, racial discrimination, voter suppression, poverty, and education reform.

Learning about the BLM movement's mission can also help young people understand how they can use their voices to challenge existing systems of power that are reinforcing oppressive structures. The BLM movement is an important reminder that we must always strive for progress towards equity and freedom for all people.

As young activists, it's our responsibility to stay informed on current events so that we can fight against injustice wherever it exists. With these efforts, we're better equipped to create meaningful change in our communities by taking direct action towards achieving social justice.

As we continue forward with this work, let us remember that together we have the power to ensure a brighter future for generations to come. Moving on from here then - finding ways to take action - will be key in helping us achieve our goals of creating true equality for all people.

Finding Ways to Take Action

Taking action is the only way to create a more just and equitable society; it's time to make our voices heard and fight for what's right! One great way young black children can take action is through joining organizations and groups that are dedicated to social change.

Organizations like Black Lives Matter, NAACP, Color of Change, and others are all actively fighting for justice in society. Joining such an organization not only gives young black children a platform to use their voice but also provides them with support from other members in the group. They can work together to brainstorm ideas on how best they can bring about change.

Young black children should also look into ways of getting involved in local community activism. This may involve attending protests or rallies, volunteering at events or fundraisers, or helping out with initiatives like voter registration drives. Connecting with local activists will help young black children understand the issues being addressed on a grassroots level and learn more about how to take part in meaningful dialogue with their peers and other stakeholders.

Young people have incredible power when they come together around a shared goal – this is why taking action is so important! It's time for young black children everywhere to stand up for what's right and demand justice in their communities.

As we join forces with allied organizations, mobilize our own networks, and reach out to our representatives we can make real progress towards true equity in society. From there we can move forward towards creating lasting positive change on both local and global levels.

Joining Organizations and Groups

You can make a real difference by joining organizations and groups that are devoted to meaningful causes, allowing you to connect with like-minded people and become part of a larger movement for justice.

This is an opportunity for young black children to join forces with others who share similar values and beliefs, creating the potential for more powerful collective action. Through these connections, young black children can learn from the experiences of those committed to social change while also contributing their own ideas and energy to help create lasting impact.

Joining together in this way gives them the chance to amplify their voice on important issues while also providing support for each other as they work towards common goals.

In addition, many organizations and groups offer resources such as training programs, mentorship opportunities, or advocacy campaigns that can help equip young black children with the skills necessary for effective activism. By accessing these tools they'll be better able to understand how systems of oppression work and how individual actions can lead to systemic change.

Furthermore, learning from those already engaged in activism will provide valuable guidance about how best use their voices and take action in meaningful ways that reflect their values. Being part of an organization or group dedicated to social justice provides young black children with a platform to express themselves freely without fear or judgement while also connecting them with other activists working towards the same objectives.

With this type of support structure in place, it becomes possible for them to exercise their rights as citizens more effectively while making a genuine contribution towards positive transformation within their communities.

Exercising Their Rights as Citizens

Gaining a sense of empowerment and understanding your rights as a citizen can help you take meaningful steps towards making an impact. As young black children, it's important to understand the power that comes with being citizens.

We have the right to vote, which allows us to make our voices heard in government decisions.

We have the right to protest peacefully, which allows us to demonstrate against unjust laws or policies.

We have the right to freedom of speech and expression, so we can raise awareness about social issues affecting our communities.

We have the right to access public education and other resources that can be used for furthering our activism initiatives.

By understanding these rights and exercising them in a responsible manner, we can become more effective activists for social change that has real-world implications.

As such, it's essential for young black children everywhere to educate themselves on their rights as citizens in order to maximize their potential for making an impact on society's injustices and inequalities.

With this knowledge under their belt, they'll be better prepared to move onto educating others about social issues they're passionate about.

Educating Others about Social Issues

Inspired by their newfound understanding of their rights as citizens, they can ignite a spark of hope in others to take meaningful steps towards creating lasting social justice. Young black children can use education to inform and inspire people on social issues that affect them. They can teach others how to recognize injustice, advocate for marginalized communities, and unite the community together in order to build solidarity.

Education	Advocacy	Solidarity
Learn about social issues and injustices	Raise awareness and support other activists	Unite everyone under one cause
Identify sources of information	Speak up against discrimination	Work together towards a common goal
Research strategies for social change	Reach out to decision makers	Create lasting relationships with allies

The education process is an important tool in the fight for equality. Through taking classes or researching online, young black children will discover an array of resources that they can share with those around them. With this knowledge they can create workshops or seminars which offer insight into the many challenges facing society today. In these forums they have the opportunity to educate others on how they should respond when faced with injustice or prejudice. Moreover, it allows them to bring attention to topics that are often overlooked which helps foster greater understanding among different groups of people.

Their advocacy efforts also provide opportunities for real change within their local communities. By raising awareness through organizing protests or speaking out at public meetings, young black children have a voice that cannot be ignored when demanding concrete solutions from lawmakers and policymakers. Furthermore, they are able to showcase examples of successful initiatives taken by other advocates which may inspire new approaches while highlighting areas where progress still needs made. All these actions help promote dialogue across cultural divides while encouraging collaboration between individuals who may not always agree but still find common ground through mutual respect and understanding .

These combined efforts demonstrate why it is so essential for young black children become active participants in this movement towards equality. By exercising their right as citizens while educating others about social issues, they are laying down a foundation on which future generations can build upon . As momentum grows within their own neighborhoods, so too does the power of their collective voice as it echoes throughout society. This call-to-action serves as reminder that only when we come together will our shared vision full potential be realized.

Utilizing Social Media as a Platform

You can use the power of social media to amplify your cause, by encouraging engagement and evoking emotion through alliteration. Platforms like Twitter, Instagram, and YouTube provide an effective way for young Black children to spread their message about social change.

By creating content that allows them to share their stories and experiences with a wider audience, they can help raise awareness of important issues in their communities. From showing support for organizations dedicated to fighting racial injustice to using hashtags that create conversations on the latest news topics, social media is an excellent tool for amplifying activism efforts.

Not only can young activists use these outlets to share information but also engage people in meaningful dialogue. This includes offering suggestions for further action or providing resources that may be needed in order to get involved. Additionally, giving recognition and appreciation to those already doing work on the ground is another way of leveraging social media platforms as a powerful tool for advocacy and activism.

Young Black children have the ability to make an impactful statement about pressing issues by utilizing various features of different social media sites. As more people join this movement, it will not only bring attention but also drive tangible results towards achieving positive change in society.

Through collaboration with key influencers within their networks and beyond, they have the potential to mobilize large numbers of allies who are passionate about making a difference—all without leaving home. With these tools at hand, now's the time when young Black activists can take charge and create real lasting progress toward justice and equality.

Participating in Demonstrations and Protests

By taking to the streets and participating in demonstrations or protests, young Black children can be a visible force for justice and equality. Demonstrations and protests are an effective way to draw attention to an issue or injustice. They also provide a platform for voices to be heard and allow people to express their opinions on matters of social change.

Protesting allows young Black children to boldly state that they won't accept the status quo. It's a powerful way for them to show solidarity with other activists in their community while making sure their demands are being heard by decision-makers.

Protests give individuals who may not have access or influence the opportunity to make their voices heard by those who do have power and authority over them.

Demonstrations and protests are essential tools in the fight for social justice. They bring attention to pressing issues while also empowering individuals from marginalized communities by giving them agency over their own lives. Additionally, it provides an outlet for people of all ages, backgrounds, and walks of life — especially those within the Black community — to come together in pursuit of change that affects us all.

In order to move forward, it's important that we continue using protesting as a tool for positive change in our society today. Volunteering for causes is another avenue that can be used to help push these efforts further along.

Volunteering for Causes

Volunteering for causes is an effective way to show your support and provide tangible assistance in the fight for justice, allowing you to take a stand without having to take to the streets.

Whether it's working with local organizations or offering services related to legal aid or medical care, any form of volunteering allows young black children to have a direct impact on their community.

This can be done in person by speaking with local charities and non-profits that need volunteers or through virtual means such as donating funds online or writing letters of support.

Volunteering also provides young black children with more knowledge about how social change works and what they can do directly within their communities, giving them a platform from which they can further educate themselves on issues of injustice and oppression.

By taking part in this form of activism, young black children will not only gain valuable experience but will also help build solidarity amongst fellow activists while sparking meaningful conversations around race and inequality.

Moving forward, another way for young black children to become activist for social change is by writing letters and signing petitions. These are typically done either in person at events or gatherings organized by local organizations or online via platforms such as Change.org making it accessible from anywhere in the world.

The key here is that these actions should always be targeted towards those who are able to actually make changes: politicians, business leaders, school administrators etc., since this method relies heavily on public pressure being placed upon these people in order for true progress to be made.

Writing letters and signing petitions allows young black children to raise awareness about social issues that are important to them while also encouraging others to join the cause as well – something that can have an even greater impact than if done alone.

Writing Letters and Signing Petitions

Now that we've explored volunteering for causes, let's look at another way young black children can become activists for social change: writing letters and signing petitions.

Writing letters is an easy way to get involved in making change. By writing letters to elected officials, you can make your voice heard and express your opinion on important issues such as racism, economic inequality, or any other topics related to social justice.

You can also write letters to the editor of newspapers and magazines, expressing your opinion on articles or news stories related to social justice. This is a great way for young people to be seen and heard by the public.

Signing petitions is another important form of activism that young black children can take part in. Petitions are forms of collective action that allow individuals from all over the world to come together in support of a cause or issue they care about.

By signing petitions, you can show solidarity with others who share similar beliefs and help drive meaningful change on important issues like racism and economic inequality.

Young black children have the power to make a real difference when it comes to creating positive social change through their activism efforts -- and writing letters and signing petitions are two great ways for them do just that! From voicing their opinions in written form or joining forces with thousands of others around the world in support of an issue, these tools offer powerful opportunities for young people looking to make a difference.

Frequently Asked Questions

How can young black children stay safe while participating in demonstrations and protests?

We, as young black children, understand the importance of participating in demonstrations and protests to bring about social change. However, it is crucial that we stay safe while doing so.

We should always make sure to attend with a group of friends or family members for safety purposes. Furthermore, we must wear protective gear such as masks or helmets and carry water bottles for hydration.

We should also take note of the resources available in case things become dangerous - like having emergency numbers ready to call if needed and knowing where the nearest medical facilities are located. Finally, familiarizing ourselves with our rights when interacting with law enforcement can help us protect ourselves and remain safe during these events.

What are some effective ways for young black children to spread awareness of social justice issues?

We, as young black children, have the power to spread awareness about social justice issues and bring attention to the cause.

Did you know that over 1 million people attended the Women's March in 2017? This impressive statistic shows just how powerful our collective voice can be when we use it to make a stand.

We can use platforms like social media and blogs to share stories of injustice, connect with people who are also passionate about the cause, and encourage others to join us in creating positive change.

We can also take part in marches or peaceful protests where our presence will show that we care and demand justice for those most affected by systemic racism.

By using our voices effectively and standing together, young black children can help create a more equitable society for all.

How can young black children become involved in the Black Lives Matter movement without joining an organization or group?

We, as young black children, can get involved in the Black Lives Matter movement without joining an organization or group.

We can start by educating ourselves and our peers about social justice issues. We can read books that focus on the history of the black experience in America and research current events related to race.

We can also participate in peaceful protests and rallies with friends and family. We can share stories of injustice online to help raise awareness, volunteer at local organizations dedicated to fighting for racial justice, and send letters to representatives advocating for change.

Additionally, we can create art that highlights social issues and organize events such as fundraisers or marches in support of Black Lives Matter.

What are the most important rights that young black children should be aware of as citizens?

We, as young black children, are aware of the importance of standing up for our rights and making our voices heard.

We must remember that we have the same rights as every other citizen in this country, and it's up to us to protect those rights.

As such, it's essential that we know what these rights are - from freedom of speech and press to the right to vote - so that we can advocate for them when necessary.

By using a powerful figure of speech like "our future depends on us protecting our present," we can remind ourselves why being aware of these important rights is crucial.

How can young black children use their voices to effect change in their communities?

As young black children, we can use our voices to effect change in our communities. We can join organizations that are fighting for social justice and actively participate in rallies, marches, and protests.

We can also write letters to legislators or newspapers advocating for policy changes or starting movements on social media to spread awareness of the issues we care about. By using our voices and taking action in any way we can, we have the power to make a difference.

Conclusion

As young black children, we have the power to create real and lasting change in our communities. We can make history by standing up for what's right and speaking out against injustice. Our voices are strong and when we come together, they become even louder.

With every letter written, protest attended, organization joined, and petition signed, we're making a difference that'll be felt for generations to come! So let's keep striving forward until justice is truly served in this world!

Let's show everyone that our collective force is greater than any oppressive system or individual ever could be!

Resources for Young Black Children

Category	Resources
1. Books:	- "Little Leaders: Bold Women in Black History" by Vashti Harrison
	- "The Youngest Marcher: The Story of Audrey Faye Hendricks, a Young Civil Rights Activist" by Cynthia Levinson
	- "Malcolm Little: The Boy Who Grew Up to Become Malcolm X" by Ilyasah Shabazz
	- "The Hate U Give" by Angie Thomas (for older readers)
2. Websites and Online Platforms:	- **Teaching for Change:** Offers resources, booklists, and articles to help children understand social justice and activism.
	- **Scholastic's Social Justice Book List:** Curated list of books that explore themes of social justice and activism for different age groups.
	- **Facing History and Ourselves:** Provides educational resources to promote civic engagement and social justice.
3. Documentaries and Films:	- "I Am Not Your Negro" (2016): A documentary based on James Baldwin's unfinished manuscript, exploring the history of racism in the United States.
	- "Selma" (2014): A historical drama focusing on the 1965 Selma to Montgomery voting rights marches led by Martin Luther King Jr.
	- "Hidden Figures" (2016): A film celebrating the achievements of African-American women mathematicians at NASA during the Space Race.
4. Educational Games:	- "Mission US: Flight to Freedom": An interactive game that takes players through the Underground Railroad, teaching about slavery and abolition.
	- "Activate: Games for Social Change": A collection of games that aim to inspire and educate players about social issues.
5. Community Organizations:	- **Black Girls Code:** A nonprofit organization that introduces young girls of color to computer programming and technology.
	- **Boys & Girls Clubs of America:** Local chapters often offer programs focused on leadership development and community service.
6. Art and Creativity:	- Encourage artistic expression through drawing, painting, or writing about social justice issues.
	- Explore music that speaks to social activism and discuss lyrics with them.
7. Mentorship Programs:	- Connect them with mentors who are involved in social activism or community organizing.
8. Local Community Events:	- Attend local events, workshops, or talks related to social justice and activism.

Books by Author

AI, Race, and Discrimination: Confronting Racial Bias in Artificial Intelligence

ASIN: B0CHCP31ND

From biased hiring processes to skewed criminal justice systems, the impact of AI-driven discrimination is far-reaching and profoundly damaging.

As artificial intelligence becomes an integral part of our lives, its inherent biases are proving to be more insidious than anticipated, magnifying the very inequalities it was meant to address.

The First Black Trillionaire: HOW BLACK KIDS MASTER ARTIFICIAL INTELLIGENCE

ASIN: B0CGYY82KL

Teaching artificial intelligence (AI) to young Black children holds significant importance, as it has the potential to cultivate fairness in access, empower with technology, and create pathways to future careers.

By integrating AI education early on, Black children can acquire the essential skills and insights needed to navigate the digital landscape actively. This empowers them to engage meaningfully with the technological progress that is reshaping our society.

I HATE MY JOB: A Journal for Documenting Workplace Discrimination and Harassment

ASIN: B0CDNPT4T7

Employees have the right to work in an environment free from discrimination and harassment, and employers have a responsibility to prevent and address this behavior in the workplace.

Made in the USA
Monee, IL
21 December 2023

50260585R00273